A CULTURAL HISTORY OF WESTERN EMPIRES IN ANTIQUITY

A Cultural History of Western Empires
General Editor: Antoinette Burton

Volume 1
A Cultural History of Western Empires in Antiquity
Edited by Carlos F. Noreña

Volume 2
A Cultural History of Western Empires in the Middle Ages
Edited by Matthew Gabriele

Volume 3
A Cultural History of Western Empires in the Renaissance
Edited by Ania Loomba

Volume 4
A Cultural History of Western Empires in the Age of Enlightenment
Edited by Ian Coller

Volume 5
A Cultural History of Western Empires in the Age of Empire
Edited by Kirsten McKenzie

Volume 6
A Cultural History of Western Empires in the Modern Age
Edited by Patricia Lorcin

A CULTURAL HISTORY OF WESTERN EMPIRES IN ANTIQUITY

Edited by Carlos F. Noreña

BLOOMSBURY ACADEMIC
LONDON • NEW YORK • OXFORD • NEW DELHI • SYDNEY

BLOOMSBURY ACADEMIC
Bloomsbury Publishing Plc
50 Bedford Square, London, WC1B 3DP, UK
1385 Broadway, New York, NY 10018, USA
29 Earlsfort Terrace, Dublin 2, Ireland

BLOOMSBURY, BLOOMSBURY ACADEMIC and the Diana logo are trademarks of Bloomsbury Publishing Plc

First published in Great Britain 2018
Paperback edition published 2023

Copyright © Carlos F. Noreña and Contributors, 2018

Carlos F. Noreña and Contributors have asserted their right under the Copyright, Designs and Patents Act, 1988, to be identified as Author of this work.

Cover design: Raven Design
Cover image © DEA / G. DAGLI ORTI / Getty Images

All rights reserved. No part of this publication may be reproduced or transmitted in any form or by any means, electronic or mechanical, including photocopying, recording, or any information storage or retrieval system, without prior permission in writing from the publishers.

Bloomsbury Publishing Plc does not have any control over, or responsibility for, any third-party websites referred to or in this book. All internet addresses given in this book were correct at the time of going to press. The author and publisher regret any inconvenience caused if addresses have changed or sites have ceased to exist, but can accept no responsibility for any such changes.

A catalogue record for this book is available from the British Library.

A catalog record for this book is available from the Library of Congress

ISBN: HB: 978-1-4742-4258-5
PB: 978-1-3503-5820-1
ePDF: 978-1-3502-9034-1
eBook: 978-1-3502-9033-4

Series: The Cultural Histories Series

Typeset by RefineCatch Limited, Bungay, Suffolk

Printed and bound in Great Britain

To find out more about our authors and books visit www.bloomsbury.com and sign up for our newsletters.

CONTENTS

ILLUSTRATIONS	vii
ABBREVIATIONS	xii
GENERAL EDITOR'S PREFACE	xiv

Introduction   1
Carlos F. Noreña

1 War   39
    Michael Taylor

2 Trade   63
    Sitta von Reden

3 Natural Worlds   87
    Nicholas Purcell

4 Labor   109
    Elio Lo Cascio

5 Mobility   131
    Sailakshmi Ramgopal

6 Sexuality   153
    Caroline Vout

7 Resistance   177
    Lisa Pilar Eberle

| 8 | Race | 201 |
| | *Emma Dench* | |

NOTES	223
FURTHER READING	229
NOTES ON CONTRIBUTORS	263
INDEX	265

ILLUSTRATIONS

INTRODUCTION

0.1 Victory Stele of Naram-Sin, Akkadian King, *c.* 2250 BCE (detail). Photographer: Rama. Accessed via Wikimedia Commons, CC BY-SA 2.0.   10

0.2 Old Kingdom Pyramids on the Giza Plateau, Egypt, mid-third millennium BCE. Photographer: Ricardo Liberato. Accessed via Wikimedia Commons, CC BY-SA 2.0.   11

0.3 The Parthenon atop the Acropolis, Athens, mid-fifth century BCE. Credit: De Agostini Picture Library/Getty Images.   18

0.4 A Hellenistic-Style Colonnaded Square in Rome: Restored Plan of the Porticus Metelli, 140s BCE. Drawing by John R. Senseney. Reproduced by permission of the artist.   26

0.5 Denarius of Julius Caesar, DICTATOR PERPETUO ("Permanent Dictator"). Rome, 44 BCE. Reproduced by permission of the J. Paul Getty Museum (78.NH.315.6).   27

0.6 Sacrificial Altar with Image of Cow's Head. Lugdunum, Gaul, mid-second century CE. Musée gallo-romain de Lyon-Fourvière. © Morburre, Accessed via. Wikimedia Commons, CC BY-SA 3.0.   31

0.7 Statue of Trajan in military dress, Colonia Ulpia Traiana (mod. Xanten, Germany), *c.* 110 CE. Xanten Archaeological Park. © Hartmann Linge. Accessed via Wikimedia Commons, CC-BY-SA 3.0.   33

CHAPTER 1

1.1 A citizen army: Roman citizen soldiers stand by to register for the census. Altar of Domitius Ahenobarbus, Rome, *c.* 100 BCE. Musée du Louvre, Paris. Public domain. Accessed via Wikimedia Commons. — 43

1.2 Military culture: Dice-tower from the frontier: "Picts defeated, enemy destroyed: Play safe!" Vettweis, Germany, fourth century CE. Rheinisches Landesmuseum (Inv. 85.269). Accessed via Wikimedia Commons. — 54

1.3 Close combat on the Danube: Fully-armored Roman vs. naked Dacian. Tropaeum Traiani, Adamklissi, Romania, 108 CE. Accessed via Wikimedia Commons. — 56

1.4 A distant campaign: Barely visible details of Trajan's Dacian campaigns. Trajan's Column, Rome, 113 CE. Accessed via Wikimedia Commons, CC BY-SA 4.0. — 57

CHAPTER 2

2.1 Excavations at Myos Hormos, Egypt. Photograph © Andrew Peacock. — 64

2.2 Map of the western Red Sea coast. © Jean-Pierre Brun. — 65

2.3 Storehouse (*horrea*) at Ostia. Photograph © Parco Archaeologico di Ostia Antica. — 75

2.4 Denarius of C. Julius Caesar Octavianus, Lugdunum mint, *c.* 4–2 BCE. © University of Freiburg, Germany. — 79

2.5 The Madrague de Giens shipwreck, second century CE. Photograph © Bruno Baudoin. — 83

CHAPTER 3

3.1 Temple of Hercules Victor at Tivoli, Giovanni Battista Piranesi, 1748–1778. Legate of Mr. J.W.E. vom Rath, Amsterdam. Public domain: courtesy of the Rijksmuseum. — 97

3.2 Tunnel giving access from the edge of Naples to the ports and cities around Puteoli, Cumae, and Baiae. — 101

ILLUSTRATIONS ix

3.3 The Aqua Claudia. Central Italy, mid-first century CE.
Thomas Cole, oil on canvas, 1832. Kemper Art Museum,
Washington University in St. Louis. Public domain. Accessed
via Wikimedia Commons. 103

3.4 Hadrian's Villa. Tivoli, mid-second century CE. Piranesi,
etching, *c.* 1769. Metropolitan Museum (37.17.4). Public
domain. 105

CHAPTER 4

4.1 Funerary monument of P. Longidienus, shipbuilder. Ravenna,
late first century BCE/early first century CE. National Museum of
Ravenna. Public domain. Accessed via Wikimedia Commons. 115

4.2 Monument of the Secundini, Igel (near Trier), third century CE.
Accessed via Wikimedia Commons, CC BY-SA 3.0. 116

4.3 Floor mosaic showing a fish-sauce container. Villa of
A. Umbricius Scaurus (7.16.15), Pompeii, first century CE.
Accessed via Wikimedia Commons, CC BY-SA 3.0. 117

4.4 The tomb monument of M. Vergilius Eurysaces, the baker.
Rome, third quarter of first century BCE. Accessed via
Wikimedia Commons, CC BY-SA 4.0. 117

CHAPTER 5

5.1 Private letter on papyrus (P. Oxy. 43.3094). Oxyrhynchus,
Egypt, *c.* 217–18 CE. POxy: Oxyrhynchus Online.
Photograph © Egypt Exploration Society. 136

5.2 Prisoners under Roman control. Trajan's Column, Rome,
113 CE. Credit: Leemage/UIG via Getty Images. 139

5.3 Funerary stele of Aulus Capreilius Timotheus, slave-trader
("body merchant," SŌMATENPOROS). Amphipolis, early
second century CE. Drawing by Margaret M. Andrews.
Reproduced by permission of the artist. 140

5.4 Roman military diploma, bronze (*CIL* 3.854 = *CIL* 16.26).
Carnuntum, Upper Pannonia, June 13th, 80 CE. Public
domain: GNU Free Documentation License. 145

5.5 An Urban Landscape: Thamugadi, Numidia, early third
century CE. Accessed via Wikimedia Commons, CC BY 2.0. 148

CHAPTER 6

6.1 Roman woman in the guise of Venus. Tomb of the Manilii,
Rome, 100–10 CE. Vatican Museums (Mag. Nr. 267).
Photograph © Vatican Museums. 157

6.2 Marble relief with an erotic scene in a boat. First century
BCE–first century CE, provenance unknown. British Museum
(Inv. No. 1865, 1118.252). Photograph: © The Trustees of
the British Museum. 160

6.3 Panel showing Claudius overcoming Britannia. South portico of
the Sebasteion, Aphrodisias, first century CE. Photograph: New
York University Excavations at Aphrodisias: Guido Petruccioli. 161

6.4 Panel showing Nero suppressing Armenia. South portico of the
Sebasteion, Aphrodisias, first century CE. Photograph: New York
University Excavations at Aphrodisias: Guido Petruccioli. 162

6.5 Floor mosaic showing Europa riding on a bull. Lullingstone
Roman Villa, Kent, fourth century CE. Credit: De Agostini
Picture Library. G. Wright/Bridgeman Images. 163

6.6 Floor mosaic showing Dido and Aeneas. Low Ham Roman
Villa, Somerset, fourth century CE. Credit: Somerset Co.
Museum, Taunton Castle. UK/Bridgeman Images. 164

6.7 Tombstone of Regina, second century CE. Credit: Arbeia
Fort & Museum, © Tyne & Wear Archives & Museums. UK/
Bridgeman Images. 167

6.8 Floor mosaic showing Ganymede being carried off by the
eagle. Bignor Roman Villa, fourth century CE. Credit: The
Tupper Family, Bignor Roman Villa. 169

CHAPTER 7

7.1 Denarius of the emperor Otho, PAX ORBIS TERRARUM
("Peace in the World"). Rome, 69 CE. Münzkabinett,
Staatliche Museen zu Berlin (Inv. 18215169). Photograph ©
Münzkabinett. 180

7.2 Fresco showing a riot at the Pompeii amphitheater. Villa in Pompeii (1.3.23), 59–79 CE. Credit: De Agostini Picture Library / A. DAGLI ORTI / Getty Images. 183

7.3 Tetradrachm showing implements for Sukkot celebration. Bar Kochba coinage, Judaea, 134–5 CE. Münzkabinett, Staatliche Museen zu Berlin (Inv. 18204073). Photograph © Münzkabinett. 196

7.4 Tetradrachm showing Zenobia as SEBASTE ("Empress"). Palmyrene coinage, 272 CE. Münzkabinett, Staatliche Museen zu Berlin (Inv. 18252812). Photograph © Münzkabinett. 197

CHAPTER 8

8.1 An image of Roman triumph over defeated and bound barbarians. Gemma Augustea, Rome, 10–20 CE. Accessed via Wikimedia Commons, CC BY-SA 3.0. 203

8.2 East stairway of the Apadana, showing diverse subjects bringing gifts to the Persian king. Persepolis, late sixth/early fifth century CE. 209

8.3 Statue of togate Augustus (the "Via Labicana Augustus") as Pontifex Maximus. Rome, late first century BCE/early first century CE. National Museum of Rome, Palazzo Massimo alle Terme (Inv. 56230). Public domain. Accessed via Wikimedia Commons. 213

8.4 Menorah inscribed on stone column. Synagogue, Ostia, mid-first century CE. Accessed via Wikimedia Commons, CC BY-SA 3.0. 220

Every effort has been made to trace copyright holders and to obtain their permission for the use of copyright material. The publisher apologizes for any errors or omissions and would be grateful if notified of any corrections that should be incorporated in future reprints or editions of this book.

ABBREVIATIONS

AE	L'Année épigraphique
BNJ	Brill's New Jacoby
CIL	Corpus Inscriptionum Latinarum
CLE	Carmina Latina Epigraphica
Coll. Mos. et Rom. Leg.	Mosaicarum et Romanarum Legum Collatio
CPL	Corpus Papyrorum Latinarum
CPR	Corpus Papyrorum Raineri
FgrH	Die Fragmente der griechischen Historiker
I. Delos	Inscriptions de Délos
I. Eph.	Inschriften von Ephesos
IG	Inscriptiones Graecae
IGLS	Inscriptiones Graecae et Latinae Syriae
IGRR	Inscriptiones Graecae ad Res Romanas Pertinentes
ILG	Inscriptions latines de trois Gaules
ILS	Inscriptiones Latinae Selectae
O. Did.	Didymoi Ostraka
P. Col. Zen.	The Zenon Papyri
P. Oxy.	Papyrus Oxyrynchus
P. Yadin	Yadin Papyri
P. Yale	Yale Papyrus
RDGE	Roman Documents from the Greek East

RIB	*Roman Inscriptions of Britain*
SB	*Sammelbuch griechischer Urkunden aus Ägypten*
SEG	*Supplementum Epigraphicum Graecum*
SIG	*Sylloge Inscriptionum Graecarum*
Suppl. Ital.	*Supplementum Italicum*
T. Sulp.	*Tabulae Pompeianae Sulpiciorum*
Tab. Vind.	*Vindolanda Tablets*

GENERAL EDITOR'S PREFACE

Histories of empire have been transformed in the last three decades by a combination of new methods, new archives, and a new generation of scholars who have come of age in a postcolonial world. The impact of these historical forces on how imperialism is understood has been remarkable. For decades the province of geopolitics, diplomacy and the "official mind," imperial history is now just as likely to be told from the bottom up as from the top down. The rise of cultural history has played a significant role in how we think about and narrate imperialism from the ancient world to the twentieth century. With an emphasis on evidence drawn from literature, the arts, life-writing, and a host of fragmentary sources, cultural historians think through patterns of representation and experience that shape the conditions in which histories of all kinds—economic, political, social—happen. They investigate often overlooked subjects and offer new angles of vision on familiar topics through a cultural lens. The ambition of *A Cultural History of Western Empires* is to advance conversations about the work of culture in shaping how empire took root, took shape, was maintained, and faced challenges whether its regimes were of long or short durée. Indeed, no thoroughgoing histories of the subject can afford to ignore the influence that culture has had on the shape of empires in local, regional, and global contexts.

The geographical remit of *A Cultural History of Western Empires* is indicated in its title. As compelling a topic as the wide variety of imperial formations is, and as interconnected as west and non-west have been along the axis of empire from Greece to Beijing and back again, the authors in this volume explore empire's cultural histories in a broadly western European setting. And while the differences between French and German and English imperial experiences are often notable, what is equally striking are the features that cultures of labor, trade, sexuality, race, war, mobility, natural worlds, and resistance share across imperial locales. Even allowing for specificities of time and place, there is a value to taking a very long view of the concept and practice of *imperium*—not simply to note commonalities or differences but to be able to discern through lines across such widely distinctive terrains as the Frankish kingdoms and the world of the post-Versailles settlement. In no small respect, attention to cultural forces, identities, rhetorics, tropes, relationships, and imaginaries make this kind of discernment possible. Reading for culture—which is to say, developing the capacity to plumb a variety of sources and archives for evidence of how meanings and forms were constantly made and struggled over across a range of domains—reveals the work of historical forces that have undergirded and, at times, have redirected or undone imperial power. Empire simply cannot be understood in all its limits and possibilities without an analysis of its cultural histories.

This is a work of scholarly synthesis rooted in the original scholarship and intellectual vision of the volume editors and their contributors. Its audience is students seeking a comparative, interdisciplinary, and evidence-based account of how empires worked at multiple scales. Readers will get a sense, then, of the cultural impact of large-scale territorial expansion and hegemony *and* of the meaning and experience of conquest and colonization in more intimate environments. Contributors have written their essays to make available a broad overview of their theme or topic. Each one draws on a range of materials and case studies to make a larger argument about the history of cultural formations and influences that pertain to their subject. The series is structured around six time periods: Antiquity, The Medieval Age, The Renaissance, The Enlightenment, The Age of Empire, and the Modern Age. These are conceptual and pedagogical, signaling a periodization that modern Western imperialism itself has played an important role in shaping and sustaining. Casting Rome as an imperial touchtone and colonized territories as "ancient" or "medieval" in temporal terms remains an important cultural resource for contemporary empire building, and it draws on a long cultural legacy that contributors both address and challenge. Each volume takes up the chronological parameters assigned in critical conversation with the historical evidence, allowing readers to see the pros and cons of thinking about empire itself as a maker—and breaker—of time periods. Of equal significance, each volume is organized with the same chapter titles so that readers can either follow a theme across time frames—mobility in the Enlightenment as compared to the twentieth century, for example—or read through a single period by exploring the range of thematic lenses on offer. This combination of diachronic and synchronic affords us a unique opportunity to cultivate comparisons that are as deep as they are broad, and to appreciate the indispensability of cultural history to practically all aspects of imperial regime making and unmaking across this particular swath of the global past.

Such a purposeful focus on culture at this juncture in the history of the historiography of empire is worth remarking on. As an object of historical inquiry, culture is arguably the carrier of a number of historical forces that attention to politics or economics alone cannot capture. Though embedded in and constitutive of every aspect of imperial geopolitics, race, gender and sexuality were long invisible to the historians' eye because they were considered trivial, or at best inconsequential to, the workings of real power. Cultural history practices, which bring new forms of seeing and reading as well as new subjects to our sightline, open up the imperial archive to aspects of the past which, in turn, shed new light on old paradigms. Thinking with and through culture also reorients our gaze, pulling us toward sources—diaries, images, discursive motifs—in a diverse array of formations and spaces that illuminate dimensions of hegemony and power otherwise invisible: dismiss-able, even, as immaterial because they are ostensibly "only cultural." What the collective example of this series accomplishes is to suggest how, why, and under what conditions culture has been a maker of imperial history—indeed, that empires have been done and undone by the cultural forces they sought to control but which were not always completely in their grasp. As twenty-first-century forms of imperial power emerge, claiming historical newness and relying on past models of conquest and occupation all at once, we need narratives that insist on the power of histories attuned to the ideological and material work of culture more than ever.

Culture is at the dynamic heart of all imperial histories. It operates in spaces of high command and conjugal intimacy; in ceremony and in ordinary life; in military documents and botanist's texts; at court and on the plantation; through trade routes and refugee settlements; in the pronouncements of empresses and the movements of the lowly beetle; in the signing of treaties and the violence of the battlefield and the inner workings of the household. Thinking through cultures of empire, in turn, throws us back on the protocols and presumptions of the discipline by encouraging us to be ever vigilant about where—in what spaces and through what repertoires—history happens. Empire is not, perhaps, unique in this regard. The irony is that while imperial ambition and self-regard have often been steeped in convictions about the power of culture to conquer and colonize, imperial narratives on a grand scale are often the most impervious to the argument that culture matters. What follows is a wide-ranging and lively set of arguments about how and why that has been incontrovertibly so from antiquity to modern times.

Introduction

CARLOS F. NOREÑA

The kaleidoscope of ancient empire: violently torn from their homeland and everything they had ever known, and resettled in a strange landscape half a thousand miles away, a family from Tyre on the Levantine coast learns how to cultivate crops in the upper Tigris river valley . . . an Egyptian priest wakes up before sunrise to prepare the morning's ritual performances in honor of the local deities of Abydos . . . Darius the King, the Persian Great King, is depicted, victorious over a winged lion, on a cylinder in Sardis in West Asia . . . a Macedonian soldier, who has not seen his home for over a decade, enjoys a Greco-Persian feast in the ancient city of Babylonia . . . a successful Italian merchant on the small island of Delos commissions a bronze statuette of the Greek god Hermes . . . the son of a large landowner in Lugdunum in central Gaul recites lines from Vergil's *Aeneid*, from memory . . . thirteen slaves from beyond the edges of the Mediterranean world, settling down for the night in a small room on a farm in western Sicily, use gestures and sign language to communicate with one another . . . a crude monument on a desolate hillside in the lower Danubian plain commemorates the Roman conquest of the kingdom of Dacia . . . a shipment of olive oil from southern Spain arrives at the port of Ostia and is prepared for transshipment up the Tiber river to the megalopolis of Rome, home to a million people . . . a mosaic in the dining room of a Mediterranean-style villa in eastern Britain recounts the Greek myth of Perseus and Medusa . . . a stonecutter in Hippo Regius in North Africa carves a small cross into the humble tombstone of a Christian shopkeeper . . .

These vignettes of the experience, infrastructure, and aesthetic of ancient empire may seem disparate, but they are all variations on a set of themes that will be encountered again and again in this volume. What links them together is a particular scale (both temporal and geographical), a particular type of convergence, a particular form of ideology and, above all, a particular degree of systemic power, centrally organized, which influenced the lives of everyone who lived in the polities examined in the chapters that follow. The fundamental alienness of this world—in its chronological remove from the present, and in its organizing principles, so different in so many ways from everything we take for granted today—requires a bit of scene-setting. In order to understand ancient empires and their very lively cultural histories, that is, we need to think about where these large-scale political systems came from and what happened to them, and how they shaped everything from the labor and mobilities of their mostly anonymous subjects to their sexualities and consciousness.

EMPIRES AND STATES: A TYPOLOGY

Before we turn to these questions, however, it will be worthwhile to pause for a moment to tackle the problem of what, exactly, an empire is, and the ways in which it is and (more to the point) is not like the modern nation-states that most of us now inhabit.

As a political form, an empire can be seen as a type of state—or, perhaps better, as a particular stage in a long-term process of state-formation. We may define a state as a set of centralized institutions and associated personnel, normally backed by armed force, that exercises ultimate decision-making authority over a particular territory.[1] Over the long sweep of western history, states have come in several different shapes and sizes. In the ancient world, the two most common iterations of the state were the city, or city-state, and the empire (or what we might call the "empire-state"). City-states, empires, and nation-states all qualify as states, on this definition, but with important differences in the scale and depth of state power, on the one hand, and in the sociospatial distribution of culture, on the other. Let us consider both in turn.

In most ancient cities, the central state apparatus exercised intensive power over a limited space, usually an urban core and a surrounding rural territory. Within these circumscribed limits, the state and its agents could achieve a high degree of social control. In ancient empires, by contrast, the central state exercised extensive power over a far-flung space, often embracing several geographic regions. But logistical constraints normally precluded anything but the most rudimentary administrative control over these territories. The reach of state power, in other words, tended to be narrow but deep in city-states, and wide but shallow in empires. The modern nation, on this typology, is characterized by a central state that exercises intensive power over an extensive territory. We usually associate empires with both size and power, but it is important to recognize that the centralized administrative power of a nation-state, precisely in its combination of spatial extent and social depth, dwarfs that of even the largest and most aggressive ancient empire. In world-historical terms, the modern nation-state is at the leading edge of the long-term growth of state power (long-term evolution of state power: Mann 1986–2012).

A related way to think about the location of power within states is to consider the relationship between territoriality and sovereignty. Here empires stand apart from both ancient city-states and modern nation-states. In city-states and nations, the state asserts its authority equally, and for the most part successfully wields it, over the entirety of its territory. This is straightforward for city-states, given the limited spatial extent of the area under administrative control. Modern nation-states, too, especially in the industrial and post-industrial West, can rely on advanced infrastructure, communications networks, and information systems to regulate activity anywhere and everywhere within their borders. In principle, that is, the sovereignty of, say, the state of France is no more valid or effective in Paris than it is in any other corner of the country. This is decidedly not the case in empires, which are characterized instead by "lumpy" sovereignties, very uneven administrative capacities, and fuzzy boundaries (Benton 2010). In this respect, traditional classroom maps with monochromatic depictions of imperial territories—"The Roman empire at its Greatest Extent!"—are highly misleading. Empires, especially ancient ones, could never achieve the sort of blanket coverage implied by those cartographic representations. What most empires attempted, instead, was control over strategic locations and key resources. In practice, this entailed the projection of power outwards from a central core, diminishing in effectiveness as a measure of functional distance from the center, and not terminating abruptly at a clearly marked border, but rather petering out haphazardly in a loosely defined frontier zone. In empires, in other words, state power was normally concentrated at the center, and imposed unevenly across ever-widening circles of subordinated peripheries. In fact, this structural opposition between center and periphery is a defining feature of ancient empire as a political form (e.g., Doyle 1986: 35–40; Howe 2002: 30; Reynolds 2006: 152).

The other key variable that helps us to distinguish between different types of state is the sociospatial distribution of culture within them (Gellner 1983). Because of their small scale, ancient city-states were usually comprised of culturally homogenous populations. Language, religion, consumption, the practices of daily life, and "worldview" were all widely shared by the members of these communities (with the important exception of slaves). The same is true of modern nation-states, despite their size and social complexity. Since the early nineteenth century, the combination of mass education and mass literacy, both driven by the imperatives of capitalist economies, has generated distinctive national cultures that reach from the top of the social hierarchy to the bottom. Citizens of modern nations, that is, wherever they are located, and wherever they fall on the socioeconomic spectrum, will normally share a common core of cultural attributes, especially language, that makes them more or less "interchangeable." Ancient empires, in sharp contrast to both ancient city-states and modern nation-states, embraced multiple subject populations of widely divergent cultures, languages, consumption patterns, and belief systems. Indeed, most subjects of ancient empires, scattered across widespread landscapes and ecologies, with very different histories and local traditions, would have had little way to relate to or even communicate with one another. In a world without mass education, and with comparatively rudimentary infrastructure, it could hardly have been otherwise. An important exception to this pattern is typically found in the uppermost social strata of ancient empires, it is true, where an empire-wide elite often participated in an empire-wide high culture. And this sort of cultural cohesion at the apex of the social hierarchy, a form of premodern imperial "cosmopolitanism," is one way to approach the cultural history of ancient empires, as we will see (below, 29–33). The vast majority of imperial subjects, though, inhabited what were in effect different universes. So cultural diversity was another defining feature of ancient empires (Goldstone and Haldon 2009; Burbank and Cooper 2010; Lavan *et al.* 2016).

From this brief typological survey we can now sketch a working definition of "empire." Let us define an empire as a type of state, distinguished from other states (or from other stages in the state-formation process) by its combination of territorial extent, internal cultural diversity, and control by a dominant center over a succession of increasingly remote and variably subjugated peripheries.[2]

STATE-FORMATION, EMPIRE, AND CULTURE IN ANCIENT WEST ASIA

A synthetic definition of this sort can help us to grasp the essential features of empire, which facilitates comparative analysis, but it does not explain how or why this particular political form arose in any one time or place. These are key questions for this first volume in the series, especially with respect to the Roman empire—the prototypical empire in western history and the western imagination, and the focus of the essays in this volume. In order to set ancient western empires in general and the Roman empire in particular in their proper historical contexts, then, we will need to sketch the long-term evolution of imperial state-formation in the ancient world, first in West Asia ("The Near East") and then in the Mediterranean basin. The rest of this Introduction is meant to serve both as an "origin story" and as a comparative lens, exploring the problem of where western empires came from, and highlighting some of the ways in which the Roman empire was typical and some of the ways in which it was unique.

The earliest durable frameworks for social and political organization that we can recognize as states (on the definition above, 2) are found in ancient Sumer (Mesopotamia; modern Iraq) around 3200 BCE. For tens of thousands of years up to that point, humans had lived in small, mobile groups, acquiring food from nearby resources ("hunting and gathering"), and moving constantly in the ongoing search for new resources. A major rupture occurred sometime between about 9000 BCE and 5000 BCE with the domestication of crops and the emergence and rapid spread of small-scale farming. This agricultural revolution (sometimes called the "neolithic revolution"), which arose independently in the Fertile Crescent and a handful of other regions around the globe, laid the foundations for the permanent inhabitation of specific sites. But these early communities were still incapable of producing large agricultural surpluses. The next big breakthrough came in the late fourth millennium BCE with the mastery of alluvial agriculture in the lower Euphrates and Tigris river valleys. Here the systematic control of the two rivers' floodwaters, by means of intricate networks of canals and levees, generated the sorts of agricultural surpluses necessary to sustain large, urban populations of non-primary producers. This demographic concentration in sites that qualify as "cities" both required and enabled an increasingly complex division of labor, which in turn promoted social stratification. Important technological innovations, such as the wheel and bronze metallurgy, helped to drive urban infrastructure and monumentalization, while the emergence of writing facilitated the entrenchment of political authority in permanent administrative structures and institutions, above all kingship, which was crucial for the centralized coordination of large-scale labor. The state, as an instrument of organization and coercion, had been born (Diamond 1999: chs. 4–10; Trigger 2003; Yoffee 2005; Garfinkle 2013; Liverani 2014: chs. 4–6; Scott 2017).

City-states, as effective social and political "containers" for the populations of Mesopotamia, proliferated dramatically, in terms of both numbers and size, over the course of the third millennium BCE. Though these city-states participated in a broadly shared, "Sumerian" culture, especially in terms of language, religion, and art, the cities themselves were politically independent (shared culture and political autonomy are common features of city-state clusters: Hansen 2000). And these cities were highly competitive with one another, as each engaged with the others in a zero-sum contest over important material resources (water, timber, metals) or control over profitable trade routes. As a result, warfare, presumably on a small scale, was probably endemic in early Mesopotamia, but at no point did any one city come to control other cities outside of its own immediate hinterland.

This multipolar world of independent city-states was transformed in the last quarter of the third millennium BCE with the rise, for the first time in world history, of territorially extensive conquest states. The first was centered in the city of Akkade (still unlocated, but probably near modern Baghdad), which rose to regional domination under the founder of its ruling dynasty, Sargon, around 2350 BCE. Through military conquest, the creation of a standing army, and the imposition of a series of garrisons in strategic locations, the royal court at Akkade achieved centralized control, for about 150 years, over many of the cities, and their respective material resources (especially grain), of Mesopotamia and neighboring regions. For the first time in western Eurasian history, that is, a single city dominated an entire region. Following the demise of the Akkadian state around 2200 BCE, the political geography of Mesopotamia reverted to the earlier framework of multiple independent city-states. A second and more robust phase of centralization began around 2150 BCE, with power and authority now concentrated in the city of Ur ("The Third Dynasty of Ur," or Ur III). A comprehensive proto-bureaucratic apparatus, well documented from surviving tablets, underpinned an elaborate fiscal regime, with inner and intermediate zones supplying tax grain and livestock, respectively, and an outer zone, connected to the ruling family at Ur through dynastic marriages, serving as a buffer region. Also important was agricultural intensification throughout Mesopotamia, catalyzed by a new system of corvée labor, which financed both a standing army and the monumentalization of the capital city. The dynasty at Ur eventually collapsed, too, sometime around 2000 BCE. We do not know enough about either Akkade or Ur III to provide narratives of rise and fall, but what the two cases illustrate is the enormous challenge, in a world of limited technology and infrastructure, of projecting centralized state power across space and (especially) over time (Sallaberger and Westenholz 1999; Liverani 2014: chs. 8–9).

We can trace a related but ultimately different trajectory of territorial consolidation and political centralization in Egypt (Manning 2013). There, too, the mastery of alluvial agriculture in the late fourth millennium BCE was translated into a regular, annual agricultural surplus that sustained an ever-larger number of settled communities throughout the Nile river valley and the Nile delta region. The unification of these communities, under the towering authority of a monarchic ruler who came to be known as the Pharaoh, embraced both regions, which were always conceptualized as "Upper" and "Lower" Egypt, respectively. Virtually from the moment of political unification c. 3100 BCE, under King Narmer, the culture of both Upper and Lower Egypt looks broadly similar, characterized by shared language, visual idioms, religious customs (especially death ritual), and material cultural assemblages. The state in Egypt eventually comprised a hereditary monarchy at the head of a differentiated administration of officials, regional governors ("nomarchs"), and military generals; priests, who controlled local temples and their landed estates, were nested within this ruling apparatus in a somewhat opaque way. Centralized power in ancient Egypt rested upon the methodical extraction of revenues from royal land and grain tax from private land. This supported the administration, monumental royal building programs, and, by the New Kingdom period (c. 1500–1000 BCE), a large standing army, which propelled imperialist expansion into Nubia, the Levant, and West Asia.

Because the Pharaohs promoted an ideology of timelessness and changelessness, it is difficult to write a detailed, diachronic history of the state-formation process in Egypt. What we can say, though, is that just as in Mesopotamia, so too in Egypt, periods of political centralization alternated with so-called "Intermediate Periods" in which the centralized authority of the state temporarily broke down. Where Egypt diverges from the Mesopotamian pattern is in the remarkable longevity of its essential political and territorial structure, which stretches across nearly three millennia; in the greater concentration of autocratic power in its monarchic regime; and in the relative cultural homogeneity of its subject population. In these ways, then, ancient Egypt does not fit neatly into the typology of states presented above (2–4)—the result, surely, of its functional "insularity" and radically distinctive riverine and desert ecology.

The history of West Asia for the two thousand years following the rise of Akkade *c.* 2350 BCE can be schematized as a replication, on an ever-larger scale, of the Mesopotamian pattern of the third millennium BCE, as (ultimately) the entire macroregion, from Anatolia, the Levant, and Egypt in the west to the Hindu Kush and the Indus river valley in the east, oscillated between periods of political tessellation and fragmentation, on the one hand, and periods of consolidation and hegemonic centralization, on the other (Barjamovic 2013). The world of West Asia in the first half of the second millennium BCE was mostly a multipolar one, with multiple independent city-states competing for regional preeminence, but several different city-states, especially Assur (*c.* 2000–1800 BCE) and Babylon (under Hammurabi, 1792–1749 BCE), did manage to achieve something like supraregional hegemonies during this period. A number of large, territorial states also formed around the edges of the Fertile Crescent, especially in Anatolia, where the Hittites enjoyed a long-lived regional ascendancy (*c.* 1650–1200 BCE) (Bryce 2013: 161–75); Egypt, too, was an important regional presence in this period. Following the disruptions that rocked much of West Asia around the turn of the first millennium, usually associated with the coming of the mysterious "Sea Peoples" (cf. Cline and O'Connor 2012), much of the Fertile Crescent came under the control of the Neo-Assyrian state (934–610 BCE) and its successor, the Neo-Babylonian state (626–539 BCE). Both states, especially the Neo-Assyrians, employed a variety of coercive tactics, including forced population transfers, and both projected centralized state power over large territories, including into the very different cultural world of Egypt. The Neo-Assyrians and Neo-Babylonians may be seen, at a minimum, as "proto empires," and should probably be regarded as fully imperial states (Liverani 2014: chs. 27–31).

The evidence for West Asia from the late fourth millennium down to the middle of the first millennium BCE is fragmentary and often intractable, but one big trend line is clear: over time, phases of consolidation and centralization were characterized by ever more hegemonic applications of state power across ever-larger territories. This two-thousand-year trajectory culminated in the Achaemenid empire, the first state in western Eurasia to meet even the most stringent definition of "empire." Centered in the Persian heartland (Fars, in modern Iran), and rising rapidly through a series of explosive conquests under Cyrus the Great (r. 559–530 BCE), the Achaemenid empire came to embrace the entirety of West Asia, from the Mediterranean to the Indus, and from the Caspian Sea to the Persian Gulf. Built on conquest, the empire was consolidated through a sophisticated administrative machinery and far-reaching communications apparatus, especially the famed royal road network. Especially striking is the stability and endurance of the Achaemenid empire, which persisted until it was conquered by Alexander the Great and his Greco-Macedonian army in the 330s BCE (below, 19–20). It had been the largest and most stable empire in world history up to that point (Briant 2002; Kuhrt 2007a; Wiesehöfer 2013: 199–202, 208–15).

Asking how the Achaemenid empire managed to control such a large territory for two centuries brings us to the general problem of how any ancient imperial system achieved and, crucially, maintained such territorial control. We have already noted that unlike city-states or modern nation-states, empires—especially in antiquity—did not possess the infrastructural capacity necessary to exercise total, "top-down" control over their territories. Instead, most aimed at channeling as many material resources as possible toward the center, on the one hand, and into the hands of the empire's sociopolitical elite, on the other (these two imperatives could conflict, of course, and required a delicate calibration of interests), and at dictating the external relations (what we would today call "foreign affairs") of the empire's many constituent parts, usually a mix of cities and tribal affiliations, especially those located in strategically sensitive locations. Imperial states achieved these (limited) ends, as we see throughout the history of West Asia and Egypt, through a mix of coercion and consensus.

Coercion denotes the capacity of the central state to enforce its will through the actual or threatened use of armed force (various perspectives, mostly drawing on Weber, in Giddens 1985: 35–60; Tilly 1985, 1992: 68–70; North *et al.* 2009; Scheidel 2013: 5–9). The organization and deployment of such force was crucial, and was normally managed through an institutional framework, especially an army. Smaller-scale applications of force were important, too, for internal policing, the enforcement of judicial punishments, and so on. What distinguished territorial conquest states and empires from the city-states and tribal groupings they controlled was the ability to bring such centralized coercion to bear across ever-larger territories. Important early steps in the evolution of this capacity included the Akkadian network of military garrisons, and the subsequent rise of standing armies (under Ur III, the Hittites, and New Kingdom Egypt, for example). Over time, the incidence and brutality of organized violence seems to intensify, too, especially under the Neo-Assyrians. Most striking, though, is simply the increased scale of imperial force. In this respect, the Achaemenid empire reigned supreme, as the Persian Great

King could raise field armies from throughout his immense realm that could number, according to the Greek historian Herodotus (3.90–8, 7.60–97), well over one million soldiers (for more detail, see Taylor's chapter, this volume). Even if Herodotus' numbers are inflated (as they surely are), it is clear that the armed force at the disposal of the Achaemenid state was an order of magnitude greater than that of any other state in the long history of ancient West Asia.

More germane to this volume, and to this series, is the role of consensus in the making of empire—no less important, it must be stressed, than "hard power" in explaining the rise and replication of imperial structures. For it is very clear from the historical record of ancient empires that coercion, while (obviously) necessary in order to bend unwilling subjects to the will of the ruling regime, was not by itself sufficient for the long-term maintenance of imperial power. Some degree of consensus, whether sincere or merely "performed," was also necessary. If coercion is a matter of armed force, then consensus is a matter of belief, representation, discourse, and meaning, to be located, *inter alia*, in religion, ritual, literature, art, architecture, and space (and, ultimately, in politics). Coercion is the product of institutionalized violence. Consensus belongs to the domain of culture.³

Though our evidence from this period rarely takes us down to the level of individual, subjective experience, and to the beliefs or attitudes of any one person in any one polity, we can make some plausible guesses about how different actions undertaken by the states and empires of ancient West Asia might have induced an intersubjective consensus in the starkly asymmetrical political systems that prevailed there. Here I draw attention to just three such legitimating mechanisms. The first is the visual representation of power and hierarchy—especially important in a world of limited literacy (Feldman 2005; Cheng and Feldman 2007). Small-scale objects, such as the Warka vase (*c.* 3000 BCE) or the Standard of Ur (*c.* 2600 BCE), both of which depict processional scenes centered on authoritative figures, or the Naram-Sin Victory Stele (*c.* 2250) (Figure 0.1), which represented the Akkadian king, Naram-Sin, trampling over defeated enemies and wearing a bull-horned helmet (a symbol of divinity), reflected—and, as I am suggesting here, helped to constitute—an emergent social order, with a clear differentiation between rulers and followers. More dramatic as visual expressions of hierarchy were the monuments built under royal authority. Especially resonant were the royal palace complexes constructed in most "capital" cities, emblematic of political and economic centralization, and the massive and visually imposing tombs erected for rulers. There are several impressive examples from West Asia, especially the rock-cut tombs of the Achaemenid kings, but the most dramatic monumental statements of royal power and authority are the pharaonic tombs from Egypt, above all the pyramids from the Old Kingdom period (*c.* 2700–1500 BCE), clustered around the Giza Plateau (Figure 0.2), but also the vast burial complexes from the New

FIGURE 0.1: Victory Stele of Naram-Sin, Akkadian King, *c.* 2250 BCE (detail). Photographer: Rama. Accessed via Wikimedia Commons, CC BY-SA 2.0.

Kingdom period in the Valley of the Kings. Such structures stood as enduring symbols of a social and political order with a monarchic ruler firmly ensconced at its apex (Root 1979; Briant 2002: 165–203; Kemp 2006, chs. 2–3; Kuhrt 2007b; Feldman and Heinz 2007).

A second set of legitimating mechanisms can be grouped under the general rubric of standardization. This took various forms, including the regularization of weights and measures, which facilitated exchange across ever greater distances, and the homogenization of scripts, time-keeping mechanisms, and calendrical systems, all of which helped to universalize and normalize the ways in which widely scattered individuals situated themselves in (the same) time and space (Robson 2007). The production and imposition of universal law codes, of which that of Hammurabi is the best known, was another official process that influenced imperial subjects to orient themselves to a shared, and centrally determined, set of norms (Roth 1997).

FIGURE 0.2: Old Kingdom Pyramids on the Giza Plateau, Egypt, mid-third millennium BCE. Photographer: Ricardo Liberato. Accessed via Wikimedia Commons, CC BY-SA 2.0.

A third process that must have worked to generate some degree of consensus in imperial authority was the diffusion of an increasingly uniform set of objects, practices, and beliefs that we can identify as "religion." That religion (broadly defined) was a focal point for the organization of these societies is manifest from the articulation of space in most cities, in which religious structures normally occupied a commanding position. Thus we can trace a line from the ziggurats that originated at Ur and spread throughout Mesopotamia to the enormous temple complexes—some the size of small towns—that proliferated throughout Egypt. The tight linkage between religious and political authority in these states is especially relevant. Royal inscriptions from mid-third millennium Mesopotamia, for example, portray the king as a temple-builder and a protector of the city in the name of a protecting deity (many examples in Frayne 2008). In Egyptian royal ideology, Pharaohs, as direct heirs of the sun god, Ra, were incarnations of sacred power, and also served as living guarantors of *ma'at* ("truth, right behavior, balance") (Ferguson 2016). The regular collocation of divine and royal statues in most Egyptian temples also helped to blur the distinction between Pharaohs and gods. We find a different relationship between religion and power in the Achaemenid empire. There the state promoted (or, perhaps, tolerated) a high degree of religious pluralism. But even this pluralism was a royal prerogative. The most famous expression of religious "freedom" in the Achaemenid empire comes from the Cyrus Cylinder, recording Cyrus' capture of Babylon, and its protecting deity Marduk, in 539 BCE:

> I, Cyrus, king of the universe, mighty king, king of Babylon, king of Sumer and Akkad, king of the four quarters, son of Cambyses, great king, king of Persia, grandson of Cyrus, great king, king of Persia . . . I set up, with acclamation and rejoicing, the seat of lordship in the palace of the ruler. Marduk, the great lord, daily I cared for his worship . . . The city of Babylon and all its cult centers I maintained in well-being . . .

Here the empire's ultimate control over local religious experience is explicit (Kuhrt 1983). More broadly, and throughout the political systems we have been considering, it was through the intermingling of human and divine power, and the royal prerogative in managing the relationship between men and gods, that imperial subjects came to be bound to a cosmic order in which the ruler at the center stood as a lynchpin. The universalization and sacralization of monarchic and imperial authority that resulted must have conduced to a widespread acceptance of the basic legitimacy of these imperial states.

In the large-scale political systems of ancient West Asia and Egypt, then, a mix of coercion and consensus secured centralized control (such as it was) over ever-larger territories, resources, and peoples. The vital institution that tied all of this together—critical, that is, both to the coordination of armed force and to the making of an imperial ideology—was kingship (Assmann 2002: *passim*; Briant 2002: chs. 5–8; Trigger 2003: 71–91; Garfinkle 2013: 107–10; Bryce 2013: 164–6). Monarchic rulers, ranging from the conquerors of Akkad to the Pharaohs of Egypt to the Great Kings of the Achaemenid empire, were the very embodiments of centralized authority and imperial domination. They were not formally accountable to anyone, nor did there exist any practical or even imaginable alternative to their totalitarian power. The politics of these ancient West Asian and Egyptian states, in other words, were absolutist in nature, defined by the simple, binary relationship between ruler and subject. In this first stage in the long-term development of the state in western Eurasia, the nexus between empire, monarchy, and subjection was airtight.

INTERLUDE: POLITICAL CULTURE(S) IN THE ANCIENT GREEK WORLD

States in the Mediterranean basin arose in the shadow, and under the influence, of both Egypt and especially West Asia, but with the emergence of representative government and the concept of citizenship in early Greek city-states, ancient Mediterranean state-formation developed along a divergent path, culminating—chronologically and in terms of scale—in the Roman empire. Here we will review the major stages in this process in the ancient Greek world, with a focus on the revolutionary new political cultures that developed in this period.

The story begins on the Greek peninsula and in the islands of the Aegean Sea. Evidence for agriculture and the domestication of animals here goes back to the seventh millennium BCE, with the first settled communities appearing in the mid-third millennium, roughly coincident with the development of metallurgy and the production of bronze tools and weapons. These small communities were forerunners of the two great "civilizations" of the Greek Bronze Age (c. 3000–1050 BCE), the Minoans and the Mycenaeans (Cline 2010). Minoan culture (c. 2000–1350 BCE) was centered on a string of palaces located around the island of Crete (Bennet 2013: 237–42). The largest and best preserved of these palaces, at Knossos, contained a series of large-scale storage facilities, which hints at the palace's role as a center of redistribution. This was facilitated by the technology of writing and the archiving of detailed palace inventories written in a still untranslated script known as Linear A. There is no evidence for the political system of Minoan Crete, but the palaces must have performed at least some of the coordinating functions of a state. Following the near-total breakdown of Minoan culture c. 1425 BCE, for reasons that are unclear, only Knossos was rebuilt. The key difference in this second stage of Minoan palace culture was that the palace inventories were now being written in a new script, Linear B, a proto-Greek language. Linear B tablets are also found, in larger numbers, on the Greek mainland, especially in the Peloponnese. This is the writing, and language, of the Mycenaean civilization (c. 1600–1200 BCE), centered on the great palaces at Mycenae, Tiryns, Pylos, and Orchomenos (Bennet 2013: 243–52). It was another Bronze Age culture anchored in a large-scale redistribution complex, but the palaces of this civilization were not really ceremonial centers, as at Knossos, but rather imposing fortresses. The warrior spirit at the heart of this culture is also reflected in the predominance of weapons and martial imagery in the grave goods discovered in the chamber tombs throughout the Mycenaean world. There did not exist any territorially extensive states in the Mycenaean period (much less empires), but rather a shared culture and series of independent settlements orbiting around these palaces, which were presumably ruled by chieftains or warrior kings.

Mycenaean civilization collapsed in the late second millennium BCE, at about the same time as the widespread regional turbulence that shook the major polities of Egypt and West Asia (above, 7). Whatever the cause of this systemic breakdown, which is still debated, the outcome was a rupture in the state-formation process throughout the Greek peninsula, which entered into a period of stagnation known as the Dark Age (c. 1100–800 BCE), characterized by demographic decline, diminished settlements, an impoverishment in material culture generally, and the disappearance of literacy (Snodgrass 2000). But in the aftermath of this breakdown, social organization did not start up again entirely from scratch. For a constructed and collective memory of the lost world of the Mycenaean warrior kings, as it was later imagined, had been enshrined in the Homeric epics, the *Iliad* and *Odyssey*, which recounted the exploits of rulers such as Agamemnon, Achilles, and Odysseus, and which canonized a heroic code of individual achievement and competition for *kleos* ("everlasting fame"). Collectively produced, most scholars now believe, by several generations of wandering bards, these epic poems helped to generate a broadly shared ethos in which individual competition, achievement, and social hierarchy were central (Nagy 1979; Fowler 2004). A sense of communal Greek identity based in part on these principles gathered momentum in the eighth century BCE, with the rise of inter-city athletic competitions at religious sanctuaries (originating in Olympia in 776 BCE, according to the traditional chronology); a long-term colonizing movement (beginning *c.* 750 BCE) that brought Greek settlers far and wide, with concentrations of colonies on the Black Sea coast and in southern Italy and Sicily; and the reemergence of literacy, with a new alphabet borrowed from the Phoenicians (Osborne 1996: 70–136; Shapiro 2007, esp. chs. 8–10). It is this dynamic phase of ancient Greek history that witnesses the rise of the *polis*—a seminal development for ancient Mediterranean state-formation in general, and a key element in the deep structure of the Roman empire.

The Greek term *polis* (plural *poleis*) can refer either to a nucleated settlement or to a set of governing institutions; it often refers to both simultaneously, and is therefore best translated as "city-state." Like the city-states of ancient West Asia, Greek *poleis* were independent, self-governing communities that exercised control over an urban center and a surrounding rural hinterland. In the wake of demographic expansion and economic growth in the eighth century BCE, the *polis* as a political and social form proliferated both within the core of the ancient Greek world (the Greek peninsula, the Aegean Sea, and the west coast of Asia Minor) and, as part of the colonial movement (lasting down into the early sixth century BCE), throughout the Mediterranean basin. By the fourth century BCE, there were some 600 Greek *poleis* in the Greek core and another 400 or so along the Black Sea coast and in the central and western Mediterranean. Most ranged in size from about 1,000 to 6,000 permanent inhabitants; larger *poleis* reached populations of about 30,000, while the largest of all, Athens and Sparta, might have surpassed 200,000. Together these *poleis* formed vibrant city-state clusters, like those of ancient West Asia, and despite their political independence, they participated in a widely shared city-state culture (especially in terms of language, myth, and religion) (Hansen and Nielsen 2004).

Where the Greek *polis* differed radically from earlier instantiations of the city-state in the ancient world was in its formalized, and highly elaborated, condition of membership. Membership in a *polis* came to be understood above all in terms of citizenship, which entailed a robust set of rights and responsibilities, legally defined. Citizenship in the *polis* was limited, it is true, to adult males, but all citizens (so circumscribed), regardless of wealth or family background, enjoyed legal equality, and all in principle participated in the governing of the community, with collective responsibility for communal finance, religious institutions, and military defense (Hansen 2006, 2013). As Herodotus put it in an imaginary speech in defense of democracy (3.80.6):

> But the rule of the multitude has in the first place the loveliest name of all, equality, and does in the second place none of the things that a monarch does. It determines offices by lot, and holds power accountable, and conducts all deliberating publicly. Therefore I give my opinion that we make an end of monarchy and exalt the multitude, for all things are possible for the majority.

The contrast with ancient monarchies and the monopolization of decision-making authority by the ruler, which Herodotus is careful to draw out here, is sharp.

The ancient Greek world, then, was a world of independent city-states, from the rise of the *polis* in the archaic period (*c*. 800–479 BCE) through the heyday of city-state culture in the classical period (479–323 BCE). The political character of Greek *poleis* varied considerably, of course, and with this variability came differences in the level of collective participation in civic affairs. A simple typology of constitutions, derived from the Greeks themselves, distinguishes between executive rule by one, by the few, or by the many (e.g., Plato, *Statesman* 302c-d; Aristotle, *Politics* 3.7). The dominant political form of the archaic period was what the Greeks called "tyranny," one-man rule exercised, according to Aristotle, contrary to customary law and in the personal interests of the ruler (*Politics* 3.7–8). The emergence of tyranny in the mid-seventh century BCE, a form of government eventually established in every major Greek city-state with the exception of Sparta (ruled, anomalously, by two kings), threatened the prospects for a genuinely representative politics in the ancient Greek world (Osborne 1996: 192–7). But tyrannies had mostly disappeared by the middle of the sixth century BCE, in almost every case collapsing after exactly two generations of autocratic rule, and usually supplanted by oligarchic regimes in which executive authority was controlled by an inner circle of wealthy families. Even in oligarchies, though, citizens could influence the public decision-making process through their participation in popular assemblies and other political institutions (Simonton 2017). Collective management of the *polis* was of course most vigorous in democratic city-states, of which classical Athens stands as the glimmering exemplar. Born out of a series of complex institutional reforms enacted in 509/8 BCE—some framed in response to a phase of tyranny at Athens (546–510 BCE)—the classical Athenian democracy was a remarkable achievement of communal governance. At Athens, democracy (*dēmokratia*, from *dēmos*, "people," and *kratos*, "power") was not representative, as in most modern democratic states, but direct. In principle (and very nearly in practice), that is, all citizens, enacting their will through a suite of public institutions, were responsible for deliberating on and passing legislation, and for managing a system of courts. And with the important exception of military generals, who were elected, all key executive posts in the government were filled by ordinary citizens chosen by lot. Citizens fulfilling their democratic duties even received pay for their service (introduced in 451 BCE), which meant that the poorest Athenians could participate right alongside their wealthiest neighbors—and on an equal footing. In the long-term sweep of state-formation in the ancient world, this was a truly groundbreaking political system (Ober 1989; Hansen 1999; Rhodes 2004).

The classical Athenian democracy bears directly on our theme in three ways. First, Athens was the ancient Greek *polis* that came closest to creating something like an "empire." What scholars normally call "the Athenian empire" was a regional hegemony that Athens established over many of the islands and coastal cities of the Aegean Sea (Rhodes 2009; Morris 2009; Ma *et al.* 2012). It was formed, in its first phase, in the aftermath of the successful Panhellenic ("all Greek") defense of the Greek peninsula against a large-scale invasion by the Achaemenid Persian empire (481–79 BCE, following an earlier failed expedition in 490), when leadership of the coalition was transferred from Sparta to Athens (478). The Athenians rapidly converted the instruments of a common military enterprise against the Persians, with a common treasury on the island of Delos, into instruments of Athenian domination over other Greeks. Cities unwilling to join the so-called Delian League were coerced into joining (from as early as 472), and those which attempted to secede were forced back in (from 470). Common funds were increasingly monopolized by Athens—the treasury was even transferred from Delos to Athens, probably in 454—and used to finance an ever-larger navy (and a program of monumentalization in Athens itself, of which the Parthenon is the crowning glory: Figure 0.3). Naval power, commercial wealth, administrative interference (including the requirement that "allied" cities conform to Athenian weight and monetary standards), and jurisdictional control underpinned a hegemonic system over much of the Aegean world that the Athenians themselves called an *archē*, "rule." The system peaked in the mid-fifth century BCE, which triggered Athens' great rival, Sparta, at the head of its own coalition of city-states, to declare war—responding, according to Thucydides (1.23), from fear of growing Athenian power. Following its catastrophic defeat at the hands of Sparta and its allies in 404 BCE, the Athenians rebounded quickly, and eventually forged another (slightly less) hegemonic system, the "Second Athenian Sea League" (378–338 BCE), which disintegrated after the Macedonian conquest of the Greek peninsula (below, 19). In neither phase of its hegemonic power in the Aegean, however, did the Athenian *archē* constitute a full-fledged "empire," at least on the definition above (4). It was indeed built upon a set of peripheries subordinated to a dominant center, but in cultural terms the Aegean was largely homogenous, and the territorial extent of the system was rather limited—certainly by comparison with canonical premodern empires. The Athenian *archē* does, nevertheless, represent a potent convergence of democratic government and imperial expansion, which will shed some useful light, as we will see, on the growth of the Roman empire.

Another important convergence, and a second way in which classical Athens bears on the theme of state-formation and empire—again, especially relevant to the Roman case—is the structural relationship at Athens between citizenship and slavery (Vlassopoulos 2009; Rihll 2011). Classical Athens has been identified as a true "slave society," one in which chattel slaves—humans owned by other humans as property—were essential to the overall operation of the social, political, and economic order (Patterson 1982). And it is from precisely the moment that the most famous Athenian law-giver, Solon, canceled debts and abolished slavery as a punishment for indebted Athenian citizens (early sixth century BCE), an important step on the road to democracy, that we can trace the rise of chattel slavery on a large scale at Athens. Some Athenian slaves came from other Greek city-states (normally as enemies defeated in warfare), but most originated from beyond the Greek world. They had no legal standing or juridical identity. The slave, in Aristotle's formulation, was simply a "possession," but one "with a soul," to be distinguished from inanimate objects (*Politics* 1.2.4). They performed a wide range of functions: domestic (household service of various kinds), urban (mainly in the commercial, banking, and retail sectors), and rural (especially agricultural labor). The Athenian democracy could not function without slaves. For it was only because of the essential labor they provided that citizens had the necessary leisure to participate in the time-consuming processes of self-governance. What we find in the wealthy and powerful Athenian city-state of the fifth and fourth centuries BCE, then, is a conjoining of democracy, empire, and slavery.

The third way in which classical Athens is relevant to our story is in yet another convergence there, this one between democracy, imperial expansion, and cultural production. In the same dizzying period in which an Aegean hegemony was being created and a democratic constitution elaborated, Athens was presiding over a remarkable cultural efflorescence that laid many of the foundations for what we now call "western civilization" (Boedeker and Raaflaub 1998; Lapatin 2007; Henderson 2007). The fifth century BCE in particular was an embarrassment of riches. At the center of Athenian cultural life was dramatic performance in the theater—a mirror, in some ways, of democratic "performance" in the assembly—in which the main forms were tragedy, cultivated by the trio of Aeschylus (*c.* 535–455), Sophocles (*c.* 497–406), and Euripides (*c.* 480–406), and comedy, in which the major exponent was

FIGURE 0.3: The Parthenon atop the Acropolis, Athens, mid-fifth century BCE.
Credit: De Agostini Picture Library/Getty Images.

Aristophanes (c. 446–386). This period also witnessed the coming into the mainstream of philosophical discourse. The key figure here is Socrates (c. 470–399), who encouraged his fellow citizens to question all received wisdom. His ideas were set down in writing for later generations by his pupil, Plato. Several canonical literary genres took shape in fifth-century Athens, including historiography. Thucydides (c. 460–400), who recounted the cataclysmic confrontation (as he framed it) between Athens and Sparta, was the leader in this field. The fifth century also witnessed striking developments in visual culture, with striking innovations in sculpture, ceramic arts, and monumental architecture (Figure 0.3). Some of these texts and art forms were critical of Athenian society, democracy, and the imperial project, but as a large and wealthy imperial center, Athens was a magnet for writers, artists, and thinkers of all kinds. Indeed, cultural production was as essential to Athenian democracy, and its energetic civic sphere, as any of the city's political institutions.

Athens was always an outlier. For much of the archaic and classical period, the Greek world was comprised of smaller, less powerful, and less culturally creative city-states, many of them independent, others entering into alliances or formal groupings—such as the Peloponnesian League, with Sparta at its head (Cartledge 2002), or the various federal states that were formed in central Greece and the Peloponnese (Mackil 2013)—but all organized as largely self-governing communities with some form of representative politics. Around the edges of this world, by contrast, there lay a constellation of larger territorial states arranged rather differently, usually under monarchic regimes. These states always threatened to encroach upon the autonomy of the Greek *poleis*. At the beginning of the fifth century BCE, for example, the Persian Great King launched not one but two unsuccessful invasions of the Greek mainland—minor setbacks on the distant fringe of an empire that stretched to the Indus Valley, from the Persian perspective, but formative events for the coalescing of a Greek identity (defined, in part, by opposition to the "barbarian" East) (Miller 1997; Rhodes 2007). More decisive for the long-term development of state-formation in the Greek world was the kingdom of Macedonia to the north (Hammond 1989; Hatzopoulos 1996). Large, wealthy in precious metals, timber, and horses, and teeming with manpower, the Macedonian kingdom under Philip II (r. 360–336 BCE) embarked on a concerted program of imperial expansion that eventually brought its armies to the doorstep of central Greece. This led to a series of armed conflicts that culminated in the Battle of Chaeronea (338 BCE). At this decisive battle, one of the major turning-points in ancient Mediterranean history, the coalition of Greeks was routed by the Macedonians, and the political independence of the Greek city-states came to an end. The *poleis* of the Greek peninsula were now, in effect, under the sway of an alien power, the Macedonian kingdom.

Two years after the Battle of Chaeronea came another equally momentous event: the assassination of Philip II and accession to the Macedonian throne of his son, Alexander III (r. 336–323 BCE). Alexander's short life and explosive career, the stuff of legend already in antiquity, beggars description (Bosworth 1993; Roisman 2003; Badian 2013). At the head of his Macedonian troops, he reasserted control over the southern Balkans and Greek peninsula (336–334); at the head of a joint Greco-Macedonian army, he attacked the Achaemenid empire—nominally as a campaign of vengeance for the Persian invasions of the early fifth century—and within a single decade had conquered the whole of West Asia (including Egypt, and stretching as far east as the Hindu Kush), shattering an old world that had stretched back for several millennia and ushering in a new one that brought East and West together in a dynamic set of overlapping, hybrid political and cultural systems. Alexander ruled over his vast realm as a new sort of monarch, bridging Macedonian, Greek, and Persian traditions and ideologies—propelling the diffusion of Greek culture throughout West Asia, while simultaneously reimagining Macedonian kingship in an increasingly Persian and West Asian idiom (above all in terms of the divinity of the ruler)—and attempting to forge a new, Greco-Macedonian and Persian elite to rule over this gigantic polity.

But this was a short-lived project. The breathtaking (and still unparalleled) speed and scale of Alexander's conquests, and his death at the age of thirty-two (in 323 BCE), without having named a successor or outlined plans for what to do next, left an unwieldy and wobbly realm that splintered almost immediately. The narrative of the next fifty years is complex and confusing, but the trajectory is clear (Bosworth 2002). One by one, Alexander's surviving generals in the high command carved out smaller territories for themselves, most of them in the former Achaemenid empire, and by the last decade of the fourth century BCE had begun ruling these territories as monarchs in their own right, having appropriated the title of "king" (*basileus*) for themselves. Shifting alliances and near-constant warfare between the main contenders left three major states—the Ptolemaic kingdom in Egypt, the Seleucid kingdom centered in the Fertile Crescent (and extending far to the east), and the Antigonid kingdom in Macedonia, founded, respectively, by Ptolemy I (r. 305–282 BCE), Seleucus I (r. 305–281), and Antigonus I (r. 306–301)—and a host of smaller polities which managed to survive in their midst. This is the period that historians since the nineteenth century have referred to as the "Hellenistic" age, from the death of Alexander to the Roman conquest of the last surviving kingdom, Ptolemaic Egypt (323–30 BCE). As a stage in the development of the ancient Greek state, the Hellenistic kingdoms stand out for their territorial scale and political organization as dynastic monarchies, in both respects representing a major departure from the smaller, more intimate, and more collective frameworks of the *polis*. Like the earlier West Asian states on whose former territories most of these kingdoms stood, they were monarchic regimes with a strong, ritual focus on the person of the king, and based on centralized bureaucracies (especially in Ptolemaic Egypt), elaborate tributary apparatuses, and large, standing armies (Manning 2010; Ma 2013; Kosmin 2014). The Hellenistic kingdoms are also characterized by the imposition of an alien, Greco-Macedonian ruling elite atop a diverse, subjected, and indigenous population, and in this respect prefigure the later European colonial empires of the early-modern and modern periods.

STATE, CULTURE, AND COSMOPOLITANISM IN THE ROMAN EMPIRE

We come now to the nexus of state-formation, empire, and culture in the Roman world. The eight chapters that follow explore different points of this convergence and its effects, examining war and conquest (Taylor) and its structural antithesis, resistance (Eberle); some of the different engines of economic performance and social and geographical mobility in the Roman empire, ranging from slavery and labor (Lo Cascio) to the short- and long-distance movements of both objects (von Reden) and people (Ramgopal); a vital dimension of the lived (and represented) experience of the Roman empire, sexuality, with deep implications for the problem of imperial subjectivity (Vout); one of the main discourses that effectively interpellated many of the empire's millions of inhabitants, race (Dench); and the geographical and ecological settings within which all of this played out, and which were themselves transformed (literally) by empire (Purcell). Together these chapters offer a bold new cultural history of the Roman empire, juxtaposing key topics that are not always considered under the rubric of "culture." This section of the Introduction is designed to provide a comprehensive historical and interpretive framework for these free-standing chapters, drawing on the main themes that have guided the discussion thus far.

A crucial preliminary point that must be emphasized is that Rome began as a city-state and ended up as an empire. This trajectory can be charted along two interrelated axes. In the first place, Rome began its imperial expansion in Italy and the Mediterranean as a republican city-state, with a form of representative politics that recalls the collective decision-making institutions of the Greek *polis*. It eventually controlled a far-flung territory and, as a polity, was no longer, in practice, a city-state. But one of the defining features of its empire-state was the spread throughout of Roman citizenship, as we will see, a clear inheritance from the republican phase of its development. A closely related development, and a second key axis of imperial state-formation at Rome, was the transformation of its internal political system. For at the height of its imperial expansion, as a republic, the republican government imploded in a series of civil wars, replaced by a dynastic monarchy under the first emperor, Augustus. This is not surprising. In the premodern world, as we have seen, empire and monarchy normally went together. We will continue to probe that structural relationship in a moment. But here I want to observe that the republican origins of the monarchic system at Rome were never entirely effaced, and this had all sorts of secondary effects on the political culture of the Roman empire. In its combination of imperial citizenship and republican ideology—both crucial for the political and cultural system of the Roman imperial state—the Roman empire, especially in light of its size and longevity, stands apart from all other ancient empires.[4]

According to its own scholars, Rome's history begins with the foundation of the city in 753 BCE, a tradition indirectly supported by the archaeological record, which indicates the growth of a nucleated settlement there in the mid-eighth century (Holloway 1991; Cornell 1995: chs. 3–8). The city was originally ruled by kings, according to this same literary tradition, but this "regal period" came to a sudden and violent end in 509 BCE (traditional date), when the monarchy was abolished and a republic founded in its place (Cornell 1995: ch. 9). The political history of the early Republic (509–264 BCE) was shaped by the so-called "Struggle of the Orders," a multigenerational conflict that pitted the patricians, a closed aristocratic caste, against both wealthy plebeians, who wanted access to high office, and their poorer counterparts, who were fighting for basic social and economic rights. After nearly two centuries of internal conflict and negotiation (to 287 BCE), the plebeians ultimately prevailed on both counts, gaining political and legal equality and emancipation from harsh socioeconomic conditions (Raaflaub 2005). Their leverage stemmed in large part from their service in Rome's citizen militia. Warfare in the fifth century was on a small scale, and was normally a matter of defending the rich agricultural territory of Latium against raids by the tribal peoples of neighboring regions. A sea-change came in the early fourth century, with Rome's first aggressive conquest, of the nearby city of Veii, and its first territorial expansion beyond Rome's own agricultural hinterland (396 BCE). Equally significant was the development in this campaign of one of the key mechanisms that would fuel subsequent warfare: the imposition of a property tax (*tributum*) on Roman citizens, which covered the high costs of continuous fighting, and which served as a sort of investment on the returns to be gained from conquest (Nicolet 1976: 16–19; for subsequent developments in the *tributum*, Northwood 2008; Taylor 2017).

Rome's growing regional power and increasing domination of the neighboring cities of Latium, nominally allies, impelled the latter to declare war in 341 BCE. Rome's victory in the resulting Latin War (341–338 BCE) created a blueprint for further expansion in Italy (and abroad). Two key principles informed the obligations imposed upon defeated enemies. First, Rome entered into treaty relationships with communities individually rather than collectively. Second, it created a new category of allied cities which possessed *civitas sine suffragio*, "citizenship without the vote" (Mouritsen 2007). This was an arrangement whereby the citizens of defeated communities retained their local citizenship, but also acquired a form of Roman citizenship with certain privileges, including protection under Roman law, and certain limitations, in particular the exclusion from voting in Roman assemblies. In addition, these communities did not pay taxes to Rome, but rather contributed soldiers which fought in allied contingents alongside Roman troops. In principle, this arrangement entailed an incorporation rather than subjugation of defeated Italian enemies; in practice, it meant that the Roman war machine began to grow exponentially. In this way Rome transcended the bounds of a traditional city-state—in which all the prerogatives of the citizens were jealously guarded, as in classical Athens—and eventually came to draw on the manpower of the entire Italian peninsula (Rich 2008; Taylor, this volume). This institutional innovation helped pave the road to empire.

Long before Rome launched its astonishing run of overseas conquests, however, its manpower was severely tested in Italy itself, again and again, down to the end of the third century BCE (Cornell 1995: ch. 14). In a series of bloody conflicts fought against various peoples in the mountainous and less urbanized parts of the Italian peninsula, especially the Samnites of the southern Apennines (326–304, 298–290 BCE), Rome prevailed and, in the process, reinforced its hegemony over most of central Italy. In the south, it successfully fought off the invasion of Pyrrhus of Epirus, a minor Adriatic potentate who came to Italy at the head of a professional Hellenistic army only to be overwhelmed by Rome's seemingly endless supply of troops (280–275 BCE). This victory ensured Roman control over the whole Italian peninsula south of the Po river. The turning-point in Rome's rise as a regional power, though, came in the second half of the third century BCE with the epic confrontation between Rome and the dominant state in the western Mediterranean, Carthage (Hoyos 2011). Like Rome, Carthage was a city-state that had forged an empire, with control over much of north Africa, the larger islands of the western Mediterranean, and long stretches of coastal Spain. Its power was based on naval supremacy and commercial wealth (Ameling 2013). The first extended conflict between the two states lasted nearly twenty-five years (264–241 BCE), with Rome victorious in the end. In the aftermath of its victory, Rome began laying claim, with varying degrees of formalization, to its first overseas territories: Corsica (238), Sardinia (238), and Sicily (227). Soon afterwards the two sides clashed again, and this time the stakes were higher (218–202 BCE). The Carthaginian invasion of Italy under its daring leader Hannibal, the annihilation of several Roman armies, and the occupation of the southern peninsula for over a decade (217–204 BCE) very nearly terminated Rome's ascendancy. Once again, though, the Roman manpower advantage proved decisive, as the Carthaginians were defeated in multiple theaters, including southern Italy, southern Spain, and north Africa. Following its decisive victory over Carthage, at the climactic Battle of Zama (202), Rome annexed extensive territories in the Iberian Peninsula (Richardson 1986; Curchin 1991: 24–54), and within a couple of generations added a large swath of north Africa itself. By the middle of the second century BCE, Rome was the unrivaled imperial power in the western Mediterranean (Harris 1989).

By the mid-second century BCE Roman power had also become entrenched in the eastern Mediterranean. This was a world of fierce rivalries, diplomatic intrigues, and deep histories, dominated by the Hellenistic kingdoms introduced above (19–20): large, wealthy, centralized states that, collectively, wielded far greater infrastructural capacity than Rome. The narrative history of Roman intervention here is complex, and the underlying motivations of Roman expansion in the east still debated (Harris 1979; Gruen 1984; Ferrary 1988; Kallet-Marx 1995; Eckstein 2005). But there is a pattern. On several occasions, Rome responded to calls for (armed) support from smaller states, especially the minor kingdom of Pergamum (northwest Asia Minor) and, entering in this way into the vortex of Hellenistic power politics, fought a series of ever-larger wars against Hellenistic kings. Major victories over Philip V of Macedonia (in 197 BCE, at Cynoscephalae in central Greece), Attalus III of the Seleucid kingdom (in 189, at Magnesia in Asia Minor), and Perseus of Macedonia (in 168, at Pydna in Macedonia) left Rome in de facto control over the Greek peninsula and much of Asia Minor. Yet Rome did not formally annex any of these domains.

Even after dismantling the Antigonid monarchy in 168, it created four new republics in Macedonia rather than occupy the region. In the next generation, though, something changed. In 148 BCE, following a minor victory over a pretender to the Antigonid throne, Rome formally annexed the territory of Macedonia, incorporating the whole region into the Roman imperial state as a new province. This was Rome's first real foothold in the east. Two years later, in response to some low-level, anti-Roman unrest in central Greece, Roman armies destroyed the city of Corinth—the very same year its troops had razed Carthage to the ground, once and for all eliminating its ancient north-African rival (146). Rome was now a Mediterranean-wide imperial power that was prepared to project devastating force far and wide in order to safeguard its expanding interests. What happened?

Part of the answer lies in a new set of attitudes and conceptions of the imperial project that coalesced over the course of the second century BCE. The Roman terminology for what we call "empire" is especially relevant here (Richardson 2008). The key terms are *provincia* and *imperium*. *Provincia*, the root of our word "province," originally denoted the sphere of competence assigned to a Roman official, whether or not it had a spatial dimension (the treasury, for example, was one official's "*provincia*"). By the end of the second century, however, the geographical sense of the term came to prevail, as reflected in Roman public laws, and there developed a notional association between a Roman official, his *provincia*, and a given territory claimed and administered by the Roman state. *Imperium* underwent a similar semantic development. It originally referred to a specific, legal competency with which certain Roman officials were invested, denoting in particular the capacity to exercise military command outside of Rome. Eventually, though, *imperium* evolved into something like the modern idea of a composite, territorial empire. It is difficult to know what drove these semantic shifts. We may infer, nevertheless, that Roman officials, equipped with these sorts of cognitive tools for conceptualizing the different areas controlled by the Roman state, became increasingly invested in a policy of territorial annexation (Harris 1979: 131–62). The long-term effect of this cognitive and strategic shift was the provincialization of the entire Mediterranean basin, with Rome at the center. What this meant in practice was the cobbling together of a permanent administrative and military apparatus to control and govern overseas territories, now defined as provinces. Provincial governors and Roman armies ensured that order was kept and that taxes were collected—defeated communities in the provinces were not, like their Italian counterparts, incorporated into the Roman imperial state as (junior) partners. They were subjects. But they did enjoy a high degree of local autonomy. This was not because Rome was especially progressive or enlightened, but because the state lacked the infrastructural means to rule these communities in a direct, "top-down" manner (a common weakness of premodern empires, as we have seen). Provincial government in the Republican period, in fact, was mostly haphazard and amateurish in nature (Lintott 1993: 5–107; Brennan 2000: *passim*; Nicolet 2000: *passim*).

Running in parallel with these semantic, cognitive, and administrative shifts was the intensifying engagement of Roman aristocrats with the Greek cultural tradition, and the large-scale adoption of Greek cultural forms in Rome (Zanker 1976; Gruen 1990, 1992; Wallace-Hadrill 1990b, 1998, 2008). This is a curious and anomalous development. In most imperial systems, culture is diffused downwards and outwards from the top and the center, from the conquerors to the conquered. In the case of Rome's Republican empire, by contrast, the major flow of (high) culture went in the other direction, as the Roman elite over the course of the middle Republic (264–133 BCE) became increasingly "Hellenized." As the late-first-century BCE Roman poet Horace put it in a famous line: "Captured Greece (*Graecia capta*) captured the savage conqueror | And brought the arts to uncultured Latium (*agresti Latio*)" (*Letters* 2.1.156–7). Greek culture was influential in several different spheres. Statues and paintings carted off from defeated Greek cities helped to shape emergent Roman visual idioms. In terms of architecture, monumentality, and public space, the city of Rome began to take on the appearance of a grand Hellenistic city, with the spread of Greek-style porticoes, colonnaded squares, and extended urban axes embellished by uniform façades and arcade architecture (Figure 0.4) (see Purcell's chapter for the effects on landscape). Different Greek philosophical schools, especially Stoicism, were eagerly embraced at Rome. In no area of Roman Republican culture was Greek influence more pronounced, however, than in literature (Feeney 2016). Latin literature was born in the mid-third century BCE with a handful of tragic and comic plays, in the Greek manner, now lost. The first Latin author for whom we have some complete works is the poet Plautus, who wrote comedies adapted from Greek originals (first half of second century BCE). Another important early author is Plautus' contemporary, Ennius, whose *Annals*, an epic poem on Roman history, was closely modeled on Greek prototypes. Perhaps the clearest indication of Greek influence over Roman literary forms is the decision of the Roman senator Fabius Pictor to write the first ever prose history of Rome, in the late third century, not in Latin but in Greek. Latin literature (and Roman cultural production more generally) would eventually develop along its own, independent path, but the early debt to Greek models was profound.

By the middle of the second century BCE, then, the Roman state, ever more cosmopolitan in its cultural horizons, controlled a handful of territories around the Mediterranean that, collectively, constituted what the Romans themselves came to think of as an "empire." And it acquired and managed these territories not, like earlier West Asian polities or contemporary Hellenistic kingdoms, as a monarchic state, but rather as a republic, with a lineup of annually elected

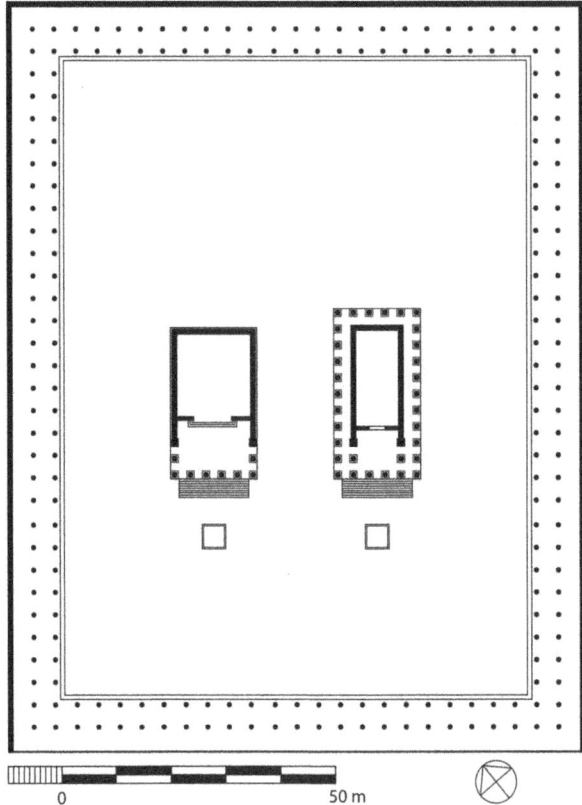

FIGURE 0.4: A Hellenistic-Style Colonnaded Square in Rome: Restored Plan of the Porticus Metelli, 140s BCE. Drawing by John R. Senseney. Reproduced by permission of the artist.

officials and a host of interlocking governing institutions formally controlled by the Roman citizen body, the *populus Romanus* ("Roman People") (Millar 2002: chs. 3–6; Hölkeskamp 2010; Mouritsen 2017). It would not last forever. The history of the late Republic (133–44 BCE) is a history of intensifying imperial expansion, rising inequality at Rome, large-scale violence throughout Italy, and the bloody collapse of this republican system (Brunt 1988; Steel 2013).

Imperial expansion continued in the second half of the second century BCE, with new territories added in southern Gaul and Asia Minor, and then accelerated through the first century, with gigantic new acquisitions in Anatolia, Syria, Cyprus, and the Levant, in the east, and most of continental Gaul, in the west (Badian 1968). Material wealth flowing into Italy as a result of these Mediterranean-wide conquests, monopolized by a metropolitan elite, led to the formation of large, profit-driven, slave-worked agricultural estates (*latifundia*) throughout the peninsula, which permanently altered an older landholding system of small, subsistence farms worked by peasant families (for the changing labor regime in Italy, see Lo Cascio's chapter in this volume). Attempts to address the resulting agrarian and socioeconomic problems led both to small-scale internal violence at Rome—the assassination of Tiberius Gracchus, who pushed for a redistribution of public land in Italy in 133 BCE, is the conventional beginning of the late Republic—and large-scale external violence throughout Italy, as Rome's Italian allies (*socii*) waged a brutal and ultimately successful revolt, the Social War (91–88 BCE), gaining as a result full Roman citizenship (Keaveney 1987; Mouritsen 1998).

Interwoven with these structural problems was the dangerous rise of aristocratic Roman generals, ambitious and competitive. By exploiting the increasingly desperate troops at their disposal, who looked to them as patrons, they began to challenge one another and, increasingly, the state as a whole (Steel 2013: 80–210). A sequence of devastating civil wars ensued, pitting pairs of senatorial generals and their followers against one another: Marius vs. Sulla (80s BCE); Pompey vs. Julius Caesar (49–45 BCE); Mark Antony vs. Octavian (30s BCE). As the stakes in these conflicts grew, the winners—bona fide warlords, all of them—accumulated ever more personal and political power. Sulla revived the archaic office of dictator, which had been employed in emergencies when the normal republican system of checks and balances was too cumbersome, to reform the political system in an autocratic manner (Flower 2010: 117–34). Caesar followed suit, but elevated his standing still further by having himself declared *dictator perpetuo*, "dictator for life" (Figure 0.5), and by accepting a flood of honors (titles, privileges, statues throughout the city of Rome) that set him far above his peers, and that even assimilated him to the gods (Koortbojian

FIGURE 0.5: Denarius of Julius Caesar, DICTATOR PERPETUO ("Permanent Dictator"). Rome, 44 BCE. Reproduced by permission of the J. Paul Getty Museum (78.NH.315.6).

2013: 1–128). Octavian, Caesar's grand-nephew and adopted son, understanding the political implications of Caesar's assassination at the hands of disaffected aristocratic rivals (44 BCE), sought to rule not as dictator (nor as king, as some thought Caesar wanted), but rather as a *princeps*, "leading citizen." Having brought the cycle of civil wars to a close, Augustus (as he chose to be called; see Figure 8.3 for his depiction as civilian official) trumpeted the slogan of *res publica restituta* ("the commonwealth restored") while simultaneously laying the foundations of a ruling dynasty (Syme 1939; Osgood 2006; Galinsky 2012). His unexpectedly long life and protracted reign (27 BCE–14 CE) foreclosed the possibility of any real alternative. Indeed, the historian Tacitus commented that at the time of Augustus' death, there was no one left who had any memory of a properly functioning republic (*Annals* 1.3). From the "Age of Augustus" onwards, Rome conforms to the expected premodern link between monarchy and empire.

Following a final, explosive burst of aggressive expansion under Augustus, which brought Egypt, most of the Balkans, and northwestern Iberia under Roman imperial control (Gruen 1996), and some smaller accretions in the next few decades around the perimeter of the Mediterranean, the tempo of imperial conquest slowed considerably. Invasions of Britain under the emperor Claudius (r. 41–54 CE), and the kingdom of Dacia (modern Romania) under Trajan (r. 98–117), were the exceptions to the new pattern. Under its monarchic rulers, Rome had become a stable, tributary state (Bang 2013). It is this extended period—from the Age of Augustus through the early empire (to 70 CE) to the middle or "high" empire (to the third quarter of the second century CE)—that forms the core of most of the essays in this volume. Instead of presenting a continuous account of these centuries, therefore, I want to focus instead on the underlying dynamic of imperial control as it operated during this period, before turning in the final section to a brief account of the later Roman empire and the different post-imperial state systems that followed, which mark the transition to the Middle Ages.

The Roman empire, at its maximum territorial extension (at the end of Trajan's reign), covered some 2.5 million square miles. This immense realm, subdivided for administrative purposes into about forty provinces, embraced the entire Mediterranean basin (with several deep projections into its continental hinterlands). On the one hand, this is just the Roman empire "on paper." As I have stressed, ancient empires could not govern such spatially dispersed territories in a comprehensive manner. On the other hand, for several centuries the Roman imperial state did manage to control the most strategic sites in the Mediterranean and continental European worlds (cities, fertile plains, mines, ports, contested frontier zones, and so on); to direct the flows of resources in ways that were conducive to the replication of the "system" (see von Reden's chapter); and to wield ultimate decision-making authority over a subject population of somewhere between fifty and seventy million persons (Scheidel 2007a). It was a formidable achievement. The mechanisms of control were not so different from those by which the larger ancient West Asian polities ruled their territories. Given the slow pace of technological change in antiquity, this is not surprising. Like its predecessors, that is, the Roman state presided over the territories, resources, and peoples under its sway through a mix of coercion and consent.

The logic of coercion in the Roman empire was identical to that of the other imperial states we have considered. Through the organization and targeted projection of armed force and the tactical application of other coercive mechanisms (for example, courts, judicial punishments, and routine policing in the larger cities), the Roman state evidently induced the necessary degree of obedience in its subjects. Some of that obedience must have stemmed from fear. On the local scale, public executions of convicted criminals, staged in the amphitheater for the entertainment of paying spectators (normally as the early-afternoon prelude to gladiatorial combat), served as exemplary reminders of Roman order and the perils of subversion (Coleman 1990; Fagan 2011). And on the imperial scale, armed revolts against the Roman state were suppressed with awesome force (see Eberle, this volume); official responses to the several Jewish uprisings (66–73, 115–17, 131–6 CE), for example, were ever more brutal, culminating in the expulsion of the Jews from their ancestral homeland. Frontier defense and the maintenance of a large, professional standing army naturally required a monumental investment of both manpower and financial resources. The Roman imperial army of the mid-second century CE was composed of perhaps 450,000 soldiers, and claimed somewhere between two-thirds and three-quarters of annual state expenditures (further details in Taylor's chapter). On any reckoning, the Roman army was one of the foundations of imperial rule.

Not even the Roman army, however, was sufficient by itself to ensure the long-term stability of imperial rule. Coercion and fear can only go so far. Just as in other premodern states, so too in the Roman empire, some element of consensus was also necessary. Consensus in the Roman empire fulfilled the same core function as it did in any other ancient empire—normalization, legitimation, belief, and sociopolitical stability—but the means by which this consensus was spread and replicated, and above all the particular modalities of its public expressions, were unique to Rome. Normative buy-in to the Roman imperial order is reflected above all in the empire-wide spread of a Roman culture, a process that historians often refer to as "Romanization" (see Versluys *et al.* 2014 for a range of recent perspectives on this controversial concept). Romanization can be seen as a type of ancient cosmopolitanism that worked to bind center and periphery—or, perhaps better, key sectors of the center and periphery—together into a single political and cultural system. And this cosmopolitanism depended, as we will see, on the peculiar political structure of the Roman empire and its republican, city-state heritage.

What we call "Roman culture" (a convenient shorthand for "Italic culture") refers to a distinctively Roman (or Italic) complex of objects, practices, and beliefs. Conventional indices include Roman urbanism and the monumentalization of public space; Roman architecture, both civic and domestic; Roman religion (deities, objects, modes of worship); the Latin language (especially in public inscriptions, many examples of which appear in the chapters that follow); Roman nomenclature; Roman material culture (from jewelry and luxury goods to ceramics and table wares; see von Reden's chapter for the logistics of trade and the nature of Roman imperial "consumption"); Roman art and visual idioms (illustrated in almost every chapter in this volume); Roman taste (as reflected, for example, in clothing, portraiture, and hairstyles); Roman dietary habits and foodways; and Roman burial practices. From one end of the Roman empire to the other, one could find people speaking Latin, using Roman law in a Roman-style forum (central public square), hosting Roman-style dinner parties in Roman-style houses using Roman-style utensils, sacrificing and making vows to Roman gods (Figure 0.6) and burying their dead in the Roman manner (for some examples of Roman tombs and funerary monuments, see Figures 4.1, 4.2, 4.4, and 5.3). The geographical extent of this Roman imperial culture is remarkable.

Roman culture never wholly supplanted local cultures, of course. Each region and each locality had a traditional culture that interacted with the metropolitan culture in a thousand different ways. Those interactions were especially dynamic in the Greek East, which continued to find meaning and value in its own language, culture, and carefully curated past (Woolf 1994; Whitmarsh 2010; for the West, Woolf 1998; Johnston 2017). But even in the eastern half of the empire there existed a recognizably "imperial" culture that was not so different from what one could find anywhere, at least in the cities. Understanding how this imperial culture was formed and sustained is the key question for our purposes. Adoption and replication was driven at a structural level by what has been called a "grand bargain" between the Roman state and the local elites of the empire (Scheidel 2015b). Because the central state lacked the means to govern its vast territories directly, it relied instead on the empire's cities, and in particular on their municipal elites, to undertake most of the day-to-day management of the empire, especially in the maintenance of order and collection of taxes on behalf of the imperial regime. In addition to new channels of upward mobility (see Ramgopal's chapter) and the implicit armed backing of the central state, the main reward these local elites received for their service was the Roman citizenship—a direct inheritance from the empire's republican roots (Ando 2016). As a juridical status, Roman citizenship gave them the full protections of Roman law. More important, perhaps, was the symbolic

FIGURE 0.6: Sacrificial Altar with Image of Cow's Head. Lugdunum, Gaul, mid-second century CE. Musée gallo-romain de Lyon-Fourvière. © Morburre, Accessed via. Wikimedia Commons, CC BY-SA 3.0.

dimension of Roman citizenship. For it allowed these local elites to advertise their membership in the imperial "power set." This helped them to differentiate themselves from the local masses and, as a result, to reinforce their power over them. And this incentivized the elites in turn to adopt many of the other trappings of Roman culture, which served the same purpose. The spread of Roman culture, that is, can be largely explained in instrumentalist terms. These local elites did not want to "be" Roman because Roman culture was intrinsically desirable; they wanted to be seen as Roman because that was practically useful (Millett 1990; *contra* MacMullen 2000, arguing for the inherent attractiveness of Roman culture).

The figure of the Roman emperor was an indispensable catalyst of this process. Like any monarch, the emperor was a peculiarly resonant symbol. As such he attracted a steady stream of discursive statements and public gestures from various "constituencies." The two main vehicles employed by local elites to honor the emperor in the civic sphere were imperial cult and imperial statuary. "Imperial cult" is a catch-all term for the objects and practices through which provincial communities exalted the reigning emperor and (some of) his deceased predecessors. Temples, priests, processions, and rituals—especially live animal sacrifice—were all mobilized to express a stance of veneration toward the emperor. The cumulative effect was not only to invest the emperor's authority with divine sanction, but also to generate an empire-wide network of cult centers that provided the Roman world with a form of "symbolic glue" (Hopkins 1978: 197–242). The erection of honorific statues for the emperor, which proliferated in the public spaces of every settlement in the Roman world, large and small, had a similar result (Figure 0.7). The dedicatory inscriptions carved onto the statue bases, thousands of which survive, indicate that emperors were celebrated above all for their virtues (justice, piety, generosity, foresight, moderation, and so on) and for their material benefactions, real and imagined. In the collective consciousness of the empire's inhabitants, that is, the emperor of the first two centuries CE was an ethical exemplar and civic benefactor (Noreña 2011, forthcoming b). This, too, was a Republican inheritance. Unlike an Egyptian Pharaoh or Achaemenid Great King, that is, a Roman emperor—at least in the early and high empire—was always imagined at least in part as a civilian magistrate with impeccable Republican credentials. The imperial titulature, with its meticulous delineation of specific legal prerogatives, is an excellent index of this commitment to the language and ideals of a representative politics. It is true that the emperor wielded a type of monarchic power that was frankly incompatible with republican values. But it did not matter. The systematic construction of the emperor as a representative of the *populus Romanus* made him available as an ideal model for imitation by local elites. As a result, they based their authority in part on that of the emperor, and also played the role of civic benefactors in their own communities, expending their private resources on urban development—and almost always along Roman lines.

Romanization in the first two centuries CE, then, was generated by a particular strategy of imperial rule, which depended on the systematic collaboration between the central state and local elites, and by a particular model of emperorship, which emphasized the putatively civilian component of Roman monarchy. Both the strategy and the model stemmed from Rome's past as a republican city-state. And both help to explain why Rome's metropolitan culture was replicated from one end of the empire to the other, and why, as a result, its urban culture was comparatively homogenous. This was an imperial cosmopolitanism, in brief, of assimilation rather than subordination (to borrow a useful distinction from Lavan *et al.* 2016). But it was an assimilation, and an imperial culture, produced by and for an educated, urbanized, land-owning

FIGURE 0.7: Statue of Trajan in military dress, Colonia Ulpia Traiana (mod. Xanten, Germany), c. 110 CE. Xanten Archaeological Park. © Hartmann Linge. Accessed via Wikimedia Commons, CC-BY-SA 3.0.

elite. There was some "trickle down" of Roman imperial cultural forms to lower rungs in the sociopolitical hierarchy, to be sure, but without the same impact on the political system. In the Roman empire, with its pronounced asymmetries of power, only the upper strata participated meaningfully in the making of an imperial culture that tended to the perpetuation of their own privilege.

ENDS AND AFTERMATHS OF EMPIRE

"In the second century of the Christian era," Gibbon wrote in the first sentence of his *Decline and Fall of the Roman Empire* (1776), "the empire of Rome comprehended the fairest part of the earth and the most civilized portion of mankind." For this influential vision of the "golden age" of Rome, gently ruled under the careful and enlightened stewardship of the Antonine emperors, Gibbon could draw inspiration from many contemporary voices, such as that of the second-century Greek orator Aelius Aristeides, whose speech in praise of Rome ("To Rome") stands as the most eloquent panegyric of the "high" Roman empire. Two hundred and fifty years later, at the end of the fourth century CE, the Roman empire—though deeply changed in both administrative and cultural terms—was still mostly intact. By the middle of the fifth century CE, though, the Roman empire, as an integrated political system, was in trouble. In the western empire in particular, important territories around the edges (Britain) and in the interior (western Gaul, western Iberia, North Africa) had been lost to central control, and a large and dangerous Hunnic state had been established across central Europe and the western Eurasian steppe (Heather 1991; Kim 2013). A century later the Mediterranean-wide Roman empire had disappeared forever, replaced in the west by a number of smaller "successor states" ruled by Germanic kings (Wood 2013), and continuing on in the east in what came to be known as the Byzantine empire (Haldon 2013; Sarris 2015).

The story of the long transition from the Roman empire to these successor states, and from Antiquity to the Middle Ages (to employ the conventional periodization), is complex and often opaque. A detailed account is of course beyond the scope of this Introduction. One simple way to sketch the outlines of this history is to frame it in terms of ruptures and continuities. Most of the big ruptures that separate the Roman empire of the second century CE from the various successor states that followed in its wake occurred in the realm of political economy. The first point to note is that the Roman empire very nearly collapsed during the so-called "third-century crisis," an extended period of military, political, and economic turbulence that lasted nearly fifty years (235–84 CE) (Ando 2012). The period witnessed a bewildering number of emperors and usurpers (the distinction, of course, was often a point of dispute) and continuous warfare: chronic civil wars between the various contenders for the throne, heavy frontier pressure, and the temporary breaking away of large territories in the east (centered on the wealthy caravan city of Palmyra) and west (most of Gaul, Britain, and the Iberian Peninsula). These problems were compounded by a demographic contraction, as the Mediterranean basin was hit by a plague (for links with the better known "Antonine Plague" of the mid-second century CE, Bruun 2007), and by financial disarray, as the central state, low on resources, indirectly caused an inflationary panic by drastically reducing the silver and gold content in the official coinage. Cities atrophied, especially in the western empire, a process that eventually led to a "ruralization" of power, as fortified villa-estates emerged as new centers of social and economic power, increasingly detached from the empire-wide urban systems upon which the early Roman empire had rested. From the perspective of the central state, the situation was dire.

Around the turn of the fourth millennium CE, under the emperors Diocletian (r. 284–305) and Constantine (r. 306–337), the Roman state was more or less reinvented and put back on a stable—but very different—footing (Jones 1964; Kelly 2004; Lenski 2012: chs. 8–10). The size of government was dramatically increased, which enabled the imperial regime to impose a more coercive and unmediated form of administrative control over its subjects. Through a form of systematic collusion between central state and local landowners, for example, tenants were increasingly "tied" to the land they worked by a series of oppressive legal mechanisms, including the right of landlords to shackle tenants suspected of flight, and the treatment of tenants as *servi terrae*, "slaves of the land" (see Lo Cascio's chapter for changing labor practices in this period). Aggressive conscription swelled the ranks of a massive army, which was sustained by a new tax system in which revenues were collected in kind and transferred directly to imperial officials. A revised monetary system, based on a reduced but stable new gold denomination, the *solidus*, underpinned a late-antique "gold economy" in which high-ranking governing elites were paid in gold, while the rest of the empire's population made do with base-metal coins (Bainaji 2007). In the long history of the Roman empire, the gap between wealthy and poor, powerful and powerless, was never so pronounced as it was in this period (Grey 2011; Harper 2011; Brown 2012; Bainaji 2015).

As a result of these developments, then, the world of the Roman empire in the fourth and fifth centuries CE was quite different in its texture and rhythms from what it had been in earlier centuries. Economic performance was in decline. Indices include the number and size of cities, the extent and vitality of trading networks, and the quality of the material cultural assemblages found in both urban and rural contexts (Ward-Perkins 2005). The "grand bargain" between central state and local elites was no longer so appealing to the latter. It became ever more difficult for the imperial regime to extract taxes and manpower from increasingly autonomous landlords, especially in the western empire. A demoralized army—hampered, perhaps, by divided loyalties, as the central state came to depend more and more on Germanic conscripts (mercenaries, in effect)—was incapable of defending the empire's borders against incursions, especially along the Rhine-Danube frontier. All of these factors led to the final collapse of centralized authority in the fifth century CE. The "fall of the Roman empire" is conventionally dated to 476 CE, when the Germanic warlord Odoacer successfully deposed the reigning emperor in the west, Romulus Augustulus, and began to rule in his place, but in fact the erosion of imperial control was a slow process, several generations in the making. We should remember that the imperial system was developing along a very different trajectory in the east, as the Byzantine empire, centered on the new capital city of Constantinople, managed to preserve territorial control over much of the eastern Mediterranean world—though in an often tense relationship with the enormous empire to its east, the Persian Sassanian empire (224–651 CE), which was a successor of sorts to the Achaemenid Empire of the first millennium BCE (Wiesehöfer 2013: 205–8, 218–26; Payne and Soroush 2014; Payne 2015, 2016). In the west, by contrast, the trend toward political fragmentation and polycentrism was gathering momentum. The age of ancient Mediterranean empire was over.

Alongside this history of large-scale political and economic change, though, there is another, "competing" history of the whole period from, say, 200 to 800 CE, which historians now refer to as "late antiquity" (canonized as a field by Brown 1971). It is a story of continuity, above all in the realm of culture. In the post-Roman kingdoms in the west, for example, rulers made selective use of Roman law, which propagated many of the normative frameworks within which subjects of the Roman empire had lived their lives (Charles-Edwards 2000). Regional versions of Latin ("vulgar Latin") were still spoken throughout the western Mediterranean world, only slowly breaking up by the end of this period into the separate dialects that would eventually form the Romance languages (Adams 2012; Dinkova-Bruun 2012). By far the most consequential bridge between 200 and 800 CE, however, is the spread and triumph of Christianity as the dominant religion of the whole area under consideration (Brown 2013). The shift from the polytheistic "paganism" of classical antiquity, and the omnipresence in the urbanized Mediterranean world of open-air, collective, civic rituals organized around the public veneration of state gods and goddesses on behalf of the community as a whole, to the monotheistic Christianity of the late Roman world and beyond, and the private, personalized worship of a God who promised the salvation of the soul, is of course one of the great revolutions in world history. But insofar as Christianity developed as a religion of empire, but also continued to grow after the fall of the empire, it represents a binding link—or, perhaps better, *the* binding link—between the Roman empire and the medieval world.

Early Christianity was a religion of empire in at least two senses. First, its rapid growth and geographical spread were enabled and propelled by the institutions of the Roman imperial state. Rome's urban and administrative network, for example, provided an organizational architecture for early Christian communities, which were widely scattered and did not yet form a single "Church." In addition, the empire-wide spread of another urban religious phenomenon, the Roman imperial cult (above, 32), provided a sort of template for the dispersal of a coherent set of beliefs and practices. And when the emperor Constantine adopted the Christian god as his personal god, he invested Christianity with the towering authority of Rome, while also directing all sorts of more prosaic favors to Christian communities, especially tax immunities. A second way in which we can see early Christianity as a religion of empire is through its deep embedding in urban administration and civic life more generally. Especially relevant here are the various public roles played by bishops (Rapp 2005), who not only oversaw their individual congregations, but who also effectively replaced the local elites of the early empire, through their civic benefactions (often presented as charitable gifts to the poor), and who also complemented the provincial governors, especially in their jurisdictional capacity (a prerogative confirmed by Constantine). Also significant, of course, is the changing urban landscape of late antiquity, and the emergence of the Christian church—modeled after the Roman basilica—as the salient architectural form in cities (and, increasingly, in the countryside: Bowes 2008: 125–88).

In the end, however, it was the spiritual dimension of early Christianity that ensured its survival after the collapse of the Roman imperial system in the west. Christian liturgy, Christian art and visual culture, and the sacred books of the Christian Church held a magnetic and enduring appeal for the followers of Christ. And yet the association with temporal and earthly political power never disappeared entirely. Almost a thousand years before Gibbon, "musing," as he put it, "amidst the ruins of the Capitol while the barefooted friars were singing Vespers in the temple of Jupiter," and suddenly inspired as a result to write his *Decline and Fall* (in October 1764), the subjects of Charlemagne, the Holy Roman Emperor—crowned as such by Pope Leo III on Christmas Day, 800, in St. Peter's Basilica in Rome—could already look back on an ancient history of imperial power and Christian piety, and imagine themselves the heirs to a new Roman empire.

CHAPTER ONE

War

MICHAEL TAYLOR

Ancient empires were established through violent conquest and maintained through armed coercion.[1] But war was endemic to the ancient world more broadly, and therefore we should ask whether there was something distinctive about *imperial* warfare, as opposed to the organized violence between smaller political entities, such as modest city-states, petty kingdoms, or various tribal groupings. This chapter suggests two fundamental features of imperial warfare: first, massive resource superiority, and second, the distance of war from the imperial core, a fact that complicated how imperial regimes recruited troops, supervised operations, and commemorated victories.

Empires deployed manpower, money, and material on a scale that far exceeded what non-imperial states could muster. Ancient authors themselves used resources, sometimes vastly exaggerated, as a means of conceptualizing imperial power. The fifth-century BCE Greek historian Herodotus, for example, analysing the first great world empire in human history, Achaemenid Persia, could report that the Persian king enjoyed an annual income equal to 14,560 talents (*c.* 415 tons) of silver, and commanded an army 1.7 million strong for his invasion of Greece (3.90–8, 7.60–97, with Laird 1921 and Armayor 1978 for discussion of Herodotus' sources). Herodotus' basic point is valid even if his numbers are bogus: the Persian king enjoyed resources unimaginable for any Greek city-state. When Athens had an empire of its own, in the fifth century BCE, Thucydides describes how the Athenian general Pericles accounted for the fiscal resources for the empire—some 600 talents (seventeen tons) of silver annually—and proclaimed these adequate for the looming war against Sparta (2.13.3–5; Pritchard 2015; cf. van Wees 2013 for Athenian finance in the Archaic period). In trying to make sense of the sudden rise of Rome, the historian Polybius reported that the Romans in 225 BCE had on their militia rolls some 770,000 men of fighting age, a combination of Roman citizens, Latin colonists, and Italian allies (2.24, with Brunt 1971 and de Ligt 2012). Writing after Rome's empire was firmly established, the historian Tacitus (*c.* 100 CE) analysed the warrior peoples of the Germanic frontier by highlighting their striking material scarcity. He noted, in implicit contrast to the well-equipped Roman legionaries, how the otherwise warlike Germanic peoples suffered from a critical poverty of iron, so that few warriors wore body armor, donned metal helmets, or wielded swords (Tacitus, *Germania* 6.1–4, with Todd 1996: 36–46; for Roman military equipment, Bishop and Coulston 2006).

Greater resources also allowed imperial powers to maintain professional armies that invested in the "human capital" of soldiers and officers. The process was often halting, as Rome retained the structures of a civic militia until the reign of the first emperor, Augustus (31 BCE–14 CE), who instituted a series of reforms that created a professional force, especially the requirement that soldiers serve continuously for twenty years, allowing them to accumulate skills through training and combat experience.[2] The historian Josephus, who had faced Roman legionaries on the battlefield as a Judaean general from 66–7 CE, marveled that "it would not be wrong to call their exercises bloodless battles, and their battles bloody exercises" (*The Jewish War* 3.5.1). That imperial warfare was resourced in a lopsided fashion is not surprising: not only did the creation of empires require substantial "venture capital" in terms of men, money, and material, but over the long run a self-perpetuating virtuous cycle arose in which conquest generated resources, which in turn fueled either new conquests or the maintenance of current borders.

The second defining feature of imperial warfare was that it usually (though not always) took place at some remove from the society of the imperial core. Between 203 BCE, when the Carthaginian general Hannibal evacuated Italy, and the Gothic invasion of Italy in 408 CE, no foreign enemy made a significant territorial incursion into Italy south of the Po River Valley (civil wars were another matter). Imperial states therefore did most of their fighting well outside of the traditional homeland. Well-resourced wars and all their accompanying destruction took place on the periphery, in the liminal space of frontier regions, or, ideally, beyond them. The military prowess of empire was expressed far from the center, away from the gaze, and indeed supervision, of the inhabitants of the metropole. Thus, the paradox of imperial warfare: The most powerful polities of the ancient world saw less warfare in their own "backyards" than did weaker powers clinging to geopolitical survival in an anarchic environment, in which the enemy could appear quite literally at the city gates. War was a far more immediate experience for, say, the inhabitants of feuding *poleis* in Crete or the tribal societies of continental Europe than it was for a citizen living in Rome during the *pax Romana* (cf. Goldsworthy 2016 on the "Roman peace").

DEPLOYMENT AND RECRUITMENT: CORE AND PERIPHERY

One useful way to parse ancient empires is to borrow the core-periphery model of world systems theory pioneered by Immanuel Wallerstein to describe modern, capitalist empires and the hierarchies of production, distribution, and extraction (Wallerstein 1974–89). The model of empire with an (inner/outer) core and (inner/outer) periphery is useful when applied to pre-modern empires, although primarily focused on the impact of primitive transportation and communication technologies (Woolf 1990). Thus, the city of Rome and Italy as a whole would respectively form the inner/outer core of the Roman empire during the Principate, with demilitarized interior provinces and militarized frontier provinces forming the inner/outer periphery.

Most ancient empires were formed by states that succeeded in mobilizing the superior resources of their core territories. Athens combined the fiscal resources from the silver mines of Laurion with the motivated rowers of her large citizen body, which stood as high as 60,000 adult males at the outbreak of the Peloponnesian War in 431 BCE (Hansen 1988). Even this was small compared to the enormous militarized citizenry of Republican Rome, which numbered in excess of 300,000 adult citizen males at the outbreak of the Second Punic War.[3]

States with imperial ambitions that lacked resources in their core regions, particularly manpower, simply did not become empires. Perhaps the best example of the phenomenon of under-resourced imperial pretensions was Sparta after the Peloponnesian War (431–404 BCE). Despite having the most militarized society in the entire ancient Mediterranean, Spartan attempts to control the Aegean in the early fourth century BCE quickly fizzled. There were many reasons behind Sparta's failure to establish itself as anything beyond a regional power, including diplomatic and strategic error. But the most salient deficiency was the lack of Spartans, especially full Spartiate citizens (*homoioi*), to carry out increasingly ambitious expeditionary operations. By the mid-fourth century BCE, Sparta had fewer than 1,000 full Spartiate males (Aristotle, *Politics* 1270a.30–31), and with any hope of Aegean empire shattered, struggled to remain even a regional power in the Peloponnese (for demographic decline, see Ober and Weingast forthcoming).

Imperial states with ample resources in their core regions needed to project power into their expanding peripheries. This led to logistical problems concerning the transport and supply of large forces operating increasingly far from home. Each empire had its own logistical limits, and major military defeats often signaled that they had run up against them. While the logistical sophistication of the Achaemenid empire was readily apparent in its network of royal roads and detailed bureaucratic system, it lacked the infrastructural capacity to successfully project its forces into the Greek mainland, with the dramatic bridge over the Hellespont proving a showy but insufficient stand-in for more coherent seaborne power-projection assets. The Athenian debacle in Sicily (415–413 BCE) signaled that Athens lacked both the manpower and logistical capabilities to maintain a substantial military force into the central Mediterranean: notably, the Athenians only brought thirty cavalrymen in one horse transport vessel.[4] Geography certainly favored Roman logistics: located roughly in the center of the Mediterranean basin, Rome could project its power, via sea lanes, with equal ease to the east and west (Scheidel 2014). Yet Rome struggled to maintain its forces beyond the Mediterranean basin, as illustrated by the failed Parthian campaigns of Crassus, Mark Antony, and, eventually, the emperor Julian, all derailed by insurmountable logistical problems. In the North, operations across the Rhine river were hampered by a grossly inadequate transport network, which stymied Roman strategic mobility and resupply, leading the emperor Tiberius in the early first century CE to abandon attempts to reconquer Germany (cf. Tacitus, *Annals* 1.63). A successful Germanic campaign, like those of the emperor Domitian, involved building roads (Frontinus, *Stratagems* 1.3.10).

Various strategic deployments were employed based on the constraints of time and space. Achaemenid grand strategy, for example, maintained weak military forces in the periphery, under the command of vetted governors (satraps). The Persian king himself retained control of a central standing force of Persians, 10,000 (or perhaps 12,000) infantry (the "Immortals" and "Apple Bearers") and 2,000 cavalry (Charles 2011, 2015). These doubled as both a strategic strike force which the king could bring to bear against any salient threat, and as a professional cadre for offensive operations. For major wars, the Great King personally levied enormous field armies from across the empire. The weakness of satrapal armies meant that they were often incapable of responding to initial frontier incursions, for example the lackluster response to a modest Spartan expeditionary force in Asia Minor in the 390s BCE. Far more seriously, Alexander the Great completely overwhelmed a satrapal army at the Granicus river in 333 BCE. By the time the royal field army had completed a ponderous, empire-wide mobilization process, Alexander had already conquered Asia Minor, an Achaemenid possession for nearly two centuries.

Rome became an imperial power in the third and second centuries BCE because of an expanded citizen body, bolstered by an intensive program of colonization and land distribution, and the exploitation of Rome's Italian subjects (*socii*) through conscription. During the First and Second Punic Wars (264–241 BCE; 218–202 BCE), Rome suffered enormous losses, but was still able to defeat Carthage after protracted struggles. In the second century BCE, Rome leveraged its manpower pool to maintain massive strategic deployments in multiple theaters, fielding between six and thirteen legions across the Mediterranean from 200–167 BCE, comprising roughly 75–200,000 Roman and Italian soldiers (Brunt 1971: 454).

FIGURE 1.1: A citizen army: Roman citizen soldiers stand by to register for the census. Altar of Domitius Ahenobarbus, Rome, c. 100 BCE. Musée du Louvre, Paris. Public domain. Accessed via Wikimedia Commons.

During the Republic, Rome maintained these deployments on a power-projection model. It did not maintain a professional standing army in the periphery on permanent duty. Rather, amateur citizens were conscripted in Italy and deployed in temporary legions that disbanded at the end of the campaign (Figure 1.1). Even as Roman and Italian peasants organized their family life-cycles to accommodate a heavy period of military service by young men, the heavy expeditionary deployments of the second century BCE were disruptive.[5] Long, bloody, and unprofitable campaigns in Spain, especially from 153–133 BCE, proved particularly onerous and unpopular (Rich 1983). Furthermore, the number of citizens who could be conscripted for protracted periods without shutting down the agrarian economy was still limited, so that Roman imperial activities were actually somewhat under-resourced.[6] This constraint was particularly felt in the east, where the Romans proved reluctant to annex and directly administer territory. This hesitation was disguised under the lofty slogan of "freedom for the Greeks" (Dmitriev 2011; Polybius 18.46.5–13), but it was also a policy of convenience, as it was difficult to scrounge up an annual deployment of two to four additional legions (20,000–40,000 men, counting allies) conscripted from an already stressed peasantry. In the aftermath of the Third Macedonian War (171–168 BCE), Cato the Elder captured this problem with a quip that "the Macedonians must be free, because they cannot be defended"

(Scriptores Historiae Augustae, *Hadrian* 5.3, with Gruen 1984: 429 for the difficulty of defending Macedonia from barbarian incursions). The result was that Rome re-entered the Greek East on multiple occasions between 205 and 146 BCE, at which point a permanent garrison was established to occupy Macedonia.

The militarized and politicized peasantry of the Republic ultimately proved a dangerous liability to the Roman state as its politics increasingly destabilized over the course of the first century BCE. The availability of tens of thousands of heavily armed and militarily competent Roman citizens fueled the civil wars of the 80s, 40s and 30s BCE. In order to demilitarize Italy and prevent any prospective rival from quickly raising an army, the final victor of the civil wars, Augustus, demobilized tens of thousands of soldiers in the provinces, as colonists, and created a new professional army that would be permanently stationed in the periphery. A force of professional soldiers (about 125,000 citizens in twenty-five legions at the time of Augustus' death in 14 CE) serving for longer periods (first sixteen, then twenty years) was far less disruptive to the agrarian economy of the imperial core than was mobilizing nearly every single able-bodied male for shorter and discontinuous periods of time. Professionalization also shifted the danger of large, organized military forces away from the politically volatile core, which housed the senate and urban plebs, the two other groups in the empire with the potential for organized collective action against the emperor.

To a degree, military dispositions after Augustus resembled the satrapal dispositions of the Achaemenid empire, with standing forces in frontier regions commanded by trusted subaltern officers (*legati Augusti pro praetore*, "legates of Augustus with praetorian rank"). In the imperial core, Augustus kept a special force of privileged troops, the Praetorian Guard (de la Bédoyère 2017). This unit consisted of nine cohorts, roughly 9,000 men, analogous to the Persian king's Immortals. But there were important differences between Roman and Achaemenid dispositions. First, the satrapal armies in the periphery of the Achaemenid empire were relatively modest garrisons, deployed for local defense and police purposes. By contrast, the Roman legions in the provinces represented potent and experienced field armies, far superior in both numbers and fighting quality to the Praetorian cohorts. This disposition left the empire vulnerable to civil war in moments of dynastic collapse, in particular in 69 and 193 CE.

Armies posted to peripheral regions inevitably began to recruit locally. This was partially a matter of convenience, but a successful empire also faced the problem of a core population increasingly unfamiliar with the routine practice of warfare. Those living in frontier societies, ranging from the Greeks on the Achaemenid fringe to the Germans on the Roman frontier, were schooled in frequent fighting, and therefore needed little additional training or acculturation to prove effective killers in the service of empire.

The frequent deployments of the middle Republic (264–133 BCE) had produced a heavily militarized citizen body in Rome. Even so, Roman generals relied on local forces in the periphery to supplement their expeditionary forces, especially providing scouts, light infantry, and cavalry (Prag 2007). By the Julio-Claudian era (14–68 CE), auxiliary cohorts of provincial troops totaled approximately 150,000 men, roughly half of the Roman army. Tacitus puts auxiliary strength at only slightly less than that of the citizen troops (*Annals* 4.5), but the exact ratio would have varied from province to province. By the end of the second century CE, very few legionaries hailed from Italy itself (Forni 1953). By the late empire (from 284 CE), recruitment had shifted outward again, with the distinction now made between soldiers and units recruited from within the empire (where virtually all inhabitants enjoyed citizenship after 212 CE), and soldiers recruited from beyond the frontiers. While this so-called "barbarization" of the army has long been cited as a source of military decline, it was in fact the continuation of a long trend in Roman military history which saw a significant portion of troops recruited from the outside, first the Italian *socii* of the Republic, then the provincial auxiliaries of the Principate, and finally the barbarian *foederati* (allies bound by treaty) and *laeti* (non-Roman settlers in the empire who supplied troops) of the late empire (Elton 1996b).

By the late Roman empire, strategic deployments came to resemble a series of concentric circles, radiating out from the inner core to the outer periphery. In the late second century CE, the emperor Septimius Severus permanently stationed a legion in Italy as an additional military bulwark to his new dynasty. During the Third-Century Crisis (235–84 CE), emperors began to assemble a cadre of units around them that evolved into the mobile field army (*comitatenses*). By the fourth century CE, Roman military deployments had become increasingly layered. On the outer periphery were the *limitanei* (soldiers in frontier zones) and *ripenses* (soldiers on river frontiers), who served as border garrisons, even if their numbers (and perhaps their fighting quality) were insufficient to stop major incursions (Isaac 1990). A series of mobile field armies (*comitatenses*) were posted in the inner periphery, providing a defense-in-depth. By the mid-fourth century CE, emperors personally commanded a reserve field army (*praesentales*). The system in theory allowed for a great deal of flexibility in dealing with threats, as *limitanei* could be rolled into comital armies (with the title of *pseudocomitatenses*) in order to concentrate forces, while the praesental armies served as centralized strategic reserves and also a bulwark against civil war. This flexible echeloning of armed forces continued in the Eastern empire into the seventh century CE.

COMMAND AND RULE

A critical aspect of deploying forces in the imperial periphery was ensuring that they obeyed the orders of the government in the core. Empires needed to effect command and control of sizable military forces over great distances, requiring some degree of decentralized decision-making authority and delegate command. Sovereignty in non-monarchic empires was usually in theory and to a degree in practice assigned to the people themselves, so expeditionary leadership was accomplished by elected magistrates. From 502/1 BCE onwards, the Athenians annually elected a board of ten generals (*strategoi*) who were able to stand for office repeatedly. This allowed some men—most notably Pericles, who held the office continuously for fifteen years—to obtain a pre-eminent position within the democracy (Plutarch, *Pericles* 16.3). In the Roman Republic, the people elected annually two consuls and two to eight praetors, endowing them with *imperium*, the legal capacity to command armies, from which our word "empire" is derived (see most recently Vervaet 2014). Also elected were the quaestors who served as quartermasters in Rome's armies, as well as the military tribunes who served as staff officers in the consular legions. In Carthage, generals were in some cases directly acclaimed by armies themselves, most notably when the Carthaginian army in Spain nominated Hannibal to command in 221 BCE, a fact subsequently ratified by the citizens' assembly in Carthage (Polybius 3.13.3–4).

While the citizen body might elect its commanders, there was always the risk of misconduct once commanders had removed themselves from the surveillance of the core. In some instances, the citizen soldiers themselves acted as the eyes and ears of the rest of society. Carthaginian soldiers on several occasions crucified generals believed to be cowardly or ineffective (Polybius 1.11.5, 1.24.6). Roman soldiers affirmed that their commanders had actually won a major victory by spontaneously hailing him as an *imperator*, a prerequisite for requesting a triumphal celebration.

Further accountability awaited generals upon their return to the metropole. The Athenians routinely subjected their commanders to a rigorous review (*euthuna*) of both expenditure and conduct (Aristotle, *Constitution of the Athenians* 48.4, 54.2). Misconduct and incompetence could result in massive fines, exile, or even capital charges. Thus Miltiades, the hero at Marathon, was prosecuted and convicted for a botched attack on Paros the very next year (Herodotus 6.136; Plutarch, *Cimon* 4.3). Thucydides took to writing history because he had been exiled for his failure to adequately support operations around Amphipolis (Thucydides 5.26.5). In one of the most controversial instances of democratic accountability, an Athenian jury condemned six successful generals after the victory over the Spartans at Arginusae in 406 BCE for failing to rescue survivors and retrieve the dead (Xenophon, *Hellenica* 1.7.1–35).

Accountability was less rigorous in Republican Rome, owing to the entrenched position of Roman aristocratic families and the deferential nature of Roman voters. Rare prosecutions did happen in response to egregious misconduct, for example against Publius Claudius Pulcher for religious violations prior to the catastrophic loss at Drepana in 259 BCE (Polybius 1.52.3). Yet Roman generals more often faced little democratic accountability for major failures. When the consul Gaius Terentius Varro returned to Rome after losing his entire army at Cannae in 216 BCE, for example, he was honored for "not despairing of the Republic," and continued to hold important commands throughout the war (Livy 22.61.14). Roman voters themselves were willing to elect to further office men who had previously suffered military setbacks, so long as they comported themselves honorably in the face of defeat (Rosenstein 1990). This lack of accountability may have at times proven an advantage, as Roman generals could operate without the onerous fear of being second-guessed for the necessary tactical risks a commander in the field must assume. By contrast, the Athenian generals in Sicily in 415–413 BCE led their armies to total annihilation for fear of being tried and executed for dereliction of duty if they failed, against their own better judgment, to press home the attack (Thucydides 7.48.4).

Accountability in Republican Rome focused less on the outcome of campaigns than on fiscal impropriety, corruption, and abuse of power. By the early second century BCE, Roman commanders were expected to account strictly for booty taken on campaign (Churchill 1999). Following a shocking incident in Spain in 150 BCE, in which a commander promised a band of Lusitanians clemency, only to massacre them and pillage their belongings, the Romans set up a standing court for the prosecution of corruption (*quaestio de repentundis*).[7] Sadly, this court rarely proved a genuine tool of accountability, as it was instead hijacked as an instrument of vicious political competition. Cynical use of the tools of accountability helped to push the faltering Republic over the brink: Caesar crossed the Rubicon largely because he feared prosecution and condemnation should he return to Rome a private citizen (Plutarch, *Caesar* 46.1; see Gruen 1969 for a history of the courts after the reforms of 149 BCE).

Caesar, subsequently Dictator for life (*dictator perpetuus*), proved the culmination of a trend toward military dynasts that had been brewing for a century. Ironically, the Roman people in their voting assemblies played a key role in elevating this new generation of increasingly autocratic commanders. In 107 BCE, the people elected Gaius Marius as consul, and overrode the Senate to assign him the command against the Numidian king Jugurtha. When a new Germanic threat loomed, the people elected Marius to five more consecutive consulships. In 88 BCE, the people even passed a bill to give Marius, then a private citizen, command in the east against Mithridates VI, an act which sparked the first great civil war when the consul who had been given the command by normal mechanisms, Sulla, turned his army against Rome.

Sulla established himself as Dictator and paradoxically sought to restore the aristocratic system of shared commands, but his reforms could not withstand either the requirements of imperial warfare or the chronic instability of

Roman politics. Sulla's best general, Pompey, borrowed the old Marian ploy of using popular laws to obtain unprecedented long-term commands, the first against Mediterranean pirates in 67 BCE, and then a command against Mithridates the next year. The result was that Pompey effectively became the generalissimo of the last generation of the Roman Republic. In 59 BCE, Pompey's ally, Julius Caesar, used a popular law to obtain a five-year command in Gaul, subsequently extended. In 55 BCE Pompey himself was granted another unprecedented command, being allowed to command his legions in Spain remotely through lieutenants (*legati*), while simultaneously overseeing the grain supply in Rome.

In the late Republic, then, soldiers were not just serving for long periods, but were also serving for long periods under the same generals. In the middle Republic, the centurion Spurius Ligustinus, who served for twenty-two years between 192 and 171 BCE, had soldiered under many commanders, naming five different generals to whom he owed promotions or honors. No single Roman aristocrat could claim his total loyalty (Livy 42.34). How very different was the centurion Gaius Crastinus, who was loyal to Caesar alone, presumably after serving under him in Gaul for much of the past decade. In 49 BCE, Caesar promoted Crastinus as senior centurion (*primus pilus*) of the tenth legion. The next year, Crastinus urged his fellow veterans to fight against other Roman citizens on behalf of "our commander," and fell fighting at the battle of Pharsalus in 48 BCE (Caesar, *Civil War* 3.91, 99). Ultimately, the imperial model of the middle Republic, with commanders overseeing modest armies, in geographically constrained areas of operation and temporally limited commands, made civil war unlikely. The late-Republican model, however, of military dynasts with large armies, geographically expansive areas of operation, and extended commands enabled civil violence on a massive scale.

Ancient monarchs, ranging from Achaemenid kings, the Hellenistic successors of Alexander the Great, and the Roman emperors from Augustus onwards, encountered a new set of problems around integrated rule and command. In particular, how could a monarch simultaneously rule the entire empire while also commanding armies in peripheral regions? Command by proxy was an inevitable feature of monarchic empires, although such proxies could prove a serious danger if they accrued either too much coercive force or gained too much political capital on account of military victories. Take for example the cadet prince Cyrus, the governor of Achaemenid Anatolia in the last decade of the fifth century BCE and an architect of Athens' defeat in the Peloponnesian War. As a result, he commanded a series of garrison forces, and also had access to a large pool of Greek mercenaries. With both political capital and coercive force, Cyrus marched from his peripheral command in an audacious, and nearly successful, attempt to unseat his reigning brother, Artaxerxes (described in Xenophon, *The March Up Country* 1).

At the inception of the Roman imperial monarchy, Augustus left the Republican system of provinces largely in place. Those provinces with sizable military forces, instead of being governed by elected (or prorogued) magistrates, were now appropriated by the emperor himself, governed remotely through lieutenants, *legati Augusti pro praetore*, exercising the emperor's delegated power on the model pioneered by Pompey.

Early in his career Augustus chose to supervise critical military operations himself, personally commanding armies in the Balkans and Spain. These operations added to his military glory, and also absented him from Rome during a period when his status as monarch was not yet universally welcomed. As he aged, he relied on close family members for important campaigns, in particular his stepsons Tiberius and Drusus and, later, his grandson Gaius. This strategy was later imitated by the emperor Vespasian, who, upon settling in Rome as emperor, placed his son Titus in command of the Jewish War. A major assignment was a high-profile way to groom a successor: Tiberius and Titus both ascended the purple themselves.

Tiberius, despite long experience as a successful field commander, chose to remain in Italy during his reign (14–37 CE). Remote command through proxies had distinct advantages, above all because it allowed the emperor to remain in (or near) Rome, and to focus on domestic politics and imperial administration. The emperor's "paperwork," involving vast quantities of correspondence from across the empire and managed with only a small staff, consumed significant energies (Millar 1977). Furthermore, it was difficult for the emperor to process intelligence about frontier operations spread across three continents, so while emperors employed rudimentary grand strategy (such as the troop strength in each province, and military instructions), they relied on provincial governors who enjoyed significant operational leeway.[8]

Tiberius' immediate successors largely followed suit, save for brief campaigns (e.g., Caligula's erratic northern expedition and Claudius' two-week "safari" in Britain) which were more political stunts than close supervision of military operations. While emperors monopolized the constitutional right to command, some of the glory of military victory inevitably accrued to the legate who was directly in charge of victorious operations. Emperors accordingly placed limits upon commemoration and public display by subordinates. 19 BCE saw the last triumphal parade by a non-member of the imperial family, although successful generals were given the less conspicuous honor of triumphal garb—the costume for private display without the public parade. Still, a successful commander could be a potential liability to a politically weak emperor. Nero liquidated his most successful general, Domitius Corbulo, on the paranoid suspicion that he might prove a rival. Shortly after Corbulo's dutiful suicide, another of Nero's generals, Galba, marched on Rome with his army, forcing Nero's own suicide in 68 CE. The emperor's paranoia was not necessarily unfounded.

Nero's death created a vacuum of power which triggered the so-called "year of the four emperors," as Galba was soon murdered and replaced by his former ally Otho, who was in turn deposed by Vitellius, commander of the legions on the lower Rhine. Final victory went to Vespasian (r. 69–79 CE), a man from such an obscure background that Nero had felt comfortable entrusting him with the massive army necessary to crush a major revolt in Judaea.

Vespasian's son, Domitian (r. 81–96) became the first Roman emperor since Augustus to engage in long-term personal command of military operations, spending nearly two years reorganizing the frontier on the lower Rhine. The emperor Trajan (r. 98–117) massed troops from across the empire for two major campaigns across the Danube in the kingdom of Dacia (modern Romania), followed by an invasion of Mesopotamia, all under his personal supervision. His successor Hadrian (117–138) eschewed such military adventures, but nevertheless spent extended periods in the provinces. The results of his personal review of the Legio III Augusta in Lambaesis are preserved on a lengthy inscription (see Speidel 2006 for text and translation). Antoninus Pius maintained himself near Rome for the entirety of his reign (138–161), a reaction, perhaps, to the expeditionary and peripatetic tendencies of his predecessors. Yet a new military crisis pushed his successor Marcus Aurelius back into the field, as Germanic invasions prompted him to spend most of his reign (161–180) on the Danubian frontier fighting the Marcomanni and Quadi (Birley 2012).

Neither Trajan nor Marcus Aurelius had worked their way up the ranks in the army. Instead, they both came from families who had worked their way up the social ladder in Rome over the course of generations. The same could be said for Septimius Severus, the commander of the Pannonian legions who used his army to win the next round of civil wars in 193 CE. While an effective general, Severus was not a career soldier but instead a wealthy provincial striver (originally from Lepcis Magna in North Africa) who had combined successful administrative positions with an advantageous marriage to put himself within striking distance of the throne. Once emperor, however, Severus further entrenched the notion that the emperor's primary job was to command in the field, spending most of his reign campaigning in the east and in Britain. His deathbed advice to his sons was to "get along with each other, enrich the soldiers, and scorn everyone else" (Cassius Dio 77.15.2).

As the paradigm of soldier-emperor crystallized, it became less clear why the emperor should be recruited from the ranks of the Roman Senate at all, rather than from the senior echelons of the army itself. In 235 CE, Severus Alexander was murdered by his own soldiers, who elevated the general Maximinus the Thracian to the purple, heralding a new breed of emperor, selected not because of his social standing in the imperial core, but rather on the basis of his professional military competence out on the periphery (and his ruthless ability to stage a military coup). Military command literally usurped imperial rule.

There were two great risks to this new model. The first was that the emperor became increasingly unmoored from the imperial core, evidenced by the rise of frontier capitals like Trier, Milan, Thessalonica, and Nicomedia at the expense of Rome. Recruitment from the ranks of the army meant that emperors hailed from a very different social background from that of the empire's landed elite. Most critically, the legitimacy of the emperor more than ever before was yoked to his superior ability to command, a fact that had to be proven on the battlefield against rival candidates. Civil war became a routine form of imperial election. These internecine conflicts made the empire especially vulnerable to external threats that would have been manageable in other circumstances. The series of civil wars that wracked the empire from 235–84 CE allowed several major foreign incursions. The Sassanid Persians invaded Asia Minor and sacked Antioch, while Goths and other Germanic invaders overran the Danubian frontier, raiding as far as Greece and Anatolia.

It was difficult for a single emperor to deal with multiple threats personally, and it was increasingly perilous to entrust a large army to a subordinate who might become yet another usurper. Shortly after his election by the army in 284 CE, the emperor Diocletian sought a new solution: multiple emperors would rule at once. Diocletian hoped to bypass the hereditary principle, recruiting new emperors into a college of four on account of their military prowess and transforming the emperorship into a self-perpetuating junta of senior generals. The so-called Tetrarchy functioned well enough under the guiding hand of Diocletian, but quickly degenerated into civil war following his voluntary retirement in 305 CE. Yet the advantages of joint rule caused the ultimate victor, Constantine (306–37 CE), to divide the empire between his sons (ultimately not harmoniously) and subsequently prompted the emperor Valentinian (364–75 CE) to share the burden of rule with his brother Valens (364–78 CE). While briefly sole emperor, Theodosius (379–95 CE) sought to continue this trend by splitting the empire between his underage sons Honorius and Arcadius.

Both boys grew up to be ineffective men, creating a vacuum of imperial power. Child emperors became the norm during the fifth century (McEvoy 2014), allowing a new breed of warlord to arise—senior military commanders, often of barbarian origin, who wielded real power behind the throne, in a manner not dissimilar to the shoguns of medieval Japan (MacGeorge 2002). The result in the West was an irrevocable dissonance between military command and rule: now the legitimate ruler was a nobody, while senior generals such as Stilicho, Aetius, and Ricimer wielded enormous powers in perilous games of power politics. In the West, this unstable solution resolved itself when the *magister militum* (Master of the Soldiers) Odoacer overthrew the boy emperor Romulus Augustulus in a palace coup in 476 CE and proclaimed himself king of

Italy. A similar dynamic prevailed in the East during the fifth century. The cycle was broken in the East, however, by the reemergence of a strong emperor in the person of Zeno, who solidified his power, coincidentally, in 476. While Zeno's reign was tumultuous, he succeeded in reuniting military command and imperial rule, paving the way for the survival of the East Roman empire for nearly another millennium.

WAR AND CULTURE IN ANCIENT EMPIRE

Imperial societies were militaristic by any measure: created largely by success in war, they needed to celebrate and inculcate martial values in both their political classes and in their broader populations as a matter of self-perpetuation (Lendon 2004). But the immense geographical distance between the core society itself and its peripheral wars tempered the militarism of even the most warlike empires. Let us take the example of the Roman Republic (Harris 1979; cf. Eckstein 2005 for militarism as an endemic feature of the ancient Mediterranean). The period of the Roman Republic saw near constant warfare based on the mass mobilization of the citizen body. We would therefore not be surprised to see the impact of warfare on culture both high and low. It manifested itself in the spectacle of the triumph, the great victory procession featuring captives, loot, the triumphal general, and his victorious army (Beard 2009; Östenberg 2009; Lang and Vervaet 2014). Militarism pervaded the folk tales the Romans themselves told, for example about the heroic sacrifice of Horatius Cocles, killed helping the Romans cut the Tiber bridge to ward off an Etruscan invasion (Polybius 6.55; cf. Livy 2.10, who has Cocles swim to safety). War even helped to define Roman home décor (Welch 2006), from the display of captured arms and armor, to elite homes jammed full of captured artwork, to domestic decorative ensembles teeming with military violence, like the set of fragmentary reliefs from the Latin colony of Fregellae showing a fight between legion and phalanx (Coarelli 1996). By the third century BCE, military victory began to impinge upon Roman onomastics, too, as when the Roman general Manius Valerius took the surname (*cognomen*) Messalla to celebrate a victory at the Messana during the First Punic War (*Fasti Capitolini* 54). The list of imitators was long. By the late Republic, the pre-eminent plebeian clan of the Caecelii Metellii alone could claim members nicknamed Balearicus, Macedonicus, Numidicus, Delmaticus, and Creticus, each reflecting a conquest. The organization of the most powerful Roman voting assembly, the *comitia centuriata*, evoked military units (*centuriae*), and owed its origins to an army assembled to elect the generals who commanded Rome's armies. Meeting on the Campus Martius ("Field of Mars"), it did not begin its deliberations until a garrison had been installed in an over-watch position on the Janiculum hill, a piece of archaic symbolism ensuring that the "army" would not be ambushed while it deliberated. Even the Latin word for voting, *suffragium* (hence the English "suffrage") may derive from soldiers clashing their weapons as a form of assent (Vaahtera 1990).

As pervasive as war was in Roman culture, we should take a moment to marvel at what Romans did not do. They did not, for one thing, carry weapons in public. Indeed, the center of the city was encircled by a ritually demilitarized zone, the *pomerium*, where armed soldiers were forbidden to enter, except when marching in a triumphal parade. While happy to watch servile gladiators butcher each other in the arena, Roman citizens themselves did not fight duels to the death such as Europe's medieval warrior aristocracy would later do, nor were Roman men buried with weapons and armor when they died.

When Quintus Caecilius Metellus eulogized his father Lucius, a successful commander in the First Punic War (264–241 BCE), he named ten areas in which the deceased had surpassed all others. Lucius had enjoyed great success in war: during the First Punic War, he had captured the city of Panormus (Palermo), and had triumphed riding a chariot drawn by captured Carthaginian elephants. Still, when his son listed his virtues, the vast majority—seven out of ten—were essentially civilian, rather than martial, in nature. Sure enough, the son claimed that his father had been "the foremost warrior, the stoutest general, and a man who had accomplished great deeds as a commander." But he was also the "best orator" who "had enjoyed the highest offices, was supremely wise, was the most prestigious senator, obtained much money by honest means, left behind many children, and was the most distinguished man in the city" (Pliny the Elder, *Natural History* 7.140).

A century later, the young Scipio Aemilianus received a difficult lesson that success in war was not the only source of cultural currency in Rome. Scipio was a genuine war-hero. As a seventeen-year-old cavalryman, he distinguished himself at the battle of Pydna (168 BCE), riding so far out in pursuit of the fleeing Macedonians that he was feared lost, only to return drenched in the blood of slain enemies (Plutarch, *Aemilius* 22.3–8). But Aemilianus subsequently learned to his dismay that his ostentatious heroism was insufficient to launch a political career. Having contented himself upon his return with private recreation, he was saddened to realize that his comrades judged him "lazy and slothful" because he did not occupy himself in the law courts (Polybius 31.23.11). Even at the height of overseas conquest, an aristocratic war-hero might be harshly judged for not spending enough time in Rome as a lawyer.

Always a civic elite at heart, the Roman aristocracy became further demilitarized as Rome's Mediterranean empire grew. In 153 BCE, a shocking incident occurred when not enough candidates declared to fill all twenty-four positions as military tribunes, officials who served as legionary staff officers (Polybius 35.4.4). A dangerous and unpopular war in Spain was the immediate cause of this shortfall, but the incident signaled that elite youths might have other priorities than military service. By the first century BCE, the wealthiest class of Romans ceased to serve as cavalrymen, so that the "knights" (*equites*) became a commercial and administrative class rather than a fighting force (McCall 2002).

The ultimate result of Augustus' military dispositions was that the culture of the frontier armies became profoundly alien to the inhabitants of much of Italy. Soldiers, rather than being agents of Romanization, were instead absorbed into the hybridized cultural spaces of the frontier zones. Whereas an Italian would most likely eat pork accompanied by wine, a soldier on the frontier would more likely eat beef washed down with beer (King 1999; beer: *T. Vind.* 2.182, 190). On his way to his barracks he might pass severed heads impaled in front of Roman military installations.[9] The soldier might play dice with a tower (designed to randomize throws) labeled "Picts defeated, enemy destroyed: Play safe!" (Figure 1.2). By the late empire, soldiers were wearing barbarian-style trousers and long-sleeved tunics, rather than the short-sleeved tunic dominant in the Mediterranean. These are seemingly minor points, but collectively they

FIGURE 1.2: Military culture: Dice-tower from the frontier: "Picts defeated, enemy destroyed: Play safe!" Vettweis, Germany, fourth century CE. Rheinisches Landesmuseum (Inv. 85.269). Accessed via Wikimedia Commons.

manifest the growing cultural gulf between soldiers on frontiers and civilians in the imperial core. When soldiers flooded into Italy to fight civil wars, they appeared as profound outsiders to both common and elite Romans. In 69 CE, for example, several Roman citizens decided to sneak up and cut the belts of some Batavian auxiliaries, a sort of workingman's prank (Tacitus, *Histories* 2.88). The pranksters were shocked by the murderous rage this gag evoked, and paid with their lives for the ever-widening gap between the militarized periphery and the demilitarized core.

COMMEMORATION, FAR AND NEAR

Where should imperial powers commemorate the violence and sacrifice associated with distant campaigns? While ancient states did commemorate battles or wars near the places where they were fought, few would be able to experience these monuments. Peripheral memorials in some instances targeted an audience of deployed imperial agents (primarily soldiers and veterans) along the frontier: Trajan's Adamklissi monument in Moesia (modern Romania), for example, included a list of the dead and an altar honoring fallen comrades as well as metopes featuring gritty depictions of combat, and was likely intended as a site for veterans and active soldiers (Figure 1.3) (*CIL* 3.124124; Richmond 1967; Rossi 1997; Turner 2013). Nonetheless, official monuments to slain Roman soldiers were rare, and troops on the frontiers largely commemorated fallen comrades at their own initiative and expense (Hope 2003).

Most peripheral commemoration was primarily directed at imperial subjects, as advertisements of power and control. In 168 BCE, the Roman general Aemilius Paullus commemorated his victory over the Macedonians with a pillar at Delphi, an emphatic statement about the new realities of Roman hegemony (Kähler 1965; Taylor 2016). Pompey's victory monument in Spain and Augustus' Alpine *tropaeum* ("trophy") at La Turbie had similar functions (Hölscher 2006; Formigé 1949). Even graveyards could be transformed into powerful statements. The Romans notably left exposed the bodies of Macedonians killed at the battle of Cynoscephalae in Thessaly (197 BCE), and the bleached skeletons lay for over five years as symbols of Roman power (Livy 36.8). The exposed remains of Germanic invaders killed by the Romans at Aquae Sextiae (102 BCE) served a similar purpose (Plutarch, *Marius* 21.3). Conversely, Germanicus' burial of the long-exposed Roman bodies at Kalkriese and the erection of a high barrow over them represented a territorial claim as well as an act of domestic piety. This symbolism was legible to the Germans, who dug up the barrow and re-scattered the bones as soon as his armies withdrew back across the Rhine (Tacitus, *Annals* 1.61).

But how to commemorate remote victories (and on occasion mourn distant defeats) in the imperial core? Imperial societies had to find ways to bring the war

FIGURE 1.3: Close combat on the Danube: Fully-armored Roman vs. naked Dacian. Tropaeum Traiani, Adamklissi, Romania, 108 CE. Accessed via Wikimedia Commons.

home. The Athenians developed an annual ceremony repatriating the ashes of the dead with great fanfare (the occasion of Pericles' famous funeral speech: Thucydides 2.34–46), and inscribing the names of citizens slain abroad on public casualty lists in the city (Arrington 2011). The Romans transformed the triumphal parade, a procession that probably began as a purification ritual for soldiers returning from battles fought within miles or even meters from the city, into a means to recapitulate victories that had taken place far from the view of the city's inhabitants. All of the key players in these campaigns were reassembled for the urban audience: enemy captives were driven before the procession, and the spoils of war were paraded in a sort of theatrical accounting before being deposited into the treasury. Next came the general himself, dressed in a special robe, riding a four-horse chariot, followed by his victorious army. The soldiers doubled as witnesses, able to back up the claims their commander had made about his victory (Livy 31.49.10; cf. Pittenger 2008 for contested triumphs). In addition, floats and murals provided bystanders with representations of enemy cities and landscapes, and sometimes of the battle itself and its aftermath (Holliday 1997).

FIGURE 1.4: A distant campaign: Barely visible details of Trajan's Dacian campaigns. Trajan's Column, Rome, 113 CE. Accessed via Wikimedia Commons, CC BY-SA 4.0.

Still, the triumph often failed to make distant wars intelligible and relevant to Roman bystanders. The poet Ovid was a sardonic eyewitness to the last set of triumphs before the ritual effectively lapsed in 19 BCE (henceforth only occasionally revived for members of the imperial family). In his poetry, Ovid suggests that a triumph was a good place to pick up a girl, and part of the "art of the lover" was to help her interpret the difficult representations of far-off battlefields. Yet the would-be *amator* might find that the foreign terrain and events baffled not only the pretty girl, but even himself! The poet advises him to make up names and explanations about events on the periphery ("if she asks about what you don't know, reply as if you did!"), which were increasingly illegible to the privileged inhabitants of the metropole (Ovid, *The Art of Love* 1.6).

The high empire saw two monumental attempts to bring the war home to the Roman people: the columns of Trajan and Marcus Aurelius, which featured combat scenes from the emperors' respective wars against the Dacians and the Marcomanni (Figure 1.4). Ironically, both columns also recapitulated the problem of legibility in the core, as the content of the scenes, after the first few registers, would have been little more than a vague impression of combat to viewers craning their necks upwards to gaze at the reliefs as they spiraled into the sky (Trajan's Column: Coulston 2008; Leppard and Frere 2017. Column of Marcus Aurelius: Ferris 2009; Kovacs 2009; Beckmann 2011). Victory celebrations could be so generic (bound prisoners, triumphant armies, and so on) that one monument might even be handily substituted for another: the Arch of Constantine, for example, was decorated with *spolia* culled from victory monuments erected earlier by Trajan, Hadrian, and Marcus Aurelius (Pensabene and Panella 1999; Ferris 2009).

False triumphs were one of the hallmarks of a bad emperor. Domitian, for example, was accused of putting wigs on slaves to masquerade as German prisoners in his triumphs (Tacitus, *Agricola* 39). This problem was not unique to imperial Rome, and at least one Roman traveler was said to have witnessed a duplicitous scene dating back to the Achaemenid empire. The first-century CE philosopher Apollonius of Tyana supposedly saw an old tapestry hanging in Babylon displaying the very successful Persian campaigns in the Aegean, including the capture and sack of Naxos and Eretria in 490 BCE, as well as the victory at Thermopylae and the capture and destruction of Athens in 480 BCE. These were plausible enough victories to celebrate, but the tapestry conveniently omitted the Persian reverses at Marathon, Salamis, and Plataea![10]

DECLINE AND FALL

Military defeat was the leading reason for the collapse of several imperial powers in the ancient Mediterranean. Sparta destroyed Athens' Aegean empire with its victory in the final phase of the Peloponnesian War. Alexander the Great violently conquered the Achaemenid empire. Rome annihilated Carthage in 146 BCE. Most ancient empires did not suffer from any sort of prolonged "decline and fall." Rather they were ended through sudden, massive military defeats, even if some form of sub-imperial state survived in the aftermath.

The Western Roman empire did not suffer any sort of sudden and irrevocable shock. Instead, it saw a long period of military and political instability before it fragmented into independent kingdoms ruled by Germanic kings. While simplistic narratives of "decline and fall" do not adequately capture the complex transformations of the period, it is nonetheless indisputable that Rome was increasingly incapable of maintaining its Mediterranean hegemony by the late fourth century CE, a fact starkly illustrated (but not caused) by the costly defeat at Adrianople in 378 CE, when migrating Goths rebelled and destroyed a Roman field army, killing the emperor Valens who personally commanded it (Potter 2004: 526–75). The destruction of an army and even the death of an emperor should have been a crisis from which an adequately resourced and politically stable Roman empire could recover, as it had from the destruction of so many armies and the combat deaths of more than a few emperors.

Resource deficiency lay in the background of the western empire's military difficulties. The administrative split between West and East, present in some form from the third century CE, the organizing principle of the Tetrarchy, and permanent in the dynastic arrangements of 395 CE, made it more difficult to transfer resources around the empire against any serious threat, be it a Germanic incursion in the West or a Sassanid Persian invasion in the East. The debacle at Adrianople illustrates the breakdown in cooperation that resulted when two emperors brought a split personality to imperial decision-making. The Goths could have been handily defeated had Valens waited to unify his field army with another force being brought from the west by his teenaged co-emperor (and nephew) Gratian. But Valens bristled at being viewed by his own court as dependent upon the aid of a mere boy and therefore sought to defeat the Goths by himself, losing everything (Heather 1991 and 2010 for Goths and barbarian groups in the implosion of power in the Western Roman empire). The divided empire could work at cross purposes: in the 440s CE, the eastern empire began paying the Hunnish warlord Bleda a hefty indemnity after a series of military defeats. His son Attila, so resourced, launched an invasion of the western empire, ravaging Northern Gaul, and even advancing as far as Italy before his death in 452 CE (Kelly 2009).

There was also greater competition for resources that in other times might have gone to the armies. The late empire developed a large bureaucracy without necessarily developing an efficient one, and corruption may have siphoned off funds that could have gone to armies. Ramsay MacMullen has postulated that the late Roman army was inexorably weakened as corrupt officials and commanders appropriated pay and rations of non-existent soldiers for their own enrichment (MacMullen 1988). Chris Wickham has suggested even deeper structural problems in the empire, as an increasingly powerful class of landowners succeeded in competing successfully with the late Roman state for both manpower and money (Wickham 1984). A recruit to the army meant the loss of an agricultural laborer for the late Roman landlord, who had the clout to protect a class of dependent tenants (*coloni*) from conscription. Meanwhile, powerful landlords wrested a greater proportion of the agricultural surplus as rent, which before would have gone to taxes. As a result, the late Roman state struggled to mobilize and concentrate the resources necessary to defend the empire.

The long-running migration crisis that plagued the empire in the late fourth and fifth centuries CE was severe: the Hunnish migrations had disrupted the peoples of Central and Eastern Europe, setting in motion an array of subsidiary migrations like a billiards cue. Such mass migrations were part of the fundamental human dynamics of Iron Age Eurasia. Between 112–101 BCE the Romans had faced a serious threat in the form of the Cimbri and Teutones, but these had been repulsed through a coordinated response, in particular the joint consular armies, some 52,000 men strong, at Vercellae (Plutarch, *Marius* 25.4). In 60 CE, the governor of Moesia had successfully settled some 100,000 Bastarnae and Roloxani across the Danube (*CIL* 14.3608). The Marcomanni and Quadi had threatened Italy at a moment of demographic crisis owing to a massive plague, but a strong emperor was still able to concentrate military resources to defeat them. The *Volkswanderung* was a serious problem, but one that might have been managed with a focused and adequately resourced response. But the political dysfunction of the late empire, especially in the West, prevented a concerted movement against these threats. Warlords and usurpers instead encouraged armed bands of barbarians to move about the empire in order to exploit them in their own internecine conflicts (Kulikowski 2000). The collapse of the western empire was caused by political decentralization and destabilization, resulting in the dissipation of resources for armed forces and the failure of military coordination as second-order effects.

War proved an immediate presence even for the most demilitarized aspect of late Roman society, the Christian clergy. In *c.* 400 CE, a Roman teenager in Britain named Patricius was kidnapped by Irish raiders and taken to Ireland as a slave. Even as he escaped and returned to Ireland as a bishop, his would be a world of thuggish warlords, not stable empire. Around the time St. Patrick was born, another inhabitant of Roman Britain, the monk and theologian Pelagius, migrated from the faltering frontier to the safety and comfort of Rome. In 410 CE, a Gothic army sacked the city of Rome, seeking concessions from the emperor Honorius. Pelagius fled as a war refugee to Carthage, intensifying a theological clash with Augustine, the bishop of Hippo, over the nature of salvation. Augustine's own *City of God* in no small part sought to respond to pagan allegations that Christian neglect of the traditional gods had led to Gothic sack (*On the City of God* 1–5). An early chapter dealt with the problem of whether Christian holy women raped in the sack were permitted to commit suicide (1.16–28). As Augustine himself lay on his death bed in 430, at the age of seventy-five, Hippo was besieged by Vandals, who had crossed the Rhine in 406 and then been admitted into Africa by the renegade general Boniface as part of a dispute with the *magister militum* Aetius. Establishing their own kingdom, the Vandals captured Hippo shortly after Augustine's passing, next took Carthage, and even sacked Rome in 455.

An anecdote from the hagiography of the fifth-century CE saint Severinus of Noricum aptly captures the dynamics of imperial implosion. On the Danube frontier, menaced by Germanic warlords, a group of Roman soldiers stayed in their garrison despite the fact that they were no longer being paid by the bankrupt imperial court. The unit sent messengers to Italy seeking wages, but these never returned. According to the supernatural tale in the *Life*, Severinus began to weep spontaneously in his cell and alerted the townspeople to the bodies of the soldiers floating down the bloodstained river (Eugennipus, *Servinus of Noricum* 20). Warfare had become both poorly resourced and terrifyingly close.

CHAPTER TWO

Trade

SITTA VON REDEN

In the middle of the second century CE, a Greek-speaking merchant from Egypt undertook a trade journey to Muziris on the western coast of Southern India. The ship on which he undertook the long trip through the Red Sea along the Arabian Peninsula and into the Indian Ocean was based in Myos Hormos, a port town on the east coast of Egypt (Figures 2.1 and 2.2). In order to finance the large enterprise, the trader had taken out a maritime loan either from a professional moneylender or, more likely, from a large agrarian estate owner who combined, like many other members of the Roman imperial elite, agrarian business with trade (Rathbone 1990). An excerpt of a fragmentary papyrus containing a supplement to the loan contract reads as follows:

> I will give your camel driver (. . . .?) for the extra charges of the journey to Koptos; and I will convey (the goods) through the desert under guard and protection up to the public tax-receiving warehouse at Koptos, and I will place them under the authority and seal of yourself, or of your agents or whichever one of them is present, until their loading at the river; and I will convey them down to the warehouse for receiving the quarter-tax at Alexandria, and likewise will place them under the authority and seal of yourself or your men. For all the payments (for the ship?), from now to collection of the quarter-tax, and of the desert transport and the carrying charges of the river-workers and the other incidental expenses (------ ?) on occurrence of the date for repayment specified in the contract of loan to the trip for Muziris, if I do not then duly discharge the aforesaid loan in my name, that then you and your agents or managers are to have the option and complete authority, if you so choose, to carry out execution without

notification or summons to judgement... (text and translation from Rathbone 1990).

The back (*verso*) of the papyrus contained a full list of commodities imported and valued for the twenty-five percent tax the Roman administration claimed on commercial imports into the empire. Only a short portion of the account is preserved, giving the values of Gangetic nard (an aromatic essential oil), tusks, and ivory splits measured by weight. The ship had loaded around four tons just of ivory, while 135 tons are given as a total weight for another missing item. This was clearly a large consignment of high-value goods. Other items will have been pepper, spices, pearls, silk, precious stones, exotic animals, and tortoiseshells, as we know from a trading manual dealing with the Indo-Egyptian trade route that went via Arabia (*Voyage Around the Erythraean Sea* 56; see below, 83–5, and *Digest* 39.4.16). The total value after tax amounted to almost seven million sesterces (6,926,852 Egyptian drachms), as we learn from the end of the papyrus. This was seven times the census of a Roman senator, the equivalent of a large estate in Italy, or the cost of an aqueduct in Asia Minor (Harris 2007; Sidebotham 2011). A hundred and twenty ships annually were involved in the Indian Ocean trade from Egypt, according to the geographer Strabo (2.5.12). Strabo wrote during the Augustan period, and this trade even increased over the following

FIGURE 2.1: Excavations at Myos Hormos, Egypt. Photograph © Andrew Peacock.

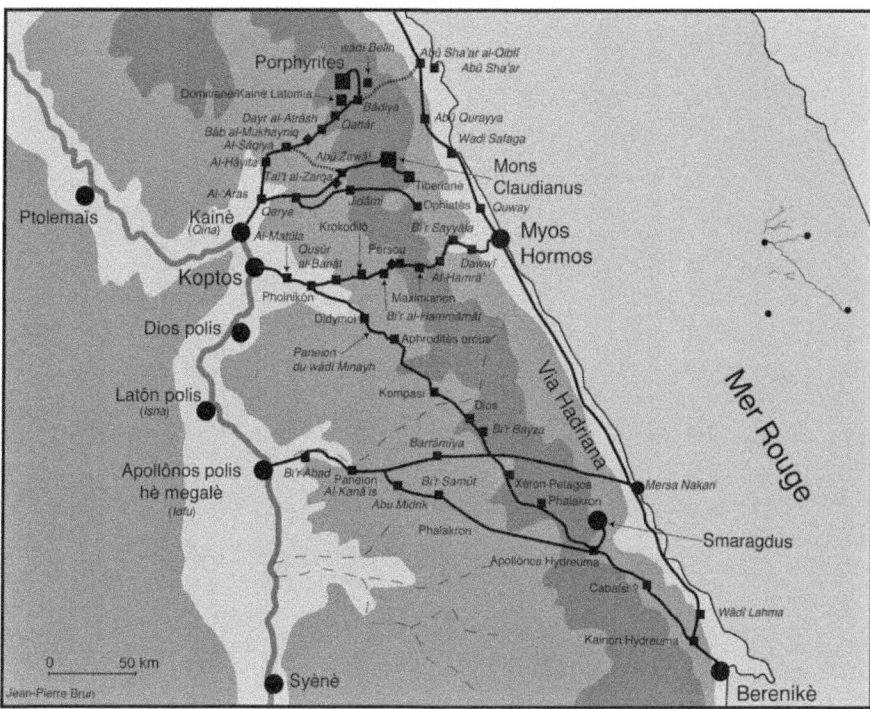

FIGURE 2.2: Map of the western Red Sea coast. © Jean-Pierre Brun.

one hundred years (Sidebotham 2011: 218 and *passim*). Not all shipments will have had the size and value of the one known to us from the Muziris papyrus, of course. But nothing indicates that it was a unique adventure.

The Muziris papyrus sets an agenda for the study of trade in the Roman empire. It gives an idea of its spectacular scale, its geographical reach, value, financial and social organization, as well as state interest in it: the enormous tax of twenty-five percent was not meant to prohibit imports from outside the empire, but rather to take a just share from its profits (cf. Cottier *et al.* 2008 for customs duties at provincial borders). Yet, more important, the papyrus also raises a number of questions: How was trade in luxuries related to trade in mass products? How did long-distance trade interlock with regional and local trade networks? Who financed trade? And most important, in what ways was the development of trade connected to the development of an empire? Beneath its surface, the Muziris papyrus hints at various possibilities. We need to look at regional exchange networks that were connected to larger circuits; at hubs of exchange, like Alexandria and the city of Rome as centers of consumption; and at the role of a central state that extracted taxes and tolls, but also provided infrastructure such as roads and ports as well as a unified coinage and a legal system in which contractual partners could trust one another. As financial, legal, and physical infrastructures expanded, and the exchange of knowledge between regions intensified, the conditions for trade were much improved.

TRADE IN THE ROMAN ECONOMY

Markets can be regarded as the most efficient distribution systems for goods. But in antiquity, many goods did not pass through marketplaces, nor did all markets function according to the modern market principle of free supply and demand. The greatest problem of ancient markets was the potential lack of information. Demand could be very volatile due to seasonal change or temporary events, such as festivals, visits of the emperor, or armies passing through a region. Supply was equally unpredictable due to unforeseen climatic factors, military factors, or the incapacity of local producers and traders to respond to unusual levels of demand. Moreover, information asymmetries between buyers and sellers, such as uncertainty about the adequacy of price setting or the quality of the product on offer, were among the most widespread concerns of consumers supplying themselves via the market (Bresson 2016). In order to make markets function at all, ancient states moderated information asymmetries by promulgating rules of fair exchange, and by controlling standard weights and measures, the validity of media of exchange, and, at times of food shortage, prices of essential goods; but official price controls for goods other than grain were rare (Rathbone and von Reden 2014). This market oversight justified (among other things) the imposition of harbor tolls, importation taxes, or market fees. Sometimes states or cities attempted to attract to, or ban certain groups of people from, local markets, or prohibited the export of particular local products.[1] Markets could also be controlled by social asymmetries and through patronage, privileging, protecting, or threatening individuals in ways that affected their business (Bang 2008; Curtin 1984; Morley 2007a). Foreigners in particular could suffer from serious disadvantages, such as lack of legal and social protection in competitive market environments (Terpestra 2013). Other forms of distribution thus coexisted with market exchange and trade: There were networks of kinship, friendship, and patronage, all of which included some mutual material exchanges; landlords (and the emperor) exchanged goods between different units of their estates or with employees and agents as part of their wages; diplomatic exchanges involved money, precious metal, and other valuables between states; there was state-organized acquisition, requisitioning, and distribution of tax in kind; and there was the state-organized grain dole of the city of Rome (*frumentatio* or *annona*).

These very different kinds of movement of goods are difficult to distinguish archaeologically, while in the perception of contemporaries their distinction was often neglected. Political writers and rhetoricians of the Roman empire, for example, emphasized the massive imports to Rome as part of an imperial rhetoric of abundance. But they had little interest in the economic mechanisms behind the imports. Take the praise of Aelius Aristeides, a famous Greek orator living most of his life at Smyrna in Anatolia during the second century CE:

> Whatever the seasons may grow and whatever countries and rivers and lakes and arts of the Hellenes and non-Hellenes produce are brought from every land and sea . . . Whatever is grown and made among each people cannot fail to be here at all times and in abundance . . . The city appears as a kind of common emporium of the world. Cargoes from India and, if you will, even from Arabia Felix, one can see in such numbers as to surmise that in those lands the trees will have been stripped bare and that the inhabitants of those lands, if they need anything, must come here and beg for a share of their own . . . Arrivals and departures by sea never cease, so that the wonder is not that the harbor has insufficient space for the merchant vessels, but that the sea has enough, if it really does (*Orations* 26.11–12, 13) (cf. Morley 1996: 3–6 for the imperial context of this oration).

The supply of the mega-city of Rome with food and the standing armies far away on the frontiers could not be achieved just by free commerce. Both were parts of an economy in which the state, provincial governors, agents of the emperor (*procuratores*), and local merchants cooperated in order to meet extraordinary demand. The grain dole for the urban plebs of Rome, beginning in the late second century BCE on the initiative of popular tribunes or individual magistrates, and feeding by the time of Augustus about one-fifth of the city's roughly one million inhabitants with free grain, played an important role in the state-organized economy during the imperial period[2] Similarly, the provisioning of mobile and standing armies could not be left entirely to the uncertainties of local markets. One of the most difficult questions to answer is whether the demands of the state, or markets, were the driving factors of the Roman economy. But the opposition is badly framed. The two economies were interconnected in various ways, while there were forms of supply that are not easily classified within either of the two categories. If we wish to understand the success of the Roman imperial economy, we need to understand the ways in which markets and state institutions operated in common to meet high levels of demand.

EARLY TRADE IN THE MEDITERRANEAN

Archaeologically we see extensive networks of exchange in the coastal regions of North Africa, Europe, and Egypt as well as in the Near East from the Bronze Age (*c.* 3000 BCE) onwards. There is little doubt that much, though not all, of this exchange was genuine trade and that the search for metals was its major motivation (Dietler 2007; Broodbank 2013). Another ecological factor stimulating trade in the Mediterranean was its maritime geography, which allowed for relatively safe travel over short and middle distances. The Mediterranean region, furthermore, is characterized by a large number of micro-climatic environments favoring diverse local production and specialization. There was enough agricultural variety, especially of vines and oil, to stimulate exchange for variety and choice, while food shortages did not hit large geographical areas simultaneously. The Mediterranean Sea, moreover, is well connected to continental hinterlands by an abundance of navigable rivers, comparable only to the Northern Black Sea region where, too, we find a concentration of Greco-Roman trade. Since the late Bronze Age there was also a high human mobility in the Mediterranean and the Near East, which favored the spread of consumption habits and cultural knowledge.

Italy and the regions that became part of the Roman empire were agrarian economies developing within these ecological and demographic parameters and constraints. Local subsistence economies dominated, while rural trade in subsistence goods and tramping in relatively small ships of up to seventy-five tons was the most common form of exchange. Yet in order to understand the growth of trade in pre-industrial empires we need to understand how the host of small agricultural units and local exchange networks came to be integrated into larger economic circuits (Eisenstadt 1963: 30–3; Mann 1986: 25; Morley 2007a). Demand and power were the twin engines of trade in the Roman empire. Efficient satisfaction of demand helped to legitimize the empire and was thus a key to Roman power. It sustained armies on campaign, maintained the Roman frontiers, and supplied the cities with food, water, and building materials. Successful distribution improved standards of living in the city of Rome as well as some provinces and created incentives for taking part in the imperial system. As the empire consolidated, not only the Italian but also provincial elites participated in agrarian and industrial production of scale. They extended loans for maritime trade, increased production, and engaged in the re-export of exotic luxuries. The Muziris papyrus is a vivid example of this. Roughly from the Augustan period onwards, there are indications that the empire came to be integrated more closely into an economic system in which some regions became major suppliers of other regions. This affected local production, choice, and possibly even prices.[3] Scholars have described the increasing economic interdependence of regional economies in the Roman empire in different terms, calling it an "integrated" economy (Hopkins 1980), a "market" economy (Wilson 2009; Temin 2013), or a "global" economy (Woolf 1990; Morley 2007b; Pitts 2015). We shall return to this question later. First, we need to ask how the Roman economy developed out of smaller regional economies into an empire-wide system of distribution until its (partial) disintegration toward the end of the third century CE.

TRADE NETWORKS AND THE COMING OF ROME: FIFTH TO SECOND CENTURY BCE

In 500 BCE Roman interest in trade was still negligible, but trade in the Mediterranean was thriving. Carthage dominated the coasts of North Africa, western Sicily, and southwestern Spain up to Gades. Corinth, Aegina, and Athens frequented maritime routes in the Aegean, reaching into Thrace, the Black Sea, and Western Asia Minor in the North, and to the Levant and Egypt in the South. Greek cities had colonized Cyrene in eastern Libya, the eastern parts of Sicily, southern Italy, and the southern coast of modern France. Etruscans were active in northern Italy, southern France, and across the Alps. Greeks, Macedonians, and Persians traded with tribal groups in eastern continental Europe and the Northern Black Sea region; spice and incense trade connected the Arabian Peninsula and India with Egypt and the Levant (cf. Morel 2007: 492–4 for Etruscan trade connections). There were at that time very active networks of heterogeneous trading groups for which ethnic designations like "Greek," "Etruscan," "Carthaginian," or "Phoenician" are inappropriate (Dietler 2007: 249).

"Phoenician" traders may have had access to the Forum Boarium in Rome, the city's earliest market (Morel 2007). In the first quarter of the fifth century, Rome began to expand its territory, conquering Veii and maintaining friendly relationships with Caere, a Carthaginian ally located near the Italian coast. These connections may lie behind the first Roman treaty with Carthage (dated by the literary tradition to the sixth century BCE). It is, however, only a century later that Rome expanded aggressively into the western Mediterranean trading *koine*. In the late 350s, Rome defeated Caere and Tarquinia, while the coastal colony of Ostia was founded at the mouth of the river Tiber. In the early 340s, a second treaty with the Carthaginians was ratified. Rome pushed into Latium and Campania in the 330s, coming into contact with the large Greek commercial center of Neapolis (Naples). It was also at that time that Rome began to use coined money: square bronze bars (*aes signatum*) in the areas of northern Italy where the Etruscans dominated, and round pieces in Campania where they exchanged with Greeks. Roman interest in coastal towns and coinage was not driven by trade, but expansion led to increasing involvement in interregional and long-distance trading networks that had been active for centuries.

Let us linger a little longer on the trade networks of the pre-Roman period. These are vital to understanding the first phase of Roman expansion and trade in the fourth to second centuries BCE. Take for example the trade of Massalia (Marseille), a Phocaean foundation of the sixth century BCE. Because of its relatively limited agrarian hinterland (*chora*), trade was the most important source of income of this sizable Mediterranean town. Wine, drinking cups, and trade amphoras were the most important commodities circulating along the southern coasts of France and further inland. But some of Massalia's exports reached as far as the regions of Switzerland, continental France, and Germany, where we find plenty of archaeological evidence for independent local and regional exchange before the Roman conquest (Elton 1996a: 77–9). Massilia's commercial activities from the sixth to the second centuries can be distinguished into three different dimensions: an intense local exchange network with the Gallic hinterland in which above all agrarian produce, wine, and drinking vessels circulated, but also medicines, fish, precious stone, and other local and regional products. The second dimension of trade developed along the maritime routes toward Spain on the one hand and Etruria on the other. Several secondary colonies of Massalia developed along the coast of the Languedoc and toward the Rhône delta, all of which being trade and consumption centers themselves, but also functioning as transit zones of precious metals, above all silver and tin. A third dimension of trade was long distance, linking Massalia with Phocaea (its nominal mother city) and its trading network in Asia Minor and the Black Sea, as well as Athens, the hub of the Aegean in the fifth and fourth centuries BCE. Along these routes tin and silver were resources to which Massalia had access, while conversely profiting from the fine ceramic wares produced in Chios, Rhodes, Corinth, and, above all, Athens.[4]

The multipolar trade network of the Phoenician and Carthaginian colonial world provides another example. It reached from the Levant via North Africa to sites in Sicily, Sardinia, and Spain. Most Carthaginian trade and that of its colonies was local in the first 300 years, showing the typical pattern of an agrarian regional economy with only some long-distance connections across the Mediterranean (Pilkington 2013). However, successful colonization of the coastal regions of Cyrenaica (eastern Libya), combined with the intense connections between Sicilian colonial cities and mainland Greece in the fifth century BCE, allowed Carthage to create a powerful empire expanding across the western Mediterranean, and even affecting the Aegean. Arguably, Carthage was one of Athens' major supplier of grain before it was eclipsed by the Bosporan kingdom in the fourth century BCE (Pilkington 2013).

With the Macedonian conquest of the Persian Empire under Alexander the Great (334–323 BCE), trade in the Mediterranean reached an unprecedented scale. In the third century BCE, Alexandria gained from the territory of Egypt an estimated tax income of six million *artabas* of grain (c. 240 million liters) to which must be added financial capacity derived from monetary taxation (at least equivalent to the tax income in kind), and unknown quantities of private surplus for distribution in the eastern and western Mediterranean as well as the Near East.[5] Alexandria developed into a commercial and cultural hub with a population of about half a million, while Rhodes, closer than Athens to the western Asian coast, took over from the Piraeus the role of being the major Aegean port of exchange. Alexander's conquests, moreover, linked the vast road network of the Persian empire to the Mediterranean, spread Greek language, coinage, markets, and administrative practices to western and central Asia, the Far East and northern India. Mesopotamia and many coastal cities on the Persian Gulf became accessible to Greeks (Kosmin 2014). Ptolemy II built several harbor towns along the western coast of the Red Sea and re-opened a canal which the Persian king Darius had constructed between the northern tip of the Red Sea and the eastern branch of the Delta (Sidebotham 2011). In Egypt, we can also observe how Greek law and monetary practice gradually transformed local economies, making commercial transactions legally safer and more recognizable to Greek traders (Manning 2007). The Greek communication and trading networks in former Persian territories were patchier, imperial coin systems and administrative control more localized, and the volume of trade lower than at the height of the Roman empire. But it is important to bear in mind that the Romans conquered highly developed economic systems that were linked regionally and interregionally prior to their conquest and territorial annexation.

From the time of the Second Punic War (218–201 BCE), Rome became part of the Mediterranean Hellenistic–Carthaginian economic system. The links between Rome and these interconnected worlds of exchange and trade became stronger when Rome asserted its control over the Greek cities of southern Italy and Sicily, and even more so as Roman power spread into the Aegean and Asia Minor. Among the many indices of Rome's increasing role in the eastern Mediterranean are the eastward movement of Italian amphoras, the presence of Italian merchants in Alexandria (*ILS* 7273), and the commercial settlement of Romans, Italians, and their freedman on Delos (*I. Delos* 1699). By 166 BCE, Rome had gained so much power over the Greek world that it could grant the status of free port to Delos. The measure clearly aimed at attracting more trade in the eastern Mediterranean toward the West. Astymedes, a Rhodian envoy pleading for mercy before the senate, bewailed that Rhodes had lost eighty-five percent of its harbor tax, dropping from one million drachmas to just 150,000 (Polybius 30.31.10–12). This implies a drop of the formerly substantial annual volume of Rhodian trade from 50 million to just 7.5 million drachmas. Delos became a booming commercial island as a result. This can be inferred from the wealth and status of bankers, the statues erected in their honor, and the ostentatious financial gestures they made on the island (Andreau 1999: 49). One of the most important long-term consequence of the Roman re-orientation of Aegean trade was the spread of Greek financial sophistication to Rome and Italy (Harris 2006).

CONSUMPTION AND EMPIRE: 200 BCE–200 CE

Territorial expansion, the acquisition and taxation of a growing number of provinces, improved lines of communication, transportation, and monetization, but also migration, increasing numbers of standing armies, and the unprecedented growth of the city of Rome were the most important and interdependent factors stimulating trade in the Roman empire. It is difficult to separate driving factors from secondary effects. Arguably, concentration of resources and functioning supply systems are the precondition for military expansion; yet it can also be argued that military expansion spurred economic development by mobilizing local resources. Urbanization and the growth of towns can be regarded as the result of better supply systems sustaining larger populations in urban environments, just as urban growth stimulates agrarian production and trade in agrarian hinterlands. We have little direct information about the early economic development of the city of Rome, which allowed its citizenry to turn into a successful war machine. It is assumed that conquest and predation were the major sources of Roman wealth. By the mid-second century BCE, in any case, Polybius perceived Rome as a world empire (1.3.3). We suggested in the previous section that down to the early second century BCE, Rome's prosperity derived from the reparations conquered cities had to pay, and from its involvement in trading networks that had been active before the Roman conquest. From about the second quarter of the second century, however, Rome transformed the Mediterranean economy into something quite different from what it had been before. Cash-crop production, consumption, and trade throughout the Mediterranean increased substantially. The political price the Roman state had to pay for this transformation was civil war and the loss of a Republican government.

Figure 2.3: Storehouse (*horrea*) at Ostia. Photograph © Parco Archaeologico di Ostia Antica.

During the last two centuries BCE, the city of Rome developed into a mega-city of about one million people. This was truly gigantic. It doubled the size of Alexandria, which had been the largest Mediterranean city in the Hellenistic period (323–30 BCE), and its urban population was not reached by any European city before 1800. Alexandria had been able to grow because of its exceptionally fertile hinterland, combined with a highly controlled system of taxation, in cash and in kind, channeling surplus into the city for consumption and export. Rome, by contrast, did not benefit from any of these advantages. Although the Italian peninsula is fertile in regions like Umbria, Campania, and the Po valley, it nowhere reached the yields of agrarian systems based on artificial irrigation, such as Egypt, North Africa, or Mesopotamia. Rome also did not attract traders for any significant amount of export. The supply of Rome with food, clothing, housing, heating, and construction materials for public baths, palaces, and temples was thus an unprecedented imperial and economic feat. The growth of the harbor at Ostia, with its warehouses, food markets, porticoes, aqueducts, and long-distance roads from the beginning of the second century BCE onwards, provides the archaeologically visible witness of the change. This change was spurred by taxation and rents derived from imperial possessions, but it also transformed local production and trade throughout the empire.

The degree to which imperial power contributed to the prosperity of Rome is impressively illustrated by the fact that the city experimented with grain doles (*frumentationes*) to the urban plebs while at the same time granting tax exemption to Roman citizens living in Italy (Rickman 1980; Erdkamp 2005). In 167 BCE, the citizens of Rome were exempted from tribute, and so were the Roman citizens of Italy after the Social War (91–89 BCE). From the time of Augustus, 200,000 inhabitants of Rome constituted the *plebs frumentaria* (recipients of the grain dole), a privileged group of people receiving five *modii* of grain monthly without payment (Erdkamp 2005: 258–316). Rations were sufficient to feed more than one person, but even on a conservative calculation, no more than a third of the Roman population can have benefited from the dole. The total volume of grain needed to feed the city has been estimated at 30,000,000 *modii* (c. 200,000 tons) per year, of which the state grain supply provided just 12,000,000 (or 80,000 tons). Grain came from Sicily, Sardinia, North Africa, and Egypt, partly in the form of tax in kind and partly from the vast imperial estates whose tenants had to hand over up to one-third of their crop (Erdkamp 2005: 206–57; Lo Cascio 2007: 639–41). Not all of this grain was shipped to Rome, however, serving other imperial markets as well. Conversely, local governors could buy additional grain, if the *annona* (state supply) was not sufficient. Yet although state interference in the distribution of grain was considerable, large parts of the urban supply with food and other goods were left to commercial exchange.

It is important to understand the interplay between state intervention and private enterprise (Lo Cascio 2007: 640–9). The administrative structure set up by Augustus to oversee the grain supply was headed by the Prefect of the Grain Supply, who had offices in Rome, Ostia, and Puteoli, where most ships coming in from Africa and Egypt called port. The Prefect was in charge of the collection of food, its storage, transport, distribution, and marketing. He set up contracts with private shippers (*navicularii*) and grain dealers (*negotiatores frumentarii*) who were often in fact the same people. Special incentives were given to those who contracted with the state. The emperor Claudius (41–54 CE) provided indemnities to shippers who lost their loads when transporting grain to Rome, and granted privileges to those carrying over 10,000 *modii* to the capital. Citizens gained exemption from the *lex Papia Poppea* (a law strengthening marriage), while citizens with Latin rights gained citizenship (Suetonius, *Claudius* 18.2–19.1). In the second century CE, *navicularii* investing more than half of their property in ships serving Rome received exemption from public liturgies (obligatory unpaid offices) (*Digest* 50.6.6.6.). Supervision of the grain supply extended to other professional activities, such as grain measurers, bargemen, and bakers in Ostia and Rome (Lo Cascio 2007: 641). Toward the end of the second century, contractual relationships of *navicularii* and the office of the Prefect turned into a liturgy: *navicularii* were now obliged to use part of their ships in the service to the state grain supply. Just as in the case of army supply, the supply of the city of Rome with grain was not left to the vagaries of the market, while in the last decades of the second century CE state control was further extended. But while the state interfered strongly in the grain supply, it did not develop a parallel economy but instead relied on commercial facilities and structures that were already in place. Moreover, although the state grain supply was an enormous administrative task and would not have been possible without substantial imperial exploitation, it provided only a fraction of the city's demand.

Consumption in the city of Rome transformed agrarian production and marketing in Italy and North Africa, and later in other regions as far apart as Western Asia, the Black Sea, and Spain (Mattingly 1994; Bowman and Wilson 2013). With the exemption of all Italians from *tributum* (poll tax and land tax), we can be certain that dramatic economic change in Italy resulted from marketing incentives rather than tax pressure. Grain was not the focus of the new productive activity, but for fresh food, oil, wine, textiles, wood, and some luxuries, Italy's privileged position made it a major supplier of Rome (Morley 1996). By the time of Augustus, the immediate hinterland of the capital was densely occupied with farms and villas engaged in the breeding of poultry, fish, and bees; the growing of fresh vegetables, fruit and flowers; and the raising of exotic animals and growing of exotic foods (*pastio villicata*) for the urban market (Marzano 2011). Despite a focus on horticulture, oil and wine production were important in the hinterland of Rome as well. It has been estimated that over thirty percent of the wine and twenty-five percent of the oil consumed in Rome and Ostia were produced in the immediate hinterland of Rome (*ibid.*). Single or double presses dominate sites in Latium, while multiple presses indicative of large agricultural units engaged in mass production are rare. Peasant farming and large estates dispersed into small units characterized the landscape of the *suburbium* and the wider hinterland of Rome. Most of the presses that can be dated suggest a wave of investment in the late Republican and early imperial periods. Columella, an agrarian writer and owner of a large estate in the proximity of Rome in the first century CE, gives ample evidence for the intense interest the Roman elite took in profit-oriented agrarian production, especially of olives, wine, and wood, but also of gardening products (e.g., *Agriculture* 1.16.3) (see also Lo Cascio, this volume, for the changing labor regimes of this production). So-called *villa* agriculture developed all over Italy during the second century BCE and became the hub of commercial production, income, and elite consumption not just in Italy, but also in North Africa, Gaul, Britain, and Germany. Cash-crop production did not serve just the city of Rome. We mentioned above the trade of wine and olive oil to armies in other provinces. Late Republican Dressel 1A amphoras stamped with the mark "*SES*," for Sestius, a senatorial family with estate holdings in Cosa in northern Etruria, have been found in numerous sites along the coast in northern Italy, Gaul, and up the Rhône valley (Wilson 2008a). Rome was just one focus of local and regional marketing activities taking place both within Italy and along its well-connected harbors to the hinterland during the late Republican and early imperial periods.

It is also worth looking at local distribution patterns in order to understand the connection of local and regional marketing in relation to the growth of towns (Figure 2.3). It should be remembered, first of all, that not all produce reached the city by way of independent merchants, and that many urban residents supplied themselves via their own or their *familia*'s rural estates without the intervention of merchants and markets (see above, 66, and Petronius, *Satyricon* 38, 48, with Morley 1996). There were also several ways of marketing produce without using independent merchants: an estate owner or *vilicus* could use his own agents for transporting and selling produce in markets at further distance. Many merchants and other professionals (such as moneylenders, bankers, shippers, and animal drivers) involved in trade were slaves or freedmen endowed with the mandate to act as they saw fit. Indeed, it has been suggested that the merchant and debtor of the loan of the Muziris papyrus was somehow related to the estate owner and moneylender to whom he rendered account (Rathbone 1990). Another option was to sell produce at the farm gate, or even in advance of the crop. In the case of farm sale, the seller shifted the costs and risk of transport to the buyer, while in the case of advance purchase he even transferred the risk of a poor harvest to the buyer (who in turn could speculate on higher retail rates). Cato, Pliny the Younger, and the Roman jurists all seem to take for granted that most agrarian produce was sold at the farm gate (Morley 1996: 166). There were, however, regular markets in local towns, and periodic market days in villages and the countryside. The main purpose of these so-called *nundinae* was to cater for the economic (and social) needs of country residents who rarely traveled to town. Yet it is likely that they were also frequented by merchants and intermediaries who purchased goods for higher-order markets. We happen to have a series of fragmented calendars of periodic markets (*indices nundinae*) dating to the first century CE (MacMullen 1970; Morley 1996: 169–74). One gives a list of towns where markets took place, another is a list of dates when markets in different places were held, and yet another seems to indicate the movement of one market from one place to the next on subsequent days. Without doubt, these calendars served merchants or agents who aimed to visit markets in different places day by day. In several *indices* Rome is included, suggesting that one market in the city was linked to the rural marketing system. Morley (1996: 166–74) suggests that the city was a market for goods which were also sold at rural *nundinae,* just as there was in Rome a market for goods bought up in rural markets. In other words, Rome stood at the head of a "dendric" marketing network with goods traveling both ways along the routes between interrelated markets.

TRADE AND THE ROMAN ARMY

Under the Republic, Roman wars were fought almost exclusively in the Mediterranean region where trade, markets, and taxation had generated enough income to finance substantial armies and campaigns (Erdkamp 2005). Provisions for the Roman armies were organized by armies and governors *ad hoc* and for limited periods of time. From the speeches of Cicero and other sources we hear of Sicily, Sardinia, Spain, and Greece being burdened by extraordinary taxes in kind, violent predation, and grazing rights for animals (e.g., Cicero, *Letters to Atticus* 9.9) (Alcock 1993: 19–24). But provincial surplus was used not only to feed armies passing through but also to supply the city of Rome and the markets of other provinces (Garnsey 1988: 215; Erdkamp 2002a: 50). Only when war became more regular, Roman expansion more systematic, and frontiers more far-flung, from the time of Augustus onwards, did more regular patterns of army supply evolve, including regular provincial taxation in kind. Military presence in the frontier zones also helped to develop more stable infrastructures for the provisioning of troops. Our most important bodies of evidence come from Egypt, Dura Europos in Mesopotamia, and Vindolanda in Britain during the first and second centuries CE. This evidence allows us to reconstruct various practices of army supply, although it is still difficult to assess, let alone quantify, their respective impact on commercial trade and markets. The principle that holds true for all provinces, however, is that local governors and imperial agents were in charge of the supply of staples in a flexible combination of regular taxation in kind, cooperation with local traders, and irregular requisitioning. We hear very rarely about special officials dealing with the supply of the troops, which implies that in the early years of the imperial period this was part of the wider portfolio of provincial administration. A certain Gaius Caecilius Martialis under the emperor Trajan (98–117 CE) is the first official explicitly stated to have dealt with the *cura copiae* (superintendency of supply) during the second expedition against Dacia (*AE* 1934.2). It is also at this time that an official dealing with the transport of provisions is mentioned for the first time (*ILS* 9471). The period from the second half of the second century CE onwards was the beginning of further change. The following one hundred years were marked by almost continuous warfare, an increase in the size and number of armies, and several signs of economic stress in almost all places of the empire. From the time of the Severan period (193–235 CE) onwards, Roman provincial administrations developed a regular system of requisitioning in kind (Mitthof 2001). Gradually there developed an administrative system, known as the *annona militaris* (grain supply for soldiers) for supplying armies exclusively on the basis of tax in kind and requisitioning. At first this was implemented to supply the increasing number of mobile troops, but from the fourth century onwards, the entire army was supplied by the system.

The creation of Roman frontiers in the imperial period had complex effects on the economies of peripheral regions (Lo Cascio 2007; Cherry 2007). Increasing demand for bulk goods such as food and fodder and for other essential goods such as clothing, firewood, pack animals, meat, cheese, vegetables, salt, and some others created new markets and institutions for the distribution of goods from other parts of the empire (Bowman 1994; Cherry 2007). The supply of essential bulk goods, especially grain, was organized with the help of state personnel, as we have noted, but other goods were supplied through local markets and merchants. Olives and wine in many regions of the empire reached the soldiery via longer distance trade, as olives and many varieties of grapes do not normally grow beyond the Mediterranean climatic zone. Campanian wine containers have been found in sites on the northern frontiers of the Roman empire, Baetican oil amphoras in Britain, and the Po valley was well located to supply troops at the Rhine and Danube (Morley 1996: 71). We often hear of *negotiatores* (merchants) active in frontier zones before troops were stationed there (Elton 1996a). Thus, Cassius Dio describes a Roman expedition against the Celts because they had arrested and killed traders who had entered the country to trade peacefully with them (53.26.4). Traders also accompanied moving troops—and could be attacked and killed together with the soldiers. There is no evidence that the Roman army established entirely new commercial patterns, but new levels of demand combined with better infrastructure, better communications, and an influx of money through armies whose stipends were paid in cash must have intensified trade.

The logistics required to supply armies with grain were substantial. In the early imperial period, a legion was composed of about 5,000 infantry and one hundred cavalry. The daily requirement of a single soldier has been estimated at about four *modii* of grain (700–1,000 grams), supplemented by other foods. Horses required up to 4.5 kilograms of grain and up to 4.5 kilograms of green fodder and chaff per horse. In total, this produced a maximum requirement of 6,500 kilogram of grain and 450 kilograms of forage daily, or 195 tons of grain and 13.5 tons of forage monthly (Elton 1996a). The greatest logistical problem was thus the scale of demand in sometimes remote regions. To quote just one example: in the year 6 CE, Tiberius had gathered ten legions in Pannonia in addition to fifteen auxiliary units, more than 10,000 veterans, a great number of volunteers, and the cavalry of the local king—a greater army than had ever been assembled, according to Velleius Paterculus (2.113.1). But as Velleius himself notes, it was impossible to control and manage a large army like this. One of the reasons will have been the difficulties of supplying such a number of men and animals with food and fodder.

The question of the relative involvement of markets and state agents in the supply of armies before the emergence of the *annona militaris* is still a matter of controversy.[6] Strategies probably varied from province to province, if not in principle then in practice, as did the products to be supplied. Egypt, for example, was rich in grain as well as having a highly developed system of taxation and distribution in kind. Here, the evidence suggests that armies were supplied mainly through tax-grain and forced purchases. In Britain, there is less evidence for the administration dealing with the army supply, but there was also much less taxation in kind. Here we hear more frequently about entrepreneurial contractors (*conductores*) with whom the troops cooperated in order to obtain essential goods (Whittaker 2004). Yet entrepreneurial contractors are known from Egypt (and other provinces) as well, so there is no reason to assume that army supply differed between provinces in principle. Some provinces simply had more productive capacities than others, and there were different local institutions established for dealing with exceptional and irregular demand. Grain required the largest degree of planning and coordination; for wine and oil, many regions could rely on established trade and marketing structures reaching far beyond the region. Local markets, moreover, supplied needs of special products whenever they were available (Elton 1996a; Bowman 1994).

TRADE, CONSUMPTION, AND ACCULTURATION

Roman expansion and imperial consolidation went along with cultural processes that have been termed "Romanization," "becoming Roman," or "Roman globalization" (Woolf 1993: 169–205; Pitts 2015). Each of these terms implies a different approach to the spread of material culture that archaeologically marks the centuries during which the Romans dominated the Mediterranean and much of the Afro-Eurasian landmass. We cannot discuss the cultural meaning attached to the consumption of imported goods, and the greater homogenization of consumption regimes in the Roman empire, here. Suffice it to say that changes in consumption were part of a multi-dimensional process driven by different cultural and political dynamics and different social groups, as well as by Roman state power (Pitts 2013). These changes affected elite culture in both Rome and the provinces, and the consumers of mass products. They also affected different levels of life, such as urban building, infrastructure, agricultural technology, the culture of eating, and cult practices. Most towns in the Roman empire adopted theaters, baths, aqueducts, and recognizably Roman religious architecture. Roman gold and silver coinage became attractive as prestige objects beyond the Roman border. Conversely, private elite houses and *villas* were filled with imported luxuries, such as special marble, pearls, glass, ivory, spices, exotic foods, pigments, unguents, animals, fine tableware, and precious fabrics from different parts of the world.

People also became more mobile (see Ramgopal, this volume). Provincial elites sought political careers in Rome, while imperial administration and control shifted staff and military zone in which the silver denarius currency circulated as the only precious metal coinage (Figure 2.4) supplemented by a few local base-metal currencies (von Reden 2010). Egypt maintained its Ptolemaic monetary system, but it was linked to the Roman currency system by fixed rates of exchange. It has been argued that the need of provincial populations to pay taxes in cash spurred local monetization, production for markets, and market exchange (Hopkins 1980). But this is just one of the explanations for the unprecedented circulation of goods in the Roman empire. Another, and possibly more important, explanation is that the Roman empire

FIGURE 2.4: Denarius of C. Julius Caesar Octavianus, Lugdunum mint, *c.* 4–2 BCE. © University of Freiburg, Germany.

became a "World System" within which local elites and populations positioned themselves through the consumption of particular goods (Woolf 1990).

The transformation of elite consumption in this process, as well as of religious and urban building, has left the most visible traces in the local archaeological records, as have the roads, harbors, and ships that facilitated trade and distribution of the most spectacular commodities, in terms of value, finances involved, and income generated. The Muziris papyrus provides the most impressive example. Nevertheless, for the transformation of regular production and marketing patterns, changes in mass consumption are more important. One sad aspect of ancient trade that affected both elite and mass consumption, but has left few traces in the archaeological record (though clearly in literary and documentary texts), is the slave trade. Although difficult to quantify, the traffic in human beings probably formed the single most important part of regular commercial trade in the Roman empire, and rendered conquest and economic development twin concepts (Scheidel 2012; Lo Cascio, this volume).

Oil, wine, and fish-sauce (*garum*), all transported in amphoras, as well as ceramic utensils and fine tableware (*terra sigillata*), were further items of mass consumption, supplied by long-distance trade. Ancient shipwrecks, too, can be used for analyses of trade, as long as they had metals, stone, or goods transported in non-perishable containers on board (Parker 1992; Wilson 2009). Some stoneware, like sarcophagi, decorated columns, and portrait sculpture developed into everyday items of long-distance trade as their decoration and execution became more standardized for mass-distribution (Wilson 2008a; Russell 2013: 141–200). In total, these independent groups of evidence show not only a significant increase in trade from the second century BCE onwards, but also fundamental changes in production and distribution patterns. From the late first century BCE we can establish competitive trading routes for archaeologically visible goods such as stone, tableware, oil, and wine transported in amphoras (Morley 2007a; Russell 2013).

The distribution of *terra sigillata* is one of the best indicators of changing patterns in production and trade in the course of changing patterns of consumption under the Roman empire (Peacock 1982; Wilson 2009; Harris 2011; Panella and Tchernia 2002). *Terra sigillata* was valuable enough to be imported from further distances. But given the quantities in which it was produced and distributed, it was not a very exclusive luxury product. It served a well-off Italian and provincial middle-class that had enough financial means to acquire goods from a wider than local origin (Harris 2011). Production of *terra sigillata* in Italy began in Arrezzo (northern Italy) around the middle of the first century BCE. From there it spread within a few decades to workshops in southern Gaul (above all La Graufesenque). By the first century CE, central Gaulish workshops in Lesoux, Vichy, Lubié and Toulon-sur-Allier also adopted the technique of producing red-glazed ("Samian") ware. Italian *sigillata* was exported into the western Mediterranean and Gaul from the second half of the first century BCE onwards (Wilson 2009). From the last decade of that century, *terra sigillata* produced in southern Gaul came to dominate the markets of continental Europe. Italian ware still supplied the western Mediterranean coastal regions. Yet its production decreased noticeably when so-called African "red slip" manufactured in northern Africa became more popular in the markets of the western Mediterranean (*ibid.*). African red slip, however, did not enter inner-Gaul, Germany, or Britain, where Samian ware continued to be most widely distributed during the first and second centuries. *Terra sigillata* is a good, but not the only, example of a commodity that changed from an imported good to being locally produced and eventually taking over the markets of the center from where it originated. If we consider that *sigillata* was only a by-product of mixed cargoes that also included perishable goods, these patterns also suggest that despite the greater connectivity of markets within the empire, regional distribution systems remained noticeably distinct.

THE ORGANIZATION OF TRADE

Very different social groups were involved in Roman trade. We find peasants shifting small amounts of goods in local markets and coastal harbors, professional merchants engaged in medium-size trade journeys financed with money borrowed from local moneylenders or banks, and wealthy members of the elite, including emperors, who controlled an economy of scale with the productive capacity of their estates as well as their financial means. Although Roman senators from the time of the middle Republic were formally prohibited from engaging in maritime trade, either actively and or financially, above a moderate limit (Livy 21.63.3; Tacitus, *Annals* 6.17), they engaged in large-scale business through agents, freedmen, and other intermediaries. Cato the Elder, for example, headed a financial consortium of fifty members sharing the volume and risk of trade journeys (Plutarch, *Cato the Elder* 21.6).

Most maritime trade other than the coastal tramping was third-party financed (Rathbone and Temin 2008). The Romans adopted from the Greek world contractual instrument of a maritime loan which was secured by the value of the cargo (and the ship, if the trader was also the ship owner) rather than other assets. A trader borrowed a certain sum of money, usually for a round trip. The loan was returned at the end of the journey, probably as soon as the cargo was sold. If, however, the ship or cargo were lost en route through *force majeur*, the loan no longer had to be repaid. Maritime finance thus shifted the financial risk of maritime trade from the trader to the moneylender who in turn could claim higher than usual rates of interest. While by law normal interest rates were not allowed to exceed twelve percent per annum, maritime loans were excluded from this rule (Paul, *Opinions* 2.14.3). Maritime loans have often been regarded as financial insurance policy for the dangers of maritime trade, but they are better described as a response to the social organization of ancient trade in which traders, financial intermediaries, and ship owners cooperated within interrelated social networks of friends and social dependents. These networks provided information and economic and legal protection in a potentially dangerous and uncertain business environment (Verboven 2007; Bang 2008; Terpestra 2013). It is for this reason that we do not normally find banks involved in maritime loans.

Down to the first century BCE, banks in Rome and Italy were just minor enterprises whose major business was money changing, deposit banking, and short-term lending for purchases made at auction (Andreau 1999: 30–49). During the imperial period, bankers' business increased in value but never reached the scale of private financial intermediation. We happen to have two bankers' archives buried in Herculaneum and Puteoli during the catastrophic eruption of Vesuvius in 79 CE (Andreau 1999: 71–9; Jones 2006). One of their owners, Gaius Caecilius Iucundus, had his bank in Pompeii, and the majority of the loan agreements he had stored were related to rental debts and purchases made at auctions. The family business of the Sulpicii in Puteoli reached larger dimensions. At the time of their death, they had 1.28 million sesterces on loan. Surprisingly, however, despite running a bank in the busiest harbors of southern Italy, only two of the extant documents concern maritime trade (*T. Sulp.* 51–2). Neither of them is a maritime loan.[7] One of the major differences of Roman imperial trade in comparison to its early modern European counterpart was not so much its scale, then, but rather its financial organization. Personal financial intermediation was the corollary of a cascading business structure in which large numbers of small exchange networks fed into higher-order long-distance trade.

A recent analysis of Mediterranean shipwrecks of the Roman imperial period helps us to understand the interdependence of local and long-distance trade (Rice 2016a) (Figure 2.5). Until recently, scholars have made little effort to relate the mass of local tramping to the large-scale trading ventures carried out in great ships of up to 500–1,000 ton capacity. They were simply regarded as two different spheres of exchange (see, however, Morley 1996). Yet the composition of cargoes, and the provenance of the containers and ships in which produce was transported, both suggest that some harbors functioned as emporia concentrating on produce supplied by various, often very small, local distribution systems. They acted as regional and interregional collection points of agrarian produce and other commodities before they were shipped long-distance. Rice distinguishes between three scenarios reflected by different types of wreck evidence: (i) a single type of commodity from a local production zone assembled at a harbor and loaded on a single ship; (ii) a cargo composed of

FIGURE 2.5: The Madrague de Giens shipwreck, second century CE. Photograph © Bruno Baudoin.

local material supplemented by products that were not necessarily local but had been gathered at the emporium market; and (iii) a ship loaded with cargoes which were re-exported between emporia and which had little or no connection to the local production zone and the port of export. Places of production did not serve places of consumption directly but focused instead on the sales markets of regional ports. The decision of what to transport was in the hands of the shippers and merchants who frequently specialized in a particular type of trade or route. Honorary decrees and funerary inscriptions confirm the professional specialization of *negotiatores* (Rice 2016b). One merchant praises himself for having traveled around Cape Malea, at the southern tip of the Peloponnese, to Italy seventy-two times in his lifetime (*IGRR* 4.841). The repetition of the same journeys would have increased safety and efficiency of trade, as routes became familiar, trading contacts more established, and networks of knowledge consolidated.

The route to India, with which we started this chapter, reflects both the importance of network knowledge, and the interconnection of local and long-distance trade routes. The commercial trip to Muziris may easily give the impression of a direct journey taking goods from Egypt to India and back to Egypt. Yet the *Voyage Around the Erythraean Sea*, a trading manual put together in the first century CE, tells a rather different story. It was written in Greek by an ambitious Egyptian who aimed to share his expert knowledge of the route between the Red Sea, southern Arabia, and west India with other, possibly new traders in the region. The very existence of this manual suggests that the trade between Egypt and India was booming and attracted new merchants to participate. In plain language, the treatise maps the sites and harbors along the African, Arabian, and Indian coasts, giving the distance between each port, the navigational techniques required for approaching, the conditions for anchoring, the nature of taxes to be paid, and, above all, the goods that are in demand or ready to export:

> ... on the very last bay on the left hand shore [at the southern tip of the Arabian Peninsula] is Muza, a legally controlled port of trade[8] on the coast, about 12,000 *stades* in all from Berenike [the Egyptian port of the southern Red Sea] if you follow a course due south. The whole place teams with Arabs–shipowners, or charterers, or sailors–and is full of commercial activity. For they participate in the trade across the water [i.e., Africa] and Barygaza [on the east coast of India], using their own outfits ... (24) The emporium of Muza, though without a harbor, offers a good roadstead for mooring, because of the anchorages with sandy bottom all around. Merchandise which can be marketed there are purple cloth, fine and ordinary quality, Arab sleeved clothing, either with no adornment or with the common adornment, or with checks or interwoven with gold thread, saffron, *cyperus*, cloth, *abollai*, blankets in limited number with no adornment as with traditional local adornment, girdles with shaded stripes, unguents moderate amount, coinage considerable amount, wine and grain, limited quantity because the region produces wheat in moderate quantity and wine in greater. To the king and the governor are given: horses and pack mules, gold ware, embossed silver ware, expensive clothing, copper ware. Its exports consist of local products–myrrh, the select grade of *stacte*, the Abeirian and Minaean, white marble–as well as the aforementioned merchandise from Adulis across the water. The best time for sailing is September, that is, Thoth, though there is nothing to prevent leaving even earlier (*Voyage* 21 and 24, transl. Casson 1989).

Just as the shipwreck evidence suggests, the long journey between Egypt and Arabia, and on to India, was made up of a host of smaller transactions connecting several zones of production, exchange, and consumption. Trade in mass-consumed agricultural products, and trade in special products and luxuries, each pointing again to different groups of consumers, were both part of a complex system of exchange to which long-distance traders responded on their journey. Moreover, neither the routes of exchange, the timing, nor supply and demand, seem to have joined up randomly, but were communicated within the trading networks of traders "in the know." Only for outsiders were the markets, teeming with commercial opportunity, filled with an incomprehensible and undifferentiated crowd. In such an environment, the *Voyages* was revolutionary: it made network knowledge available to a wider group of people.

CONCLUSION

We started this chapter with the question of the interdependence between state, empire, and the growth of trade. We have seen that a simple opposition between markets and the state as driving factors for the unprecedented mobilization of resources in the Roman empire does not help to explain the much more complex mechanisms by which trade and distribution developed. We are lacking the data to quantify the relative volume of goods moved by means of state-organized business, long-distance trade, or local or regional exchange networks. Even if we had these data, however, it would be difficult to disentangle the interrelated webs of exchange in which state personnel, private entrepreneurs, and the emperor all participated. We have seen that the Roman economy from the second century BCE onwards was able to absorb existing trading networks into a larger economic system that had the capacity to supply an increasing number of people, larger armies, and the growing metropolis of Rome. Agrarian production both on large estates and in smaller agrarian units increased substantially, while the extraordinary monetary wealth of Italian and provincial elites increased the financial capacity of long-distance trade. Yet social and political structures particular to the ancient world led to economic behavior and rationality rather different from the market ideology of modern nation states (Bang 2008). The power of the imperial state, its traditional responsibility for the urban grain supply, the perseverance of rather small local exchange systems, and network knowledge remained important constituents of a system of distribution and exchange that successfully maintained the coherence of a vast imperial space over 500 years.

CHAPTER THREE

Natural Worlds

NICHOLAS PURCELL

This essay revisits a central theme in the cultural imagination of the Roman imperial age—the ethically ambiguous but politically beguiling goal of overcoming Nature by ingenuity, daring, and technical skill, in order to achieve the apparently impossible. Such an achievement was one which Roman rulers famously made their own, and which is attested both by their own grandiloquent claims, and by a rich, and predominantly critical, tradition. Caligula's bridge of boats—Claudius' botched draining of the Fucine Lake—Nero's ambition to cut through the Isthmus of Corinth—all of these remain in our times among the most cherished anecdotes of Roman imperial ambition and folly.

Such displays are often viewed in a somewhat reductive and even frivolous light. Outdoing or surpassing the natural order, whether seen as superb achievement or hubristic excess, can seem fantastical, an artifact of the hypercultivated elite literary mind-set. It is, however, worth enquiring more seriously into the cultural traditions which made it appealing to spend enormous resources on works of this kind. Alongside the historical evocations, the cultural one-upmanship, the pursuit of enormous scale, and the simple pomp of logistics, manpower, and ingenuity, certain ideas of utility and the common good underlay many Roman challenges to Nature, and alongside the playful building of mountains or rivers in miniature, or the conversion of land into sea or sea to land, Roman interventions in the dispositions of Nature need to be related to a second, and more conventionally historical, subject—the large and various set of patterns in Roman social and economic interaction with the environment as they can be traced over many of the long centuries of Roman history, and the thought connected with them.

The self-justification of the people who run empires is a complex, shifting, and elusive historical subject. As Roman power grew, in what ways did Romans acquire, develop, and elaborate their own sense of exceptionalism or superiority, and deploy it in the interests of a theoretical rationalization of their domination of others? The struggle against the natural world was an ingredient in such thinking, and can therefore help us characterize Roman hegemony, and contribute to the long-running debate on the nature of Roman imperialism. Communities always seek to discern, elaborate, and display their special merits. Exceptionalism has a history, though: one in which there is a comparative habit, and in which the terms with which excellence is measured and asserted are characteristic of, and specific to, cultural milieux and periods. Who cares about each criterion? Who appoints rivals, and judges between them? Who is listening, and why are they interested? Above all, how is the "natural" order of normality understood, against which noteworthy achievement and, eventually, primate status may be calibrated? And who gets the credit?

EARLY ROME AND NATURE: THE MYTHISTORY

The history of Roman exceptionalism begins with a deduction—what we can intuit of the community's pride from the ambition and grandeur of its interventions in the natural and built environments in the seventh and—especially—the sixth centuries BCE. The centerpiece of this case is the creation, toward the end of the latter century, of a dramatic new sanctuary on the Capitoline Hill. There were three elements in this extraordinary transformation of civic space. The temple itself, shrine of three principal deities, was intended to be marvelously huge, and impressively beautiful in its fittings (above all in representational terracotta) and (no doubt) furnishings. To emphasize the scale of the project, the temple was elevated on a high platform, itself a daunting logistical challenge, on the summit of the hill. And finally, to make the first two items possible, the hill itself had to be shaped, and an approach-road carved to permit the movement of the stone for platform and foundations, and the timber and fired clay elements for the superstructure. All this (including the approximate date) we know from the archaeology of the platform, and the architectural practicability of a temple on this scale has now been vindicated against a long skeptical tradition. But the work required a very high degree of sophistication, in the manipulation of woodwork and fired clay, the specialities of the Italian peninsula in the archaic age, rather than the carving of limestone or marble.[1]

No direct evidence survives for the character of the claims made by the builders and first users of the Capitoline temple. But we can guess what they were striving for, in scale, grandeur, and intricacy, from what we know of the conditions in which cities elsewhere in the contemporary Mediterranean world reshaped their sites and embellished them with striking architecture. Thus a recently published inscription from fifth-century Caulonia in south Italy speaks of a new temple as offering "beautiful order" (*kosmos*) for the citizens, and "astonishing wonder" (*thauma*) for the outsider (Ampolo *et al.* 2014.). The scale (and accompanying technical virtuosity) of Rome's initiative was a statement in this language, to be situated on a register of challenging bigness which was being explored across the Greek world with temples from Ephesos and Samos in Ionia to Akragas in Sicily. Such construction made various claims on behalf of the builders. The building proclaimed devotion to the gods, and their favor; it expressed the skill at design and planning of those in charge of the project; it spoke eloquently of the resources of the community in raw materials, and not least in human (and, no doubt, animal) labor; and it displayed a boldness in changing the layout of the place itself, through the rearranging of the raw materials and the transformation of the appearance of the world, as far away as the great building was visible. In the Roman case, the isolated hilltop site confirms that this visibility was a significant aim of the planners.

The transformation of the Capitol suggests an early date for one of the more unusual elements in a distinctively Roman exceptionalism: the emphasis on the particularity and special character of this particular place, of Rome, and, within Rome, of the Capitol—what Livy (1.55) was to call the "majesty of the locality itself" (*maiestas ipsius loci*). Livy's remark belongs in a quite late phase of a long and intricate history of theorizing precisely this unique specificity: it is because it is rash to retroject later aspects of that theory to the sixth century that I have so far limited myself to what we know of the sixth century without even attributing the temple to the gods who were later to underwrite all Roman success at war and peace, Jupiter Optimus Maximus, whose final epithet was Capitolinus, Juno Regina, and Minerva. But it is not unreasonable to suppose that deities with those names, in dialog with their counterparts in Greek and other Italian religious practice, were early recipients of cult in this place.

From the later tradition about their cult and its meaning comes another set of assertions and explanations which is central to the present enquiry. Stories about the building of the temple and the discovery of the miraculous head (*caput*) which gave its name to the hill explained how this precise place was uniquely predestined by fate and divine favor to be the center and pivot of human affairs. Those stories go back at least to the first age of Roman historiography in the second half of the third century BCE. In that age, too, if not before, much was made of Rome's survival in the face of the disastrous Gallic invasion of nearly two centuries before, which could have led to the abandonment of the whole site of the city, had fate and the gods not forbidden it. Roman tradition dated to that age further ambitious works of terracing, revetment, and platform-building around the sacred precinct of the Capitol, extending the summit of the hill by engineering (Livy 6.4.12). Landscape works of that kind became a commonplace of sanctuary architecture across the Italian peninsula, and foreshadow the *opera pensilia*, "hanging construction," which would be one of the hallmarks of the architectural challenge to Nature when it was used in villa design or urban planning, in the age of Roman work with concrete and brick. But this is to anticipate.

The Capitol rose high above the left bank of the Tiber, just upstream of places where it could be forded (and—perhaps not much later—bridged). Being so close to a major river posed the Roman community challenges which did not have many parallels among cities of the first half of the first millennium BCE. The Tiber was Rome's main route to the sea and all the opportunities of Mediterranean communications, and the management of the environment around its river-bank harbor went back to the sixth century. Unusual in the ancient Mediterranean in having so close a relationship with a major perennial river, from the first Rome had to cope with flood-plains, marshes, drainage, alluviation, and inundation, an intrinsically unstable environment (Purcell 1996).

Roman historical tradition associated the age of the building of the Capitoline temple with major environmental engineering in the deep valleys below—the creation of a level space for the Forum, and the canalization and roofing-over of streams to form underground culverts, of which the Cloaca Maxima became the most famous (Hopkins 2012b). Archaeologists now assign a somewhat earlier date to the first reclamation and reconfiguration of the valley floors, but works of this kind remained a constant element in the continuous reshaping and manipulation of Rome's site. Indeed, the amazing skills called for by such underground hydraulic works became a commonplace of Greek praises of Rome in the early imperial period (e.g., Dionysius 3.67.5). In west central Italy, however, relatively abundant rainfall makes the management of water a central preoccupation, and Rome's neighbors too specialized early in ambitious works to channel run-off, to protect from flooding, and to conserve and redirect water for productive purposes (Bergamini 1992).

Jupiter was also god of Rome's close neighbors, the Latins. The mountain-summit cult-place of their federal deity stood on the Mons Albanus, high among the volcanic hills and crater-lakes fifteen miles south-east of Rome. Comparison between the Alban Mount and the Capitol was natural, and given cultic shape which promoted conceptual convergence after the incorporation of the Latin festival into the Roman civic calendar from the suppression of Latin independence in 338 BCE. This remarkable landscape was the setting for another emblematic story of Rome's precocious capacity for changing the dispositions of Nature. The tale is a strange one, and links the level of water in the Alban Lake with the capacity of the Romans to capture the Etruscan city of Veii, their closest neighbor to the north. Its monument was the *emissarium*, the drainage tunnel through the lip of the lake which made its water available for irrigation in the coastal lowlands below the Alban Hills, and which is indeed a very striking engineering achievement.[2]

To what extent the emission of the Alban Lake was really a distinctively Roman project is in fact unclear. The soft volcanic rocks and the tempting presence of such large natural reservoirs of water made this a widespread technology from Lake Bolsena to Lake Nemi. Another use of this technology was the creation of "artificial rivers," the derivation of springs into constructed culverts and channels carrying water-resources from region to region across impressively long distances. The first of Rome's characteristic aqueducts, which became another stock symbol of the Roman capacity to change Nature, though far less spectacular architecturally than the great projects of the Augustan and imperial city, was attributed to the censor Appius Claudius at the end of the fourth century BCE. Another, actually bearing the name of a real river, the Tiber tributary Anio, followed quickly, the work of another larger-than-life political and military figure, Manius Curius Dentatus, the conqueror of the Sabines.

In reflection on the horizons of individual peoples or communities, and whether (or how) they could be transcended, such ancient thought foreshadowed modern scholarly discussion of regional carrying capacity. If some form of interdependence was perceived as normal (and this view was common), what were the consequences for political and military decision-making? Roman accounts of the earliest years of the Republic, for example, had a prominent place for stories of how the city was repeatedly required to draw on cereal production from relatively far afield. This could be seen as a survival of a genuine annalistic record, or as a retrojection of much later political debates about food supply. But it was also an element in just this kind of reasoning about size and dependence. The early Roman community was imagined in a dynamic relationship with the resources of a wider world. The quest for famine-relief was conducted in an even-handed, even suppliant mode; but in the growth of Roman population, and the mobilization of resources on various terms of dependence and exaction which it must imply, the joining-up of interests and resources across the region inherent in the archaeological record of archaic Roman ambition contains the beginnings of long trajectories of coercion and subordination.[3]

Roman tradition also made much of inter-regional demographic mobility in creating the first population of the city, and its elite. It was believed that Rome's own first strategies of daughter-settlement establishment began very early, in the beginning of a self-perception crisply summed up by the younger Seneca: "wherever the Roman has conquered, he lives" (*Consolation to Helvia* 11.7). In fact archaeology and epigraphy support a picture of mobile Italian populations in general, of the kind enshrined in the complex tradition on the Italian Sacred Spring, in which surplus populations are ritually expelled to make new communities. There is little place here for self-sufficient, cellular territories. The demography is dynamic: opportunities for new connections and exploitation are numerous and constantly in demand. Mobilization and redeployment of people are powerful instruments for creating new human landscapes.

If we ask, therefore, in what conceptual orders Rome claimed special supremacy already in the sixth century BCE, it is reasonable to discern a theological and cultic exceptionalism, a bid for a supra-local topographical pre-eminence, a wish to display several different kinds of human political control, and, finally, a vindication of all three through the unmistakable and permanent products of human skill—what later Romans would call *ars* ("skill, technique, craft, art").

"Nature," then, could be used to refer to the whole bundle of conditions within which the Roman People operated—or, since they were by no means uniformly favorable, with which they contended. That included their setting, its place in the world, its physical conditions, the layout of weather, water, productive possibilities, and threats from all these angles (cf. McInerney and Sluiter 2016). Something of this comprehensive way of assessing a people appeared explicitly in Peripatetic philosophical thought, as in the historicizing Aristotelian theory of the fortunes of peoples, and their vulnerability to disease or environmental change. But in this ethnography, peoples had their own intrinsic character, with specific qualities and talents—a distant forerunner of the vision Vergil gives to Anchises in the sixth book of the *Aeneid*. Such a character included who these peoples were, and how many. It also included what we might call "self-location," a sense of a wide world which was susceptible of "joining up," and of the vocation of Rome within that geography of communications. Greek learned opinion started to observe and appraise Italian peoples during the fourth century BCE, and their evaluation and approval shaped the self-perceptions of those they observed.

338–202 BCE: MOLDING A LANDSCAPE OF COMMUNICATIONS

The Tiber river had made Rome a central place, and its valley formed a corridor for the early trail by which salt from the coastal lagoons could be distributed to the pastoral communities of the peninsular interior (Giovannini 1985). That nodality was part of the city's natural endowment, and it too could be improved by labor and ingenuity. Here, too, there were local precedents. A Greek geographical text of the middle of the fourth century BCE, which we know as the "Coasting-voyage of Pseudo-Scylax," tells of a road joining together the two sides of Italy across mainly Etruscan territory. After the Roman conquest of Latium, the link between Rome and the Alban Hills was expressed by a built highway, the Via Latina (the Latin Way), which foreshadowed later Roman road-building in its geometric straightness, and which closely linked visually the two hilltop cult-places, Capitol and Latin sanctuary, between which it ran

(Rodríguez-Almeida 2002). The conception, with its linkage of festivals, of sanctuaries, of cults, which created or articulated a "sacred landscape," is itself a notable step in the reworking of environment (Grandazzi 2010; Bertrand 2010).

The elaboration of the instruments of infrastructural control went hand in hand with an ineluctable pressure of which we are inclined to make too little—that of making sense of ever more widely scattered settlements, longer distances for the collection of information, the calibration of resources, and the movement of people or materials. A nucleated city of a few thousand people with its surrounding territory is relatively easy to docket and to order, but make it the heart of a web of dependent settlements, first at a day's journey, soon at two or three or four days' journey from the center, first involving a few thousand hectares, later impinging on the resource-bases of ten or a hundred times that, and the demands of making sense of reciprocal rights and obligations become far more complex. This expansion of scale is a crucial element in the Roman investment in communications.

Much more celebrated than the Latin Way is the much longer Via Appia, conceived a generation later by Appius Claudius the censor (once again), to join the new settlements of Roman citizens in the Falernian territory of Campania to the mother-city (Humm 1996). This was a new departure in ambition and swagger, if it was not wholly without precedent as an idea. Bearing the Aqua Appia in mind, we can see the projects as a package of showy manipulations of the landscape, explicitly linked to the taming, the bringing in hand, of new people and new places as part of a Roman hegemony which was acquiring a new—and innovative—character. Just as Appius' plan, moreover, was linked to the new Roman settlements of the conquered zones, so his successor Dentatus made major changes to the recently subjugated Sabine landscape, appropriating the land and disposing of it by public sale, and he too constructed a road there, as well as providing Rome with a second aqueduct.

The building of the Capitoline temple in its transformed landscape had already advertised the demographic felicity of Rome. The new projects of the turn of the third and fourth centuries BCE—land-divisions, aqueducts, and roads—likewise displayed the Roman People, their military power, their number, their geographical reach, their economic impact, and their knowledge and energy. This is the age of the last rural allocations of Roman populations which the Romans called *tribus*. Bringing the number of such subdivisions of the *populus Romanus* to thirty-five, these new creations advertised the size and intricacy of the Roman polity (no Greek community had anything like so many equivalent units), and their names, derived from the locality and its main geographical features, vividly expressed a territorial claim. The rhetoric of foundation, incorporation, organic interdependence, was continued in the numerous city-foundations with which the practices of creating new *tribus* were replaced down through the third century BCE, reshaping the settlement-geography of territories all over Italy.

The Capitoline Temple had been a triumph of *ars*. In order to outdo what Nature provided, skill, ingenuity, and know-how were essential. Rome shared with other polities of west central Italy in the spectacular elaboration of an architecture of timber and terracotta which can be shown to have been the subject of a quite different virtuosity from the stone-carving of the east Mediterranean, but nonetheless hugely impressive, and with a long legacy. The control of such expertise was a significant ingredient in Roman statecraft. But all too little can be said about where it resided and how it was managed even in the later Republic. Who surveyed the lands of the new *tribus*? Who counted and registered soldiers, their equipment, support, and deployment? Who built and accounted for booty and the monuments to victory, new temples to the favorable gods, which it helped pay for? Who drew up the contracts for the Via Latina or the Aqua Anio Vetus? How did they learn their craft? Who paid them what, and on what basis?

We have a new insight into such questions from the unlikely source of the bronze rams of Roman warships lost in the battle of the Aegates islands in 241 BCE (Prag 2014). The legend "approved by the quaestor" was cast into each piece. This can hardly not be evidence for the prehistory of the important Roman institution of public contract, or *locatio*, which included a formal appraisal. Here is the everyday infrastructure of Roman organization, and no doubt part of the explanation of Roman success in the third century BCE. Food-supply, fuel and building-materials, metals and military equipment, all these needed organizing, alongside the labor and service of people and animals, and the tradition hints at the precocity of Roman care for public accumulation, tallying, and recording. Artisans and their organization come together to suggest where we might seek an "official mind" in Roman imperialistic behavior (cf. Robinson *et al.* 1961, for this idea in a rather different imperial context).

In mid-Republican Rome, the practical and the utilitarian by no means excluded the domain of religion. In my list of what the colossal temple architecture of the early city had proclaimed, the religious implications came first, and later Romans made even stronger claims about the place of their temple and their city in the divine order than they did about the ingenuity and force in overcoming natural limitations which their project represented. The two claims were interrelated, as the gods and Nature were part of the same system. Jupiter the protector of Rome always remained Jupiter the god of lightning and thunder. The immovable sanctity of the Capitoline temple derived from its Olympus-like vocation as a preferential home for Jupiter, who was depicted and conceived of as specially immanent there. That extraordinary privilege was the centerpiece and foundation of Roman reflections on their special place in time, in space, in the *orbis terrarum* ("the world"), and in the cosmos as a whole.

Plebeian know-how and aristocratic ideology clashed at the end of the fourth century BCE, when Appius Claudius' scribe Flavius published to the whole community the formulae of the law and the workings of the calendar. A shrine dedicated by Flavius was recorded as bearing a date in an era since the building of the Capitoline temple, suggesting that the Roman sense of history was already shaped by the cosmic claims of Jupiter. Jupiter's beneficent influence was expressed in the cult on the Capitol of virtues and abstractions deriving from and clarifying his power—Concord, Good Faith, Wise Counsel, Abundance. Gradually, theology and imperial self-justification combined in an increasingly Greek philosophical register, of which the classic summary is Melinno's second-century BCE Hymn to Rome, seen both as city and as abstract Power (*Rhōmē* in Greek), holding sway by land and sea, encompassing the universe, superior to Time itself (Bowra 1957).

The claim to superiority which was visible in the original creation of a monumental sacred landscape came to be expressed as a unique position for the city and its people in the layout of the world, a layout which reflected the divine order as well as the human or the merely physical—in so far as those things could be separated. The struggle with lesser aspects of Nature was just an echo of this breathtaking one-upmanship.

A NEW NATURAL HISTORY OF ROMAN IMPERIALISM?

Within less than a century from 338 BCE, Romans had domesticated both a strikingly wide range of landscape-changing initiatives, and taken decisive steps toward integrating their self-perceptions with the elite cultures of the Hellenic world. If some of the rather obvious aspects of the transformation of natural landscapes through draining, land-division, the relocation of people, and the construction of roads and aqueducts, were part of the world-view of the Romans who planned and executed such schemes between 320 and 280 BCE, the question inevitably arises of which theories and experiences of such activities were accessible to these planners, especially from Greece, but perhaps also from Carthage (Quinn 2017; Feeney 2007). Roman experience of Homer is of course certain from the mid-third century BCE. When Roman historiography began, a generation later, the influence of Herodotus is palpable, and Herodotus is especially rich in reflection on the encounter between humanity and Nature, above all in his descriptions of the overweening behavior of monarchs in West Asia and, principally, of the Persian Kings whom the Greeks had defied at the beginning of the fifth century BCE. It would be entertaining to think of Appius Claudius reading about the Royal Road as well as contemplating Pythagorean principles; but perhaps Herodotus appealed to the generation of Fabius Pictor just because he spoke to an already developed sense of what could be achieved by a determined people in shaping their landscapes. What is clear is that during the third century, Roman leaders accommodated their self-presentation more and more to the contemporary norms of the rulers of Hellenistic kingdoms, who in turn were the political heirs of Alexander and the cultural inheritors of the Persian world which he had overcome.

Indeed, long before Alexander, Greek rulers, whether of kingdoms or city-states, had deployed many of the strategies of which the Romans became proud. The similarities between the Roman system of *tribus* and the doctrinaire reorganization of the territorial institutions of Athens at the end of the sixth century BCE were noted in antiquity. A century later, Archelaus of Macedon had centralized his kingdom using the landscape of urbanism and the building of roads. Greek overseas settlements offered a template for the relocation of people and their integration into new landscapes, including through complex allotted landscapes, often presaging Roman practice in the geometric regularity of their subdivisions. There was a whole spectrum of possibilities for the relationship between such new communities and the metropolis. The profile of the conqueror and the display of conquest could be seen either in the institutions of the ancient Spartan double monarchy, to which many likened Rome's consuls, or in the—often consciously Persian—style of military kings. In the age when history-writing appeared at Rome, generals took on these modes of behavior. Marcellus the conqueror of Syracuse and Scipio the foe of Hannibal, for example, staged newly magnificent triumphs. In Greece itself, Flamininus' diplomatic spectacle or Paullus' remarkable festival at Amphipolis for the conquest of Macedon made the point explicitly. At the end of the second century BCE, the naval commander Marcus Antonius boasted in the best Xerxean tradition of how he saw to the transportation of a whole fleet from sea to sea across the barrier placed in his way by Nature at the Isthmus of Corinth (*ILLRP* 342; Pettegrew 2016: 124–30).

Meanwhile, the rulers of the Greek Mediterranean were watching Rome, and Rome was keen to explain its excellences. Allies of Rome from the beginning of the third century BCE advertised the Roman virtue of Good Faith (*Fides*) in Greek on their coins. Around the same time, the Rhodians glossed their treaty with Rome with the useful explanation that the god of the Capitol is the deity worshiped above all by the Romans. Philip V of Macedon advised his subjects of the dramatic success of the Romans' urban and demographic policies across peninsular Italy (*SIG*^{3} 543). King Antiochus IV of Syria adopted his own version of the Roman version of spectacular triumphal pageantry, also recognizing the deities who so helped the Roman state. In honor of Olympian Zeus, indeed, he attempted to complete that god's gigantic temple in Athens—and to meet the challenge of the superstructures, employed Roman architectural and constructional experts, working in the tradition of those who had long ago succeeded in roofing the Capitoline' temple.

So complex was the *va-et-vient* of imitation and prescription across the world in which Roman power waxed, that, in the case of Rome's loyal allies the kings of Pergamon, it can be hard to tell whether their famous landscape-changing architecture was a homage to the great works of terracing or excavation which became normal for sanctuaries in Italy during the second century BCE, or one of the prototypes of that architecture. Nor is it clear in this case that the fashion for sculpting hillsides, and extending them with platforms on vaulted substructures, should really be regarded as Roman in a strong sense, though they became a feature of the mainstream Roman architectural tradition. Here, as with the hydraulics and road-building, integration and mobilization of resources, Rome was a leader in an Italy which shared and propagated similar languages of power and display. The key exhibit of the colossal architecture of sculpted Nature, Italy's answer to the acropolis of Pergamon, is the massive terraced and porticoed sanctuary of Fortune the First-born at Praeneste, and it is significant that it was built when the city was technically independent, and that we have no idea who paid for it or got the credit for the transformation of the whole site of the city (see Figure 3.1 for a second great temple complex of this kind).

FIGURE 3.1: Temple of Hercules Victor at Tivoli, Giovanni Battista Piranesi, 1748–1778. Legate of Mr. J.W.E. vom Rath, Amsterdam. Public domain: courtesy of the Rijksmuseum.

Hellenistic manipulation of the environment transmitted from West Asian royalty two further important elements of Roman environmental management. The pairing between managing people and managing the land, disposing of the cultivator as well as the cultivated, was an ancient monarchic habit, involving the replacement of (often destroyed) communities or peoples with forcibly resettled groups often from far away. Roman resettlement policy after the war against Hannibal became more aggressive and more spectacular in scale, and served as a precedent and model for the still larger transfers and repopulations of the imperial period (Broadhead 2000; Boatwright 2015). The second theme which the Romans made their own was a consequence of both cultural emulation and the availability, after imperial victories, of economic power on an unprecedented scale. It was the link between the control of Nature and the life of luxury, and here we are on the edge of those aspects of the morally depraved antagonism to Nature which is so familiar an observation of later Roman literature in Latin and in Greek. The geographer Strabo could already in the Augustan period note the extravagance of the "Persian palaces" of the Romans. The transformation of the Italian landscape by Roman villa design was certainly seen as analogous to the grandiose luxury of Achaemenid Persia.

Assessments of the imperialism of the Roman Republic have become skeptical about the structures and institutions which accompanied Roman victory.[4] It is now widely held that the systems which characterized the imperial systems of the Caesars should not be casually retrojected into a period when *imperium* itself, "command," was still that of the Roman People, and the jobs of those who wielded it on their behalf were labile and opportunistic, recreated according to circumstances, and slow to acquire institutional uniformity. A military logic of aggression or response to threat was paramount, and accounts for most "imperialistic" decisions. Empire was therefore only accidentally spatial. Such a view of the Republican hegemonic system has appealed on various grounds. It is popular with those who take a realist view of Roman military engagements; it chimes with the general realization that—even for the imperial period—close engagement with Roman law can lead scholars to exaggerate the regularity of institutions and practices.

There may, however, be other things to look for when the territorialities and institutionalisms of past scholarship have been set aside. We might instead seek patterns of behavior which were seen by Romans and by others as amounting to something distinctively different from other hegemonial practices on offer around the Mediterranean and in West Asia, not so much in governmental institutions as in social and cultural practices, the dialectics of persuasion and acceptance, or example and imitation, of aspiration and commendation, of self-positioning and legitimation. Such patterns were messy, because they were in constant reflection and refraction through the mutual scrutiny of often hostile polities. But the mess had themes and traditions and order, of a complex and fluid kind.

The understanding or manipulation of the layout of the human and physical worlds, of ethnographies, demographies, political histories, social patterns, and cultural systems, alongside climates, landscapes, regions of differential prosperity, and geographies of communication, formed one of these languages of imperialistic reflection. Others might be sought in religion, in familial strategies, in social and cultural languages, even in the worlds of elite learning and reflection on custom, prescription, precedent—and *artes*. Those most celebrated lines of the *Aeneid*, after all, make *ars* the marker of the distinctive character of peoples, and though Vergil makes Romans excel in the craft of building an empire through measured aggression, and precisely not in the more practical skills of the artist, the artisan, and the technician, other claims could be made.

Such an approach offers contexts for the imperialism of the middle Republic in the worlds which preceded it and followed. Early Roman acquisition of advantage across the landscapes of production and exchange in west central Italy and the Tyrrhenian Sea were not a matter of territorial conquest, but they were imbued with ideas of the order of things within which success could be won, congruent with those of new Greek communities in adjacent milieux. There are major questions still to be asked, let alone answered, about the dissemination of new notions of Nature and human dialogs with it in early Greek communities, and still more about the transmission and reception of such ideas in communities in dialog with the normatively Hellenophone world. It does not seem unlikely that such ideas formed part of the "apoikic package"—a standard kit of self-representations and convergent institutions shared by Greek overseas settlements in the western Mediterranean—which those in dialog with aggressive and often successful Greek interlocutors encountered across the Mediterranean from the eighth to the sixth centuries BCE, a package which included economic, social, and political institutions interleaved with technologies of conceptualization and communication, of dealing with the divine, and of war. Beyond the conquest of the Mediterranean, likewise, it was out of discursive practices of this kind that the newer modalities of the empire of the Caesars developed—to my mind a more plausible vision than leaving Caesar and Augustus to invent a new imperialism out of whole cloth.

Urban form itself should be seen in this context. As Varro said, "divine Nature gave us the countryside, but human skill built the cities" (*On Agriculture*, 3.1.4). The built environment was a key stage for the display of all the *artes* and the bid for excellences in each, a setting in which the merits of different interventions and different solutions to practical and aesthetic issues could be debated, within communities and, by comparison, imitation, and rivalry, between them. That *kosmos* and wonder evoked by the citizens of Caulonia in the fifth century BCE became a feature of an accumulated world of cities increasingly synonymous with the power and capability of the empire as a whole. Cities represented one of the most substantial changes in the landscape, and their universal presence and spectacular visibility was a standard commonplace of a prosperity and taste which was, by the second century BCE, definitely seen as Roman. Nor was it only the dramatic architecture of urban nuclei which promoted this effect: the cities were part of a matrix of managed landscapes and enhanced communications which served to diminish distance, overcome separation, and generate the experience of comparability, even uniformity, which suggested an imperial cohesion.

THE AMBITION TO TRANSFORM THE WORLD

Roman intervention in the landscape of cities had developed organically. In the middle of the first century BCE, however, in the powers of Pompeius Magnus and the early institutional vision of Julius Caesar for the organization of settlements and landscapes, as in their other actions, a change of scale is visible. Interventions and personal displays which had been made piecemeal now began to be delivered more regularly and across wider spaces. The precedent was set for the structural transformation of the Roman world in the long ascendancy of Caesar Augustus, "father of cities," as Horace called him, with whose initiatives the transition from the individual to the systemic in the manipulation of natural and human environments was largely accomplished.[5]

Some of the wealthiest Romans of the last years of the Republic built their "Persian palaces" around Rome, drawing on, appropriating, and reworking the historic associations of the landscape which their predecessors had first appropriated. But the place where Lucullus had indulged his Xerxes-like tastes was a second zone of volcanic wonders, the Bay of Naples, which had developed as a privileged location for Roman luxury vacationing. With the removal of naval threats from the seas around Italy, coastlines became a prime location for the ostentatious reworking of Nature, turning sea into land and land into sea, making new experiments with "hanging" architecture, and displaying the remarkable natural curiosities of an area of hot springs and sulfurous exhalations. In the last years of civil war, Marcus Agrippa chose to transform this environment spectacularly, converting crater-lakes at Avernus, Lucrinus, and Misenum into harbor-basins for the Caesarian fleet, linked with adjacent cities by roads in long tunnels carved deep into the (conveniently soft) volcanic rocks (Figure 3.2). The Portus Iulius thus deployed the sensibility to natural wonder, and the languages of power over Nature which had been developed for private luxury, explicitly to serve the public interests of the Roman People, and the achievement was lauded by the loyal Augustan poets.

The order of Nature, we see again, was not simply the rivers and the mountains, the gulfs and islands of the coast, the layout of lands with their different climates and products. It also concerned the basic location of

FIGURE 3.2: Tunnel giving access from the edge of Naples to the ports and cities around Puteoli, Cumae, and Baiae.

everything, human or physical. Nature was seen as establishing peoples and landscape features in their own separate places. The achievement of imperial power was to overcome the separation, and join up the world. So building a great new highway, such as Domitian's link from the Via Appia to Puteoli, the great port of the Bay of Naples, challenged Nature not just by crossing rivers where they had never been bridged before, or hacking its way through mountains in deep cuttings, but by changing where the places linked actually were. That is what was said by the people of Puteoli specifically about this road: "the Flavian and Augustan *colonia* (colony), by the generosity of the greatest and godlike emperor, relocated nearer his own City" (*AE* 1973.137). Spectacular new communications shrank the world.

The civil strife of the mid-first century BCE had raised the possibility that alternative capitals might be found for the Roman hegemony. The Augustan peace involved a deliberate emphasis on the ancient tradition of the unique centrality in the world, and eternal vocation to domination, of the city of Rome and Italy as its backdrop. The city's centrality in the ever smaller world of easy communications was now constantly emphasized, as in the text from Puteoli. At Rome, as a product of all this accessibility, the Roman People was displayed afresh as wonderfully numerous, and constantly to be marveled at when on display in the huge spectacle-architecture of the capital. The age was presented as golden, a revival of all that was good in the past, and deliberately choosing to evoke the glorious beginnings of the city, with huge new temples, new aqueducts (the first for more than a century), road-building on an unprecedented scale, but now using in addition all the techniques of Hellenistic literature and knowledge to prove the imperial destiny of Rome, justified astronomically, geographically, climatically, and historically, through the control and gathering of information and the best, rarest, and most valuable artifacts and materials from all the circle of the lands. *Natura*, which provided for the distribution of the amber, pepper, marble, or incense which was gathered in to the metropolis, had a prominent role in such systems of ideas, and its wonders were celebrated in the literature of the early empire, culminating in the very first *Natural History*, the Enquiry into Nature of the elder Pliny, written in the years before the author's death in the eruption of Vesuvius in 79 CE (Figure 3.3).[6]

This huge work attempted summation of knowledge, and its contents can seem chaotic, but it would be a mistake to think of it as an unsorted or directionless compilation. The title expressed a paradoxical unification of the two competing domains which make up my subject, and which enabled Pliny to present, in what was, as far as we know, an original manner, the triumph of Italians and Romans, as being inseparable from the dispositions of Nature. At the same time Pliny remained throughout strikingly skeptical or critical of the impositions which Roman imperial success made on the natural order. Here is a natural-science equivalent of Tacitus' uneasy blend, less than a generation later, of confident assertiveness about imperial victory with consciousness of the moral failings of Romans and the real damage done by Roman conquest. The work thus reflects the same unease about the encounter of Nature and imperial might which was felt by the authors who described the grandiosity (or

FIGURE 3.3: The Aqua Claudia. Central Italy, mid-first century CE. Thomas Cole, oil on canvas, 1832. Kemper Art Museum, Washington University in St. Louis. Public domain. Accessed via Wikimedia Commons.

megalomania) of Roman emperors' schemes for making their mark on the landscape.

Although Julius Caesar in tradition and (perhaps) reality had set the scene for such initiatives, and though Augustus had not failed to set his stamp on the map of Rome, Italy and the provinces, it is with the last three Julio-Claudian emperors that the projects which have given emperors such a name, good or bad, are most to be associated. Three *grands projets* stand out. Gaius' bridging of the sea between Puteoli and Baiae, surpassing Xerxes in the same landscape that his grandfather Agrippa had transformed for the Portus Iulius; Claudius and the draining of the Fucine Lake in the central Apennines by way of a great *emissarium* which revisited those mythical works of the early Roman and Etruscan past (on which the erudite emperor was an expert); and Nero's canals, joining Campania (yet again) and Rome, or cutting through the Isthmus of Corinth, as Xerxes (yet again) had done at Mount Athos.[7]

The last word, however, goes to the destruction and rebuilding of Rome itself in 64 CE, and to the narrative of Nero's Golden House, which informs parts of my theme. For the ambition of Nero's architects, Severus and Celer, was, says Tacitus, "to attempt by means of craft (*ars*) what Nature had refused" (*Annals* 15.42). What this meant in practice was imitating many different kinds of landscape, "an artificial lake like a sea, surrounded by buildings designed to look like cities, and a range of countrysides, ploughed fields, vineyards, pasture, woodlands, with every kind of domesticated and wild animal" (Suetonius, *Life of Nero*, 31). Nero's Nature, we observe, included control of water, and themes common to the "Persian palaces" tradition of great Roman villas; but it also created a new human landscape, and it astonished above all by setting down the whole gigantic complex right in the middle of Rome.

The Flavians did away with less of the spirit and atmosphere of Neronian Rome than might have been expected. Following Vespasian's patron Claudius, their contributions to the cityscape had a community-orientation which had not been conspicuous under Nero, but the monuments with which they replaced the Domus Aurea shared with the latter a belief in enormous scale and virtuoso architecture, and a capacity to transform the landscape completely. The creation of the Colosseum and its—wholly new—urban setting, sculpting hills, leveling valleys, changing skylines, was in many ways consonant with the vision of the emperor whose landscapes it obliterated.

In the records of imperial challenge to Nature, a rather different place is occupied by Trajan. Patterns across the empire in intervention in the human and physical landscape can of course never be assessed, but there can be no doubt that the reign of Trajan saw a level of publicity for top-level projects of this kind which is hard to parallel. Precedents are to be found for every aspect of what he did in this regard, framed as it was with Domitian's Campanian road before, and Hadrian's incomparably ambitious villa-landscape at Tivoli (Figure 3.4). And yet the sheer quantity of Trajan's interventions, and the high profile which they have in the very abundant epigraphic and literary record of his rule, are very striking. This is not a coincidence—this was a regime very interested indeed in making itself visible—and it is important that such a prominent streak in what it chose to broadcast as "the glitter of the age" (as the younger Pliny called it) was work of the kind we are discussing.

From the cutting away of the site of his Forum in Rome itself, marked by the height of his famous column, Trajan's new roads—in south Italy (where it was the Via Appia itself which was reworked), in Arabia, in Lusitania, or the Sacred Way at Didyma in Asia (Ehrhardt and Weiss 2011)—canals—in Egypt (where the Nile and the Red Sea were linked), in Bithynia, at the Iron Gates on the Danube—and harbors at Portus, Ancona, or Tarracina, present a tremendous dossier of power and utilitarian zeal for joining the world up. But they also evoke a suite of cultural allusions. The elder Pliny had called the Caucasus mountains, which for him held off the teeming mobile peoples of the steppe beyond Roman control, an architectural project of Nature (*Natural History* 6.30). Now interventions such as Hadrian's Wall across the whole island of Britain built architecture to imitate or enhance natural frontiers.

Trajan's works did not attract the opprobrium with which the mighty shows of the Julio-Claudian emperors were recalled. His successor Hadrian got away

FIGURE 3.4: Hadrian's Villa. Tivoli, mid-second century CE. Piranesi, etching, c. 1769. Metropolitan Museum (37.17.4). Public domain.

with a villa far larger and more ambitious in its architecture, its scale, its expense, and its cultural allusiveness, than Nero's Golden House—though admittedly on a green-field site rather than in the heart of the metropolis. Hadrian's villa, alleged to encapsulate the sites and wonders of the whole empire in replica, summed up the reign of the emperor who joined up the world in his own journeyings more than any other. The exceptional, the megalomaniac, the transgressive, were only the pinnacle of practices which were widespread, and which, in the usage of the Antonine emperors, became routine. Later "bad" emperors were not stigmatized for their gigantic transformations of landscape, which had become normal, and were scarcely noticed, until their gradual decline and disappearance toward later antiquity.

NATURE AS ENEMY

Over the period covered by this sketch, from 650 BCE to 150 CE, it was possible to form the impression that the world within which history happened, though full of local diversity, was in a steady state which could gradually be circumscribed by human provisions. The main exogenous variables with which historical actors had to contend were demographic—the aggressions of mobile peoples from outside the Mediterranean world, such as those of the Gauls which had threatened Rome in the early fourth century BCE. That impression was an illusion. The order of things was unfortunately not static, but prone to disaster and crisis, both sudden, and—as was in fact recognized by the theories of Peripatetic science—gradual, as communities were prone to obliteration through the slow worsening of their environmental conditions. Greek and Roman observers noticed the effects of such processes on other peoples' history, which could pattern their relations with Rome: the migrations of the Cimbri and the Helvetii over the two generations before Caesar's Gallic War are examples.

Responsiveness to the dispositions of Nature meant coping with such things too, and the Romans perceived themselves as capable of making the effort to intervene to correct such negative events or processes. Here, too, is a subject on which our information is casual and erratic. It ranges from the responses to the alluviation and waterlogging of the Pomptine landscape to the emergency measures taken after the eruption of Vesuvius. It takes in the perception of the dangers of epidemic disease, and the realization of the repeated risks of urbanism—fire, and flood. In many cases, if not most, the comprehension of the threat was much too simple and schematic, and the confidence with which the remedy was undertaken largely mistaken.

We have seen that coping with the more active threats of the natural order, from the floods of the Tiber to reconstruction after earthquakes, was an integral part of the ways of thinking and decision-making that we have been examining.[8] It is a question, therefore, how far and for what reasons, such physical challenges played a part in the decisive changes in organizational capacity which accompanied the departure of the Roman state of late antiquity from the behaviors of its predecessors. Of all those earlier challenges, high-mortality disease was probably the one which was least understood and in front of which ancient systems were most helpless, so there is some plausibility in seeing the plague which devastated the empire in the reign of Marcus Aurelius (*Historia Augusta, Marcus* 13.3–6; Duncan-Jones 1996) as a threat which could only overwhelm both *ars* and—even more important?—the perception of competence and control which had become traditional over so many centuries.

Between the enormous monumentality of triumphant Roman power, social or physical, and the struggle with the real and incomprehensible workings of Nature, climatic, demographic, geomorphological, and biological, which could not ultimately be won, the battleground was the precarious productive environment of the Mediterranean world and its margins to east and south. Scale was a good symbol of how the war might have been won, since integration and reciprocity, interdependence and entitlement, on a suitably hard-to-imagine-scale were no doubt the best remedies available with ancient technology to achieve the advantage and preserve social and cultural order. It was a battle which was lost in part because of factors which the Peripatetics understood well, incomprehensible and ineluctable change in the natural world, in epidemiology, demography, and climate, but also through the pathologies which interrupted the constructive process of sharing, with pride and greed. Skill and knowledge, *ars* and *ingenium*, had made possible massive and highly visible environmental change, replicated and comparable across huge areas of the Greco-Roman world. The power it represented was based on greed and all too often manifest in destructive war.

The themes of this long narrative were perhaps never again so prominent after the disaster of the Antonine Plague of the 160s CE. There were economic and political reasons for that, but also a growing crisis of confidence, which was also manifest in religious change. For all that, when the empire began to be Christian, something of the older style of environmental intervention survived. Christians took on Roman sacred time, and Roman religious space, but also the possibility of building new landscape. Rome's periphery was punctuated by a series of great churches—a new landscape of city-institutions was shaped by the sees of bishops—the narratives of the martyrs patterned a historical continuum—pilgrimage joined up the new world as the roads and sea-routes of the empire had one—the landscape of the New Testament was reworked as a new kind of provincial space which was also a new sacred heartland. But the power of which the changes spoke was no longer primarily that of the Roman People and its rulers.

CHAPTER FOUR

Labor

ELIO LO CASCIO

The idea that the unification of the Mediterranean world under the aegis of Rome and also that—seven centuries later—the dissolution of the unique political entity that had been created in this area of Eurasia represent two of the fundamental breaks in the continuum of the history of the West is widely shared but also controversial. It is a shared idea to the extent that the legacy of the Greco-Roman world is considered fundamental to the history of the West. But it is controversial insofar as the classical world no longer seems to be the model of Western civilization itself—its radical diversity and the insuperable distance from today's globalized world needs to be underscored. In any case a comparative approach is directed at identifying structural analogies with prior and subsequent empires located in other areas of the world, like the Qin and Han empire, the Mughal empire, and the Ottoman empire (Scheidel 2009; Morris and Scheidel 2009; Bang 2008). Yet it is not so much the structural analogies but rather the differences vis-à-vis these other empires, beginning with those that are geographic and environmental, that justify looking at the specificity of the experience of the Roman empire and various aspects of the life associated with it; these differences provide the subjects of the chapters of this cultural history. The goal of this chapter is to identify the manners and forms with which work activity was performed in the Roman world; the scenarios and conditions under which it was performed; and the perception of it on various levels—from individual and social utility to moral judgment—as it relates to the specific activities performed.

LABOR AND SLAVERY

It is a truism that ancient society was strongly affected by the presence of slavery, which permeated its economy, social relations, and cultural aspects, and influenced the perception and social consideration of human labor. One can gauge the dominant and conditioning role of slavery in those societies defined as the genuine slave societies of antiquity, Greece and Rome. They are set apart from other societies with slaves or other modes of labor dependence for two reasons: the first is the sheer quantitative dimension, and the second is captured by the expression "chattel slave," i.e., a slave bought at market for a price.

The first criterion has raised some controversy in the most recent historiographical debates. As recently as a few decades ago, historians of the most diverse orientations, and in particular, the Soviet scholars, took it for granted that the ratio of slaves to the entire population was very high, on the basis of indirect indications provided by some ancient authors such as Seneca. In his *On Clemency* (1.24.1), for example, Seneca recalls that at one time it was thought in the Senate that one should reserve a particular type of clothing for slaves; the project was suspended because of the realization that it would have made evident to slaves their own numbers compared to those of freemen. Gibbon had already concluded that slaves represented half of the entire population of the empire from this testimony and from other references that seemed to point in the same direction, including those in Tacitus (regarding the significant number of the *familia*, "slave household," of Pedanius Secundus: *Annals* 14.43); Pliny the Elder (regarding the slaves of Caecilius Isidorus, *Natural History* 33.135); and Apuleius (regarding the slaves of Pudentilla, *Apology* 93.4).

More recently, various ingenious approaches have been attempted to arrive at more dependable indications of the size of the slave population. An attempt was made to estimate it on the basis of the demand for various uses of slave labor in agricultural and mining activities, for example (Scheidel 2005a). In any case, it seems to be an acceptable and obvious proposition that the number of slaves in the diverse context of the Roman empire must have varied both in space and time. Thus the percentage of the slave relative to the free population must have been highest in Rome and in central and southern Italy in the period following the acquisition of the empire, and it must have been lowest in the more marginal areas of the Balkan peninsula close to the *limes* ("frontier")—both in the first phase of Roman presence and later.

Notwithstanding the difficulty of gaining calculations more solid than mere guesstimates with regard to both the size and demography of the slave population, a growing consensus deems it implausible that the rate of slaves within the overall population in Rome and the Roman empire ever approached the thirty percent or more figure that is considered the notional average of authentic slave societies of modern times, such as those in the Caribbean, the antebellum South, and Brazil (Hopkins 1978: 101, Table 11.1). That level might have been reached only in a few areas of Italy and for a relatively short time span.

CHATTEL SLAVERY AND OTHER FORMS OF DEPENDENCE

The second criterion of distinction seems more relevant, tied as it is on the one hand to the emergence of a market economy and on the other to the encapsulation of the notion of the commodification of labor, certainly a central concept in Marx's labor theory of value and in Engels' theory of the linear evolution of the forms and modes of production.

The connection between the establishment of chattel slavery and the decline of other forms of dependent labor that characterized the most ancient period of Roman history is discussed in Varro, the antiquarian scholar of the first century BCE. He proposes a classification of the various types of agricultural laborers in his text on Roman agriculture (*On Agriculture* 1.17). He observes that the *obaerarii*, the "debt-bondsmen" in the most ancient phase of the history of Republican Rome, are "even now ... numerous" in Asia, Egypt, and Illyria, evidently meaning that they are no more in Italy. Similarly, Caesar (*Gallic War* 6.13) explains to the Roman public that the *plebs* of dependent laborers of the Celtic nobility, Druids, and equestrians—variously defined as "slaves," "retainers," "clients," and "debt-bondsmen"—are to be assimilated in some manner to Roman slaves in terms of the place they occupy and the functions they perform, but that the relationship with those who make use of them is not the same as that which ties the Roman slave to his owner. It is understandable, then, why the re-emergence of forms of dependent labor like the much debated "colonate" that, whatever the specific juridical configuration of these forms, were less tied to the mercantile and monetary horizons in late antiquity, could be placed in the context of the "decline" of the empire, at least in its western part. In other words, it is understandable why the disappearance of chattel slavery, which re-emerges as a significant phenomenon only many centuries later, and in the radically different scenario of the New World, could be one of the most significant manifestations of the dynamic of the decline of the mature and complex Roman economy of the early and high empire, which was based on markets and currency.

On the other hand, the emergence of the chattel slave is not only tied to the establishment of a market and monetary economy, but also contributes to the commodification of free work. It used to be maintained that hired labor was "spasmodic, casual, marginal" (Finley 1980: 68; and see below, 122). On the contrary, the documentation now seems to demonstrate the wide distribution of salaried work in the Roman empire, in the countryside as well as in the cities, based on contractual relationships and thus the establishment of a market of free labor. That is to say that the emergence of chattel slavery and of free work based on contractual relationships are two faces of the same coin, and the outcome of two parallel processes. The commodification of jobs leads to a sharper freeman–slave contrast. This is not to say, however, that human labor, whoever the laborer, loses its servile connotations in the eyes of the elite—quite the contrary: labor or service carried out in the service of another, paid for with a wage or salary, is equated to that of chattel slaves, and the wage itself (*merces*) becomes *auctoramentum servitutis*, "the reward for a servile task" (Cicero, *On Duties* 1.150).

The slave at Rome is therefore an object, a *res* (a device, the most important technological innovation, according to Carandini 1988), and, as such, it must be used carefully. Thus Varro advises against the use of slaves in unhealthy areas, preferring day laborers instead since the loss of a slave is equivalent to an economic loss (Varro, *On Agriculture* 1.17). The slave is also, however, a human being, a member of the *familia*, potentially able to become not just free, but also a citizen and a *paterfamilias*. Indeed, the most striking feature of Roman slavery is the role played by manumission. The result and sheer frequency of manumission gives Roman society its unmistakably multi-ethnic, multiracial, multicultural flavor—a society that is keen to integrate in a relatively easy way the foreigner and the "Other," and able to effectively protect the ability of those manumitted and their offspring to climb the social ladder (see chapters by Dench and Ramgopal, this volume). In fact, manumission is key to understanding three intertwined social aspects of Rome: the perception of labor in its complexity and variety; the structure of society (its features and the limits of social mobility); and finally the evolution of the Roman economy itself in its growth and decline (see further below, 119–21).

THE CULTURAL CONSTRUCTION OF LABOR AT ROME: THE ELITE AND THE NON-ELITE

Cicero's *On Duties* (1.150–1), which presents itself as a close examination of human activities performed in non-autonomous conditions—i.e., what we define as "labor" as a whole (the word is absent in the Latin language, and the absence is evidently significant: De Nardis 2016)—is generally considered to be the most eloquent testimonial to the attitude of the elite toward work activities in general. In this extended passage, Cicero purports to relate common wisdom by making a sharp distinction within the so-called *artificia* and the *quaestus* (the activities and the types of gain) between those considered *liberales* ("worthy of a free man") and those that must be thought of as *sordidi* ("low" or "vulgar"). The latter are, first of all, the types of gain achieved by those who incur everyone's hatred through their activity, like tax collectors and money lenders. *Sordidi* are also the types of gain of all the *mercennarii* (wage laborers) from whom *operae* (work days) are bought, but not including the *artes*, the professional skills. Cicero implies the reason for this: their jobs are to be equated to those of slaves if the salary is *auctoramentum servitutis*. Retailers also must be considered *sordidi*, since they would not gain without cheating.

But also the *artes* of those who work by exhibiting professional skills, like all the *opifices* (craftsmen), should be considered *sordidae*. Especially contemptible are the *artes* procuring pleasures (*voluptates*). And even those *artes* that require a higher professional competence or are more useful, such as medicine, architecture, and teaching, are respectable only for those whose status makes them suitable in the first place. As for commercial activity, Cicero observes that if it is on a small scale, it is mean and contemptible, whereas if it is on a large scale and over long distances, it is not too blameworthy, especially if profits are then invested in landed estates. Indeed, among acquisitive activities, only agriculture is really worthy of a free man, but what Cicero evidently refers to here is not the peasant *qua* peasant, but rather the peasant farmer, who is also a citizen and soldier, whose possession of an albeit limited extension of agricultural land, measured at the census, is what defines his role in the citizen body.

This passage from Cicero seems to show that the main reason why labor was despised, in a society strongly permeated by slavery, was because it entailed personal subordination, and therefore the limitation of freedom. The fact that some activities are listed as exceptions, such as those of a doctor, architect, or teacher, is in itself quite illuminating. Cicero's claim that they are suitable to those whose social condition makes them so shows that, in a society structured by orders and personal legal status, the identity of an individual is primarily defined by the role he occupies within the social hierarchy, not by the activity itself. A similar classification is the one Seneca derives from Poseidonius (*Letters* 88.21). Seneca lists four categories of *artes*: *artes vulgares et sordidae*; *artes ludicrae* (those involved in entertainment); *artes pueriles* (those involved in education and teaching); and finally, liberal arts.

At first sight, the picture one derives from both epigraphic and archaeological evidence (funerary monuments and inscriptions) seems to point in a completely different direction. Those who commissioned epitaphs for themselves, their relatives, friends, or dependants mainly belonged to an "ambiente volgare" (low social environment)—as opposed to the "ambiente aulico" (high social environment) (De Robertis 1963). The former group presented its own work and the earnings derived from it as a value, as a reason to be proud, and as a means of self-promotion. The value of that work resided in the competence with which it was carried out, in the technical knowledge it implied, in the effectiveness by which it met the requirements of those who benefited from it, and in the opportunities that it provided for improving one's own social standing within a rather dynamic society, as Roman society indeed was.

We ought to examine some pieces of evidence which reveal a very positive attitude toward labor and toward enrichment as a means of social advancement and upward mobility. The first is a funerary monument found in Ravenna, a stele, to be dated to the Augustan age. The stele presents four figures in two niches, and below one of the niches is the depiction of a male figure dressed in an *exomis* (a particular type of Greek tunic, used by workers), holding an ax in his hands and constructing a small boat. The inscriptions on the stele reveal that the monument was for a free-born Roman citizen, Publius Longidienus, *faber navalis* (shipbuilder); for his wife of freedman status; and for two of his freedmen, who had paid for the monument (Figure 4.1). Another inscription, placed above the image of the boat, identifies the man who is depicted in it as Longidienus himself: in the inscription it is said, rather mysteriously, that he "*ad onus properat*"—literally, that "he hastens to take on himself the burden." How should we understand this rather odd expression? It seems uncontroversial that the whole monument was conceived in order to celebrate Longidienus precisely as a shipbuilder. The formula means not only that he is proud of his job, but also that he is perfectly aware that to do it best requires a constant effort. As has been recently said with remarkable incisiveness, such evidence shows "an attachment to labor as a moral value" (Courrier 2014: 273–4; see also Tran 2017); what was specifically appreciated was honesty and competence.

On this level competition could be fierce. The epitaph of Quintus Candidius Benignus, *faber tignuarius* (carpenter), underlines his ability to build hydraulic equipment, saying, "*doctior hoc nemo fuit*" ("nobody was more competent than him") (*CLE* 483). A funerary inscription in verse from Numidia celebrates the upward mobility of someone who, by his activity, was able to enrich himself and become an equestrian:

patiens laborum | frugi vigilans sobrius | qui rem paravit haud | mediocrem familiae | domumque tenuem | ad equestrem promovit gradum.

(This tomb belongs to) he who, enduring of toils, thrifty, alert, and temperate, provided something considerable to his family, and advanced a lowly household to equestrian rank (*CLE* 1868; cf. Courrier 2014: 282–3).

A famous funerary monument found in Igel, close to Trier, celebrates the activities of an important cloth merchant family in third-century CE Gallia Belgica (Figure 4.2) (see Marcone 2000; Tran 2017). Other Pompeian examples include Umbricius Scaurus' proud ostentation of his activity as a producer of *garum* (fish sauce) (Figure 4.3), or Marcus Vecilius Verecundus' as an affluent textile manufacturer (Clarke 2003; Holleran 2012). Probably the most spectacular self-representation of one's own activity as the means for enrichment and social climbing is the grandiose funerary monument of the *pistor redemptor* (baker), Marcus Vergilius Eurysaces, just outside the Porta Maggiore in Rome, with its monumental relief representing the various stages of bread production (Figure 4.4).

These examples, which one could easily multiply, represent the world of labor in a way completely different from that of Cicero and other literary

FIGURE 4.1: Funerary monument of P. Longidienus, shipbuilder. Ravenna, late first century BCE/early first century CE. National Museum of Ravenna. Public domain. Accessed via Wikimedia Commons.

FIGURE 4.2: Monument of the Secundini, Igel (near Trier), third century CE. Accessed via Wikimedia Commons, CC BY-SA 3.0.

sources, which mostly present the view of the elite. Of course, one cannot refrain from observing that only a minority of funerary inscriptions, from Rome as well as from elsewhere in Italy, mentioned the actual activities carried out by those who either received or gave the honor. However, it would be wrong to conclude from this that professions had no part in defining the personal identity of an individual.

Rather, the opposition between "ambiente aulico" and "ambiente volgare" is less sharp than it might appear at first sight. This is because both epigraphic and archaeological evidence, as we have seen, seems to acknowledge some kind of hierarchy in terms of the value of the various professions, thus showing some correspondence with what emerges from the literary sources, which in themselves are not so consistent in despising the world of work and business. Rather significant, from this point of view, is the evidence provided by Petronius'

LABOR 117

FIGURE 4.3: Floor mosaic showing a fish-sauce container. Villa of A. Umbricius Scaurus (7.16.15), Pompeii, first century CE. Accessed via Wikimedia Commons, CC BY-SA 3.0.

FIGURE 4.4: The tomb monument of M. Vergilius Eurysaces, the baker. Rome, third quarter of first century BCE. Accessed via Wikimedia Commons, CC BY-SA 4.0.

Satyricon, and especially that part of the story in which the character Trimalchio, a freedman *parvenu*, is introduced along with his guests—successful freedmen themselves. Behind the mockery of this "freedmen world" sketched by a member of the elite, which Petronius certainly was, one can catch a glimpse of a different system of values which in turn privileges commitment to work as a fundamental condition toward achieving wealth as much as social self-promotion. For example, education represents one such concrete possibility of self-promotion. Especially illuminating, in this respect, is the speech that Petronius has the *centonarius* (firefighter) Echion give (Lo Cascio 2007). This is a rambling speech, but a significant one in terms of the way in which the character presents his own high expectations for his *cicaro* (son or *alumnus*?), who has studied first Greek and now Latin, and who now, according to Echion, will have to study some law: "There's some money in law. For he's already been sufficiently contaminated with literature" (46.7). If the *cicaro*, Echion says, is not willing to study, then he will make him learn a profession, such as that of a barber or an auctioneer or a *causidicus* (advocate). And this is what he keeps telling him every day: "Whatever you study is for your own good," because "education is a treasure, and a profession lasts forever" (46.8).

Moreover, a different system of values can also be seen as mirrored in the concrete relationships between private citizens as presented by the jurists in the *Digest*, where Ciceronian prejudices seem to get totally dissolved.

LABOR AND IDENTITY: A WORK ETHIC ALREADY IN IMPERIAL ROME?

Yet another attitude was that of the intellectuals, rhetors, and teachers—the stoics Musonius Rufus (first century CE, the teacher of Epictetus) and Maximus of Tyre (late second century CE) in particular. The former underscores the positivity of the example provided by the philosopher to his own students by working in the fields, since it meant he did not have to depend on others for survival (Musonius, *Discourses* 2.26–31). To Maximus of Tyre all occupations were honorable, including trade in luxury goods or businesses related to forms of entertainment, because just as all parts of the human body are indispensable, so are all occupations to society (Maximus of Tyre, *Orations* 15.2–4; Lis and Soly 2017: 265).

The emergence of the "antichrematistic" ideology (i.e., opposition to getting rich), which surely was derived from Greek philosophy but was consistent with the craving for archaic Roman values, merits another discussion (Viglietti 2011). One could say that antichrematistic ideology is the basis for the praise of agricultural activity as the only one truly worthy of man. The praise of *frugalitas* (temperance, modesty), *parsimonia* (thrift), and even *paupertas* (poverty) as the measure of the self-sufficient farmer is an important topic in

Vergil, Livy, and Pliny the Elder, and famous figures from early Roman history such as Valerius Publicola, Menenius Agrippa, and Cincinnatus were considered exemplary. Yet, how effective was such an antichrematistic ideology, and how much did it influence the tangible workings of the various social classes? A satisfaction in one's own skills and the activities performed is expressed by those who are defined as middle class, as well as by the positive valuation of enrichment as the outcome of a "worthy effort," which reveals, as we have seen, an "upside-down" value system compared to that upon which Cicero comments.

Lis and Soly's 2012 book, *Worthy Efforts. Attitudes to Work and Workers in Pre-Industrial Europe* (Leiden-Boston), has revised the traditional picture and the narrative that seeks to explain "the rise of the West," the birth of modernity, or the arrival of capitalism through the establishment of a particular work ethic, according to the Weberian paradigm. The two Flemish scholars question this linear path, starting with the assumed contrast between classical antiquity, when the elite would have given a negative assessment of work in general and manual labor in particular, and the subsequent era, which saw the progressive growth of a more positive assessment of work, brought about by the adoption of Christian values. They recognize what they define as a "polyphony" in the positions expressed by the ancient authors: work, conceived as worthy effort, is not compared with leisure, as Cicero might make one believe, but rather with idleness, which is always censured. In this sense one can already recognize a work ethic in imperial Rome.

LABOR AND THE STRUCTURING OF ROMAN SOCIETY

Beyond the problem of perception and representation, the functioning of society and the economy are conditioned by the presence of slavery. Paradoxically, the Roman version of slavery accentuated social mobility, and made horizontal integration easier.

The keystone is manumission. More precisely, it is (a) the frequency and ease of performing manumission, and (b) the effects of manumission: the fact, that is, that the slave who has undergone manumission with certain formalities becomes not only free but also a citizen, which was not the case in Greek communities (see below, 121–2, on "open" and "closed" slave societies). In this way there was social ascension via a short circuit that in the long term favored integration within the empire (for the mobility of freed slaves, see also Ramgopal, this volume). Paradoxically, the great migratory phenomenon represented by the movement of slaves became much less dramatic in its effects because of the "escape valve" represented by manumission. Due to motivations apparently shared by the elite, the emperor Augustus tried to slow down or limit this process, prescribing that manumission should occur according to specific rules and before a magistrate, if it was desired that the slave should become a Roman citizen with full rights (see Dench, this volume). Nonetheless the prospect of manumission was the primary method used to ensure that slave revolts would remain infrequent and circumscribed following the one led by Spartacus in the late 70s BCE.

The epigraphic documentation regarding freed slaves (cf. Mouritsen 2011), when compared to that relative to the free born and slaves, has provided evidence for scholars of the social history of imperial Rome of such different orientations as, for example, Geza Alföldy (1972) and (though with some caution) Keith Hopkins (1978), to advance the thesis that the normal destiny of a slave, or at least a slave who survived to adulthood, was to be manumitted. Suggesting this conclusion is above all the overwhelming presence of freedmen in the documentation of funerary epigraphs especially of Rome, Ostia (ancient Rome's port city), and other urban centers of the peninsula's central regions, which would be difficult to explain exclusively as the result of the more well-to-do freedmen's urge for self-representation. One cannot help placing this overwhelming presence in relation to a high influx of slaves, but also to the high manumission rate to which a Ciceronian passage alludes, from which it seems one must deduce that a slave to whom responsibilities were given could expect to be manumitted just six years after being reduced to slavery (Cicero, *Philippics* 8.32; Alföldy 1972; Harris 1999).

Moreover, freedom in Rome was bought easily, and even imperial jurisdiction provided juridical protection to the buyer. To see how ordinary the purchase of freedom was, we can refer to a series of allusions in the literary sources, the juridical documentation collected in the *Digest*, and the one thousand or so manumission deeds regarding about 1,200 slaves, which are spread out over the last two centuries of the Republican era, inscribed on the blocks that support the terraces of the Temple of Apollo at Delphi (Hopkins 1978: ch. 3). In the time of the conquest of the Mediterranean region, the influx of slaves would have been continuous and significant, and the price would most likely have been lower than in the subsequent period. During this time the owners would have rapidly replaced slaves in uncertain condition, allowing them to buy their freedom with their *peculium*—the small amount of money left by the owner to the slave to use autonomously and to his own advantage (this was a form of loan originally conceived for the *filius familias*, who lacked juridical capacity and therefore was unable to perform any economic activity as long as the *paterfamilias* was alive). Naturally this frequency and ease of manumission would not have applied to all slaves at all times, regardless of their use. That is, the prospect of being freed would have been much more concrete for slaves used as servants in the urban *domus* and the suburban *villae*; it would have applied less to those who worked in teams and were often chained, on agricultural properties or as miners.

Modern commentators have asked why so many slaves were manumitted in the Roman world and why some categories of slaves were even allowed to buy their own freedom. While non-economic motives might have been involved in the decision to free one's slaves with testamentary dispositions, it is difficult to suppose that non-economic motives were the only ones. Procuring a slave was expensive, and one was not always able to amortize the expense if the slave died prematurely. Two reasons seem to lie behind this behavior that at first glance would appear contrary to economic logic. The first could explain why one would allow a slave to buy his freedom, and the second could more generally justify why one would free one's own slaves, or at least those to whom one was closest. If one's slave were to buy his own freedom, one could renew one's human capital, replacing the oldest slaves who were in worse physical condition with younger, stronger ones. Furthermore, the acquisition of freedman status did not confer absolute independence upon the manumitted slave—the manumitted slave who became a citizen continued to be obligated to give *obsequium* (deference) and specific and concrete *officia* (tasks) to the former master who became his patron, of whom he became a client. In this sense, the practice served to reinforce the institution.

The second motive is more subtle. In reality, and once again paradoxically, manumitting a slave could be the most rational economic option if the marginal productivity of slave labor dropped to the same level as that of salaried work, and the latter dropped to the level of subsistence. At this point it would have been worthwhile for the owner to choose free labor which did not involve the use of monetary capital for the purchase of a slave. In the diverse reality of the empire, and in the various phases during which, in connection with the conquests, slave manpower presented itself as a possible alternative to the use of wage labor, there must have been purely economic reasons to justify the choice between the two.

LABOR AND THE ROMAN ECONOMY

The economist and economic historian Peter Temin, in a recent essay significantly entitled "The labor market of the early Roman empire," answers positively the question whether there was a unitary and integrated labor market, covering the whole empire, basing himself on what he thinks are the peculiarities of slavery at Rome, in comparison with the other genuine slave societies (Temin 2004; the essay has been reprinted with significant additions, and the author's position significantly nuanced, in Temin 2013: 114–38). Starting from the theorizations of the anthropologist and sociologist James Watson, Temin distinguishes between "open" slave societies and "closed" slave societies. The former are those in which slaves can win their freedom and be integrated into the society as a whole. "In anthropological terms, freedmen and women are accepted into kinship groups and intermarry freely with other free persons. Closed slavery is a system in which slaves are a separate group, not accepted into general society and not allowed to marry among the general population, even when freed" (Temin 2013, 123). From this specific point of view, Rome and the southern states of the United States are placed at the opposite extremes of a continuum.

Another aspect which differentiates the Roman slave society from the other genuine slave societies is the frequency of manumission: "Slaves in the early Roman empire could anticipate freedom if they worked hard and demonstrated skill or accumulated a *peculium* with which to purchase it. Once freed, they were accepted into Roman society far more completely than the freedmen in closed systems of slavery. The promise of manumission was most apparent for urban, skilled, literate slaves, but it pervaded Roman society" (Temin 2004: 523). These peculiar features of Roman slavery make it plausible, according to Temin, to approximate slave labor to free labor, so that it becomes possible legitimately to speak of a "unified labor market" (Temin 2013: 129). Temin questions the conclusions of Karl Polanyi, who in *The Great Transformation* recognized the decisive factor for the transition to a market economy in the emergence of a labor market, which according to Polanyi did not exist before the Industrial Revolution and the Poor Laws. Temin also censures Weber, who would have considered free labor an essential component of capitalism.[1] He also questions the position of Finley and Hopkins, both of whom denied the existence of an integrated labor market, since free hired labor would have been "spasmodic, casual, marginal" (Finley 1980: 68).

It must be observed that the labor market Temin is considering, on the basis of his admittedly correct conclusions on the open character of slavery in Rome and on the ease and frequency of manumission, is the labor market of the slaves who have as an incentive the very concrete prospect of being freed and are employed in a wide range of jobs and activities, including managerial positions. In any case, Temin seems to consider just the urban jobs performed by slaves.

One might object, however, that Temin has largely avoided facing the problem of the specific development of slave and free labor in agriculture, a problem which he considers largely outside his scenario, perhaps because it does not appear to him to reveal the actual working of a real labor market. He has avoided asking why a landowner would choose to use slave in preference to free labor in the first place, as slave labor involves the cost of subsistence and the amortization of capital. Temin has taken into account just the case of the slave who, either by the incentives he enjoys or because he receives a wage like a free worker, has to be put in a sense on the same level of a free laborer. He has considered the issue by looking at the "employee" only, not at the "employer," at the determinants of labor supply, that is, and not at those of labor demand. One could say that, in this way, he has underrated the difference between the acquisition of workforce and the acquisition of the worker himself.

But if we do feel justified to put on the same level the acquisition of the worker and the acquisition of his workforce, then we need to include the analysis of the slave market in a broader and unified view of the labor market.

A UNIFIED VIEW OF THE LABOR MARKET

A unified view of the labor market has an important consequence, however. If we are ready to admit the existence of a labor market in this sense, we have to admit the possibility of an actual competition between slave and free labor: the choice by the employer to use the former or the latter is to be understood, then, as a mere economic choice (but see Temin 2013: 134–5, where this idea seems to be envisaged). Other important contributions by economists and economic historians have followed this path, recognizing that the choice between the use of slave or free labor is above all an economic choice. They have tried to understand how a slave economy works, by adopting a comparative approach, but giving pride of place to the slave economies of the ancient world and looking directly at the primary evidence. These contributions have often been ignored by ancient historians, or have had until very recently a negligible impact. I think in particular of the important essay by Stefano Fenoaltea on "Slavery and supervision in comparative perspective: a model," which appeared thirty years ago in the *Journal of Economic History* (1984). Fenoaltea proposes a transaction costs model of slavery. The model is based on the appraisal of the costs and benefits involved, on the one hand, in the supervision of laborers and in what he defines as "pain incentives," and on the other hand, in the rewards that motivate the laborers to work. "Pain incentives" are the negative incentives, for a slave, of corporal punishment and the like, and, for a free day laborer, the fear of not getting subsistence. Among the rewards that motivate the laborers to work is, for example, the prospect of being freed for a slave. According to Fenoaltea, the former case would be the best suited to the "effort intensive" activities, that is, those requiring greater worker effort, whereas the latter case would be the best suited to the "care intensive" activities. In the case of pain incentives, unfree labor can be efficient, whereas in the case of rewards, slave labor, in the long run, would turn out to be inefficient. The way in which the model has been applied to the ancient world can be criticized (and it has been criticized in a recent contribution: Scheidel 2008). But in any case it is important that Fenoaltea builds his model starting from the specific economic options of the employer in the different scenarios and advancing in this way an explanation not only of the reason why slave labor or free labor was chosen in each scenario, but also of the possible changes in the choices of the employer, when the scenario itself has changed.

Actually what happens in the Roman economy and more specifically in the agrarian economy makes the option between free and unfree labor wholly concrete, if it is true—and it is true—that the increasing employment of slave labor in the last centuries of the Republican age goes hand in hand with the increasing employment of free tenants and day laborers, since both developments are linked to the concentration and more efficient use of agricultural land. To put it differently, the employment of slave labor and the employment of free labor are to a certain extent parallel phenomena. Moreover we must admit that it is possible to trace a development in the use of slave labor, depending on its relative profitability in comparison with free labor.

Sir Moses Finley has developed a well-known thesis according to which there were three necessary conditions for the emergence of a demand for slaves and therefore of a slave society both in Greece and in Rome: (i) concentration in landholding, sufficient to require a permanent workforce; (ii) the existence of commodity production and a pretty large market sector in the economy; and, above all (iii) the "unavailability" (to be understood as psychological unavailability even before or even more than economic unavailability) of an alternative free hired labor force (Finley 1998: 154). A fourth essential condition is missing: the differentiated profitability of the employment of slave vs. free labor, depending on their respective costs (the price of the slaves and the cost of maintaining them; the level of wages or land rents in relation to subsistence for the free laborers), and on their respective marginal productivity. According to Finley (though now few Roman historians would agree), this kind of preoccupation would have been entirely absent in the choices of the employers: they would not have tended to profit maximization or they would not have had the ability to do so.

The evaluation of the respective profitability in the employment of slave vs. free labor has been considered as the decisive element in explaining the emergence and then decline of the use of slave labor, for instance by Sir John Hicks in his *A Theory of Economic History* (1969), in which he maintains that the crucial factor that induces the use of slave labor and accounts for its abandonment is change in the prices of slaves (which, as an instrument of production, imply a depreciation expense) and the cost of subsistence, in relation to changes in the level of wages paid to the free laborers. When the price of a slave is lower, frequent replacement of the slave with another is more convenient, and also the cost of maintenance is lower—close to mere subsistence. As he puts it, "When slaves are cheap and easily obtainable, it will pay to keep the sums invested in their maintenance to a minimum; but when slaves are harder to get and more expensive, so that the loss of a slave, or his inability to work, is a serious matter, it will be profitable to undertake expenditure to diminish the risk of this occurrence. It is evident that in this latter case the treatment of the slave is likely to be better" (Hicks 1969: 127).

Hicks also underlines the connection between the low price of slaves and their employment in gangs (with the frequent replacement of overexploited slaves through the market), and also the connection between high prices and the supply of slaves through slave-breeding rather than through the market. Change in the price of slaves in relation to the cost of employing free laborers, in Hicks' view, explains why slave labor was replaced by free labor in the end. "The principal reason why free labor displaced slave labor was that in the conditions when the change occurred, free labor was cheaper" (Hicks 1969: 131). It was not the consequence of a greater efficiency of the latter over the former: Hicks does not think this was a crucial factor. It was instead the effect of their respective costs, itself the consequence of a greater or smaller supply of free and slave labor. In the case of free labor the employer pays only the wage and the wage will fall very low, "to something which corresponds to no more than the maintenance of the slave," if labor is abundant. In conclusion, "If slave labor is plentiful, it will drive out free labor; but if free labor is relatively plentiful, it will drive out slavery. They are competing sources; when both are used the availability of one affects the value (wage or capital value) of the other" (Hicks 1969: 132).

One may ask, then, if our evidence allows us to reach any conclusion on the relative costs of free and slave labor in the Roman empire. In a recent contribution, Scheidel has collected data on the real prices of slaves, measured in relation to the daily wages of the free and the cost of grain, in different scenarios of the ancient world. On the basis of this material he has been able to show that slave prices were low in Classical Athens, but high in some areas of the Roman empire during the Principate (Scheidel 2005b). This must be on the whole a consequence of the difference in the demand and supply of both slave and free labor in the various situations. In very broad terms one can contend that slaves must have been in shorter supply or in greater demand in comparison with free labor in the regions of the Roman empire as opposed to the situation in Classical Athens. And such a conclusion seems to be more compatible with a scenario that includes a higher proportion of slaves in the total population of Athens and a lower one in the regions of the Roman empire. But we do not have the ability to calculate with reasonable approximation the wages of free laborers. And there is, moreover, the unknown represented by the late Republican age (133–31 BCE), for which we do not possess enough data in general, but which was admittedly the period of the fastest and most substantial increase of the slave population at least in Italy, and also, one can submit, of the most intensive demand for slaves, connected with the transformation of the Italian economy following the conquest and the enrichment especially of the ruling class. And as to the possible term of comparison represented by the real wages of the free laborers, we do not have the ability to evaluate it over time.

Can we compensate for the lack of data on the trend of slave prices and wages in this crucial late Republican period and therefore on the quantitative dimension of the supply of slave and free labor, by using as a proxy the dynamics of the slave and the free population? We can resort to this exercise, but in very broad terms and without hiding the inherent danger of circular reasoning. It must be underlined that not only are reliable data missing, but that we are not able to build independent estimates of the size of the slave population of late Republican Italy. The last attempt by Scheidel to offer what he calls "bottom-up" estimates of the putative numbers of slaves employed in the great *domus* of the ruling class (senators, equestrians, town-councilors) and of the urban population at large, and bottom-up estimates of the number of slaves employed in agriculture (600,000 and 750,000, respectively), does not appear entirely convincing for several reasons, even if one can contend that these estimates certainly suggest that the traditional ones are far too high (Scheidel 2005a, 2005b). And the main reason why these bottom-up estimates can be thought to be just plausible minima is that they assume a level of demand for domestic slaves and agricultural products compatible with a low level of free population in the towns and the countryside of the Italian peninsula. But the size of the free population of Italy is still a hotly debated topic: the controversy between the so-called "low counters" and "high counters" does not seem to have been solved. Even if the absolute numbers of the free and of the slave population are obviously unattainable, there is nevertheless an emerging consensus on the trend lines. Nobody doubts that the number of slaves in Italy was drastically increasing in the period in which the villa system was flourishing, as a consequence of overseas conquests. But the idea that the free population in the crucial second century BCE was growing, too, is also thought to be plausible even by some of the "low counters" themselves.

It is this growth in the free population that would best explain the social problems that emerge acutely in the Gracchan years (from the late 130s BCE). It is this increase in the free population, that is, that would account for the "competition" between free and slave labor which seems to emerge above all from Appian's and Plutarch's account of the Gracchan reforms and their social and economic background (Appian, *Civil Wars* 1.7; Plutarch, *Tiberius Gracchus* 8.7). But regardless of the resolution of the controversy over the free population of Italy, we can try to single out, in very broad terms, the development. A trend seems to be easily discernible, at least as far as the proportion of slaves in Italy—closely related to the general trend of the population—is concerned. One can contend that the proportion of slaves in Italy was at its highest level by far in the last two centuries of the Republic and that during this period warfare, piracy, and the related slave trade were the most important sources of slaves. The contribution of slave-breeding must have been less important at this time, even if we accept the picture given by Ulrike Roth (2007), who plausibly argues that slave families can have been a quite normal phenomenon in the Italian countryside after all. The price of slaves must have been correspondingly low. On the other hand, this is the period in which the marginal productivity of an

Italian agricultural slave must have been high: higher than the cost of feeding him and of amortizing his purchase price.

With the end of the conquests in the first decades of the imperial age there must have been a downward trend in the size of the slave population, whose "natural" reproduction was problematic (as maintained by Harris 1999 against Scheidel 1997), and whose "social" reproduction was even more problematic, given the high frequency of manumission. This downward trend was matched by the increase in the free population, so that one can contend that the total population of Italy was more or less stationary or even slightly increasing. The decrease in the supply of slaves must have had an impact on their price, thus favoring the spread of slave-breeding, itself perhaps connected (according to the traditional view) to the abandonment of the peculiar organization of the slave-staffed villa described by the agronomists. On the other hand, population pressure must have reduced the cost of employing free labor, thus favoring the replacement of slaves with free laborers, wherever this replacement was economically viable.

WHY ARE THERE STILL SLAVES IN LATE ANTIQUITY?

It is understandable, therefore, why, given the very high marginal productivity of labor in the period of Italian economic expansion during the late Republic, the employment of slaves could have been profitable. In this scenario even the wages of the free laborers must have been much higher than subsistence. On the other hand one can explain why slave labor, when it begins to be more expensive in comparison with free labor, can no longer be quantitatively important, even in the central areas of the empire. But why is slavery still present in the Roman world in the late Roman empire (from 284 CE), as Harper has recently and convincingly shown, in numbers which are still substantial (Harper 2011; cf. Harper 2010)? Why is there still a demand for slaves, generating a supply?

The explanation is to be found, at least partly, in the high marginal productivity of some types of slave labor, which cannot be easily replaced by free labor. Temin is right in stressing this as a peculiarity of slavery in Rome. Slaves better perform the tasks that require high skill and expertise (and so justify the very high prices paid for them: see, for instance, Pliny the Elder, *Natural History* 7.39.128–2). And Harper has recently pointed out that, since "slavery and free labor were institutionally different forms of labor," the use of slave labor "might reduce transaction costs (the cost of finding, hiring, and training laborers)" (Harper 2010: 213). The prospect of being manumitted, for these skilled slaves, by a free grant of the owner or by purchasing freedom, is moreover very concrete and provides a powerful incentive to operate in the best way. This is especially true, obviously, since the purchase of freedom by the slave himself receives a form of judicial protection, in particular with the rescript of the emperors Marcus Aurelius and Lucius Verus (161–9 CE), establishing the immediate manumission of the slave *suis nummis emptus*, "bought with his own money" (*Digest* 40.1.5 pr.; see also 48.19.38.4).

But is the activity performed by a substantial number of slaves really to be considered, among the factors of production, under the label of "labor?" The essential point is the existence of the slave entrepreneur, who can be either an "independent businessman" or a "manager." Paradoxically, in a sense, this figure seems to be more similar to the manager of advanced capitalism, insofar as he performs a managerial activity with capital that is not his own. This kind of trained slave with high technical and accounting skills can obviously be far more expensive and remains worth buying.

But the high marginal productivity of certain categories of slaves cannot be the only explanation for their continued use. Even where the substitution of slave labor with free labor is easy, other factors could have operated in keeping the demand for slaves high. Again the dynamics of the free population are paramount. If, as is commonly assumed, the population of the empire as a whole dramatically shrank, starting from the years of the Antonine plague (160s CE), and then failed to recover for a century or more, the cost of free labor must have tended to increase, thus urging the landowners, backed by the state, to try to tie their agricultural laborers to the land (Lo Cascio 1982; reprinted in Lo Cascio 2009: 179–91). But the higher cost of free labor must have also increased the demand for external slaves, provided that their supply had not dwindled as well.

CONCLUSION

In conclusion, it is perhaps possible to outline an evolution. The great expansion of slave labor is to be recognized, obviously, in the period of overseas conquests (last two centuries BCE), with the big influx of slaves and their low cost. This is the period of competition with free labor (the Gracchan scenario, described above, 126), of the great expansion of the villa as a unit of production, and of servile manufacture. The cessation of the conquests in the first decade CE brings about the increase of the price of slave labor, and the increase in population produces a decrease in the cost of free labor; this cost now approaches the cost of subsistence, whereas the increase in population (at least in some areas of the Roman world) raises the cost of subsistence by itself. At this point slave labor, reduced in its numbers, is mainly used in functions for which it can still be very efficient.

But this is not the end of the story. Population pressure must have depressed the cost of free labor just in some regions of the empire (e.g., Italy and Egypt), whereas in other areas the use of slave labor must have still been a viable option. And this can explain why, in some provincial regions, there were still agricultural slaves in substantial numbers during the high empire (second century CE). Moreover, a dwindling free population can explain why in the late empire as well agricultural slavery does not disappear. In this period the price of slaves does not seem to be higher than in the first two centuries of the empire. Slaves remained a not insignificant part of the labor force.[2]

CHAPTER FIVE

Mobility

SAILAKSHMI RAMGOPAL

"I sing of arms and a man who first came from the shores of Troy, made a refugee by fate, to Italy and the Lavinian coast . . ." (Vergil, *Aeneid* 1.3). The *Aeneid* opens with a description of a man and his people in flight as they make a fated odyssey to Italy. The epic goes on to reveal the topographies Aeneas crossed—land and sea—the conditions he endured—terrible storms and Juno's wrath—and the circumstances that forced him abroad: the destruction of his people and homeland by the Greeks. After stops throughout the Mediterranean, his Tiberine journey into the Italian peninsula ends with his murder of the indigenous king Turnus to allow the eventual birth of the Roman people.

A mythological chronicle of how Rome came to be, the *Aeneid* intimated the historical reality of Rome as it was under Augustus. Through war, destruction, and settler colonialism—the brutal, requisite tools of empire—Rome continued to expand after Augustus's death. By the second century CE, its north–south axis stretched from Britain to swaths of Africa, with Spain and Syria at either limit of its breadth. Within and across the borders of this empire, peoples and goods moved constantly, between house and field, native city and battleground, from port to port. The movements of the millions who lived and died in the Roman empire—movements that were undertaken voluntarily and involuntarily, seasonally or occasionally—covered short and long distances. They also determined the shape and dynamics of its cultural, economic, and political structures. Millennia later, Rome remains well positioned to speak to contemporary questions about who belongs where and when, as nation-states continue to struggle with immigration and the reality that the needs of modern refugee populations require global solutions.

However, mobility was not and never has been limited to the physical dispersal of bodies across space: it also consists of movement between social statuses and the privileges that accompany them. Social mobility in the Roman empire could occur, for example, when a woman paid for the construction of a building in her local community to enhance her visibility, or when an ordinary soldier successfully positioned and repositioned himself over time to become emperor of the Roman world. Aspirations to social mobility are particularly intriguing and important to trace in the lives of freedmen (ex-slaves), whose efforts for social integration could exert determinant forces on social hierarchies across the Mediterranean.

Drawing on archaeological, literary, and epigraphic sources that date to between the third century BCE and third century CE, this chapter offers an overview of geographic and social mobility in the Roman world. It does not aim for comprehensiveness nor, for the most part, a demonstration of historical change for any given form of mobility. Rather, it discusses a range of mobilities by encompassing categories of movement that were both permanent—such as migrations which produced diasporas—and temporary—such as short-term travel for work.

By adopting a flexible approach to the kind of movements that can fall under the umbrella term of mobility, this chapter examines how legal and social structures shaped the relationship between identity and social and physical mobility.[1] It focuses on three categories of identity: slaves, freedpeople, and women. The mobilities of these three groups were experientially distinct from those of men and freeborn men in particular, due to the manner in which structural forces governed their lives as a consequence of their particular legal and gender identities. This difference is reflected in the preponderance of free men in Roman sources and scholarship, which tends to present the experience of those who occupied such positions as normative. For a long time, the byproduct of this focus was the relative undertheorization of the physical mobility of freedpeople, slaves, non-Romans, and women. Fortunately, recent scholarship suggests a sea change with respect to all three (Bradley and Cartledge 2011; Mouritsen 2011; Bell and Ramsby 2012; Foubert 2011, 2016; Hemelrijk and Woolf 2013; Bruun 2016). Slaves are critical to any study of physical mobility.

Human trafficking was a source of coerced mobility for millions in the Roman empire. One gains a sense of the scale from estimates for Italy before the Common Era where, for example, 58,000–77,000 individuals may have been enslaved by the Romans after the Third Samnite War (298–290 BCE), and another 150,000 after the sack of Epirus (167 BCE). Armed conflict in the subsequent centuries caused even greater numbers of people to be enslaved, reflecting the expanding reach of Roman hegemony, a growing demand for slaves among Romans, and structural changes in the organization of Italy's agrarian economy. These factors eventually led to the enslavement and export of people from Asia Minor, Greece, and Dacia. The slave populations of the empire's cities boomed, prompting Galen to estimate that slaves made up a third of Pergamum's inhabitants (5.9 Kühn). These kinds of numbers demand attention to the mechanics of the mobility of those who suffered these conditions (for the Roman slave regime, see Lo Cascio, this volume).

Where studies of mobility are concerned, to set aside the little evidence we have for the movements of slaves is to treat their sufferings as trivial and to tacitly regard slavery as an acceptable feature of empire. Roman literature, art, and archaeological finds like chains and neck collars amply document the torture, overwork, rape, and death that slaves constantly faced. A discussion of enslaved mobility should not be divorced from a discussion of these atrocities: the affective dimensions of this mobility resulted from an institution that fueled an empire that was profoundly cruel, regardless of the technologies of city-building and peacemaking for which Rome continues to be admired. Slavery was a fundamental motor of mobility.

Slaves did not possess legally recognizable kin and as a result they were socially dead as far as Roman law was concerned. Consequently, while they appear to have produced and experienced social hierarchies among themselves, they could not experience social mobility in the ways that free individuals could. This was not the case for former slaves. Freedpeople, and freedmen in particular, often appear at the intersection of social and physical mobility. Since freedmen were nearly as free as the freeborn to travel, many used migration to enrich themselves and improve their social status in a society that tended to regard them with suspicion and scorn. Evidence for their strategies for social advancement is plentiful; in fact, the social marginalization of freedpeople has caused them to be anything but marginal in Roman material culture, and in literary and documentary sources. Their public self-representation, public expenditures, and occupation of special priesthoods and offices in private associations produced significant contributions to Roman art, culture, and economic systems. Together, this evidence signals a population that played a key role in the creation of social structures that deconstructed traditional ideas of what it meant to be Roman.

The substantial autonomy that Roman law and society afforded free men, not to mention their conscription as soldiers and colonists, rendered them the most mobile population of the ancient Mediterranean world and granted them the most control over their own mobility. But free women traveled, too, even if the relative paucity of evidence for their travels remains an obstacle to a nuanced understanding of where, when, why, and how they traveled. Several factors appear to have differentiated free female mobility from free male mobility. For example, women were less likely than men to make long distance journeys of their own accord. In addition, women may have often required the physical accompaniment of male guardians. These differences should not, however, relegate the discussion of female mobility to hyperspecialized subfields which position them beyond mainstream academic discourse. In fact, they merit further investigation, perhaps by marshaling comparative evidence. Evidence for the movements of women reveals the gendered quality of mobility in the Roman empire and how women's mobility (or even lack thereof) impacted the economic and social conditions of both women and their families.[2]

Braiding these themes together, the chapter concludes with a discussion of groups of merchants and businessmen called associations of Roman citizens. These associations began to form in non-Roman cities in the third century BCE with the initial goal of protecting the physical safety and business interests of their members. Their presence throughout the empire reflects the mobility that characterized the lives of many who lived in the empire. They also served as vectors of social mobility for freedmen—and, in one intriguing case, perhaps a group of Roman women, as well—who may have employed the power of collective action and Roman citizenship to augment their social status.

PHYSICAL MOBILITY

"Greetings, my lady Serenia, from Petosiris. Make every effort to come out on the 20th, the birthday festival of the god, and inform me whether you will come by boat or by donkey, so that we may send for you" (letter on papyrus from Egypt: *P. Oxy.* 1.112, third or fourth century CE); transl. adapted from Hunt and Edgar 2014, no. 403).

Three broad generalizations usefully characterize physical mobility in the Roman world: men were more predisposed to mobility than women; elites were more mobile than non-elites; and those in the employ of the Roman army were more mobile than those who were not (Bekker-Nielsen n.d.: 2). In addition to military service, countless factors caused the empire's residents to leave home. They included trade, tourism, exile, enslavement, colonization, and the practice of cult (Wierchowski 1995; Moatti 2004, 2010; Claassen 1999; Harland 2011; Collins and McIntosh 2014; de Ligt and Tacoma 2016; Lo Cascio and Tacoma 2017). The stage upon which these mobilities were enacted was the Mediterranean Sea and the deserts, plains, and mountains of its continental hinterlands (Horden and Purcell 2000: 342). The interconnectivity of these regions permitted such extensive mobility that Romans and their goods are attested at sites as distant from the empire as Arikamedu near India's southernmost tip.

Yet, interconnectivity did not mean effortless mobility. The sentiment that travel was a serious undertaking looms in writings such as a fourth century CE letter from Oxyrhynchus, Egypt, that a man named Heraclides sent to his sister

Antiochia: "I am sending Melas with a letter," he writes, "because the wind was contrary to us since you sailed, so you might let us know of your journey and security, and may the divine providence grant that you may be restored in security to your home; and do you by all means send word to us whether you have arrived so we may be more reassured after hearing about you" (*P. Oxy.* 14.1682) (transl. adapted from Foubert 2016: 294) (Figure 5.1).

The challenges that travelers faced were numerous. Money was one obstacle. Whether the empire's denizens journeyed on foot, by boat, or on vehicles drawn by animals or other human beings, they required money to feed or pay those who transported them. Money was also necessary for accommodations, and those who could not pay slept outdoors like Paul (2 *Corinthians* 11:27). Travel by land was always more expensive than travel by river or sea, and infrastructure and the weather could also pose problems. Bridges and roads were not always well maintained, and the Mediterranean Sea often endangered those who crossed it with tempests that sent many a ship to the seafloor.

Human beings were a threat, too. In a letter, Seneca the Younger encourages a life free of possessions, for only the poor are safe from bandits (*Letters* 14.9). Though his exhortation was moral, it reflects a peril of travel to which the wealthy saw themselves as being particularly vulnerable. While it is difficult to ascertain the degree to which this fear represented a reality, legal sources suggest that brigandage was not an unusual cause of death, and epitaphs demonstrate that not everyone survived encounters with highwaymen (*CIL* 2.1398 from Baetica, for example; cf. *Digest* 13.6.5.4). The bodies of some victims were never recovered for commemoration. In a letter to Hispanus, Pliny the Younger observes that travelers could disappear without a trace and that there was little that technologies of the day could do about it: "You want me to send for Scaurus and get some information from him to enquire about it . . . I am very afraid it will be pointless" (*Letters* 6.25). In Apuleius's *Golden Ass*, a humorous interlude evokes the paranoia these anxieties could produce when a group of villagers mistakes the protagonist's traveling party for highwaymen and attacks them with rocks and vicious dogs. This causes the travelers to assume the villagers are brigands in turn.

Pirates and highwaymen, whose activities depended on mobility, offer a provocative lens for considering the implications of identity on physical mobility in the Roman world. Roman law and society did not view bandits and pirates as common criminals, but as outcasts (Shaw 1984: 22–3). This did not stop people from pursuing robbery, though. For many, the choice to pursue such work may have resulted from limited options for socially acceptable work that also covered their living costs. In other words, it was hardly a choice for many. A brigand in *The Golden Ass* explains, "The reluctant could be terrified [by brigands] into enlisting, the willing would be attracted by the prospect

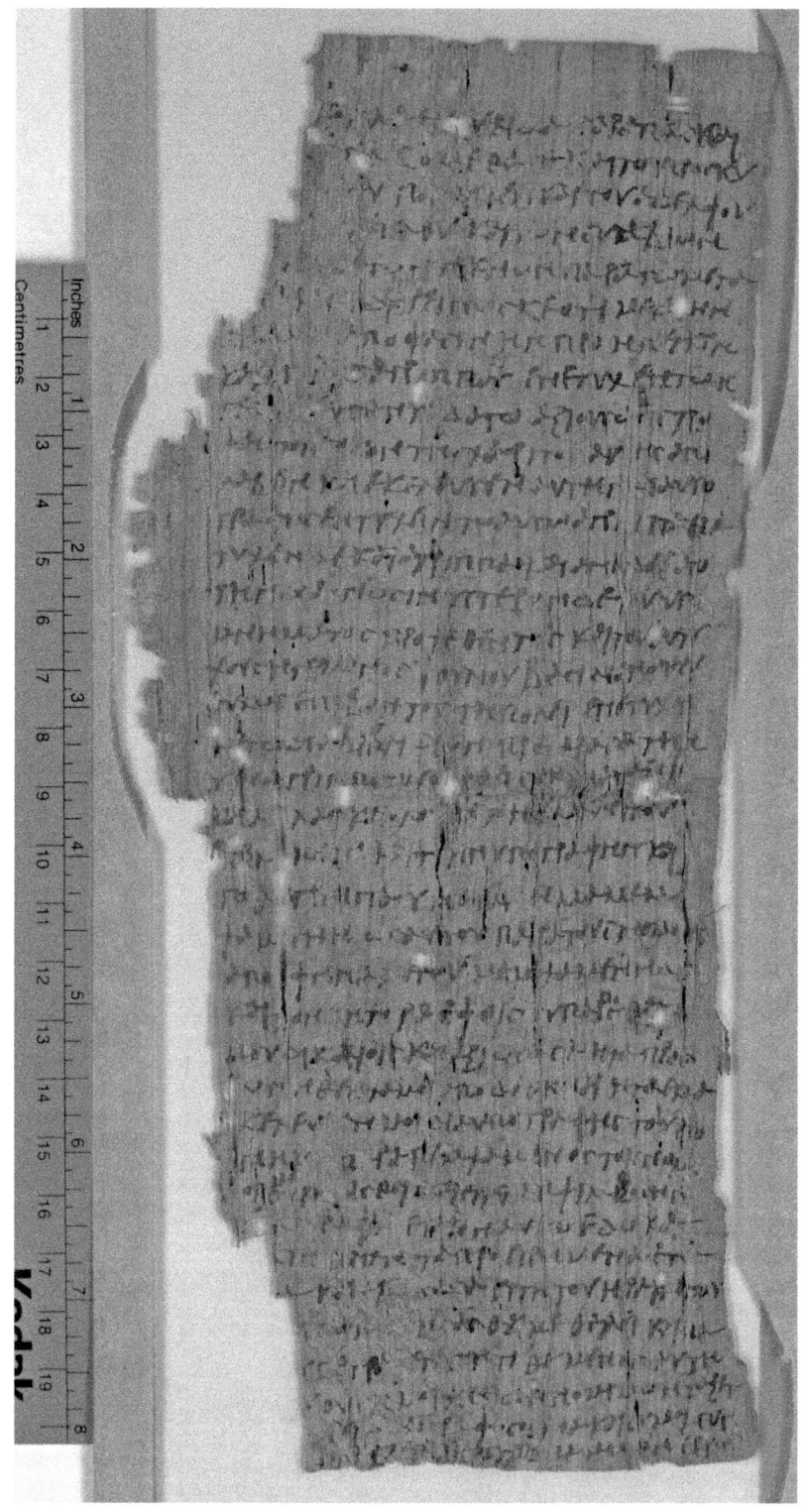

FIGURE 5.1: Private letter on papyrus (P. Oxy. 43.3094). Oxyrhynchus, Egypt, c. 217–18 CE. P. Oxy: Oxyrhynchus Online. Photograph © Egypt Exploration Society.

of loot, and there would be many who would be happy to renounce a downtrodden and slavish existence for a life of almost princely power" (7.4) (transl. Kenney 1998).

Livy's account of Romulus and Remus illustrates how poverty encouraged people in lower-income professions, like shepherding, to practice brigandage. He claims the twin brothers stole from highwaymen and redistributed what they took among their shepherd community (1.5.3). Their identity as impoverished shepherds necessitated brigandage. In their case, however, such activities were acceptable only because the brothers pursued bandits who preyed on innocent travelers and would eventually emerge as the highborn founders of Rome.

Others, like the Numidian rebel Tacfarinas, chose brigandage to resist Rome's presence in Africa in the early first century CE. Tacitus reports that Tacfarinas transitioned to brigandage after deserting the Roman auxiliaries, potentially eliminating the possibility of joining the Roman citizen community upon the completion of his service. Tacfarinas then convened a band of individuals who were "experienced with wandering and robbery for pillage and plunder" (*Annals* 2.52). These men participated in the uprising he led between 17 and 24 CE before he admitted defeat and committed suicide. Tacfarinas's alleged embrace of brigandage may reflect one of few forms of mobility open to him as a consequence of his identity as a non-Roman and victim of Roman imperialism—he was an outsider to Roman society.

The examples of Romulus and Remus and Tacfarinas illustrate some of the ways in which identity and mobility were tied to each other, as well as the potential consequences of these relationships for one's status in Roman society. In the following sections, I will take up these themes with respect to legal status and gender. What were the characteristics of enslaved mobility? How did one's identity as a woman limit one's physical movements in the Roman empire? And what strategies did women and freedpeople employ to realize their ambitions for the political prominence that men and freeborn people could access more easily?

SLAVES AND FREEDMEN

Strictly speaking, total freedom of movement was a significant characteristic of liberty that the enslaved did not enjoy. Nevertheless, the Romans did establish mechanisms to identify different groups of free people and control and surveil their movements (Moatti 2000, 2004, 2010; Moatti and Kaiser 2007; Moatti, Kaiser, and Pébarthe 2009). These included documents that could be used to track, confirm, and prevent the access of free people to particular places. Cities likely maintained lists of citizen and non-citizen residents, for example, to assess who was liable for certain taxes and *munera*, or services (Moatti 2000).

Latin communities in the early second century BCE must have utilized such lists, since they were able to pinpoint a drain on their populations as a result of emigration to Rome. Their complaints to Rome ultimately led to the *ius migrandi* ("the right of migrating"), which restricted the movements of Latins from their homes (Livy 41.8.6ff). Rome must have employed similar lists for the targeted expulsions of foreigners that occurred periodically during food shortfalls.

Other documents confirmed the right of their owners to live in and travel to certain places. Permission and special paperwork were required for Romans and non-Romans to enter and exit Egypt. For example, in a letter to the prefect of Egypt, a woman named Aurelia Maeciana requested permission to leave the province via Pharos in 246 CE, possibly to travel to her hometown of Side in distant Lycia et Pamphylia (*P. Oxy.* 10.1271). Students arriving to study at Rome at the end of the fourth century CE were required to turn over a dossier with information about their place of birth and past education to an official (*Theodosian Code* 14.9.1).

Social and legal status shaped the mobility of freedpeople. Unlike many slave-owning societies, the Roman empire granted former slaves considerable freedoms, the most notable being Roman citizenship and its contingent privileges. However, the law ensured that former slaves were never fully free. Freedpeople were ineligible to hold office, and they maintained certain obligations to their former masters, known as patrons. They could not harm their patrons' reputations or sue their children—in fact, they were expected to treat patrons with respect at all times. In addition, while Roman law does not appear to have placed explicit limitations on the mobility of freed people, their identity as former slaves could demand or benefit from physical mobilities in ways that were particular to them. For example, though freedmen were not required to relocate with their patrons if the latter chose to move, the law did require them to perform *munera* to the city in which their patron lived (*Digest* 38.1.20.1 [Paul, *Edict*, book 40]). As a result, freedmen who did not live in the same city as their patron would have been required to undertake a certain amount of travel within their lifetimes, whether or not they wanted to.

The social marginalization of freedpeople, which subsequent sections of the chapter detail, was another cause of travel that was particular to freedmen. Since wealth could facilitate social mobility, many freedmen traveled to enrich themselves through trade. An inscription from first or second century CE Vardacate in Northern Italy also reveals that their relationships with patrons could produce social enhancement through travel. The inscription indicates that the town offered local citizenship to a group of freedmen after their patrons had migrated there and received it. The condition for this privilege was to agree to perform *munera* both at Vardacate and in their previous place of residence (*Suppl. Ital.* 13.5, Vardacate no.1).

The mobility of slaves contrasted starkly with these liberties. Their movements were wholly subject to the will of other human beings, and mobility depended on when and where they were enslaved. Virtually all of the empire's slaves were either born into servitude or combatants and civilians whom the Romans had captured in war. War captives came to their owners in a variety of ways. Julius Caesar gave slaves to his soldiers as part of their share of booty, and presumably left the recipients to contend with bringing their slaves home (Livy 4.34.2; Caesar, *Gallic War* 7.89; Suetonius, *The Deified Julius* 26). Slavers, who likely traveled with the merchant communities that followed Roman armies, purchased slaves that were not gifted to soldiers and transported them to sites of sale.

State-sponsored monuments like Trajan's Column in Rome offer glimpses into these processes with images of people being forced to board ships and wearing garments like leggings to indicate distant origins (Figure 5.2). From

FIGURE 5.2: Prisoners under Roman control. Trajan's Column, Rome, 113 CE. Credit: Leemage/UIG via Getty Images.

FIGURE 5.3: Funerary stele of Aulus Capreilius Timotheus, slave-trader ("body merchant," SO MATENPOROS). Amphipolis, early second century CE. Drawing by Margaret M. Andrews. Reproduced by permission of the artist.

Amphipolis comes a stele dating to the late first century or early second century CE with an inscription that reads, "Aulus Capreilius Timotheus, freedman of Aulus, slave-trader" (Figure 5.3). The lowermost panel of the stele depicts a group of slaves walking. Eight are men joined at the neck by collars and chains; behind them walk two unchained women and children. Leading the group is a man wearing a hooded cloak—perhaps Aulus Capreilius Timotheus himself, or one of his employees. Evidently, the deceased man's experience with enslavement did not deter him from inflicting on others the cruelty he himself may have endured.

One scholar's analysis of Strabo's description of the slaves that Julius Caesar's British campaigns brought to Italy uncovers the horrors they faced as a consequence of a mobility that they and they alone were positioned to experience (Bradley 1992: 130–1). Strabo observes that they appeared not to be sedentary agriculturalists and that "the forests are their cities . . . their weather rainier than it is snowy" (4.5). As they journeyed from their homelands, they became further and further isolated from familiar landscapes, mores, and those who spoke their language—traumas that were at once physical, psychological, and cultural (Bradley 1992). Their relocation to populous, urbanized, Latin-speaking Rome came on the heels of their capture and long overland or maritime journeys in terrible conditions.

People could experience extensive mobility after they were enslaved or born into slavery, depending on the work they did. Slave-owners who traveled probably brought their slaves with them for assistance with domestic functions. Slaves who were sold by one master to another would have been forced to travel to new locations. Sales likes this routinely fragmented slave families. Some slaves gained the trust of their owners and eventually became their business agents. These men regularly traveled on their own and could have significant autonomy to invest their masters' financial resources (*Digest* 14.3, with Morley 2011: 279). But this autonomy could not have been the norm, and the freedoms these slaves may seem to have enjoyed hardly erased their obligation to accede to any and every demand of their masters.

WOMEN AND PHYSICAL MOBILITY

As the introduction of this chapter observed, women likely traveled shorter distances than men. Noteworthy exceptions include Aurelia Maeciana, who may have departed Egypt for Side, and Victoria and Maccusa, two women commemorated by an epitaph from Beroia in Northern Greece, where they died after journeying from Gaul to visit their uncle (*CIL* 3.14406). Women also accompanied their husbands to distant army and diplomatic postings.

Employment must have motivated many women to travel short distances. Non-elite women who were single, too poor to own slaves, or married to men whose earnings could not support their families probably worked for wages in addition to being the primary caretakers of their children. Women are found in all manner of work: sources document female shoemakers, artisans, weavers, independent innkeepers, dock workers, professional cooks, and, of course, sex workers. Some of this work involved leaving the house to traverse local urban centers and, in some cases, beyond the city walls. If poor women's income depended on travel to market or locations further from home, it seems possible that they traveled more frequently and independently than wealthy women, who did not need to work (Woolf 2013: 357). If this is true, then poor and non-elite women may have moved around more than scholars have considered, and perhaps as often as elite or rich women, even if the distances they covered were shorter (Foubert 2013: 392; Woolf 2013: 360).

By and large, surviving evidence locates the mobility of women in their friend and kinship networks.³ Two letters from very different geographical and chronological contexts beautifully animate some of these networks. The first is a fragmentary letter from the late first/early second century CE by a woman named Claudia Severa, who lived in Briga with her husband Gaius Aelius Brocchus, to her friend Sulpicia Lepidina, who lived with her husband Flavius Cerialis in Vindolanda. In the letter, Claudia writes, "Just as I had spoken with you, sister, and promised that I would ask Brocchus and would come to you, I asked him and he gave me the following reply, that it was always readily (?) permitted to me, together with . . . to come to you in whatever way I can" (*Tab. Vind.* 2.292) (transl. Foubert 2013: 395). The second letter dates to the third century CE and was found at Oxyrhynchus. It is written by a man named Flavius Herculanus, who complains to his former slave, a woman named Aplonarion, about a journey she did *not* make. He writes, "I was very much grieved that you did not come for my boy's birthday, both you and your husband, for you would have been able to have many days' enjoyment with him, but you doubtless had better things to do; that was why you neglected us." He reminds her of his affection for her and emphasizes that his doors are always open to her (*P. Oxy.* 14.1676) (transl. Foubert 2016: 293). Much, of course, could be speculated regarding the exact nature of that affection and Aplonarion's real feelings about her former owner.

For the most part, social mores subordinated decisions about a woman's mobility to her male guardian. Claudia Severa's letter and other sources demonstrate that men likely dictated the movements of most women and that traveling alone was often off-limits. Her letter, as well as Tacitus's accounts of imperial family members like Agrippina the Elder in Germania and Julia the Elder in Asia Minor, also suggest that it was not unusual for women to accompany husbands who traveled for military or diplomatic purposes, even if Roman society frowned upon the practice. Men also appear to dictate the movements of their wives with regard to work. A letter by a man named Philocles, who ran a what seems to be a sex work network that included many military garrisons in the desert east of Oxyrhynchus, suggests that he sometimes sent his wife out to do sex work (*O. Did.* 380). A letter from an unknown writer at the garrison of Aphrodites Orous writes to a man named Rusticus to remind him to return the wife of the former—that is, the anonymous writer—after she has completed her tenure as a sex worker at Didymoi's garrison. The writer also states that she should not have sexual intercourse with anyone without his explicit consent (*O. Did.* 406).

The women in the Egyptian evidence cited above seem to be free, and while we cannot assume they did not want to do sex work, the role that men seem to have played in their movements is an important reminder that free women were likelier to experience involuntary mobility than free men. Marriage, which was usually virilocal in Roman society, must have compelled many unwilling brides to leave their homes and even their native cities. Moreover, access to travel did not mean more voluntary travel: Claudia Severa and Sulpicia Lepidina, for example, may not have had a say in whether or not they joined their husbands at their army posts.

SOCIAL MOBILITY

"A Roman knight, are you? Well, I am a king's son. 'Then why have you been a slave?' Because I gave myself to servitude, and I preferred being a Roman citizen to paying taxes as a provincial. And now I hope I live such that I will be a joke to no one. I am a man among men; I walk about bare-headed; I owe nobody an *as*; I have never been in brought into court, no one has ever said to me in public, 'Pay what you owe me.' I have bought a small estate and collected a little plate; I have to feed twenty bellies and a dog: I purchased my fellow slave so that no one in might wipe his hands in her lap; I paid a thousand silver pennies for my own freedom; I was made a *sevir* and excused the fees, and I hope, when I die, that I won't be a corpse with anything to be ashamed of" (freedman of Trimalchio: Petronius, *Satyricon* 57, transl. Heseltine 1913).

Generally speaking, social mobility describes a person's movement between lower and higher statuses and the changes that this movement could produce in the person's social prestige, power, and influence. The nature of this movement depended on factors like citizenship status, gender, wealth, and the social status of the family into which the person was born. It also depended on whether the person was freeborn, a freedperson, or a slave. Slaves had no status to speak of, and free, wealthy men were likelier than free women, freedmen, and the poor to enjoy high status or the opportunity for upward social mobility.

The impact of each of these factors depended on the additional variables of geographic location and chronological period. In the Republic (509–31 BCE), a small minority of people sat at the apex of Rome's social structure: free citizen males who were born into senatorial families and constituted the only individuals eligible to run for office and hold state priesthoods. But the widening of Rome's geographic reach constantly altered the dynamics of access to social status, as did changes to the Roman citizen body through the emancipation of slaves and the *Constitutio Antoniniana*, which granted Roman citizenship to nearly all of the empire's free population in 212 CE.

Roman citizenship was a significant asset for those who wished to improve their social position in the Roman world. There were numerous advantages to membership in Rome's political community. Until about the second century CE,

Roman citizenship distinguished citizens from noncitizens by granting the former privileges that included the right of access to Roman law; the capacity to draw up legally binding contracts and wills; and, until the late Roman empire (from 284 CE), freedom from torture. Roman citizens were also entitled—and for a time obligated—to serve in the legions, and those who lived in Italy were exempted from the *tributum capitis* (poll tax) and *tributum soli* (land tax) after 167 BCE.[4] Only Roman citizens could hold administrative positions in Roman colonies and municipalities, and this was valuable indeed, since officeholding of any kind could generate social status.

An individual could acquire Roman citizenship in many ways. In the late Republic, some extremely wealthy provincials like Caius Iulius Eurycles of the Peloponnese and Seleucus of Rhosos, a city in Asia Minor, became citizens by providing money and ships to politician-generals like Julius Caesar and Octavian. Roman citizenship gave them access to renewed legitimacy and enhanced social and political prestige in a new world order. For Seleucus, visibility and privilege arrived as an appointment as ambassador to Octavian (*IGLS* 3.718) (Raggi 2006: 192). Caius Iulius Eurycles was appointed dynast of Sparta. The city grew in regional prominence thanks to his relationship with Augustus and it was there that he minted coins in his name.[5]

For many, Roman citizenship materialized through service in the army. While the army's legions were only open to free Roman citizen males, free non-Roman men could join its auxiliary units and receive Roman citizenship after twenty-five years of service.[6] The best evidence for these grants of citizenship comes from tablets called diplomas (Figure 5.4). These documents indicated the grant of citizenship to the recipient as well as his name, place of origin, and the military wing and cohort in the province where he was stationed. They also recorded the extension of these rights to their families under carefully prescribed restrictions. The emperor Claudius, who argued that the Gallic aristocrats of Gallia Comata should be eligible to run for senatorial office, seems to have authored some of these policies. Together, these changes suggest active attempts to incorporate conquered peoples into Rome's imperial project by giving them a stake in it via the privileges afforded citizens (Southern 2007: 56–7).

Slaves did not possess citizenship of any kind, but if they were over thirty years of age and manumitted in accordance with certain lawful procedures—such as manumission by testament—they acquired Roman citizenship. Those whose circumstances of manumission did not meet these criteria became Junian Latins. Such individuals possessed the right to make contracts that were legally binding under Roman law, but could not marry Roman citizens and did not have Roman citizenship. Slaves could also buy their freedom and, in exceptional cases like the civil wars of the first century BCE, were enrolled in the army and received freedom and presumably Roman citizenship afterwards.

FIGURE 5.4: Roman military diploma, bronze (CIL 3.854 = CIL 16.26). Carnuntum, Upper Pannonia, June 13th, 80 CE. Public domain: GNU Free Documentation License.

MONEY, FREEDMEN, AND SOCIAL MOBILITY

Former slaves occupied an inferior social status in free Roman society that was tied to their experience of servitude and which manifested in anxieties about their character. Roman literature repeatedly articulates these anxieties by depicting both freedmen and slaves as corrupt, dangerous, manipulative low-lifes (e.g., Vedius Pollio in Cassius Dio 54.23 and Seneca, *On Anger* 3.40; Larcius Macedo in Pliny the Younger, *Letters* 3.14; and the slaves and freedmen in the Plautine corpus). For freedwomen, the problem of social status was complicated by the association of female slaves with sexual availability.

Dionysus of Halicarnassus, writing under Augustus (27 BCE to 14 CE), suggests manumission occurred relatively often (4.22.4–23.7). Writing under Hadrian (117–138 CE), Suetonius claimed that Augustus aimed to keep Roman lines of descent free from the blood of foreigners and slaves (*The Deified Augustus* 40). The Augustan *lex Fufia Caninia* of 2 BCE limited the number of slaves who could be freed by testament. The subsequent *lex Aelia Sentia* of 4 CE imposed further regulations on manumissions, and reflected concerns about the ability of slaves with malignant personalities to influence their owners. This legislation appears to have enjoyed limited success if we are to believe Tacitus, who complains that a large proportion of the empire's citizen population, including its upper classes, were the descendants of slaves (*Annals* 13.26–27).

Since freedmen could not hold office, they were barred from an important avenue toward social mobility and, consequently, social integration.[7] They circumvented this problem with other strategies. Many wealthy freedmen joined the *seviri* and *Augustales*, two priesthoods that were dedicated to the emperor's worship and contained substantial numbers of former slaves. Freedmen also became officers in voluntary associations (also known as *collegia* or *synodoi*) that were organized around the shared profession of their members. By occupying these roles and making lavish gifts to the local community, many freedmen acquired prominence in the public eye and won honors like dedicated seats at the theater (called a *bisellium*) or honorific statues from the city.

Similar collective efforts by freedwomen are less well attested, but no less important. An unusual inscription from the Via Latina, which ran between Casinum and Aquinum, shows that four freedwomen with different former owners pooled their resources to start a kitchen by a sanctuary dedicated to the goddess Venus. It reads, "Flacceia Lais, freedwomen of Augus, Orbia Lais, freedwomen of Orbia, Cominia Philocaris, freedwoman of Marcus, Centuria Thais, freedwomen of Quintus, set up a kitchen for Venus, at their own cost; concession revocable" (*AE* 1975.197, 1980.216) (transl. Kleijwegt 2012: 120). In addition to providing valuable evidence for female pride in self-employment, the inscription offers a rare glimpse into the collective efforts of low-status women to garner visibility among visitors to the sanctuary.

Seneca the Younger's description of a rich man named Calvisius Sabinus as having the money and intelligence of a freedman encapsulates an elite, freeborn view that wealthy freedmen were classless buffoons whose bank accounts were no replacement for noble blood or education (*Letters* 27.5). Rich freedmen were particularly threatening to Roman society. The most notorious example of this trope in Roman literature is, of course, Trimalchio, the edacious freedman at the center of Petronius's fictional *Cena Trimalchionis* ("Trimalchio's Banquet"). Trimalchio possesses vast tracts of land, quantities of cash, and access to goods as far away as India. His assets include so many slaves that he does not know how he acquired some and, according to one guest, is unknown to a tenth of them.

Trimalchio exhibits behaviors typical of Roman literary portrayals of wealthy, freeborn, and elite Romans: he hosts a meal for friends and strangers, offers luxurious food, reflects on the brevity of life mid-meal, and shows concern for the specifics of his funerary monument. But Petronius presents the freedman's dinner as unusual. It features outlandish dishes, such as a hare ornamented with wings to resemble Pegasus, that seem both overindulgent and the likely cause of the blocked bowel movements about which Trimalchio complains. These features, along with the freedman's meditations on death and the *ekphrasis* to which the text subjects his ideal funerary monument, evoke the narcissism characteristic of the literary trope of the freedman (for freedman portraiture and tombs, see Borg 2012; see also Lo Cascio, this volume). Throughout, the narrator's descriptions suggest that Trimalchio's internal corruption and incapacity for self-discipline are the result of his prior enslavement and that this is true of all freedpeople.

Petronius's descriptions of Trimalchio and his comrades offer a vivid testimony to the ruthlessness of Roman elite snobbery: there seems little doubt that the host of the banquet would have encountered the scorn of freeborn Romans were his feast humbler and his funerary monument smaller. At the same time, Trimalchio's taste is, in fact, unassessable: one can only describe it as vulgar if one accepts the standards of the text's foolish narrator and Petronius himself as normative and inherently valid. And, even though the text portrays freedpeople as desperate for acceptance and social integration, one can detect that at least some freedpeople maintained a limited interest in the concerns of the freeborn. They may have hoped to assimilate more fully into elite Roman society, but they were also (if not more) concerned with establishing a social network for themselves in which they could see, compete with, and support each other. Trimalchio wields genuine power and respect in his immediate circles and far beyond them, and the scorn of his freedman for Ascyltos reflects the irrelevance of the latter in the social dynamics of the banquet and perhaps the wider political landscape of Campania, where local magistrates relied on keeping freedmen happy enough to help defray the cost of maintaining local infrastructure. If there is anyone who seems bereft and desirous of social integration, it is Ascyltos and the seemingly freeborn narrator Encolpius—not the freedpeople at Trimalchio's dinner (Ramsby 2012: 70).

WOMEN AND SOCIAL MOBILITY

Scholars often locate the practice of making benefactions within the male sphere of civic activities because these activities are well attested. But women made benefactions, and at least one study suggests that wealthy non-elite women were as inclined as their elite counterparts to seek the recognition they were denied as freedwomen or low status freeborn women in this way (Hemelrijk 2013: 79–80, though confined to specific geographic and chronological parameters). The contours of women's interactions with cities in this manner reveal the strategies they employed in a system that excluded them from participating directly in local politics by voting and holding magistracies. This data also presents a fuller picture of the dynamics of civic relations and the contributions of women to them.

Iunia Rustica was one of these benefactresses. She lived in the Spanish municipality of Cartima during Vespasian's reign (69–79 CE), and made gifts to the city that included public feasts, a grant of land for a bath, the restoration of public porticoes in the city, and the installation of a bronze statue of Mars in the town's forum. The city of Cartima honored her with statues of her and her son. As was common in such exchanges, she herself ultimately paid for both (*CIL* 2.1956). Another benefactress was Cornelia Valentina Tucciana of the Roman colony Thamugadi in the province of Numidia. Tucciana appears in nine inscriptions from Thamugadi, and for this reason she is the most epigraphically attested woman known to have lived in the town (Witschel 2013: 95). She and her husband, a wealthy equestrian, were responsible for at least two major building projects in the colony, and of the five public statues that eventually honored her, two came from the city (Figure 5.5).

By making benefactions to their respective cities, Cornelia Valentina Tucciana and Iunia Rustica received honors that enhanced their local prominence and that of their families. Both must have hoped this visibility would endure well

FIGURE 5.5: An Urban Landscape: Thamugadi, Numidia, early third century CE. Accessed via Wikimedia Commons, CC BY 2.0.

beyond their lifetimes (Hemelrijk 2013: 76–7). Neither, however, enjoyed it in the absence of their male kin: the commemorative dedications they and other benefactresses received often include the men in their family, even if the benefactress had made her gift at her own expense. Still, while convention seems to have dictated that public dedications locate benefactresses in the context of male kin, it does not suggest that these women became benefactresses for the sake of their male kin. There is no reason to believe free women were less competitive than free men when it came to seeking social mobility, nor is there reason to think they did not see themselves as competing *with* men.

PHYSICAL AND SOCIAL MOBILITY: FREEDMEN, WOMEN, AND ASSOCIATIONS OF ROMAN CITIZENS

"To Gaius Afranius Graphicus, freedman of Clarus, expert copyist and player of games, *curator* of the association of Roman citizens, and to his wife Tertulla, in accordance with his will" (epitaph from Gaul, first/second century CE: *CIL* 13.444).

As evidence for Roman auxiliaries shows, social and physical mobility could intersect for people who could afford and maintain some control over the latter. This convergence similarly comes to light in the behavior of groups of Roman citizen businessmen and traders known as associations of Roman citizens (for the intersection of identity and associations, see also Dench, this volume). Their formation in non-Roman cities throughout the Mediterranean world from the third century BCE through the third century CE directly resulted from the potential for long-distance mobility in the empire. These associations also represent a little examined mechanism by which freedmen and, in one curious case, perhaps even Roman women, deployed physical mobility to facilitate social mobility.

Associations of Roman citizens probably constituted minority populations in the non-Roman cities they inhabited.[8] Their first members were mobile individuals who had immigrated to cities across the empire from Italy, and they formed part of a vast expatriate population that began to take shape in the third century BCE. These associations were not institutions formed by the Roman state, though they may have communicated with Rome and the emperor himself.[9] Membership was likely voluntary, but not free, and members were men. The spread of Roman citizenship in the provinces gradually increased the number of association members from those regions.

Members of these groups would have pooled their financial resources to fund large, expensive business ventures, and they may have negotiated with local communities for privileges that improved conditions for their businesses. These negotiations likely also concerned their physical safety. However, Romans in these groups were not necessarily peaceable merchants and businessmen seeking to trade with non-Romans. They almost certainly participated in Rome's exploitative ambitions by working, for example, as tax collectors for the state. The anger of non-Roman provincials, many of whom would have lost their families and communities to Roman conquest, made itself felt in many ways before the Common Era. These expressions of resistance came to a head most visibly in 88 BCE, when provincials in the Greek East heeded the call of Mithridates VI of Pontus to kill any and all Romans in their midst. The death toll may have been as high as 150,000, and some communities, like the island of Delos, never fully recovered.

Interactions between discrete associations of Roman citizens suggest the creation of a loose, pan-Mediterranean network that reflected and facilitated the physical mobility of Romans operating within it (Ramgopal forthcoming). Merchants in unfamiliar cities faced the practical challenges of navigating local custom and law, not to mention accessing updated information about travel conditions. The presence of individuals whose shared citizenship status motivated them to offer relevant information and help could substantially alleviate these problems. Associations in this network may have also provided financial assistance and safe havens to each other in times of civil strife. An author writing under the name "Caesar" (pseudo-Caesar), for example, reports that the association of Roman citizens at Utica received and aided Romans fleeing Julius Caesar from other parts of Africa (*African War* 88).

The intersection of geographic and social mobility becomes visible in the political heft of associations of Roman citizens. Caesarian writings, for example, describe their ability to control the loyalties of cities in the west as Caesar and Pompey clashed in the mid-first century BCE. Thanks to Caesar, associations in the Dalmatian towns of Lissus and Salona became militarized entities that successfully battled Pompey's men and may have been crucial to Caesar's hold in the region. In the African town of Zama, the association of Roman citizens forced the city's non-Roman locals into supporting Pompey, despite the latter's Caesarian inclinations. This decision ultimately caused Caesar to censure and extort large sums of money from the Roman association (ps.-Caesar, *African War* 97.1).

Across the Mediterranean in the Greek East, associations of Roman citizens carved out prominent social and political positions in Phrygian cities between the first centuries BCE and CE. Inscriptions from Apameia, Kibyra, Hierapolis, and other towns list them as dedicants alongside important civic institutions like the *boule* (council) and *demos* (assembly). One inscription explicitly describes an association of Roman citizens forming a joint assembly with the city's governing institutions (*IGRR* 4.7921). The epigraphic representation of associations in these roles suggests that they enjoyed a visibility normally afforded the *boule* and *demos*, and the right to style themselves as similarly empowered political actors (Ramgopal forthcoming).

The Phrygian dossier suggests that associations of Roman citizens aggressively navigated local social and political dynamics to guarantee the physical survival and political primacy of association members. Their success partly relied on the value of Roman citizenship in the Mediterranean world. While Rome did not consistently come to the rescue of Romans abroad, the possibility of such interventions gifted Romans in the periphery with a power that many strategically deployed to manage local social and political hierarchies.

In addition, associations of Roman citizens could enhance the status and prestige of each individual member as well as the group as a whole (Ramgopal 2017). The average person could not pay for an altar or the construction of buildings, for example. But such acts came within reach if a person combined his financial resources with those of others to construct, for example, the temple and portico in the African town of Alma that an association of Roman citizens dedicated on behalf of Antoninus Pius and Lucius Verus in the second century CE (*AE* 1974.690). Those who were known to be involved in these acts (even if the inscriptions did not name all association members) augmented their local prestige by virtue of their membership in the group. Individual Romans could also achieve social visibility by holding office in these groups. Incumbents and past officeholders who held titles like *curator* and *summus curator* included this information in inscriptions like the following dedication by one Gaius Verenius Varus, which reads: "Gaius Verenius Varus, of the tribe Voltinia, four-time *curator* of the association of Roman citizens, made a dedication to Augustus and Neptune Hippius, patron of our association" (*ILG* 338).

Freedmen with money could join these associations, and they seem to have used membership in these groups to improve their social visibility and join the ranks of the provincial elite (Ramgopal forthcoming). Freedmen appear in several inscriptions. The dedication to Gaius Afranius Graphicus, for example, humorously refers to his pastimes, explicitly describes him as an officer in the local association of Roman citizens, and identifies him as the freedman of a man named Clarus (*CIL* 13.444). Others can be tentatively identified as freedmen by evidence for their tenure as *Augustales*, such as Decimus Iulius Consors and Gaius Maecius Firmus. Both served as *curatores* and *Augustales* in associations of Roman citizens in different parts of Gaul (*CIL* 13.11478; Ness-Lieb 1959, no. 25). Given the visibility that some associations of Roman citizens enjoyed, the ability of freedmen to boast a history of service in these associations may have been consequential for their local status and influence.

Though the majority of evidence for associations of Roman citizens concerns men, an incomplete dedication from the Phrygian town of Akmoneia suggests that a group of Roman women employed collective action for similar ends. The inscription appears on a stele dedicated to a local priestess named Tatia, and dates to 6/7 CE. It states the following: ". . . the wives, both Greek and Roman, honored Tatia, daughter of Menokritos, also called Tryphosa, wife of

Menodotos, son of Menelaos, also called Sillon, the high-priestess, having acted as their benefactress in all circumstances, for the sake of all her virtue" (Ballance archive no. 1955/109; transl. Thonemann 2010). The inscription concludes with a list of the men responsible for setting up the *stele* (Thonemann 2010).

It is clear that the Roman women who were partially responsible for this dedication shared some of the goals that motivated associations of Roman citizen males: to employ collective action and participate in local honorific exchanges as a strategy for augmenting their local visibility and prestige. Their Greek counterparts shared these goals. Together, Akmoneia's elite Roman and Greek women produced a dedication that commemorated them as much as it commemorated Tatia. Their actions put them in direct competition with the town's association of Roman citizen males, and may intimate an aspiration to style themselves as important political, and not just social, actors. The local network created by Akmoneia's elite Greek and Roman women is strikingly apparent in this inscription, as is their use of it for social and even political advancement.

CONCLUSION

There was no normative experience in the Roman world when it came to physical and social mobility. Legal and social structures controlled the expression of agency by women, freedpeople, and slaves when it came to their physical movements and their respective positions in Roman society, and produced striking contrasts with the mobilities of free men and in particular freeborn Roman citizen males. These analyses generate important complications in historians' approaches to mobility in the Roman world. The strategies employed by wealthy women and freedmen, for example, mirror each other, since neither was permitted the kind of involvement in political affairs that freeborn Roman men enjoyed, and both populations emerge in evidence for associations of Roman citizens, in which Romans of all kinds acquire social and political dominance in non-Roman cities. At the same time, the nature of the visibility they acquired remained distinct: women, for example, often did not enjoy public prominence in the absence of male relationships, whereas freedmen did not have to share their prestige in the same sense. To speak of mobility in the empire is to always speak of mobilities.[10]

CHAPTER SIX

Sexuality

CAROLINE VOUT

"So what is a history of sexuality a history of" (Weeks 1986: 21)? It is certainly a history of power. Even for free men and women, sexual behavior and sexual ethics depend on systems of inequalities and expectation, on the extent to which individuals can exercise their freedom to act on their impulses and imaginations. These "systems" are always in flux. We think of Michel Foucault's groundbreaking work, and the transformation that he sees in the third century BCE with the collapse of the Greek city-state and the rise of the Hellenistic kingdoms and Rome. According to Foucault, the uncertainties of public life in this period meant that sexuality became a more important part of man's self-cultivation as an independent as well as political animal. Foucault is often attacked for ignoring women, and has been criticized for apparently neglecting colonial bodies, and for being less precise than he might be about imperial co-ordinates and their effects. Can we flesh out his picture, and make the history of sexuality a history of empire?[1]

The answer to this question depends not only on identifying top-down coercive mechanisms, or centrifugal forces of principle, regulation, and exemplarity (the laws, religious principles, role-models, of a nucleus like Rome). For even if our focus were limited to the urban environment that is the eternal city, the nature of the evidence makes the moral climate, never mind the realities of individual experience, hard to gauge. A compelling answer also depends on appreciating the plethora of possibilities that constitute that lived experience, only some of which conform to, or can be measured against, societal "norms"; some of which "get off" on subverting them—on accepting that sexuality can be a "corrupter or enemy of human culture" (Nye 1999: 3) and a means of transcending culture's constraints, that it can give anybody agency. No wonder that the first Roman emperor Augustus devoted such energies to policing bodily arousal and physical processes such as childbirth in his laws on marriage (Wallace-Hadrill 1981; Treggiari 1991; Edwards 1993: 34–62; Culham 1997; Severy 2003), and that early Christianity saw sexual renunciation as an "emblem of human freedom" (Brown 1990: 481) that offered an alternative view of self and society to that enjoyed, and policed, in the past; that in saints' lives, apocryphal acts, and martyr acts, erotics became a language of sanctity (Burrus 2004; Rhee 2005).

But an empire is an extensive group of states or provinces, each of them composed of diverse peoples of different skin-colors, religions, languages, group identities, different understandings of how individuals within, and beyond, their community should behave. As far as the Roman empire is concerned, some of these peoples were citizens, and thus "Roman" in a juridical sense, while remaining Egyptian, Syrian, British; countless were slaves, whose bodies—without legal or social protection—were "devastatingly vulnerable" (Harper 2013) to abuse, including sexual abuse. Otherness can be frightening and conquest cruel: although Rome was fairly tolerant of local practices, its soldiers were as capable as anyone of exploiting their power and making their opponents' sexuality their victimhood. We might remember the Roman occupation of Britain and the rape of Boudicca's daughters or the confiscation of the handsomest of the Batavian youths "*ad stuprum*," to satisfy the sexual appetites of Flavian forces in the Rhineland.[2] We also note the sexual nature of the *language* of alterity and conquest. Not only were foreigners stereotyped as sexually deviant—the Persians are described as excessively loose in their loving, barely content with a crowd of concubines, and uninterested in sex with boys (Ammianus Marcellinus 23.6.76; Whittaker 2004: 115–28)—but Rome's provinces and borderlands were represented as female, and, in Aphrodisias in Asia Minor, Rome's defeat of Armenia and Britannia, places outside what might be perceived as a shared classical *koine*, represented in stone as rape (cf. Smith 1987).

These graphic renderings should not surprise us. The invective we find in Roman poetry and graffiti is often as violent in its sexual aggression as it is offensive in its charges of effeminacy and passivity (insatiability, curiously from our perspective, being part of this same paradigm): "I will bugger you and fuck your mouths, Aurelius, you pathic, and you queer, Furius" (Catullus, 16.1–2) (Richlin 1983). This aggression maps onto the penetrative potential of the fertility god, Priapus, to whom some eighty Latin epigrams are dedicated: his crude, ithyphallic image is a common sight in sacro-idyllic landscapes, and perhaps also in real fields and gardens, where its ludicrous phallus presumably raised a laugh by puncturing any man's masculine pretensions. The painting of Priapus weighing his manhood against a sack of money at the entrance of the House of the Vettii in Pompeii, and the statue-fountain of the same god in the garden, were but the tip of the iceberg in a world awash with images of sex scenes, of sexy bodies (avowedly masculine, avowedly feminine, and deliciously or worryingly in between) and of genitalia, and in public as well as more private spaces (Stewart 1997; Hunt 2011; Clarke 1991: 208–14 on the House of the Vettii [VI.15.1]).

Did this "permissiveness" dispense with the category of "pornography"? Most of the sexually explicit images made in Classical Athens had lent themselves to intimate, drunken viewing at the elite, male symposium, or had been sold to Italy where they honored the deceased in Etruscan tombs. In Rome, sexually explicit images were an empire-wide fabric, in civic bathhouses and bedrooms, on walls, gems, and oil-lamps, encouraging heads to spin, eyes to widen, and fantasies to run wild (Clarke 1998; Vout 2013). "Scopophilia," the love of looking at these objects, implicated everyone, including emperors, heroes, and gods: in a poem in which he criticizes his wife for being less into sex than he is, the Flavian poet Martial (*Epigrams* 11.104) imagines slaves masturbating at the keyhole whenever Andromache "rides" Hector, and Jupiter having anal sex with Juno before finding Ganymede (whose abduction was a popular pictorial motif). Often, scopophilia morphed into voyeurism, a dominating, humiliating kind of looking.

If Jupiter warns us that anthropomorphism is another dangerous seduction, that similarities between human and divine bodies are only skin deep, and that gods' bodies are governed by urges beyond mortal measure, then Venus reminds us that sexuality also links us to the gods and, simultaneously, that the Roman empire is distinct from all others in having a god of love and erotic desire as its ancestress. From the third century BCE, the role of Venus as the mother of Aeneas, Rome's mythical founder, increased in importance until, under Augustus, whose adoptive father Julius Caesar claimed to have been descended from Aeneas' son, Iulus, she became the "promoter and protector" of empire (Rives 2010: 287). Not that her maternal role as "*genetrix*" prevented her from being a "source of sensual pleasure" to gods and men (Lucretius, *On the Nature of Things* 1.1). She led by her "attractiveness" and by the "alluring love" (*blandus amor*) she inspired in all creatures (*On the Nature of Things* 1.19) (cf. Skinner 2005: 228–38).

From this perspective, sexuality is Rome's special "power base," a pervasive, crackling force that massages and enforces, by constantly threatening to destabilize the hopes, certainties, and hierarchies that make the Roman empire Roman. If sexuality had been controllable, then Cleopatra might not have slept with Caesar or Antony, nor Egypt been annexed. But to reduce sexuality's generative, potentially destructive, charisma to sex, and sex to a "pro forma" of sexual positions, orientations, prostitution, sexual health, and so on, is to rob Venus of her reach, and deny the complexities of gender. So too the tendency among scholars to answer Venus's challenges with broad-brush claims: that Rome, in contrast to Greece, privileged heterosexual over same-sex desire; that in both societies, lovers were defined less by the sex of the person they slept with than by whether they assumed the active or passive role; that sexual identity as such is a modern invention (helpful here is Ormand 2009: 1–20). Even if these conclusions are, generally speaking, true, we should have received enough hints already—about diversity, about ways of seeing and being, about change over time—to see them as crude, if not flat-lining. Can we restore the heartbeat to Roman sexuality, resuscitate its emotion and subtlety?

This chapter will take a number of texts and images as jumping off or "pulse-points" in an attempt to measure the vitality of Rome's sexual life and sexual capacity at various loci, and from various perspectives, across the empire. Some of these texts and images are more predictable than others, some representative of a picture bigger than their immediate area, and others of more purely local significance. As the macro and the micro, the complementary and the contradictory, intersect, they capture something of the complexity and dynamics of the imperial situation. These dynamics are chains of obeisance, infatuation, escapism, and command distinct from, but in dialog with, the military, political, and other administrative energies that equate to hegemony. Factors such as legislation and polytheism will steer our reading of the results, underlining that for all its influence on ensuing Western empires, the Roman empire was a world apart from our own. Close reading will bring ancient and modern sensibilities back into contact. We turn first to male–female relations in Rome itself, then move to rethink these kinds of relations in the provinces, before exploring the changing history of male–male desire, and the impact of Christianity. Between them, these data access experience, attitudes, and feelings by bringing discourses and material processes together.[3]

"I'M YOUR VENUS" (OR "PULSE POINT" 1: IMPERIAL ROME)

By the time we reach the second century CE, the Temple of Venus Genetrix in Rome, begun under Caesar and completed under Augustus, is being renovated, its walls bedecked with reliefs of Cupids. Soon, however, it is overshadowed by Hadrian's Temple of Venus and Rome, which dominates the Forum Romanum, linking the traditional heart of the city to the new sensory experience of the Flavian amphitheater. Its cult statues, back to back in adjacent cellas, make both gods tutelary deities, each of them equivalent: "the temples of the City and of Venus rise to the same height and incense is burned to the twin goddesses" (Prudentius, *The Reply to Symmachus* 1.221–2). Under Marcus Aurelius, an altar was erected in the temple precinct at which all newlyweds in Rome were expected to sacrifice (Cassius Dio 71.31.1).

Throughout this period, and just before, private individuals might also be commemorated in funerary and domestic contexts in the guise of Venus. A statuette from the Tomb of the Manilii on Rome's Via Appia is a case in point (Figure 6.1), this "goddess" not an enthroned Venus Felix or "Bringer of Good Fortune" as in the Temple, but a Venus of the Capitoline type, whose arms follow the contours of her naked body to shield her breasts and genitalia. A swirling sea creature replaces the traditional water pot at her side, drawing attention to the curves of her *contrapposto* stance; a severe portrait-head accents the goddess's idealized physicality. Strands of hair escape onto her shoulder from what is otherwise a contemporary hairstyle (Wrede 1981: 308, no. 293; D'Ambra 1996: 227–9).

For anyone who thinks that the only legitimate role available to ancient women was that of wife, daughter, or priestess in a sitcom of honor and shame

FIGURE 6.1: Roman woman in the guise of Venus. Tomb of the Manilii, Rome, 100–10 CE. Vatican Museums (Mag. Nr. 267). Photograph © Vatican Museums.

concerned, primarily, with male relationships, this statuette is provocative (Nye 1999: 18). Not that scholars have risen to the challenge, preferring to stick to the script and read her and statues like her as symbols of fertility, marriageability, and the "care of the self" that turned a girl from raw material into an accomplished matron worthy of a husband. The "grave and modest expressions" of their portrait heads are said to ground the eroticism by being almost "masculine" and to "insist on the virtues of flawless reserve and self-possession that were requisite with high birth and an elite background" (D'Ambra 1996: 229; cf. D'Ambra 2000: 111). They are thus the pin-ups of a society that put a premium on marriage and its reproductive purposes. Given high infant mortality rates, and the frequency of divorce, at least among elites, a woman's ability to produce legitimate children was her calling card.

But if sexuality is "the cultural interpretation of the human body's erogenous zones and sexual capacities" (Halperin, Winkler, and Zeitlin 1990: 3), was the statue's borrowed form (the fact that visitors to the tomb were confronted not with a representation of the *matrona*'s own body but with an obvious costume) enough to stem the seduction of its gesturing, which signals and shields the sex organs? It is a divine costume after all, and its rightful owner, Venus, a superpower, whose sexual capacities are, like Jupiter's, off the scale. In the *Homeric Hymn to Aphrodite*, composed in archaic Greece, the goddess stands before Anchises, the man fated to be Aeneas' father, trying not to terrify him by assuming the size and appearance of a mortal maiden, but instilling wonder nevertheless. In a sex scene in Apuleius' *Metamorphoses* (2.17), a novel written in Latin in the mid- to late second century CE, the slave Photis removes all of her clothes, lets her hair down, "beautifully transforms herself into the image of Venus, who rises from the ocean waves," and "purposefully shadows, as opposed to modestly hides, her shaven genitalia." This slippage, from goddess to girl, and back again, had long lent its spark to mythology and elegy, and informed encounters with Praxiteles' Aphrodite of Knidos, a statue famed for being the first monumental, free-standing female nude, on which the Capitoline Venus is ultimately based (Havelock 1995; Squire 2011: 88–109).

Configured like this, the perceived beauty and fecundity of these portrait statues is less containable, conveying upon their referents an agency that threatens always to sidestep the husband, replacing the question "What should I do?" from the women, with a more vulnerable, yet demonstrative "Who am I?"[4] Finally, perhaps, for the honorand in the Tomb of the Manilii, death has liberated her from society's fetters. Perhaps here we have a declaration of sexual identity of the kind that scholarship has tried to silence—not a "masculine" physiognomy, but an avowedly, even aggressively, female subjectivity. There was another statuette in the tomb—a muscular male nude in the guise of Mercury (Wrede 1981: 274, no. 206). But it was more common for female figures with Venus bodies to appear with men in the role of Mars (Kousser

2007). The same poem that praises the "amor" inspired by Venus, Lucretius' late Republican *On the Nature of Things* (1.32–7), recounts the story of her infidelity with the god of war, "powerful in his weaponry," who often throws himself into her lap, "completely conquered by the eternal wound of love." Follow these cues, and there is a risk that our "matron" looks more like an adulteress, and her husband like a cuckold.

A wife's adultery was grounds for divorce as well as "*infamia,*" the denial of the legal rights that normally protected citizen status. Charged with adultery, elite women were rendered the symbolic equivalent of prostitutes: Augustus' own daughter and, if we believe the ancient authors, granddaughter, were sent into exile for their extramarital affairs, and part of their property confiscated. (McGinn 1998). Under the Augustan *lex Iulia*, prostitutes were marked out as the antithesis of the "*mater familias,*" or mother of the Roman family—non-women, who must be deterred from infiltrating the upper classes even as they gave men of all classes a legitimate outlet for their libido (Edwards 1997). Perhaps past scholarship is right to be *dirigiste*, right to think that our Venus-manquée cannot be subversive. Except that several surviving literary sources make the celebrated Greek *hetaera*, or prostitute, Phryne, the model for the paradigmatic Aphrodite of Knidos, and give Phryne the credit for exploiting her beauty and exposing her breasts during her trial in around 345 BCE for "*asebeia*" or impiety. They ask that we see prostitute and goddess not as alternatives, but as a synergy.[5] Do this, and we appreciate our statue's regulation of sexuality and its explosive potential, a potential that brings the viewer's sexuality into focus. Even temples are affected by the fall out. Scratched on to the stylobate of the Augustan Temple of Mars Ultor, with its cult statues of Mars, Venus, and the Divine Julius, is an ancient graffito, depicting a male figure penetrating a female from the rear (Boyle 2003: 179). A crude assertion of patriarchy, and an acknowledgment (and caricature) of Venus and Mars' power, it forces us to confront the fact that sexuality is always political.

"LOVE IN A COLD CLIMATE" (OR "PULSE POINT" 2: ROMAN BRITAIN)

A similarly explicit sex scene, this time on a fragmentary marble relief of the late Republic/early empire, takes place on a boat in an obviously Nilotic landscape (Figure 6.2). Are the couple to be identified as Antony and Cleopatra as some scholars have assumed, Cleopatra the "prostitute queen" whom the Augustan poet Propertius imagines "is screwed even by her slaves" (Propertius, *Elegies* 3.11.39 and 3.11.30)? Or are they generic examples of Egyptian licentiousness? Either way, they engage, publicly, in an act that defines them as abnormal, not just beyond the pale, as adulteresses and prostitutes are beyond the pale, enslaved by their passions and, thus, slavish, but inescapably exiled, beyond the

FIGURE 6.2: Marble relief with an erotic scene in a boat. First century BCE–first century CE, provenance unknown. British Museum (Inv. No. 1865, 1118.252). Photograph: © The Trustees of the British Museum.

empire's civilizing remit, resolutely un-Roman. Like the hypersexual black men who populate mosaics at Pompeii (Clarke 1996), they are exotic, erotic, excessive, and alien—as alien as the Amazons of mythology, who challenged heroes and Greek masculinity more broadly by disavowing their sex, excelling in warfare, and living apart from, or in command over, men (Tyrrell 1984).

"Unrestrained sexuality was an unending threat to empire" (Levine 2004: 134). The early imperial reliefs of Claudius conquering Britannia and Nero Armenia (Figures 6.3 and 6.4) from the Sebasteion at Aphrodisias in Asia Minor, a Greek city that came under the personal protection of the emperor Augustus in the first century BCE, graphically suppress this threat as violently as the army would suppress any uprising. A strong Nero, nude apart from cloak and baldric, dominates Armenia as, in the visual record, Achilles had long dominated the Amazon Queen, Penthesilea. Nero's imperial predecessor Claudius bears down on a half-naked Britannia, pinning her with his knee and pulling at her hair as he prepares to deliver the deathblow. This is empire-building as a masculine enterprise, and a reminder, as far as this chapter is concerned, that prosecution under the *lex Iulia de ui*, the law that punished

FIGURE 6.3: Panel showing Claudius overcoming Britannia. South portico of the Sebasteion, Aphrodisias, first century CE. Photograph: New York University Excavations at Aphrodisias: Guido Petruccioli.

forcible sexual intercourse with a boy, woman, or anyone else, could only be brought if the victim was a freeborn citizen: the boots worn by these figures, Armenia's Orientalizing hat, Britannia's unbound hair, leave no doubt that they are barbarians. It is also a reminder that "rape," if that is what this is, helped to make Rome what it was—in Mars' rape of the Vestal Virgin Rhea Silvia, who gave birth to Romulus (a scene represented on the pediment of the goddess Roma's *cella* in the Temple of Venus and Rome), and in the rape of the Sabine women by Romulus' men, the "model for the whole set of institutions that we call 'Roman marriage'" (Beard 1999: 1–2). It cements, and questions, the relationship between "sex and state," "desire and expediency" (Beard 1999: 3).

Cut to Roman Britain, centuries after the conquest, and what looks, from Aphrodisias, like a binary relationship assumes an altogether different quality.

FIGURE 6.4: Panel showing Nero suppressing Armenia. South portico of the Sebasteion, Aphrodisias, first century CE. Photograph: New York University Excavations at Aphrodisias: Guido Petruccioli.

In the apse of a dining room of a "villa" at Lullingstone in Kent, a locally made mosaic, dating from the middle of the fourth century CE, presents a different rape scene in Jupiter's transformation into a bull and his abduction of the Phoenician princess, Europa, who gives her name to the landmass beyond Asia (Figure 6.5). There is little of the fear, or estrangement from her homeland, that we find, for example, in the Ovidian account (*Metamorphoses* 2.833–875). She is instead a Venus-clone on a prancing pet, led by Cupids. Not that Ovid's poetry is far away: a couplet in his style lends a commentary: INVIDA SI TA[VRI] VIDISSET IUNO NATATVS/IVSTIVS AEOLIAS ISSET ADVSQUE DOMOS ("If jealous Juno had seen the swimming of the bull, more justly would she have gone to the halls of Aeolus").[6]

FIGURE 6.5: Floor mosaic showing Europa riding on a bull. Lullingstone Roman Villa, Kent, fourth century CE. Credit: De Agostini Picture Library. G. Wright/Bridgeman Images.

The inscription is not a slavish quote, but a witty allusion, and to one of the foundational texts of Roman imperial culture, the *Aeneid* (1.50). By blending Ovid and Vergil like this, the patron turns Rome's expansionist and sexual culture back on itself, hybridizing two of its most famous exports and rendering epic elegiac. The couplet answers the question posed by Vergil at the opening of the epic as to why Juno was intent upon making Aeneas' city-building mission so difficult, and supplements, if not substitutes for, the rationale offered there by wickedly observing that had she witnessed her husband Jupiter's adultery, she would have had a better reason for trying to derail the hero. "Better reason", "*more* justly:" are her actions unforgivable, whichever way one looks at them, or had they always been justifiable? If successful, she would have stopped Aeneas reaching Latium and secured Britain's independence. We look again at Europa, center-stage, in form and company like Aeneas' mother: within the frame of the apse mosaic at least, the power is hers. An epic of empire and conquest is re-visioned as "a countervailing epic of the defeated and of republican liberty" (Quint 1993: back cover; on the politics of the Europa myth, Morales 2007).

Either that, or it becomes a story of sex, pure and simple. Take the fourth-century mosaic in the cold room of the baths at the villa at Low Ham in Somerset (Figure 6.6). Its story is unadulterated *Aeneid*, or rather an epitome of books one and four: four panels show Aeneas and his fellow Trojans sailing into

FIGURE 6.6: Floor mosaic showing Dido and Aeneas. Low Ham Roman Villa, Somerset, fourth century CE. Credit: Somerset Co. Museum, Taunton Castle. UK/ Bridgeman Images.

Carthage; Venus introducing him and Ascanius (or should that be her son Cupid in disguise?) to the Queen of Carthage, Dido; a hunt scene; and a sex scene, as Aeneas in military dress, and a similar Orientalizing hat to that worn by Armenia at Aphrodisias, the same outfit that he was wearing on first meeting, embraces a now naked Dido. Presiding, in the center, are Venus (or should that be Dido again?) and Cupids, one of them with the torch of marriage, the other with the down-turned torch of death.[7] Dido's fate and Rome's future hang in the balance, the latter erased, or revised as story of boy meets girl. Perhaps this is pornography.

Here, it is Aeneas that is the barbarian, and Dido another clone of Venus, and a Venus who, in the first of her panels, wears armlets and a jeweled bodychain of the kind found in the "Hoxne Treasure," a hoard of coins and gold and silver objects buried in Suffolk early in the fifth century CE (Neal and Cosh 2002–10, vol. 2: 255; Bland and Johns 1993: 19–21). Her "care of the self" aligns her with the wealthiest of the island's inhabitants. In this way, it is Dido who is normative, and Aeneas—in his military dress and Eastern hat, estranged from his mum—an unsettling mix of hostile masculinity and exotic effeminacy. Did the bathers side with Rome or Carthage? Did they find or lose themselves in the narrative? Can we "bridge the division between discourse and practice by relating the experiences of sexual subjects to their status as marginal—and vice-versa" (Houlbrook 2001: 501)? How marginal was this patron?

These questions have major implications for the ways in which we think about sexuality in the provinces—both that of the landowning classes, whose Latinity is evidenced by the mosaics above, and that of society more broadly. By the second century CE, the militarized zones of northern Britain were not male domains, but alive with women and children, some of these women local, and many from further afield, and not just Italy, Gaul, and Spain (see Allison 2011, 2013; Allason-Jones 1999, 2012; Sherratt and Moore 2016). Take the centurion of the Sixth Legion Victrix stationed on the Antonine Wall, who appears to have been born in Pannonia, modern Hungary, and his wife (*uxor*) Vibia Pacata, a woman of possible African origin.[8] Further south, at York, the skull of a female skeleton, buried with an array of high-status grave-goods, jet and ivory bracelets, earrings, beads, an openwork bone mount with a Christian message, a mirror, and a glass jar, likely to have held cosmetics or perfumes, has been found to display "white" and "black" features (Leach *et al.* 2010). "Roman" is a promiscuous term: "high levels of human mobility were both a direct function of empire-building and a defining feature of Roman identity" (Scheidel 2004: 1).

From the Augustan period until 197 CE, soldiers were disincentivized, if not banned, from marrying while on active service, in part, perhaps, to ensure the professionalism of the army, and in part to protect the state from having to take responsibility for their descendants (Phang 2001; Scheidel 2007b). But in practice, even ordinary soldiers could "marry" in a *de facto*, if non-legal, sense. They could also take a concubine, as well as, of course, enjoy sexual relations with male and female prostitutes and with slaves, whom the literature makes as sexually available as they were rapacious.[9] A tombstone from South Shields in the north of England, erected in the second century CE by a Palmyrene soldier or merchant, honors the dedicant's British "wife" (*coniunx*), Regina, a freedwoman from the Catuvellauni tribe in Hertfordshire (*RIB Online* 1065) (recently, Mullen 2012: 1–5, 32–5; Caroll 2012). Her former servitude is a puzzle: were some provincial women sold into slavery by their parents? And veterans often stayed where they had been stationed. A military diploma issued in 105 CE to a British foot-soldier discharging him from the cohort that had formed part of the Roman army in Moesia records him settling in Pannonia Superior, where presumably he had been stationed previously, with his Pannonian wife and their three children

(Birley 1980: 102). He was attractive not least because his children were ensured Roman citizenship (although this would change in 140 CE, when the grant of rights to auxiliaries' children was abandoned) (Waebens 2012). But this assumes that monogamy was as obvious to her as it was to those in Rome. Given the high levels of inequality in ancient society, and the potential in inequitable societies for women to think themselves better off sharing a rich man with other women than having a poor partner of their own, the Roman, and indeed Greek, premium on monogamy is surprising—until one realizes that wealthy elites could little afford to alienate the "ordinary man" by taking many wives, if the empire needed that man to serve in the army (Scheidel 2011).

Tapping these families' sexualities and sexual lives is no easy task. A closer look at Regina's sandstone tombstone (Figure 6.7) reveals none of the nudity that characterized the Flavian women discussed in the previous section, or the mythological females of our expensive Romano-British mosaics. Instead, she is seated in stately fashion in a wicker chair, modestly clad in a long-sleeved robe that reaches to her feet, and in a style that recalls Palmyrene funerary art, as well as Greco-Roman drapery. In her lap is a distaff and spindle, and, to her left, a wool basket. She is a domestic goddess, defined by her labor. With her right hand, she opens a jewelry box at her feet, not her dowry (she is a former slave after all), but proof perhaps of the security that marriage has brought her, of the "fact" that she too has jewels to rival those that drip from the bodies of Palmyrene women proper. We note the cable-pattern necklace and bracelets that she already wears. Yet she is dead, aged but thirty. The accompanying Latin and Palmyrene inscription destabilizes, if not expunges, her ethnicity (although note Caroll 2012 on the Britishness of her clothing and adornment). She is British by birth, but has become an exotic hybrid even in her country of origin.

If sexuality is linked to life-stages, then mortality rates and related factors such as age at marriage combine with diet and so on change how we view it. Whereas scholars used to think that Roman women married for the first time at the age of twelve to fifteen, that age, especially for non-elite women, has risen in recent years to closer to twenty. Much of a woman's married life was devoted to having children, and maternal mortality, like infant mortality, was high due to complications such as hemorrhage and infection. The fourth-century burials in the Roman-Christian cemetery outside Poundbury camp near Dorchester reveal that fifty-one out of the 281 women of childbearing age died just after childbirth. (Allason-Jones 1989: 36; for childbirth in ancient Rome, Todman 2007). Although newborns are underrepresented at the cemetery, data from elsewhere in Roman Britain explain the deficit by showing that it was normal to bury neo-natal infants within the social sphere of the living—not just inside the walls of the settlement, but strategically placed, often in the corners of rooms. What was forbidden by law for older children, who were perceived as possessing the cognizance to count as individuals, was permissible for babies, keeping

FIGURE 6.7: Tombstone of Regina, second century CE. Credit: Arbeia Fort & Museum, © Tyne & Wear Archives & Museums. UK/Bridgeman Images.

them close to their mothers and to social structures that would have shaped them (Millett and Gowland 2015).

All of this is a long way from the Sebasteion's image of Britannia. The Sebasteion was a religious complex dedicated to the Julio-Claudian emperors and Aphrodisias' eponymous deity, Aphrodite, who was aligned with Venus Genetrix. For the local families who funded the project, the negative implications of Rome's expansion into Asia Minor appear to have been forgotten: the claim is that, unlike the Britons or Armenians, they inhabited the same cultural and sexual space as the Romans. In reality, of course, there were no assurances. Some of the worst atrocities committed by Roman soldiers occur in texts about civil war: so Tacitus' account of what happened when troops loyal to Vitellius captured Cremona in Italy in 69 CE and respected neither "social rank" nor "age," qualities normally at the core of Roman familial and political structures, raping and murdering men and women (*Histories* 3.33.1). This rhetoric is unsurprising: civil war shattered the cohesion that constituted Roman identity. At Aphrodisias, the classical contours of the emperors' muscular torsos and the Hellenistic composition of the panels are careful to paper over the fault-lines between Greek and Romanness and the *mores* that were their make-up—fault-lines that remain live into the Byzantine period. Tacitus again, this time on Nero's institution of games on a Greek model, sees Greece as being as corrupting as Egypt, more dangerous than Britain (*Annals* 14.20): "young men were becoming degenerate with foreign pursuits, indulging in the gymnasia and idleness and disgraceful love-affairs." Empire-building may have been a masculine enterprise that proved its men's penetrative power, but as even Herodotus' Persians could see (9.122.3), it brought a luxury that risked softness.

"IT'S A MAN'S WORLD" (OR "PULSE POINT" 3: "GREEK LOVE")

Rome's expansionist drive eastwards in the second century BCE had brought it into contact with a Greek-speaking world as alien as it was seductive. There are many ways of quantifying this alien-ness but one of the key ways has been to contrast Roman *mores* with Greece's promotion of male–male desire. Whereas Rome promoted marriage, and regarded men's sexual relations with freeborn Roman men and women other than their wives as punishable, Greek society celebrated liaisons between male citizens and freeborn adolescent males, regarding this as a *rite de passage* en route to citizen status. We need only think of Harmodius and the older, bearded Aristogeiton in the latter part of the sixth century BCE, who became as famous for their love of one another as for their love of Athens and their killing of the tyrant's brother. Democracy has its own erotics (how could citizenship not be a sexual and political category, if only men are citizens?) in dialog with Athens' own imperialist lust (Wohl 2002). Foucault contributed to this sense of difference between the two societies. For him, even the Greek literature written under the Roman empire projected a valorization of marriage. Any reflection on homoerotic desire then had "lost some of its intensity, its seriousness, its vitality."[10]

Another look at the Roman period, however, reveals just how reductive this view is. "Greek" and "Roman" culture are no more strict dichotomies in this respect than active and passive, male and female. We have already mentioned Jupiter and Ganymede: staying with fourth-century Britain, the pair grace a mosaic-floor in the summer dining room of the Roman villa at Bignor in Sussex (Figure 6.8). The beautiful bronzed Trojan boy, nude except for the same soft hat as is worn by Aeneas and Armenia, is displayed to the viewers' delight in front of Jupiter in the guise of a giant eagle. This testifies to the transportational nature of an encounter with the divine, capturing something of the experience of the ineffable power of godhead in an image of an erotic union that defies human propriety, an image of bestiality. It also testifies to the attraction of the male body, and, perhaps too, or so the diners might hope, to the sexual availability of the patron's servants or cupbearers. Were they to know their Latin literature, they would know that Ganymede is a name often given to household slaves (Williams 2010: 59–64). Elsewhere on the floor, six hexagons contain dancing maenads, female followers of the wine god Bacchus, disrobed in gay abandon. They too tap religious experience, and speak of sexual license (Neal and Cosh 2002–10, vol. 3 [2]: 498–503).

FIGURE 6.8: Floor mosaic showing Ganymede being carried off by the eagle. Bignor Roman Villa, fourth century CE. Credit: The Tupper Family, Bignor Roman Villa.

At the same time, in Roman Gaul, the local-born grammarian, Ausonius, who winds up working at the imperial court in Trier as tutor to the young prince, Gratian, plugs himself into a Latin and Greek epigrammatic tradition by writing an epitaph to a young boy, Glaucias, a name already familiar to readers of Martial (6.28–9) and Statius (*Siluae* 2.1). Unlike their Glaucias, a favorite slave who was but twelve or thirteen when he died, Ausonius' honorand is sixteen, an erotically ideal age at which he looks like both boy and girl, but is about to become a man. The poem ends, "nor will you, a weeping shade, fear the Stygian lakes, but you will go either an Adonis, son of Cinyras, to Persephone, or you will be the Ganymede of Elysian Jupiter" (53.6–8).[11] Glaucias appeals to both sexes, but is himself neither, a factor that makes him more desirable by virtue of being indefinable. In other poems, Ausonius is scathing of homosexual encounters between men, and between men and boys; to call a fellow Roman a half-man or "*semiuir*" (101.1), as he does Zoilus (again a name familiar from Martial) for sleeping with his adulterous wife's boyfriends is not a compliment (see also Epigram 99). It makes him a lesser man, even as it aligns him with Hermaphroditus whom Ausonius (72.11), in debt to Ovid, describes with the same terminology (Keith and Rupp 2007: 26–8; also on Hermaphroditus, Epigrams 111–12). In Ovid's *Metamorphoses* (4.346–88), Hermaphroditus is said to be neither boy nor woman, and yet both, a body that symbolizes lack, yet has it all. In Roman visual culture, Hermaphroditus, with breasts and penis, is a "Queer" body, whose power is celebrated.[12]

Ausonius' mix of celebration and satire, and his invective elsewhere in his poetry against men who assume a passive role during sex, shows that the literature of the later Roman empire is still concerned with male–male desire in all of its shades and intensity. It also shows us that for all that boys would be boys, not all "*semiuiri*" were "half-measures," and that the Romans were attuned to the instabilities of what we now call gender. Lots of ink has been spilled on whether, contrary to Foucault and his followers, there *were* men in Rome who were stigmatized or who self-identified as "homosexuals" in our modern sense of the word (i.e., men who have a sexual *orientation* distinct from that of other men) (esp. Richlin 1993 and Taylor 1997). But the difficulty of deploying the extant evidence to answer this key question must not distract us from what the evidence does tell us, namely that the relentless enforcement of masculine, active, penetrative norms, and, counter to these, female passivity and chastity, inevitably opened up spaces for exploring sexual practices, sexual identities even, between "fixed" parameters. Images of Hermaphroditus, some of them sexually aggressive, others languorous and lovely, were one such "space" or canvas, asking—through their challenge of "what kind of body am I?"—whether there was any such thing as the normal. Whenever viewers were captivated by a body like this, they admitted that they were not who they thought they were.

Admittedly, these viewers and the viewers of our Romano-British mosaics inhabit a radically different place from that of Augustus, Ovid, or the patrons of the Sebasteion. Crucial in this story of change was the relationship of Hadrian (emperor from 117–38 CE) and his beloved Antinous, a young boy from Bithynia in Asia Minor, whose main achievement, apart from his royal liaison, had been to die prematurely in the River Nile. Soon a city was founded in his honor, and imagery of him, modest and monumental, was visible throughout the empire, including in Roman Britain. Whatever the truth about his life and his death, he captured the public imagination more than Hadrian's wife or his adopted heir, speaking to a Hellenic revival among Rome's elites, and way beyond this, to elites and non-elites across the provinces. Whereas Julius Caesar was rumored to have been the passive partner of King Nicomedes of Bithynia (Suetonius, *Life of the Deified Julius*, 49), Hadrian was elevated, his boyfriend and beard offering an alternative, more contemplative masculinity to the aggression of the military (also important here is Noreña 2007 on Hadrian's coinage). This would have been unthinkable in the Republic or early Principate. In turn, Antinous was made a god—not a sex god like Jupiter, but nonetheless resident on Olympus like the powerfully passive Ganymede (Vout 2007).

The public dimension of Hadrian's relationship with Antinous is what is innovative here: its parading of pederastic desire as a positive, socially productive force is akin to what we find on Athenian pots with their depictions of bearded men courting clean-shaven youths at the gymnasium and symposium, and in the Roman author Cornelius Nepos, who makes the statesman Alcibiades emblematic of Athenian youths, when he claims (7.2.2) that he was "beloved by many in the Greek fashion." It is worlds away from Augustus' embrace of the titles *Pater Patriae* (Father of the Country) and *Paterfamilias* (Father of the family), with the near-absolute control over all descendants, their marriage partners, family property, money, and so on that that traditional, head-of-the-household role implies (Kuefler 2001: 70–6). Not that Hadrian was not also *Pater Patriae*, nor that pederasty was anathema to Romans prior to his reign: indeed if male–male desire is key to the sexual ideology of Greek politics, and if expansion into Greece equates to the invention of the Roman empire, then in the Republic, already, Rome had to come to terms with a more nuanced homosexuality than that enacted on the comic stage (Lilja 1983; Ormand 2009: 146–63).

This need for nuance was not lost on poets writing in the chaotic half-century before Augustus secured sole power. The rumors that circulated around Caesar underline how Rome's ambitions eastwards colored a culture of invective that was already gendered. But this is only part of the story. Even the abusively virile Catullus, who threatens to rape Aurelius and Furius and render them passive, reminds them of the kisses he craves, not only from his girlfriend Lesbia but also from Juventius, a "flower" of a boy, with youth in his name (youth = "*iuuentus*" in Latin), who features in six of his poems (compare Catullus 5, 7, and 48). Here, Catullus assumes the role of boy-lover—a role that he elsewhere urges a certain Manlius Torquatus to relinquish in favor of the normative role of Roman husband and father (Catullus 61)—so as to speak with a subaltern voice outside of Rome's hegemonic power structures. Whether kissing Juventius, speaking as the Greek poet, Sappho, whose work is famed for its staging of female homoeroticism, or indeed, as he does in poem 63, as the Phrygian youth Attis, who sheds the role of ideal ephebe by castrating himself in devotion to the goddess Cybele, Catullus stimulates his and his readers' fantasy. He escapes the constraints of Roman society, while simultaneously exploring the anxieties he feels at a sense of political disenfranchisement (Skinner 1993). Despite Sappho's inclusion here, female same-sex love, though also seen as Greek, remains unreal and alien. That there is no equivalent tradition to that of Greek pederastic poetry left it less profitable to think with (although there is a growing literature, e.g., Hallett 1989; Brooten 1996; Oliver 2015).

Hadrian was not the only emperor to revise what Roman imperial power looked like, or indeed how Rome and Romanness related to the rest of the world. Every emperor did this to some degree, but by the close of the second century, African-born Septimius Severus was in control, his mother Libyan and his wife Syrian. In 212 CE, his son Caracalla granted citizenship to nearly all free inhabitants of the empire, a decision that brought restrictions as well as privileges. It reduced the pool of men with whom male citizens could legitimately have sexual relations. And it meant that at the same time as Severus' powerful widow, Julia Domna, was being accused of incest with Caracalla in Rome, the extended reach of Roman marriage law was threatening the close-kin, especially sibling, unions so popular in Egypt (Penella 1980; Grubbs 2015).

The collapse of the Severan dynasty in 235 CE brought with it fifty years of civil war, followed by the division of the empire into two, and then four "mini-empires," each with its own leader with his own charisma—only to return to dynastic rule under Constantine in the early fourth century. By then, strong imperial support for Christianity was allowing the Church to transform the moral dynamics of the social concept of shame into the theological concept of sin. Already sexual renunciation was a live issue in many Christian communities. In time, Christianity would change relations to the body, and the body and community, in ways often considered formative of Western attitudes to sex, women, and family. But Christianity was itself an intensely debated category, Christology much disputed, and the boundary between Christian culture and "pagan" culture no less fuzzy than that between active and passive, male and female. For the most militant advocates of asceticism, like Jerome, a priest and theologian perhaps best known for translating the Bible into Latin, not even the Commandment to be "fruitful and multiply" could sanction heterosexual sex within marriage (groundbreaking here, and for the next section, is Brown 1988). For the Christian poet, Prudentius, Antinous became the ultimate image of idolatry, a Ganymede "robbed of his manhood in the imperial embrace," as legislation hit male effeminacy and prostitution harder than ever (Prudentius, *The Reply to Symmachus* 273). But, to many—Christians included—the cultural capital that came from knowing the literature of the past was as powerful as ever. Ausonius' work displays "Christian" as well as "pagan" allegiance.

"NAKED BEFORE GOD" (OR "PULSE POINT" 4: A CHRISTIAN EMPIRE)

Sexuality has been described as "the most prominent and characteristic area of the Christian claim of moral superiority over Greco-Roman society and simultaneously a point of intense controversy among themselves" (Rhee 2005: 106). Monasticism, which would do as much to preserve and shape culture as it did to encourage a retreat from society's pleasures, "arrived relatively late to the western Mediterranean" (Kuefler 2001: 273), evolving out of the desert communities of Egypt, Syria, and Palestine. But its drivers existed long before the Middle Ages, in a literature that took evolving Platonic teachings on the division of body and soul to new extremes, and turned all non-Christians into possible whores. Conversely, as increasing numbers of Christians turned their backs on the male and female roles that had traditionally made them good men and women in the eyes of their peers, they risked relinquishing not only their worldly goods but tried and tested masculine or feminine identities. Christ replaced husband or wife. Monks embraced passive, or gender ambiguous, roles as "brides of Christ," or diverted the rhetoric surrounding the increasing numbers of castrated slaves who rose to chamberlain positions in the imperial court to identify as spiritual eunuchs (Kuefler 2001). In renouncing their womanhood, female ascetics and saints were often cast as anti-women—manly, transvestite, or, more curiously, as prostitutes (Burrus 2004).

The popularity of Adam and Eve in late antique art attests to the wider implications of all of this: the identification of the moment when "the eyes of both were opened, and they knew they were naked" (Genesis 3:7) as the moment when humankind first felt sexual shame and uncontrollable sexual sensation. It was not simply that the Roman empire was declining. Mankind had fallen. Whereas the incarnation highlighted God's power to transform, mankind was confronted with its own intractable physicality, which it had to work hard to escape. Human bodies were dangerous, a realization that impacts even, if not especially, on the representation of Christ's body, born, crucially, of a virgin womb. Christ was not simply man-shaped, as Jupiter had been: he was born of flesh, a problem that remains unresolvable. Throughout the fourth century, debates waged over his precise relationship to God. In 381 CE, the

Council of Constantinople summoned by Gratian's co-ruler Theodosius I, defeated counter currents to confirm the Nicene Creed (e.g., that Christ is both fully man and one with the Father and thus both entirely God and fully man) at the heart of today's Christian liturgy.

Not that Christ's body ever makes Venus's body redundant. For every image of a pagan deity that was knocked from its pedestal, another was given increased aesthetic, and perhaps also erotic, currency by being freed of religious meaning. Indeed it was often in the *binding* of pagan and Christian motifs that elites in the period of transition that is the fourth century asserted an identity. More than one scholar, for example, has seen Christian references in the inscription on Lullingstone's Europa mosaic—most plausibly a cryptogram (so the first letter of the second line, followed by every eighth letter, until the end when we run out of letters and have to stop at "S" spells "IESVS," Jesus) (Henig 1997; Thomas 1998: 47–54). Supporting this reading is the fact that the Greek hero Bellerophon, who is pictured slaying the Chimaera on the mosaic beyond the apse, also appears on pavements at Hinton St. Mary and Frampton in association with the "Chi Rho," a Christian symbol (consisting of the intersection of the capital Greek letters Chi [X] and Rho [P], the first two letters of "Christ" in Greek) which was itself depicted in frescoes of a slightly later date in a house-church elsewhere in the villa. Never mind whether "jealous Juno had seen . . .". Have viewers seen the mosaic's hidden meaning? If they have, history is rewritten again: Europa could almost be a martyr, sacrificed to death by beasts in the Roman amphitheater (Coleman 1990).

Acts of female martyrs, the lives of female saints, and ancient accounts of asceticism, many of them also addressed to women, underline, however, how far we have traveled. Engage with these ways of bearing witness to God, and it is as though society as we know it has ended. "[H]ow did it become possible for Christian writers to present life virginity as a triumph for women, when Roman society saw it as a tragedy for a girl to die unmarried or a woman to remain childless" (Clark 2004: 66)? The shift is momentous, and accompanied by an over-zealous incitement to starve oneself or, sometimes, engage in other forms of self-harm designed to choke the body and its physical processes. There was a fine line between finding a freedom from societal constraints and misogyny. Men were not immune to the effects of over-zealousness: but whereas anorexia made women infertile, it was harder to stem an erection, a difficulty that led in writing to an almost pathological confession of man's uncontrollable urges. This, in turn, objectified and vilified women further. Contrary to changes in Roman law which had led to a progressive erosion of the overarching power of the *paterfamilias*, and a world in which Roman women could share in the domains of marital consent, ownership of property, and so on, God's punishment of Eve intensified the implicit bias that spelled female submission and male dominance. In commenting on Genesis, Jerome's contemporary, Augustine, writes, in the physical sense, woman has been made for man. In her mind and her rational intelligence she has a nature the equal of man's, but in sex she is physically subject to him in the same way as our natural impulses need to be subjected to the reasoning power of the mind, in order that the actions to which they lead may be inspired by the principles of good conduct (*Confessions* 13.32.47).

I want to stay with the female body for the rest of this section, for it is here that Christian concerns about sexuality and gender stand out. It is the female body that stages the conundrum of being in the world, yet not of the world, the female body that highlights how the anti-social, anti-familial force of some early Christianity teaching is, if anything, more threatening to Roman authority, and the natural order for which it stands, than the temptations of the flesh. In this way, all female bodies are as exposed as the prostitute's body and as much of an infringement of public decency. This exposure issues an invitation to go back to basics, to reconfigure everything the Romans thought they understood about sex, and the moral, ethical, political, and religious aspects of life that shape and are shaped by it.

The multi-version *Life of Pelagia* is the story of a fabulously wealthy "prostitute" and her conversion to Christianity.[13] But it is no straightforward story of redemption: when we and those in the text first see her, she appears decked in gold, pearls, and precious stones, like a cult-statue with all of its sensational presence (*cum summa phantasia*), an epiphany almost, carried on a donkey. The Bishop, Nonnus, cannot take his eyes off her, abject at the thought that whereas she knows how to please her lovers, he and his fellow Christians are insufficiently devoted to Christ. But her desire for them is nothing compared to her "desire" (*desiderium*) for God after she hears Nonnus' preaching and seduces him into baptizing her. Even that is not enough, and soon she is leaving her possessions to the Church for distribution to the poor, ditching her baptismal dress, and, in a tunic and breeches belonging to Nonnus, heading off to Jerusalem and the Mount of Olives. There she gains fame as an ascetic, her beauty so devastated by fasting that not even those who had seen her in Antioch recognized her. All who knew her knew her as Pelagius the eunuch. Only when (s)he dies and her body, itself compared to gold and precious stone, is anointed with myrrh, is her sex revealed. The Church fathers try to conceal the "miracle," but word escapes, and is proof of God's greatness.

What are we to make of this story? For all of Pelagia's conversion and self-mortification, there was always something extraordinary about her, a sense that in Antioch already she "cometh in the name of the Lord," the donkey a reference to Jesus' own entry into Jerusalem. And when she dies, she is still as shining as she was at the beginning, a body that everyone raves about because of its transgressive femininity. She may have been a prostitute, but went on to earn a different credit by serving God. And she entices men to join her in this even in death. She is a seductive, disruptive, entity even then—an object of reverence for a new world in which what it means to act and interact as a man or woman, in Rome, Jerusalem, Antioch, or Britain, is so fundamentally redefined as to drive paganism (or so it was hoped) to extinction.

CONCLUSION

This chapter has taken a far from traditional approach to sexuality, spurning legal, medical, or historical texts in favor of a panoramic view that takes in art and literature in a journey across the Roman empire, and through time, from the late Republic to the rise of Christianity. Examination of this art and literature has enabled us to remove Rome's official clothes, bringing representation and reality, experience and discourse, together to measure the heart-rates of the empire's inhabitants. It has also highlighted how many of them remain under the radar. Archaeology and demography can help a bit, even if they too give but a partial picture. Our attempts at "testing" offer a different route from relying on "norms" or "recommended daily intakes."

As far as empire is concerned, our findings divide and conquer, level and unify, lending flesh to political ambitions, and bringing political and religious sanctions to human and divine interaction. If we want to get at what it felt like to live under Roman rule, or understand how the Roman empire differed from the Holy Roman Empire or, for example, India under the Raj, we could do worse than study sexuality, which, if done properly, sees that "Sexual acts were invariably discussed or represented as part of a larger theological, metaphysical, or ethical context" (Nye 1999: 18). Perhaps this is why there has been no real history of Greek or Roman sexuality since Foucault. It demands being an expert in multiple sub-disciplines, and accepting that ultimately, even in complex societies, sexuality remains enigmatic, regressive and primitive (Klockars 2013).[14]

CHAPTER SEVEN

Resistance

LISA PILAR EBERLE

During the twentieth century, more people than ever before encountered Roman history through (hi)stories of resistance. The different retellings of the story of Spartacus over the course of this century illustrate this point rather well.[1] Between 73 and 71 BCE Spartacus, a Thracian slave and gladiator, led an army of revolting slaves in Italy that defeated Roman legions several times before being overcome by Crassus in a battle in southern Campania. Karl Marx had famously called Spartacus a "real representative of the proletariat in ancient times" (Marx and Engels, *Collected Works*, vol. 41: 265). In the early twentieth century, Rosa Luxemburg and Karl Liebknecht denounced the vote of the German Socialist Party in favor of the First World War in a publication called *Spartakusbriefe* (Spartacus letters). The organization they founded, the *Spartakusbund* (Spartacus League), stood at the origin of the Communist party in Germany. Subsequently, in Russia and other communist and socialist countries many schools, sport clubs—Spartak Moscow and Spartak Sofia are but two examples—and sporting events, including the socialist contest attempting to rival the Olympic Games, were named after the slave revolt's leader.

In the United States, this revolt and its leader were the subject of Howard Fast's best-selling novel, *Spartacus*, which inspired the 1960 Hollywood film of the same name, starring Kirk Douglas. The film, which broke the box-office record at the time, also made nods to several contemporary political struggles (Wyke 1997: 67–70; Hardwick 2003: 39, 42). For instance, the storyline of Dabra, a black slave who was hanged for refusing to kill Spartacus in the arena, makes reference to the emergent Civil Rights Movement and its acts of civil disobedience. The most famous scene shows the slaves standing up, one after the other, and defiantly showing their unwillingness to give up their leader by saying "I am Spartacus"; it seems to be a reference to many intellectuals' refusal to inform on their friends and colleagues in front of the House Un-American Activities Committee. In fact, *Spartacus* was the first movie to break the Hollywood blacklist on writers who had refused to cooperate with that committee.

In early twentieth-century Italy, Spartacus was a widespread symbol of the *Risorgimento*, of Italian unity and nationalism (Wyke 1997: 37–47), a position that rebellions and rebel leaders in the Roman empire occupied in several other countries as well. The importance of Arminius, the general whose army destroyed three Roman legions in the Teutoburg forest in 14 CE, for German identity since the Enlightenment and especially during National Socialism comes to mind (Dörner 1995: 200–94; Wolters 2017: 174–201), as do the revolts in Judaea in the first and second centuries CE in relation to the creation of the state of Israel, especially the suicide of the last rebel holdouts in the fortress of Masada in 70 CE, which still features in the induction ceremony of the Israeli Defense Forces today (Ben-Yahuda 1995; Ohana 2012: 7–10, 24; Rajak 2016: 230–3). In short, over the course of the twentieth century, classical antiquity's ability to legitimize changing political, social, and economic orders has repeatedly been extended to include ancient moments of revolt and resistance.

Ancient historians, by contrast, have found resistance in the Roman empire a comparatively unattractive problem. While treatments of individual revolts exist, often as part of provincial histories, only two articles, both by the same author, attempt a more general analysis of such rebellions (Dyson 1971 and 1975).[2] Similarly, edited volumes, individual articles, and monographs attempt to tackle resistance and opposition more widely conceived (e.g., Shaw 1984 and 2000; Giovannini 1986; Flaig 1992; Elsner 1997 and 2001; Whitmarsh 2013; Richlin 2014). However, except for the recent focus on Roman approaches to revolts—how Romans dealt with revolts practically on the ground as well as how they conceptualized and explained them (Woolf 2011; Gambash 2015; Lavan 2017b)—no awareness of a common set of problems or an ongoing and developing debate has emerged from them. In many ways, Ramsay MacMullen's *Enemies of the Roman Order*, from 1966, remains the basic account of the subject.[3]

The political struggles of the twentieth century and the grand narratives that accompanied them demonstrably fostered the non-academic portrayals of acts of resistance in the Roman empire. Not surprisingly, these narratives also left their trace in the academic landscape. Harald Fuchs' *Der geistiger Widerstand gegen Rom in der antiken Welt*, published in 1938 on the basis of his inaugural lecture as professor for Latin philology at the University of Basel in 1933, is unthinkable without his outrage at contemporary events in Germany (Delz

1988: 80). Faced with the rise of the German Reich, Fuchs highlighted the brutality, pain, and hatred that the rise of another Reich, the Roman empire, caused and inspired (Fuchs 1938: 24). *La résistance africaine à la romanisation*, by Marcel Bénabou, provides another example. Published in 1976, in the final days of the decolonization movement, Bénabou argued that historians' complicity with imperial rule in Africa—be it by Rome or by France, Rome's supposed successor—had made them miss the "face obscure, cachée" (the dark and hidden face) of African history in the Roman period: resistance to Romanization (Bénabou 1976: 9–15).[4] The most recent example is *Brill's Companion to Insurgency and Terrorism in the Ancient Mediterranean* (2016), which draws on the insights from the burgeoning field of insurgency and terrorism studies to illuminate a range of conflicts in the ancient world.

However, the narrative, both ancient and modern, of Rome's imperial success, would appear to have left a more lasting impact on ancient historians' engagement with the problem of resistance in the empire than have contemporary political struggles. Modern historians have tended to emphasize the longevity and stability of the empire; unlike resistance, this supposed stability and how best to explain it, has even become the subject of an animated debate (de Ste Croix 1981; Lendon 1997; Ando 2000; Noreña 2011). Emphasizing longevity and stability makes acts of resistance look inconsequential in the face of imperial triumph. They become actions that seemingly lead nowhere, and as such they lose interest for historians. What is more, these modern narratives suggest that there was little resistance to begin with. But they are not alone in so doing.

Roman emperors celebrated their military successes with the erection of monuments and celebratory processions all over the empire. For example, Claudius' conquest of Britain entailed two triumphal arches, one in Rome and one in Gaul, a triumphal procession in Rome with representatives from all over the empire in attendance, an annual festival to celebrate the conquest, as well as several local replications of these monuments and festivities in provincial cities such as Cyzicus, where the local citizens and the resident Romans set up an arch and an inscription that imitated those in Rome (Cassius Dio 60.22; *ILS* 216–17). By contrast, military victories over revolting provincials—campaigns that did not add lands and peoples to the empire but maintained the existing ones instead—rarely received commemoration outside of the province in which they took place (Gambash 2015: 126–36). Tactical considerations might explain this silence, but also cultural ones. For the Romans thought and incessantly proclaimed that their victories and subsequent rule brought stability, that it was tantamount to the establishment of peace (*pax*) in the world. A coin of Otho showing Victory standing on a globe with the legend PAX ORBIS TERRARUM, meaning "peace in the world," neatly sums up this idea (Figure 7.1).

FIGURE 7.1: Denarius of the emperor Otho, PAX ORBIS TERRARUM ("Peace in the World"). Rome, 69 CE. Münzkabinett, Staatliche Museen zu Berlin (Inv. 18215169). Photograph © Münzkabinett.

ROMAN PEACE

As Hannah Cornwell has argued, in the Republican period Romans used *pax* and its various cognates to think about the (unequal) relationships they were cultivating with both gods and other peoples (Cornwell 2017: 23–34). However, during the civil wars and the subsequent restoration under Augustus, the first emperor, *pax* came to denote the absence of civil war and dissension more generally, the protection of those conquered peoples from external threats, and Rome's ability to bring *humanitas*, the Roman equivalent to "civilization" in modern imperial and colonial contexts, to conquered peoples, making them lose their supposed ferocious and bellicose nature (Woolf 1993: 176–89; Lavan 2017a: 111). At the same time, the concept of *pax* became closely associated with the emperor—the idea of *pax Augusta* preceded *pax Romana* by several decades (Cornwell 2017: 187–95). In short, *pax*, in the sense just outlined, became not only the big promise of the Roman empire but also its greatest achievement, an achievement that imperial coins such as Otho's persistently communicated to provincial populations (Noreña 2011: 108–11).

The most spectacular celebration of the achievement of *pax* was built in Rome in 71 CE. When the new emperor Vespasian had defeated all his rivals in the civil war after Nero's death, he arranged the construction of a monumental building dedicated to Peace in the center of Rome as a celebration of his conquests and the creation of peace in the empire which they entailed (Noreña 2003: 34–9). It housed spoils from the world that Rome had conquered: works of art were on display; a library housed books of a great many origins; and the temple's garden quite likely also showcased plants from all over the empire (Pliny the Elder, *Natural History* 34.84; Josephus, *Jewish War* 159–62; Cornwell 2017: 192–93). This display of spoils was also a display of control, not least over nature (see Purcell, this volume). The new emperor's achievements were the epitome of this control, amounting to the "difficult, almost physical task of holding a dynamic world in unnatural stillness" (Lavan 2017b: 36).

Romans were not alone in celebrating this achievement; provincials did, too. The inhabitants of Andalusian Ossigi Latonium, for example, founded a cult of the goddess Pax, and in Egyptian Dendera a dedication for the *pax* that Claudius had established was set up (*ILS* 3786; *IGRR* 1.1165). Several provincials also reiterated and elaborated the idea of *pax Romana* in their own writings, including Philo (*Embassy to Gaius* 48), Aelius Aristides (*Orations* 26.95–97), and Plutarch (*On the Fortune of the Romans* 2). While from the Roman point of view the achievement of *pax* was inextricably linked with conquest and victory, the many provincials who kept quiet about conquest and their defeat focused on its benefits instead. Given the inherent ambiguity of the Latin *pacatus*, capable of meaning both "peaceful" and "made to be peaceful" (Lavan 2017a: 106–10), both sides, even in dialog with each other, could continue with their own version of reality.

Just like provincials, modern historians also joined in commemorating Rome's achievement in Roman terms, starting with Edward Gibbon, who wrote about the "peaceful inhabitants" of the empire, the "most civilized portion of mankind," and continuing to this day (Gibbon 1908: 1; Cline and Graham 2011: 246). Arguably, both ancients and modern should have known better. Thomas Pekáry, for example, has gathered evidence for more than one hundred instances of collective organized violence in the empire between 31/30 BCE and 189/190 CE, including both urban and rural revolts as well as attempts to usurp power across the entire social spectrum, from slave rebellions to the deposition of emperors by the senate and parts of the army (Pekáry 1989: 136–45). More items can still be added to his list.[5]

To illustrate, at some point in the second century CE, the bakers in Ephesos were accused of causing disturbances and unrest among the *demos* (citizen body), quite likely by supplying insufficient quantities of bread (*I. Eph.* 215, ll. 2, 9; Buckler 1923: 31–3). In the first and second centuries CE, riots in reaction to food shortages are also known from Knidos, Prusa, Aspendos, and Athens (*SIG*³ 780; Dio Chrysostom, *Orations* 46.4, 6, 11; Philostratos, *Life of Apollonius* 1.15, *Lives of the Sophists* 526) (on the violence, Erdkamp 2002b: 104–7, *contra* Garnsey 1988: 30). Dio Chrysostom, a large local landowner in Prusa and the orator who tells us about the riot there, mentions that he himself was being threatened with being stoned or burned to death—stones and fire being the weapons of those without weapons in the empire: in Athens, those rioting threw rocks at an orator trying to calm them; in Aspendos they had already lit a fire for burning the chief magistrate. In 51 CE people in Rome gathered in the Forum to make known their anger about high food prices and insufficient supply (Tacitus, *Annals* 12.43; Suetonius, *Claudius* 18.2). The emperor Claudius had abuse and pieces of bread thrown at him there and only escaped with the help of soldiers.

Urban protest and rioting is also attested in contexts other than food shortages. In the middle of the first century CE, silversmiths in Ephesos had taken to the streets—or rather, as was often the case in the Roman empire, to the theater—to vent their frustration, supposedly at how Paul's message was threatening their source of income from dedications to Artemis (Paul, *Acts* 19:23–32). In 59 CE, citizens of Nuceria came to blows with the inhabitants of Pompeii while watching gladiatorial combat in the Pompeian theater, with many being left either dead or wounded (Tacitus, *Annals* 14.17). The event was also commemorated in a local fresco in Pompeii; it shows groups of men fighting inside the arena and beyond (Figure 7.2). Around 100 CE, the citizens of Cilician Tarsos thought that a group of disenfranchised linen workers had instigated riots in their city (Dio Chrysostom *Orations* 40.21–3). In the first and second centuries CE, civil discord is also known from Puteoli, Athens, and Smyrna (Tacitus, *Annals* 13.48; Lucian *Demonax* 64; Philostratos, *Lives of the Sophists* 531).

This evidence is episodic and concentrated in the Greek East. And yet, while certain cities such as Egyptian Alexandria had a reputation for frequent urban unrest (Dio Chrysostom, *Orations* 32, esp. 69–74), these episodes do suggest that the inhabitants of many more cities in the empire were familiar with the phenomenon. In fact, Apuleius's *Metamorphoses*, a novel written in the middle of the second century CE, is full of urban crowds who observed the goings of the local elites with attitudes ranging from approbation to incipient violence. These crowds as well as their calls for fire and stones (e.g., *Metamorphoses* 2.27), calls that also accompanied community demands for justice in the sources cited above, should quite likely be ranked among "the mass of vivid, concrete and realistic detail" in which Apuleius "clothed his sequence of fantastic episodes" (Millar 1981: 66). In short, the gathering of large crowds prepared to use violence to make their grievances heard was a well-known and widespread occurrence throughout all the cities in the empire.[6]

Life in the countryside does not appear to have been calm, either. Every year the harvesting season brought with it the arrival of a free and mobile workforce, which was known and feared for its drunkenness and unruly behavior, especially regarding their pay (Shaw 2013: 216–20). At the other end of the spectrum, the countryside was also often the place where groups of armed men, numbering up to a few thousand, usually under the leadership of one individual, found both their victims and their supporters. In the late first century BCE, a certain Athronges was ravaging the Judaean countryside, especially those traveling through it, around Jerusalem (Josephus, *Jewish Antiquities* 17.278–84, *Jewish War* 2.60–65). He liked to wear a diadem and divided his followers into four groups and appointed "satraps" at the head of each of them, all elements that

FIGURE 7.2: Fresco showing a riot at the Pompeii amphitheater. Villa in Pompeii (1.3.23), 59–79 CE. Credit: De Agostini Picture Library / A. DAGLI ORTI / Getty Images.

are reminiscent of Hellenistic kingship. Around the same time, a certain Mariccus, who claimed to be a god and the defender of Gaul, managed to gather eight thousand men in Gaul and plunder the Aeduan rural districts (Tacitus, *Histories* 2.61). Some of the men who joined these bands quite likely were local agricultural workers themselves, as was the case with the Bagaudae, who first appeared in Gaul and Spain in the third century CE.[7] Tacitus provides a glimpse of how they might be recruited: Titus Cortisius, a renegade member of the praetorian guard, who was seeking to enlist men to his cause, openly posted notices in and around Italian Brundisium, calling the agricultural slaves in the area to reach for their freedom and join him (Tacitus, *Annals* 4.27).

Given the cultural repertoire and claims of men like Athronges and Mariccus and the fact that they found their way into the historical narratives of Josephus and Tacitus, their armed bands quite likely present the most ambitious and successful examples of what must have been a familiar but underreported phenomenon. Cassius Dio, for instance, an important source for the history of the empire in the first two centuries CE, states that minor military disturbances were not worth reporting (51.20.5). And yet, such bands and their leaders were important factors locally and that is also where they were known. In Apuleius' *Metamorphoses*, a band of robbers at work in southern Greece as well as members of the local elite in the area are imagined to know of Haemus and his band, who had been ravaging the Macedonian countryside further north (*Metamorphoses* 7.5–7). Locally, these bands could also enjoy considerable support. The emperor Antoninus Pius (138–61 CE), at least, when advising local magistrates on how to deal with such men, included the instruction that their accomplices and backers be found out (*Digest* 48.3.6.1).

The evidence I have gathered here contributes to questioning the reality of the peaceful empire, and thus, yet again, reveals the ideological nature of the *pax Romana*. The same evidence would also suggest that modern historians' emphasis on stability is the product of both hindsight and the bird's eye perspective with which they approach the empire. The lived experience of men and women quite likely was very different. Whether they were landowners, slaves, or members of the urban poor, they were all familiar with urban protests that could turn violent as well as with armed gangs plundering the countryside. And yet, if we understand resistance as emancipatory actions that respond to domination and try to move the subject toward freedom, which is the pervasive drift of twentieth-century popular interpretations of revolt in the Roman empire, only very few, if any, of the events I have mentioned could be considered instances of resistance. In most cases, we lack the evidence to even begin assessing the question, and more generally, one should be wary of universalizing the liberal subject, a historical creature in its own right, whom one would expect to have precisely these emancipatory tendencies (Mahmood 2005: 1–39).

At a minimum, however, this evidence shows that men and women in the Roman empire practiced resistance in the sense that they did not acquiesce in the circumstances in life to which they were allotted; that they did not encounter power obediently; that they did not conform their existence to the positions that powerholders envisaged for them. Roman power was no exception. Just like the magistrates and orators I have mentioned so far, so, too, could Roman governors in the provinces come under attack. If they were lucky the crowd had prepared carrots or turnips to throw at them (Strabo 17.1.53; Suetonius, *Vespasian* 4.3). But they could also be beleaguered (Cassius Dio 67.4.6), stoned (Philostratus, *Life of Apollonius* 1.16), and killed (Tacitus *Annals* 4.45; Scriptores Historia Augustua, *Antoninus Pius* 5.4–5). Incidents such as these brought home to the Roman political elite the essential unruliness of the world over which they claimed to rule. At times, this unruliness might pose problems for the empire and its ruling elite. But, I contend, it could equally be harnessed to imperial ends, by further implicating Roman authorities, from the emperors to individual soldiers, in their subjects' lives. Acts of resistance such as the ones that I have described so far, both when the Romans were trying to quench them and when they were enabling and encouraging them, far from leading nowhere in the narrative of imperial triumph, were constitutive of Roman rule.

RULING (THROUGH) RESISTANCE: PEACE AND DREAD

Roman authorities demonstrably attempted to prevent disruptions of the Roman peace. Above all, they developed a conceptual framework for the great variety of events disturbing the Roman peace. The terms in question are *latrocinium* and *grassatura* (banditry and brigandage) and *seditio* and *factio* (insurrection and partisanship).[8] By focusing on the fact of disturbance and obfuscating its origins or motivations, this vocabulary elided all local difference and provided the basis for criminalizing such behaviors all across the empire. They were all liable to be punished with death (Brélaz 2005: 36). But the emperors also took more proactive steps. While the legions were posted at the edges of the empire, small detachments of Roman soldiers were distributed throughout Italy and all the provinces of the empire, where, among many other things, they guarded roads outside cities and hunted down armed bands (Brélaz 2005: 231–67; Fuhrmann 2012: 201–38). One of these soldiers, on his epitaph, claimed to have killed many bandits with his own hands (*IGRR* 4.886). Others became themselves the victims of armed gangs (*CPL* 112, column 2, l. 10; *ILS* 5795).

In cities the Romans mostly refrained from using military force in spite of the fact that, in Rome at least, soldiers had an overwhelming presence (Griffin 1991: 40–1); instead, they tried to limit the purview of institutions and practices that they thought underpinned urban unrest. In the early second century CE, the emperor Trajan instructed the governor of Bithynia, Pliny the Younger, to issue a general ban on *hetaireiai*, which was how Roman officials called associations of private persons that helped organize urban unrest (Pliny, *Letters* 10.96.7; Arnaoutoglou 2002: 40). Trajan also refused to authorize the creation of an association of firefighters in Nicomedia, the capital of Bithynia, on the grounds that this was exactly the type of association that could become a *hetaireia* (Pliny, *Letters* 34.1). This type of thinking led most emperors to issue often partial and temporary bans on associations all throughout the empire (de Ligt 2000: 242–52; Arnaoutoglou 2002). Another set of bans trying to prevent urban unrest concerned men and women claiming to have knowledge about the future. According to the early third-century CE jurist Ulpian, almost every emperor renewed legislation against diviners and astrologers (*Coll. Mos. et Rom. Leg.* 15.2.1–3). Pauline Ripat has argued that these laws and the expulsions of such persons from Rome and Italy and cities all over the empire do not simply reflect the emperors' fear of oracles concerning their future and demise, but reveal the role these figures could play in shaping popular opinion and action (Ripat 2011, esp. 141–51). As Ulpian put it, at times diviners practiced their art *contra publicam quietem*, "against the public peace" (*Coll. Mos. et Rom. Leg.* 15.2.3).

The examples of urban and rural unrest cited above suggest that measures such as these were never completely effective. To be sure, in certain places in the empire and for certain periods of time these phenomena quite likely decreased. Rome in the late first century CE, for example, might have been a comparatively calm place (Yavetz 1986). So was possibly Isauria in southern Anatolia, otherwise known as a hotbed for banditry, between the middle of the first and the middle of the third centuries CE (Lenski 1999; *contra* Shaw 1990). At times, when ancient observers detected such changes, they attributed them to Roman actions. According to Strabo, traders traveling from the southern Arabian peninsula to Damascus in Syria were robbed less because of Roman presence in the area (12.2.20). Today, it is impossible to know what precisely caused these changes in behavior in the respective places. It should be noted, though, that while instances of urban unrest and banditry waned in some periods and places, they waxed in others. The province of Judaea, for example, might have seen an efflorescence of armed bands in the countryside in the late 50s and 60s CE (Horsley 1981), and Leslie Dossey has suggested that the later Roman empire, which remains largely beyond the purview of this chapter, quite likely witnessed an increasingly unruly peasantry due to the alternative normative authority that Christianity in the form of local bishops and preachers were providing (Dossey 2010: 173–94). Overall, then, Roman peace was never fully accomplished; it always remained incomplete, a work in progress.

One might try to explain this incompleteness as the result of the empire's weakness as a state, a weakness that in no small part resulted from the fact that the local elites on whose cooperation Rome's power relied had an interest in the maintenance of certain forms of violence (Shaw 1984: 39–40). At the same time, it is also important to understand that this incompleteness was not a problem for the Romans—neither conceptually nor practically. As suggested above, for them, the peace they created was a thoroughly unnatural state that they achieved. As a result, its incompleteness was a given. Furthermore, any disturbance of the peace provided an occasion to advertise the virtues of Roman actions locally, to insert the imperial narrative in local settings. In fact, conflict and violence are not the breakdown of social relationships, but the creation of new ones (Simmel 2009: 227–306). In the Roman empire, some of these new relationships further bolstered the imperial order. The long-term stability of the empire and the presence of unrest do not necessarily present a contradiction, it seems.

In 1992 Turkish archaeologists discovered a spectacular monument in ancient Patara, a coastal city in ancient Lycia. A square column—about five meters high, two and a half meters wide, and three and a half meters deep—covered with two inscriptions (Şahin and Adak 2007). The inscription on the front of the monument is a dedication by the Lycians to the emperor Claudius. The second inscription is a list of roads in Lycia (and some in Asia) that, so the inscription claims, Claudius built. It is the most detailed description of a road network in a Roman province known so far. Quite likely, a colossal statue of Claudius on a horse stood on top of the column. The monument was erected in 46 CE, three years after Claudius had made the Lycian League from an ally bound to Rome with a treaty into a full-blown province (*SEG* 55.1452; Suetonius, *Claudius* 25.3; Cassius Dio 60.17.3–4). The inscriptions, however, mention none of this, explaining instead that the Lycians decided to honor Claudius because through his "divine forethought" they were freed from "sedition, lawlessness, and banditry" and had regained "concord" and "their ancestral laws" (*SEG* 57.1670A, ll. 16–25). Another dedication by the Lycians to Claudius, written on a monumental altar that was found near Bonda Tepesi in the Lycian mountains along an ancient road, sums up the idea quite neatly: the Lycians thank Claudius for the peace and for the provision of roads (*SEG* 52.1438, ll. 7–9). Quite likely, the altar was but one of many such monuments that were erected alongside Lycian roads in the late 40s CE (Marksteiner and Wörrle 2002: 562).

The inscriptions betray no sign of local specificity—in fact, they obfuscate the events that had preceded Roman intervention—and opt into an imperial narrative instead. From other sources we know that some Lycians were exiled (*SEG* 18.143, ll. 58–9), and that, as part of the events that preceded annexation, some Roman citizens were killed (Cassius Dio 60.7.3–4).[9] Whatever happened, it provided a pretense for the emperor to get involved. As a result of his involvement, Claudius could claim to have added another province to the empire and all the revenues that came from it. Locally, he could insert himself into the Lycian polity and landscape, appear as the guarantor of order therein, and demonstrate his control and might more generally. His care for the Lycian roads emblematized all of these claims perfectly. The Lycians addressed him accordingly, calling him "savior of our nation" (*SEG* 57.1670A, ll. 12–13). In short, the main result of Claudius' involvement was a carefully scripted relationship between him and the Lycians, remembered and monumentalized publicly across the entire region, that would provide the basis for any future interaction between Roman emperors and them.

If we barely understand what prompted Claudius' involvement, we can only imagine what form his actions there took. What did it take to establish the peace that the Lycians thanked him for? An episode from Caracalla's visit to Alexandria, almost two hundred years later, can provide some ideas. In 214/5 CE, Caracalla embarked on an expedition to the east during which he continuously styled himself as Alexander the Great (Herodian 4.8.1–3; Cassius Dio 78.7.1). His stay in Alexander's eponymous city could have been the highlight of his journey; instead, it was marred by a series of events that Caracalla himself described as insurrections (*Acts of the Alexandrians* 18, column 2, l. 14), most likely involving the Alexandrian ambassadors coming to greet him, the men overseeing the production of statues he had commissioned—statues that were now being defaced—as well as various slaves (Benoit and Schwartz 1948: 22–33; Musurillo 1961: 229–32). Caracalla's subsequent actions included parts of the repertoire of Roman measures against urban unrest we have already encountered. He issued a ban on certain types of associations and gatherings; he also had a wall built throughout the entire city, with guards posted at regular intervals (Cassius Dio 78.23.3). Just like the roads in Lycia, this was in part a symbolic act, demonstrating both Rome's control and her might. But the wall also had a practical dimension: the monitoring of movement in the city. Its ultimate crudeness in this function demonstrates just how helpless and clueless Roman authorities could be in the face of urban unrest. Lastly, Caracalla and his soldiers killed a large and indiscriminate group of Alexandrians, possibly even the Alexandrian youths, who had assembled in a Macedonian phalanx in honor of Caracalla's visit (Scriptores Historia Augusta, *Caracalla* 6; Cassius Dio 78.22.1–23.2; Herodian 4.9.5–8). Such acts of spectacular and arbitrary violence quite likely played a role in making Rome's subjects opt into the imperial narrative, as the Lycians had done.

In short, the incompleteness of the *pax Romana* offered emperors the opportunity to demonstrate their frightful might as well as to reiterate their redemptive claims, both crucial means for furthering the relationship with their subjects. This interplay of rule and resistance was replicated in a fractal pattern further down the imperial hierarchy. Consider, for example, two provincial inscriptions, one from Bath in Britain (*RIB* 152) and the other from Antiochia in Pisidia (*IGRR* 3.301). Both honor individual soldiers, Gaius Severius Emeritus and Aurelius Dionysius, who were stationed in the respective provinces, detached from their legions. Severus was praised for undoing the acts of insolence that had despoiled a sacred place. The Antiochians praised Dionysius "for his goodness and the peace" (ll. 5–6). In a more poetic inscription on the same monument they thanked Dionysius for "having saved the lives of many and having established peace" (Calder 1912: 80–4, n. 1). Just like Claudius, Severius and Dionysius were able to find a place in local society because of the unruly world in which they did their service. Like Caracalla, these soldiers, too, might have put Rome's frightful might on display—in a much more limited fashion, of course.

The Roman officials whose routine always combined dread and redemption were provincial governors; for the Romans not only made behavior that they thought disruptive punishable by death but also claimed a monopoly for their governors on handling such cases, an arrangement that, together with the active participation of soldiers at governors' disposal in seeking out offenders, institutionalized the Romans' claim to be the purveyors of order and stability (Brélaz 2005: 267–82; Fuhrmann 2012: 201–38). At the same time, the public manner of punishment—mostly crucifixion combined with the prolonged exposure of the body at precisely the place where the offenses had been committed (*Digest* 48.19.28.15)—made the way in which the Romans claimed to establish order the stuff of nightmares, quite literally. In his second-century CE work, *On the Interpretation of Dreams*, the diviner Artemidorus records several dreams revealing the dread that Roman justice and its display induced (1.35, 39–40, 48, 70, 77; 2.49–54). Christians, too, whom Roman governors were quite ready to consider a suspicious type of association and punish accordingly, suffered from and recounted judicial nightmares (Shaw 2003).[10] Quite likely such widespread dread also lay behind the phenomenon that local elites considered the prospect of provoking the intervention of Roman authorities a persuasive argument for de-escalating tensions locally (Dio Chrysostom, *Orations* 46.14; Apuleius, *Metamorphoses* 9.41). And yet, provincials not only dreaded the actions and decisions of Roman governors (and emperors) or threw vegetables at them to express dissatisfaction with their actions and decisions, most of the time, in fact, they surrounded them as petitioners, as men and women trying to get them to make decisions and take actions in their favor. In these interactions Roman rule was not built on suppressing but on enabling resistance.

RULING (THROUGH) RESISTANCE: PETITIONING AS REFUGE

Petitioners could approach Roman governors anywhere. A petitioner from late third-century CE Oxyrhynchus recounts how he approached the governor "as he was entering the council-building" and again "by the laurel grove" (*P. Oxy.* 22.2343, ll. 9, 11). Many people handed in such petitions: in 210 CE, the Roman governor of Egypt, on his annual visit to the Fayoum, received 1,804 petitions over the course of two days (*P. Yale* 1.61, ll.5–7). The third-century Chinese account of Roman Syria describing a "king," probably the governor of the province, being followed around everywhere he went by an attendant carrying a leather bag, into which petitions could be thrown, does not seem that far-fetched (Hirth 1975: 71). The corpus of petitions from Roman Egypt, where they have been preserved on papyri, shows that while wealth and education made people more likely to approach governors, their absence was no bar to so doing; about fifty percent of petitioners were illiterate (Kelly 2011: 150–3). Their concerns were varied but the vast majority of petitioners approached the governor as part of conflicts concerning property and private obligations; violence and theft were the most common crimes (*ibid.* 163).

By petitioning the governor, these men and women were trying get him to hear their case. Their petitions constituted attempts to take themselves and the conflicts in which they were involved out of their respective contexts, where local power relations might conspire against them. The governor's court provided them with an opportunity to change their social position by having their version of the conflict and their desired outcome validated (Bryen 2013: 126–64, 200–2). In so doing, these men and women entered one set of power relations to escape the implications of another, a dynamic that Lila Abu-Lughod described as characteristic of acts of resistance more generally (Abu-Lughod 1990: 52–3). This system of petitioning thus channeled the unruliness of Rome's subjects toward asserting and enhancing Roman rule and authority; for it created a group of people in the provinces invested in that rule and its claims—the provision of justice—while also providing an opportunity for Roman officials to assert their virtues, above all their responsiveness: together with his staff, the governor of Egypt, who in 210 CE had received those 1,804 petitions in the Fayoum, composed replies to all of them and posted them up publicly in Alexandria as well as in the Fayoum itself (*P. Yale* 1.61, ll. 7, 10–11). This dynamic of rule (through) resistance was one of the key mechanisms of Roman power. No figure embodied it more completely than the person at the very heart of the empire, than the emperor himself.

Just like provincial governors and other Roman officials, including soldiers, the emperor too was the recipient of petitions. In 293 CE, Diocletian was traveling from Sirmium in modern-day Serbia to Byzantium on the Bosporus. The *Theodosian Code* preserves more than nine hundred responses, all (re)statements of legal principles, that the emperor issued to petitioners whom he had met during this journey. As Serena Connolly has argued, most of these responses were written in the emperor's name by members of his staff whom he had taken with him on the journey for precisely this purpose (Connolly 2010: 55–60). During the same period, Diocletian might also have acted as judge of first instance or in appeal cases from governors' courts, as emperors were wont to do (Millar 1977: 507–36). Indeed, the everyday business of (good) emperors was dealing with petitioners and hearing cases (Scriptores Historiae Augustae, *Lucius Verus* 8.8–9; Herodian 1.12.5, 3.10.2).

Those coming before emperors were often described as "fleeing" to him, a rhetoric that already existed in the time of Augustus and was still intact in the age of Constantine (*FgrH* 90, F127; *Latin Panegyrics* 6[7].5.1). Indeed, some of them clasped the emperor's feet or knees, a gesture that just like the language of "fleeing" suggests submission, desperation, and hope of rescue in equal measure (Tacitus, *Annals* 4.31.1; Suetonius, *Claudius* 15.3). The repeated analogies between the way in which emperors and gods are to be approached and grant requests evoked the same cluster of ideas (Ovid, *Letters from Pontus* 3.3.131–38; Martial, *Epigrams* 5.6.7–11; Apuleius, *Metamorphoses* 7.6–7), as did the fact that statues of emperors everywhere, both alive and dead, were places of asylum where people could not be touched (Pekáry 1985: 130–5; Price 1984: 191–5). The magistrate in Aspendos, who was threatened with stones and fire, for example, saved himself by fleeing to one such statue in the city (Philostratus, *Life of Apollonius* 1.15). In Ephesos, the capital of the province of Asia, at least sixty such statues provided places of refuge (Price 1984: 174). Fleeing to one of them could eventually lead to a hearing before the emperor, or at least to general guidance from him on the case (Pliny the Younger, *Letters* 10.74; Gaius, *Institutes* 1.53). Intriguingly, in Egypt people seem to have deposited petitions at the feet of imperial statues, an act that nicely confounds the line between the worldly and the divine aspects of the emperor's power to deliver (*P. Oxy.* 17.2130, ll. 17–20; *CPR* 1.20, column 2, ll. 11–14). Together, these accounts, gestures, and acts show that enabling resistance, enabling people's attempts to escape the circumstances in which they found themselves, was a central part of the emperor's ideology. By the second century CE this ideology had diffused into the petitions that provincials were writing to other imperial officials, in which they increasingly portrayed themselves as helpless and oppressed (Bryen 2013: 96; Harries 1999: 165–6, 185–7).

Emperors, however, did maintain their singular position, especially in the city of Rome. As Flavius Josephus, born Yosef ben Matityahu, explained to the non-Roman part of his readership, games in Rome were occasions on which the people of Rome, as a crowd, petitioned the emperor for what they needed, demands that the emperor usually granted (*Jewish Antiquities* 19.24–25). These demands ranged from the lowering of the grain price and the abolishment of certain types of taxes to demands for the restoration of statues that the emperor had moved to his private quarters and for the death of Nero's teacher Tigellinus (Tacitus, *Annals* 2.87, 13.50; Pliny the Elder, *Natural History* 34.62; Plutarch, *Galba* 17). Bad emperors refused them, and Julius Caesar, who had tried to put his responsiveness on display at the games by answering petitions in writing there, was severely criticized (Cassius Dio 59.13.3–4; Suetonius, *The Deified Julius* 45). The Roman plebs demanded its due; it demanded to have its privileged position within the empire validated (Yavetz 1969: 18–32; Deininger 1979: 285–303; Cameron 1976: 155–61).[11]

But emperors also occupied a unique position within the empire more widely. For they extended the promise of rescue into power relations that were off-limits for other Roman officials: the relationship between masters and their (ex-)slave(s). Slaves regularly fled to the statues of emperors. Slave-dealers, in an attempt to increase the value of their product, regularly swore that the slaves they were selling had never fled to such statues (*Digest* 21.1.19.1). Generally, slaves' approaches to the emperor were limited to the question of their freedom—they were claiming that they were not actually slaves, that is—but the emperor Antoninus Pius also promised them an escape from their excessively cruel masters; any such masters would be forced to sell their slaves (Gaius, *Institutes* 1.53). Analogously, former slaves, often still bound to their old masters through the bonds of patronage (see Lo Cascio and Ramgopal, this volume), could not summon their patrons to appear before the court of the governor; the emperor, however, would hear and respond to their petitions (*Digest* 2.4.15).

Lastly, imperial subjects soon learned that the emperors' power could also be invoked against the demands of other Roman officials, since they too were ultimately subject to the emperor. In the late second century CE, tenants on an imperial estate in the Bagradas valley in the province of Africa Proconsularis, in the Mejerda valley in modern-day Tunisia, successfully petitioned the emperor Commodus about abuses they were suffering at the hands of the men collecting their rents (*CIL* 8.10570 = 8.14454). In the middle of the third century, villagers from Skaptopara in modern-day Bulgaria entreated Gordian III to help them prevent soldiers and other Roman officials who were passing through from imposing on them (*SEG* 14.610). Villagers such as the farmers from the Bagradas valley or the Skaptopareni might have run away, as many other people did when confronted with the demands of the imperial state, especially with taxation (Cicero, *Verrine Orations* 2.3.46–7; Joerdens 2009: 304–30), or they might have formed armed bands with which to hound Roman officials locally. In the later Roman empire they might also have turned to local bishops, whose responses could range from legal advice to the flogging of Roman magistrates (Dossey 2010: 176–80 and 191–4). Instead, the Skaptopareni and their North African peers appealed to the emperor and inscribed the response they received from him, thus turning a one-off exchange into a permanent monument of their relationship for everyone to see, designed, one might imagine, to impress and put on alert any future tax-collectors and Roman officials. The Gohareni in Syrian Dmeir even inscribed the protocol of the hearing they had had with Caracalla (*SEG* 17.759).

As much as inscriptions such as these show the potential that petitioning had as a form of resistance, they also reveal its limits. Some imperial demands simply could not be negotiated by petitioning the emperor, at least not for a large group of people. The farmers on the imperial estate in Africa did not ask to not pay their rents, for example. The dues owed to the imperial treasury were non-negotiable, it seems. Unsurprisingly, many of these unassailable consequences of imperial rule could become focal points of resistance in those moments when the unruliness of the empire's inhabitants was directed against the empire itself.

RESISTANCE AND REVOLT

The evidence for revolts in the Roman empire is notoriously difficult, in that all accounts are written either by Romans or by Greek members of the imperial elite, whose portrayals of revolts reveal more about the mind-set and agendas of their authors than about the events on the ground (Woolf 2011: 33–40; Lavan 2017b). Nonetheless, it seems clear that certain implications of Roman conquest have repeatedly served as focal points for resistance. For example, military conquest was followed by expropriation, often enabled by surveys, centuriation, and other Roman institutions, which helped Roman settlers move in (Mattingly 2011: 146–66; Eberle 2016); the revolts, or rather the guerrilla warfare, against Rome that took place in the first half of the second century BCE in Spain and in the early first century CE in the southern Maghreb, seem to have centered around demands for land and secure property rights for certain groups (Dyson 1975: 147–8; Fentress 2006: 27–9). Conquest also entailed taxation, which was not only a material burden, but also a symbol of captivity, slavery, and submission (Tertullian, *Apology* 13.6; Cassius Dio 62.3.2–3). The imposition of the census, which was the basis for levying taxes in a Roman province, provoked military uprisings in Pannonia in 10 BCE and in Judaea in 6 CE (Cassius Dio 54.36.2–3; 55.2.4; Josephus, *Jewish War* 2.11–3; 2.117; Goodman 2014: 58).

Some of the implications of Roman rule were less immediate than taxation and expropriation. In many regions Roman rule profoundly transformed local societies, creating not only winners—local elites mediating Roman rule locally—but also losers, such as the Druids in Gaul: in the first century BCE, they still occupied an important position in their respective communities, performing not only religious but also judicial functions; one hundred years later they had become a fringe group practicing occult rites in sacred groves and encouraged Gauls to join rebellions against Rome by interpreting the burning of the capitol in Rome in 69 CE to mean that the *imperium* would no longer stay in Rome and would pass to the peoples beyond the Alps (Tacitus, *Histories* 4.54; Webster 1999). Furthermore, Roman intervention in specific areas could rapidly intensify, also many years after conquest. The Bar Kochba revolt in Judaea, for example, occurred almost two hundred years after Pompey had first conquered Jerusalem. Most likely, it was a response to Hadrian's plan to re-found Jerusalem as a Roman colony called Aelia Capitolina, a plan that had not only economic and social but also cultural implications given that Jerusalem and the recently destroyed Temple was a key reference point for many, if not all Jews at the time (Goodman 2003; Tuval 2012). In short, Roman rule gave provincial subjects at all levels of society enough reasons to revolt. But unlike what both Roman accounts and nationalist interpretations of these revolts would have us believe, there were no ready-made peoples, be they German, Jewish or otherwise, keen to rebel because of their inherent love of freedom (e.g., Tacitus, *Germania* 21, 28 and 37). Instead, such revolts required organization and coalition-building among groups that could have quite different outlooks and interests; as acts of resistance seeking to challenge Roman rule, revolts required more work than all other forms of resistance considered so far. In what follows I consider the cultural aspects of this work.

In his *Agricola*, Tacitus gives Calgacus, the chieftain of the Caledonian confederacy, a rousing battle speech. "They create desolation, and call it peace" is what Tacitus has him say, one of the more incisive ideological critiques of Roman imperialism in existence (*Agricola* 30). While the speech is a piece of fiction—Tacitus simply had no way of knowing what Calgacus was saying—we should imagine that revolts against Roman rule were accompanied by an account of what was wrong with that rule. Such hostile accounts of Roman rule are legion—they include the incendiary New Testament Book of Revelation, Pagan Martyr Acts from Egypt, and Rabbinic literature from the second and third centuries (Bauckham 1991; Musurillo 1961; Goodman 2014: 66)—but they all lack a revolt to go with them. The only case where we find the two together is the revolt of the cities of Asia and mainland Greece under the leadership of Mithridates VI in 88 BCE, which provides a good illustration of the contribution that such accounts could make to the organizational work required.

As part of Mithridates' attempts to elicit the cities' cooperation, he spearheaded a major publicity campaign against the Romans: they were greedy, he argued; greed was part of their national character, an accusation that the inhabitants of Greek cities had leveled against them already one hundred years earlier (*RDGE* 33, ll. 12–13). Most dramatically, Mithridates performed this accusation and how it would end Roman rule by publicly pouring molten gold down a Roman magistrate's throat (Appian, *The Mithridatic Wars* 21). In addition, he recruited members of the Greek intelligentsia to join his cause. One of them, Metrodoros of Skepsis, an orator and philosopher known for his hatred of the Romans, wrote a work of history in which he claimed that the Romans had attacked the Volsinii because of the two thousand statues in their territory that the Romans desperately wanted (*BNJ* 184, F12). The charge of greed not only picked up on suspicions that Greeks had long had about the Romans—the idea that they were barbarians likely resonates in this charge as well—but was also able to make sense of the experiences of Roman rule that a wide range of Greeks had had, whether they be encounters with Romans in the guise of governors, tax-farmers, or creditors and settlers. Quite likely, this charge contributed to Mithridates' success in convincing many Greek cities to kill all Italians in their midst and thus revolt from Rome (Appian, *The Mithridatic Wars* 28, Valerius Maximus 9.2.ext.3; Plutarch, *Sulla* 24).

Beyond accounts of what was wrong with Roman rule, resistance movements provided alternatives. In these promises we can see the coalition-building and broad appeal that such movements had to seek. On one level, their promises were highly specific, often focused on individuals. For example, the coins of the First Servile War in Sicily in 135–132 BCE celebrated King Antiochus, the name that the slaves' leader had adopted (e.g., Manganaro 1990, pl. 85 fig. 5); as a slave he had been called Eunus, which is what Diodorus in his unremittingly negative account of the revolt constantly calls him (Morton 2013). Similarly, the legend on the coins of the rebels around Bar Kochba in 132–5 CE extolled Simon, the Prince, and Eleazar, the Priest, and promised the freedom and redemption of Israel as well as of Jerusalem (Mildenberg 1984: 365–8).

On another level, these promises could be quite general and, at times, equivocal. King Antiochus depicted Demeter and an ear of barley on his coins (Manganaro 1990, pl. 86 figs. 3–5). This image quite likely was a reference to the prominent sanctuary of Demeter in Enna, the rebel's stronghold on the island (Cicero, *Verrine Orations* 2.4.110–12), and as such it was part and parcel of the central place that the promise of prosperity and good harvests more generally played in the ideology of the revolting slaves; Antiochus might have put on pantomimes in which his soldiers acted out the roles of slaves killing their masters (Diodorus Siculus 34/35.2.46), but he understood that he ultimately also had to appeal to a wider audience: sparing those tilling the soil and promising a newly prosperous Sicily might have seemed a good strategy (Diodorus Siculus 34/35.2.48).[12] Similarly, Bar Kochba's coins showed the Jerusalem Temple, destroyed fifty years earlier, and the implements necessary for the Sukkot, a Jewish harvesting celebration (Figure 7.3)—both symbols with which a wide range of Jews might identify. Many coins also showed a star, which in Jewish tradition could be taken as a sign of the Messiah but did not necessarily have this connotation on coins (Schäfer 1981: 64–5). Both those contemporaries, who wished to see Bar Kochba as the Messiah, as some demonstrably did (y Taan 4,8 fol. 68d; Schäfer 1981: 55–7), as well as those with less millenarian inclinations, could find themselves in these coins. Notably, the Bar Kochba coins also showed a bunch of grapes, most likely a symbol of fertility and good harvests (Schäfer 1981: 66), thus serving as a salutary reminder that despite local differences, these were all agrarian societies in which the agricultural output each year affected people's experiences and livelihood in a visceral way.

FIGURE 7.3: Tetradrachm showing implements for Sukkot celebration. Bar Kochba coinage, Judaea, 134–5 CE. Münzkabinett, Staatliche Museen zu Berlin (Inv. 18204073). Photograph © Münzkabinett.

The rebels' self-portrayal on their coins, together with the very fact of their coin production, suggests that the alternative that these resistance movements were providing ultimately was that of an alternative polity—the kingdom of Antiochus, in one case, or a polity called "Israel," in the other. As a result, the type of organizing involved in bringing about such revolts as the First Servile War or the uprising around Bar Kochba can best be characterized as incipient, if ultimately failed, processes of state-formation, processes that are undeniable in the best-documented revolt in the empire: the First Jewish War from 66 to 73 CE (McLaren and Goodman 2016). Bar Kochba's letters to his administrators in Ein Gedi, an oasis near the Dead Sea, which were preserved in a cave in the Judean desert, are a unique source for tracing some of the claims and actions involved in bringing such a polity into being.

The "House of Israel" owned property, from cattle to spice-gardens, which Bar Kochba's associates were to steward according to his instructions (*P. Yadin* 50, ll. 10, 12–13). The main concern of the letters was the movement of supplies, including staples such as wheat and salt but also the necessary fruits for the Sukkot, which were to be brought to Bar Kochba's camp, "because its population was large" (*P. Yadin* 54, ll. 3–5; 56, ll. 7–9; 57, ll. 4–5). Furthermore, the property of the "House of Israel" was to profit "the brethren" and their children; Bar Kochba insisted that his associates had a duty of care toward this egalitarian-sounding group (*P. Yadin* 49, ll. 8–10). Moving from inclusion to exclusion, Bar Kochba not only promised to punish the Romans, "as is proper" (*P. Yadin* 56, l. 5); he also ordered the punishment of men from Tekoa residing in Ein Gedi—their houses were to be burned down—and a man from Palmyra was to have his sword confiscated, and Bar Kochba ordered that he be brought before him to be punished (*P. Yadin* 56, ll. 13–16). He also threatened to punish his own administrators repeatedly (e.g., *P. Yadin* 50, l. 11–12; 54, ll. 7–8; 56, l.4). The Roman empire had no monopoly on ruling via dread, it seems, and quite likely it had no monopoly on receiving petitions, either. Less than one hundred years earlier, a group of Jews in Judaea had no qualms about turning to an armed band led by Eleazar and Alexander to help them solve a problem that the Roman governor had refused to address (Josephus, *Jewish War* 2.12.2–4), and eighty years after the revolt stories were circulating in Italy about Bulla Felix, a bandit who instructed the emperor on how to be a better emperor (Cassius Dio 76.10; Riess 2015).

In fact, some polities that were built as part of revolt from Roman rule simply claimed to be the "better" Romans. In the second half of the third century CE, independent rulers emerged in the eastern and northern provinces—both regions in which the increasing attacks of enemies from beyond the frontiers called into question the legitimacy of Roman rule, thus allowing local rulers who could stop these invasions to establish themselves—and they fashioned themselves according to Roman models. Postumus and his heirs in Gaul not only displayed Roman imperial titulature on their coins and claimed to be *restitutor Galliarum*, "the Restorer of the three Gallic provinces," just as previous emperors had done; they also appointed consuls on the Roman model and even featured *Roma aeterna* ("eternal Rome") on their coinage (Drinkwater 1987: 28–9, 164–6). Beginning in 272 CE, Vaballathus, based in Syrian Palmyra, also adopted such imperial titulature (Hartmann 2001: 354–64), and his mother, Zenobia, began calling herself "Augusta" and its Greek equivalent, "Sebaste," a title that the female relatives of Roman emperors often carried (Figure 7.4). Postumus, Vaballathus, and Zenobia are part of a larger pattern in the empire, in which revolts that build toward something other than the empire seem to decline by the early second century CE while attempts to shift power

FIGURE 7.4: Tetradrachm showing Zenobia as SEBASTE ("Empress"). Palmyrene coinage, 272 CE. Münzkabinett, Staatliche Museen zu Berlin (Inv. 18252812). Photograph © Münzkabinett.

within the empire—attempts by members of the imperial elite to challenge the reigning emperor, often based on support in a particular region in the empire—continued unabated and actually intensified in the second and third centuries (MacMullen 1990; Flaig 1992). The Egyptian *Boukoloi*, who under the leadership of a priest named Isidoros, defeated a Roman army in pitched battle in 172 CE, look like quite an isolated phenomenon (Cassius Dio 71.4; Scriptores Historiae Augustae, *Marcus Aurelius* 21).

One might see this pattern as a sign of the effective consolidation of Roman imperial authority and ideology (e.g., Andrade 2013: 5746), or as a sign that provincial populations had by that point become incontrovertibly Roman. Consider, however, Zenobia, who was not only "Augusta" but also "Queen," as an inscription in ancient Greek and Palmyrene, a west Aramaic dialect spoke in Palmyra, shows (*IGRR* 3.1028, ll. 3–4). Details such as this make it hard to maintain that there was a lack of non-Roman cultural reference points, even when it came to conceptions of rule. More likely, this shift over time in the cultural expression of opposition to Roman rule is the result of changes in how the Roman army was organized. In the first century CE, auxiliary troops, which made up more than half of the Roman army, did their service close to the areas where they originated under the leadership of men from the same background. The desertion of these troops and their leaders contributed to some of the most dangerous revolts against Roman rule, including the one led by Arminius in 9 CE (Dyson 1971). But the Romans only changed their deployment of auxiliary troops, posting them in regions other than their own and under the leadership of men with whom they did not share a background, after Rhineland units had deserted *en masse* to Civilis, the leader of the Batavian rebellion against Rome in 69 CE (Keppie 1996: 396). With this change in how troops were distributed in the empire, the local civilian population and the military manpower on which many revolts were built had lost all commonalities, the Roman empire being the only cultural reference point that they shared.

Even in the case of revolt from the empire, then the history of imperial rule and resistance are inextricably intertwined. Far from leading nowhere, revolts shaped the organization of imperial power. For as Tacitus understood, the lessons that the Romans might draw from the disaster in 69 CE not only concerned the military but also the governing of frontier regions more generally (Master 2016). How these changes played out on the ground is an intriguing research question that remains to be explored. Conversely, the cultural repertoire of revolts in the empire also emerges as yet another way in which the organization of imperial power influenced the forms that resistance in the empire might take. The most intriguing example of this influence, with which I want to conclude this chapter, can probably be found in the two, or possibly three, Pseudo-Neros in the eastern provinces of the empire, who were the focal points of resistance in that part of the world in the thirty or so years after

Nero's suicide in 68 CE (Gallivan 1973; Champlin 2003: 10–12). These men resembled Nero; for example, they could play the lyre and sing at the same time as he had famously done (e.g., Cassius Dio 61.20–21). Intriguingly, they were able to recruit many followers in central Greece and western Asia Minor with the claim that they planned on reclaiming their rightful place as emperor. Most likely, the reason these men pretending to be a Roman emperor could gather such a following in these parts of the world lies in the special relationship that Nero had established with the Greek part of the empire. In 66 or 67 CE, a year or so before his death, he had stood in Corinth and proclaimed the freedom of the Greeks, which he interpreted to mean freedom from taxation (*IG* 7.2713, l.14). This promise, had it been carried through—Vespasian immediately reversed it (Suetonius, *Vespasian* 8.4)—would have given Greece the same (fiscal) status as Italy, or, as some might have hoped, it would have made Greece the new Italy. It would appear, then, that those following the Pseudo-Neros in the east had no problem with empire as such, provided, of course, that they were in the privileged position at the center.[13]

CHAPTER EIGHT

Race

EMMA DENCH

If we set out to look for race within the dynamics of the Roman empire, the most enduring model amongst ancient empires, we encounter two main challenges. The first challenge is to unthink aspects of race that are familiar within modern imperial trajectories: the absence from the Roman empire of race-based chattel slavery and imperial regimes is the biggest surprise, highlighting the particular and peculiar geopolitical, religious, economic, and scientific dynamics of sixteenth- to nineteenth-century European imperialism. Once we have done this, the second, greater challenge awaits. We have to make sense of language and tropes within the Roman empire that are all too familiar to us despite the absence of an understanding of race as a permanent, biologically determined, hierarchical characteristic. The language of blood purity, praise for "civilization" with all its eye of the beholder overtones, or expressions of revulsion for different skin-colors and physiognomies are striking examples.

To confront these challenges, I will begin by exploring the entanglement of ancient and modern worlds through the specific question of how the classical world came to be perceived as white people's history, and recent responses to this odd state of affairs. I will then consider the Roman empire as a particular case-study of ancient empires' disruption and reconfiguration of norms of self-identification within the ancient Mediterranean and neighboring lands, emphasizing specific logics and patterns. I will focus particularly on disruption and reconfiguration of ancient notions of kinship and homeland, notions that will inform modern racial theory and practice, but which operate quite differently within their original ancient contexts.

WHITE PEOPLE'S HISTORY?

It would be hard to pinpoint a moment when the history of ancient Greece and Rome became a history of white people. This is partly because that assumption, widespread in the nineteenth and twentieth centuries, and broadly scrutinized only in recent decades, has almost always been implicit rather than spelled out or argued directly. More profoundly, the specific historically and politically contingent developments in the nineteenth and twentieth century of the concept of race as a permanent, hierarchical, and biologically determined system of categorization were intricately enmeshed with ancient conceptions of the nature of identity and difference.

Skin color and physiognomy that we might associate with race are not the primary focuses of attention in ancient perceptions of sameness and difference. When skin color and physiognomy are noticed, we see a range of aesthetic reactions as well as color symbolism at play. Although we often see aesthetics and color symbolism invoked in modern societies, the significant difference here is that they are underwritten by a pseudo-science of biologically permanent, hierarchically arranged races with Caucasians at the top and whiteness to blackness in a descending order, driving and encouraged by social, economic, and even legal inequality. In classical antiquity, whiteness was generally not an aesthetically desirable feature, at least in men, for whom a variety of yellowish and light brown shades are favored. Whiteness is praised in women able to avoid the sun, but in "ethnic" contexts it is a freakishly ugly and even ghostly characteristic, associated with the "northern barbarians" (e.g., Germans, Alpine and Danube peoples, and Britons) who are featured bound and subjected in imperial iconography (Figure 8.1). While extremely black skin was regarded as equally freakish, the color of the underworld and ill omen, it was extremely white skin that carried associations with inferiority that are closer to the nexus of modern racial equations. The Romans in particular have been accused of being guilty of "Borealism." For all that, Greeks and Romans tended to assume and imply that the ideal skin color lay in the middle rather than at one of two poles in the manner of the modern evaluation of whiteness (Thompson 1989; Krebs 2011).

Amongst the factors that would ultimately encourage many modern classical scholars to assume that the Greeks and the Romans were "white" were the ancient color symbolism that associated black with ill omen and evil. Building on this, the polarizing ideology of the Crusades would imagine a division between black Muslims and white Christians, a religious and moral dualism that would only strengthen later perceptions of a racial dualism. The buildup of particular historical circumstances occasioned by European imperial ventures in the southern hemisphere and New World, technological inequalities, and black chattel slavery, would encourage the hardening of such dualism (Dee 2004; Isaac [ed.] 2009; McCoskey 2012).

FIGURE 8.1: An image of Roman triumph over defeated and bound barbarians. Gemma Augustea, Rome, 10–20 CE. Accessed via Wikimedia Commons, CC BY-SA 3.0.

The narrative of the imperial conquests and rule of European states was underwritten by classical writings and interpreted histories of classical antiquity, combined with interpretations of genealogies in the Hebrew Bible, all distorted to privilege an ingrained ethnic hierarchy. At the same time, ancient ethnography encouraged the mapping of newly encountered peoples onto ancient peoples and within familiar parameters, and would ultimately help to inform the new discipline of anthropology. For their part, classical historians, philologists, and archaeologists were keen to engage with modern theory and to demonstrate the relevance of their discipline to the modern world, even while it formed the basis of an elite education and, in the British Empire, civil service examinations. They turned to comparative studies, plotting modern imperial trajectories against that of Rome, or to race biology and its doleful hierarchical classifications, measuring skulls to distinguish invaders from the indigenous, or attributing

Hellenistic or Roman decline to "race mixture" (Diller 1937; Hingley 2000 with Edwards 2001; Harrison 2013; Skinner 2013; Vasunia 2013).

There was no shortage of alternative points of view about classical antiquity within and beyond the academy through much of the twentieth century. One example would be the adamant and to our ears problematically unselfconscious British celebration of the Romans as every bit as racially "mixed" as "we" are, one of a range of responses to contemporary Nazi and Fascist doctrines of racial purity on the Continent (e.g., Grose-Hodge 1944). Another would be long-standing Afrocentric traditions of claiming that historical figures such as Cleopatra and Socrates were black, or that the Greeks stole their cultural heritage from Africa (particularly Egypt) (e.g., James 1954). It is not always recognized that the logical basis of these claims is no weaker than the mainstream contemporary assumptions that Cleopatra, Socrates, and the Greeks and Romans in general were white, and that their legacy belonged squarely to Europe and to the west (e.g., Lefkowitz 1996; cf. Dench 2005: 222–7).

Nothing, however, prepared the academy for the shock of the publication in rapid succession of the first two volumes of Martin Bernal's *Black Athena*, the first volume an indictment of the classical academy for its racist roots, and the second a quest for the Egyptian and "Semitic" origins of Greek language and culture (Bernal 1987; 1991). There are many just criticisms to be made of Bernal's theses. These include the selectiveness of his intellectual history in the first volume and its lack of sensitivity to historical context, and the confusion between influence, contact, and ethnic origins that runs through the second volume (Hall 1992; Blok 1996; Marchand and Grafton 1997). With hindsight, however, the publication of the first two volumes of *Black Athena* seems to have functioned as a wakeup call, even if it was generally not acknowledged as such in the early years. Within and beyond the academy, it is now routine to emphasize that classical societies were multi-ethnic and multicultural. Some scholars are beginning to overcome a later twentieth-century nervousness about the anachronistic language and associations of race, along with a later twentieth-century tendency to emphasize the constructedness of identity and ancient prejudice as "only" cultural prejudice, and identify incidents and phenomena that look a little like modern racism while being distinct from it (e.g., Isaac 2004; McCoskey 2012).

BEING, BELONGING, AND CATEGORIZATION IN THE ANCIENT WORLD

Much of the narrative of Homer's *Odyssey*, a poem that looks back to a heroic, Mycenaean age while betraying a broad, recent, and contemporary context of Iron Age and archaic Greek mobility and "colonization," plays on the identification and misidentification of strangers, whose presence invites a series of questions that seek to pin down who they are and what they are doing there. These questions indicate persistent modes of locating and classifying individuals in the world of classical antiquity that will ultimately inform the modern concept of race but which are significantly different from it. The question "Who are you?" is glossed as some variation on, "Who are you among men, and from where? Where is your *polis* and your parents?" (e.g., *Odyssey* 10.325). These first questions seek to place the stranger within an immediate environment of kin and homeland, and also within the broad networks of a mobile, competitive, and heavily interactive international elite. The regular follow up questions ("From where do you sail the watery paths? For some business, or roving over the sea, like pirates risking their lives and bringing woe to strangers?" e.g., *Odyssey* 3.71–4) introduce broader characterizations: by occupation, more and less ethically inflected, including business (particularly trade) and piracy and, elsewhere, the original ethnic out-group, Phoenicians (Winter 1995; Dougherty 2001: 43–50; Montiglio 2005: ch. 5).

Later Greek and Roman reflections on kinship and homeland can scale up from the village (or the *polis* that is the basic unit in these formulaic questions of the *Odyssey*) all the way to an "aggregative" conception of common Greekness that from the sixth century BCE had begun to draw together multiple smaller units of ethnic affinity and progressively an extensive international diaspora (Hall 1997), or to the Roman citizenship, with its increasingly virtual relationship with homeland. Kinship may be interpreted as shared blood, and common homeland could be enacted through shared religious cult and festivals, as shared customs or alternatively as ancestors' tombs. These definitions are invoked in discursive contexts when identity claims are challenged or challenging: when Herodotus' Athenians are made to protest a little too much that they will never betray the "Greekness" that holds together the *ad hoc* allies against the Persian advance in the early fifth century BCE (8.144); when Polybius tries to convey the original bonds that tied together the communities that made up the Hellenistic Achaean League (2.38–42); when Cicero has his characters work through the concept and implications of first century BCE dual citizenship (Roman and local Italian town) in his *Laws* (2.5). There is a basic expectation that religious ritual, custom, and language will normally be aligned with homeland and kinship. These issues are at the core of ancient ethnographical writing, such as Herodotus' "digressions" on foreign peoples in his *Histories*, where the author uses the sometimes conflicting evidence of religious ritual, custom, language, and very occasionally physical features to distinguish peoples and to reflect on what is retained and what is lost when people relocate (e.g., 1.171–2; 4.109.1; 6.119.4; 7.70.1).

To focus on kinship in classical antiquity is to engage with a tradition of genealogical thinking that invokes original, mythological ancestors (usually gods or heroes) both to connect and to configure. Such connections will continue to be invoked throughout antiquity in public contexts underwriting diplomacy, the claims of houses, and the origins of entire peoples. Kinship was precious currency, and claims were heavily scrutinized and asserted sparingly. Kinship with contemporary superpowers such as Hellenistic kings or the Romans was rarely asserted and even more rarely acknowledged (Jones 1999; Battistoni 2010). If classical and biblical genealogical thinking will eventually inform a more insidious, binary means of imagining race in the modern era, classical genealogical thinking can at least at first sight seem enlightened. Unlike the zero-sum position of colonizing modern powers with their monotheistic religions, classical genealogical thinking encourages the writing in rather than the exclusion of other peoples. Identifications in ritual and myth of Greek gods and heroes with those of local peoples (e.g., western Sicilian cults of Aphrodite, Venus, and Astarte; Herakles, Hercules, and Melqart, in Greek, Latin, and Punic respectively) and on the part of local peoples considerably blurs the sense of any straightforward, ethnocentric projection onto a blank slate (Bickerman 1952; Dench 1995: ch. 1; Malkin 2011: ch. 4).

If we dig a little deeper, however, genealogical thinking reveals less conciliatory and ecumenical aspects. Sexual and family relationships can be complicated, antagonistic as well as bonding. In the classical world, stories of original rape and sibling rivalry write violence, hybridity, enmity, and civil war into the DNA of individual societies and international relations (Zeitlin 1986; Arieti 1997; Dench 2005: 245, 253). As the boundaries of knowledge are pushed out further in the Hellenistic and Roman worlds, particularly in the less well-mapped territories of northern and western barbarians, degrees of closeness can be subtly colored in by imagining different levels of contact: sometimes a visiting hero really does just visit without leaving offspring by local nymphs and princesses (e.g., Tacitus, *Germania* 3). Assertion of common descent can be tipped over into exclusivism as is notoriously the case in fifth- to fourth-century BCE Athens. A Periclean law of 451–50 BCE requiring that both parents be Athenian, and its revival in 403, anticipates the connection of egalitarianism with exclusivism in the early years of the French Republic, while the contemporary language of blood purity anticipates nationalist and racist discourse of the modern era (Lape 2010; McCoskey 2012: 56–8).

It is to fifth-century BCE Athens too that we can trace the sharpened division of the world into two categories, "Greek" and "barbarian." Out-groups, including Phoenicians, Lydians, and even perhaps barbarians are identified as exemplars of difference (in various measures fascinating, strange, and problematic) within the earliest Greek literary texts we have (Kurke 1992). However, Athenian claims on leadership against the Persians in the aftermath of the Persian Wars of the early fifth century BCE, claims that would soon be expressed and heard as imperializing discourse, required the existence of a full-blown "barbarian" figure. Although it was possible to distinguish different "barbarian" peoples by the standard indicators of kinship, language, ritual, and custom, and to cluster different "barbarian" peoples by broad inclinations explained by climatic and environmental factors, it was equally possible to imagine a single "barbarian" *genos* ("breed"), with an accompanying cluster of behavioral characteristics (E. Hall 1989: 160–2; J. Hall 2002: 172–204; Nippel 2002). This generalizable figure of the singular barbarian will prove to be extraordinarily useful, even while he or she will take various guises in later historical contexts.

Classical Athenian political and social culture was driven by argument: in the citizen assembly, where in theory any male citizen could speak; in law courts that fostered a litigiousness second to none; and in the theater. In the late fifth century BCE this environment encouraged an emerging science of argument in the form of the so-called Sophists ("public intellectuals"). Sophists' notorious claims to teach better argument for pay challenged the egalitarian ideal of late fifth-century BCE Athenian democracy. At the same time, they encouraged enquiry into the causes and nature of human difference, bitterly contested arguments of which we glimpse small strands in extant and fragmentary literature. Arguments raged over whether human beings were different by nature, or because of custom or environment, with varying positions on the extent to which one could expect change. Herodotus used a tag from the poet Pindar, "Custom is the king of all," as the punchline of a story about the Persian king Darius inviting "Indians" to cremate their dead fathers, and "Greeks" to eat theirs, causing equal outrage by this proposal that they should exchange funerary customs (3.38). While for Herodotus climate and environment shaped bodies and behavior, when push comes to shove custom trumps environment. Persian and Egyptian skulls varied in thickness, he found, despite the fact that both peoples lived in hot and sunny climates. Egyptian skulls were thickened by exposure to the sun, while Persian skulls were weakened by the cultural practice of wearing head coverings (3.12). The author of the Hippocratic work *Airs, Waters, Places* traces the origins of the "Asiatic" propensity to cowardice and slavish rule by monarchs to the prenatal environment: the "seed," in its balmy climate, experiences none of the shocks to its system that provoke the martial and independent characters of inhabitants of Europe (23) (Thomas 2000). Aristotle in the *Politics* argues that barbarians are natural slaves, with impaired rationality, although he abandons an attempt to argue that this slavish nature shows up in slaves' physical appearance, an argument too easily disproved by counter examples (*Politics* 1254b.28–34; Garnsey 1996: 113–14; Heath 2008).

These different modes of thinking about human variation and change could be pushed in different circumstances. Notoriously, in exhorting Greeks to bond together against the fourth-century BCE Macedonian threat, Isocrates could try to divorce character or mindset (*dianoia*) from birth or descent (*genos*) or nature (*physis*) to argue for a much more expansive (and potentially acquired)

Greekness based on *paideia* ("education" or even "nurture"). Such feats of argument take place against a subtler hum of fascination with role reversal, "passing" and pushing over the edge: the prurient Pentheus in Euripides' *Bacchae* whom the god Dionysus has to drive mad to get him to impersonate a woman (821–61; 912–44); Greek "allies" of Athens after the Persian wars of the early fifth century BCE whose condition after their rebellions are put down is described by Thucydides as enslavement, the antithesis of freedom, the idealized natural condition of Greeks (1.98.4). With rare exceptions, when ancient writers are talking about a change in condition, the traffic in these stories is all one-way, downwards, and the existence of the binary division is left unchallenged. Diogenes Laertius quotes an ancient anecdote attributed by earlier writers to either Thales of Miletus or Socrates: that the philosopher would count his blessings for having been born "first, a human being and not a wild animal; next, a man and not a woman; thirdly a Greek and not a barbarian" (*Lives of the Philosophers* 1.33). The historicity of the anecdote is not important: it speaks volumes about categories of existence from which it was hard to emerge.

If Athens, the super-sized, almost nation-like *polis* fashioned her egalitarian and imperial character by putting legal restrictions on her citizenship and promoting herself as the Greekest of *poleis*, expansionist states of the Mediterranean and Near East more regularly put their weight behind disrupting, co-opting, and redeploying the peoples under their sway. A major model for both Athens (ironically, given that the Persians were arch "barbarians" in Athenian eyes: Root 1985; Raaflaub 2009) and later kingdoms was the Achaemenid (Persian) empire, at its height between the late sixth and early fifth centuries BCE. The inscriptions and reliefs of its kings describe a world reoriented to face the king and the imperial center, arrayed neatly into distinctive peoples characterized by epithets or suitable gifts, the king's global mandate suggested by multilingual texts, the empire's fighting forces an ethnic parade of subjected peoples (Figure 8.2). It is to the Achaemenids that we owe one of several part-for-the-whole externally applied names for the Greeks, *Yauna* ("Ionians"), the ethnic group closest to the Achaemenid heartland (Kuhrt 2002).

The Seleucid and Ptolemaic kingdoms, successor kingdoms of Alexander the Great, could look two ways: to the Macedonian kingdom's styling itself as a champion of Greekness (ironically, as a people for whom the descent-based argument for being Greek had to be made), especially through Alexander's Persian conquests, and to the Achaemenid empire and, beyond that, to the Pharaohs and other Near Eastern kingdoms. The Ptolemaic court fostered and arguably even helped to crystallize the notion of monolithic Greek culture by its library collections of the Museum at Alexandria and by fostering scholars who worked on the exegesis and with the inspiration of what became classical literature in the process (Fraser 1972; Bagnall 2002; Maehler 2003). At the

FIGURE 8.2: East stairway of the Apadana, showing diverse subjects bringing gifts to the Persian king. Persepolis, late sixth/early fifth century CE.

same time, they engaged with the sacred and environmental power of the Egyptian pharaohs, and their rule was accommodated (not without tension) within self-consciously Egyptian iconography and rituals (Manning 2010; Blasius and Schipper 2002). The Ptolemaic "salt-tax" system (a type of poll tax) enshrined this dualism and stamped on it a power hierarchy by extending tax breaks to "Hellenes" ("Greeks"). While Ptolemaic Egypt has sometimes been interpreted as an "apartheid" regime, there is proliferating evidence of individuals passing as "tax Hellenes" through their occupations, and of those who used two names, Greek and Egyptian, and passed between both zones (Clarysse 1985; Thompson 2001; Clarysse and Thompson 2006). This passing did not, of course, eliminate the binary division, but arguably only reinforced it.

The prestige and cachet of Greekness that was fostered by the Hellenistic kingdoms was felt and claimed across the Mediterranean and Near East well beyond the kingdoms' territories. This was the case not least in central Italy, where the Samnites of the central Apennines constructed in the second century BCE an elegant theater-temple complex at Pietrabbondante, 1,000 meters above sea level, simultaneously evoking the urban sophistication or even palaces of the eastern Mediterranean and, through the use of polygonal or "Cyclopean" masonry, great chunks of stone, the studied old-fashionedness of their own local (and, to the Greeks, "barbarian") identities, a material equivalent of linguistic bilingualism (Wallace-Hadrill 2008: 121–3).

In rare contexts of the Hellenistic world, passing or moving between or combining cultural zones was explicitly problematized. We see examples of the verb *hellēnizein* ("to go Greek") and its cognates in fraught contexts where people cannot or should not "go Greek." In *c.* 256–255 BCE, for example, an unfortunate individual working for Zenon, agent of the Ptolemaic finance minister, complained that Zenon's Greek employees withheld provisions and mistreated him because he was a "barbarian" and did not know how "to go Greek" (or perhaps, in this context, "to speak Greek") (*P. Col. Zen.* 2.66, trans. Bagnall and Derow, no. 137). The Jewish writers of *II Maccabees* accuse the high priest of Jerusalem and others of being in cahoots with the Seleucid king Antiochus IV Epiphanes in the early second century BCE. Furthermore, they are accused of compromising their Jewish integrity by "going Greek," which involves throwing the discus, wearing the *petasos*, the distinctively eastern Greek sunhat, and exercising in the nude (3–4), a prelude to Antiochus' desecration of the Temple with unclean sacrifice in 168 BCE (Hengel 1974).

ROME THE DISRUPTOR

When the Romans crossed the sea to Sicily in 264 BCE in a venture that would launch their overseas empire, they interacted with a world familiar with established patterns of imperial rule, empire's disruption of subjects' identities, and the opportunities offered by this disruption. Alert contemporary observers noticed aspects of Roman behavior toward outsiders that were new and different. Philip V of Macedon in 215 BCE used the slightly garbled example of Roman expansion within Italy to admonish the Larisaeans of Thessaly for restricting their citizenship, endangering the well-being of their city. The Romans, according to Philip's version, had prospered, sending out almost seventy colonies, by enfranchising even freed slaves and letting them be political officials (*SIG* 3.543).

Philip's version exaggerated Roman practice, perhaps carried away by the comparative regularity of crossing the line from slave to free person within Roman society, a striking anomaly within an ancient Mediterranean context. Although ex-slaves were in fact barred from Roman political office, the routine practice of making ex-slaves citizens would be a cornerstone of a Roman expectation (however unrealistic) of legal and social mobility reflected in the egalitarian myth that rooted the Roman citizen body in Romulus' opening of an asylum to slaves as well as foreigners (Dench 2005; see also Ramgopal, this volume). Philip also exaggerates the number of colonies founded by the Romans, as well as the connection between enfranchising slaves and expansion through colonies.

The truth about how Rome expanded into Italy and capitalized on Italian manpower is, however, every bit as illuminating of the particular patterns of disrupting identity that will characterize the Roman empire. After 338 BCE, when the Romans decisively subdued other ethnically Latin peoples, they reassigned these peoples to Roman legal categories, annexing some as Roman communities. Others were designated "Latin." This new Latinity, previously an ethnic status maintained by participation in shared ritual and the intersection of self-designation and acceptance by others, was reconceived as a Roman legal category in the gift of Rome, somewhat distanced from Roman citizens but enjoying privileged rights in dealings and relationships with Roman citizens. As the Romans expanded their sway throughout peninsular Italy, a process that was complete by the late 270s BCE, Latin status was extended to peoples who were not necessarily ethnically Latin but who were multi-ethnic citizens of the "Latin" colonies founded at nodal points, disrupting and reconfiguring pre-existing Italian communities and leagues. Importantly, however, the fact that Latinity was designated by Rome and functioned as a Roman legal category did not preclude expressions of Latin grouphood in the form of distinctively Latin religious cults or myths of common ancestry. Disruption and reconfiguration was escalated in Italy by the Roman practice of making individual treaties with defeated Italian peoples, treaties that were maintained by the annual supply of quotas of troops to fight Rome's wars in ethnic units under their own commanders. This practice strengthened and clarified the "tribal" configurations of Italian peoples (Sherwin-White 1973: chs. 1–4; Cornell 1995: ch. 14; Dench 2005: ch. 3; Kremer 2007; Farney 2007).

The most profound reconfiguration was achieved by mass annexation of whole peoples, notably the Sabines in 290 BCE, initially designated "[Roman] citizens without the vote," an obscure and in this case probably punitive status, but in 268 designated full Roman citizens. While classical Greek and Hellenistic states did occasionally enfranchise outsiders (slaves or foreigners), particularly to address manpower shortages, back engineering the normal expectations of an army as a citizen militia, the scale of Roman enfranchisement even by the second century BCE was unprecedented. After the Social War of 91–89 BCE, the Romans would conduct a radical experiment by enfranchising the whole of peninsular Italy. This experiment profoundly changed expectations that citizenship consisted of the direct participation in the political, social, religious, and military rituals that created and delineated community and bound it to its homeland. One symptom of this change is Cicero's articulation of dual citizenship (Roman and local Italian town) that we mentioned earlier (Sherwin-White 1973: chs. 5–6; Mouritsen 1998; Dench 2005: ch. 2).

Rome's bold Italian experiment in statehood functioned as an important laboratory for her rapidly expanding overseas empire. As the political domination of a few individuals gave way to *de facto* monarchy in the late Republic, the Roman citizenship was increasingly in practice (although not in law) a reward granted by a powerful Roman individual and extendable beyond Italy. These factors only enhanced the honorific status that the citizenship had begun to assume (and, in extreme circumstances, the legal protections it offered, not to speak of the benefits that could be claimed), its links to homeland rendered ever more virtual by physical distance. Roman citizens far from Rome who enact this virtual community (by wearing togas, by advertising links with officers of the Roman state, or by their priesthoods of the imperial cult), while simultaneously forging and maintaining the ritual ties that bind them to their immediate, physical community, are one symptom of the Roman imperial state's reliance on local authorities for some of the most basic functions of state (e.g., tax collection, keeping law and order, and maintaining infrastructure) (Sherwin-White 1973: chs. 8–11; Smith 1998; Purcell 2005).

There was no steady stream of citizenship extensions: cautiousness and a studied concern to preserve the dignity of the citizenship by adapting traditional expectations and parading them as criteria for extensions were the mark of a "good" emperor well into the empire. Suetonius' biography of Augustus, who epitomized the "good" emperor in specifically Roman ethical traditions of monarchy (Noreña 2009), contextualizes this cautiousness with citizenship extensions within a larger reordering of society. While Augustus re-emphasizes the dignity of senators and knights, the top orders of Roman society, by a combination of purges, reviews, honors, rituals, and assignment of tasks, he more broadly invokes the ancient language of descent to promote an idealized, exclusive Roman citizenry. Suetonius glosses Augustus' paraded caution with citizenship extensions, that included legislation tightening up conditions for legally recognized manumission, as keeping "the Roman people pure and unsullied by any mixing in of foreign and servile blood" (*The Deified Augustus*, 40.3). The extreme language of blood purity is especially striking in a Roman context of historical permeability. Roman calls to preserve such purity by being cautious about manumission and other citizenship extensions do not map neatly onto the most chilling applications of modern race "science," such as race policy in the Third Reich or South African apartheid, but are nonetheless heavy, reactionary responses to the turmoil of the late Republic and civil wars, conceived of as comprehensive mixing and muddling of categories (Dench 2005: ch. 2).

Since, as we have seen, language, custom, and ritual are normally expected to align with blood or descent, it is not surprising to see Augustus also dictate the wearing of the toga, elevated to a kind of national dress for Roman male citizens, at least in the quintessentially Roman political space of the Forum (Figure 8.3). According to Suetonius, he quoted Vergil's *Aeneid* ironically at a crowd in a public assembly dressed in the drab everyday clothing of Rome: "See the Romans, masters of the world, the toga-wearing race!" (*The Deified Augustus*, 40.5; cf. Vergil, *Aeneid* 1.282; Vout 1996). We also see the criterion of language (Roman citizens should speak Latin), or participation in traditional obligations of citizens, invoked in anecdotes, actions, and legislation. Regular

FIGURE 8.3: Statue of togate Augustus (the "Via Labicana Augustus") as Pontifex Maximus. Rome, late first century BCE/early first century CE. National Museum of Rome, Palazzo Massimo alle Terme (Inv. 56230). Public domain. Accessed via Wikimedia Commons.

grants of the Roman citizenship to non-citizen military auxiliaries *after* service to Rome from the age of Claudius (41–54 CE) normalizes the age-old pragmatism of classical societies that extended citizenship in emergency situations, preserving (albeit considerably contorting) the ideal of a citizen militia (Speidel and Lieb 2007; Haynes 2013: chs. 3, 21).

At the same time, the keen social hierarchy that arguably facilitated the Roman extension of citizenship in the first place was only enhanced as imperial rule continued. As early as the second century CE, we see the explicit invocation of a binary division between *honestiores* and *humiliores* ("more honorable" and "more humble") in legal contexts, assuming greater importance than distinctions between Roman citizens and non-citizens. If the criteria for assigning individuals to either group were suggestively subjective, the consequences were very real, with harsher legal penalties for *humiliores* (Garnsey 1970). When the emperor Caracalla finally extended the Roman citizenship to almost all the free inhabitants of the empire in 212 CE, contemporaries were quick to cite ulterior motives, and we might want to emphasize the symbolic importance of creating a global community rather than the practical benefits of citizenship in the early third century CE (Sherwin-White 1973: ch. 12; Garnsey 2004; Bryen 2016).

If Philip V admired Rome's capacity to expand by co-opting outsiders within her citizenship, other observers looked on in horror at Rome's less conciliatory imperial practices. Polybius, a young, politically active Achaean noble from Megalopolis in the heart of the Peloponnese, deported by the Romans to Italy after they defeated the Macedonian kingdom in 168 BCE, is almost certainly behind the account of the Romans' settlement of Macedon in 167 that is given by the late first-century BCE Latin author Livy. Livy's account describes the Macedonians experiencing the settlement as a kind of dismemberment, the unnatural and horrific tearing apart of a single animal into four new administrative regions. The violent severance of pre-existing bonds of community by the Romans is emphasized by a detailed delineation of the regions' territories, and bans on intermarriage and buying and selling buildings and land across the regions (Livy 45.29–30). The Romans' settlement of Macedon anticipates the increasingly confident carving out or rebranding of blocks of territory as Roman provinces, defined administrative and taxation units with new, or co-opted, ethnic names (Derow 1989; Thonemann 2004; Ando 2006; Talbert 2004; Richardson 2008).

Such interventions encouraged the Romans to assume a near (but by no means total) monopoly on arbitrations over the status of individuals and community. The Romans were slotted into an age-old imperial ritual of "surrender-and-grant," whereby the autonomy that was the ideal condition of the *polis* was now the imperial ruler's to grant or deny: this ritual bridges what could have been an uneasy gap between the Near Eastern model of empire, within which there is no such thing as citizenship, and the citizenship-based norms of community in the Greek world (Bickerman 1939; Ma 1999: 112–22). The Roman presence established a re-centered and to some extent recalibrated system of prestige and honor in which local communities competed proactively (Lendon 1997).

Some of the honors dispensed by Rome had direct economic consequences (e.g., immunity from Roman taxation), but it is hard to separate economics from esteem in the traditional world-view of classical antiquity, where taxation is regularly regressive and may be explicitly punitive. In Egypt, the Romans determined the new poll-tax categories by a hierarchy of community statuses topped by the old Ptolemaic capital Alexandria. This broadened the default bottom category of "Egyptian," limited "passing," and encouraged entrenched inequalities (Rathbone 1993; Bagnall and Frier 1994). The second-century CE historian Appian encapsulated the comprehensive blow to economics and esteem by writing of Sulla's demand from the Ephesians of five years' tax up front, punishment for their support of Mithridates as their means of preserving "the Greek race (*genos*), name, and reputation (*doxē*)" (*Mithridatic Wars*, 9.62; Dench 2011). More significant for long-term trajectories of identification and self-identification is the Jewish tax imposed on all Jews after the destruction of the Temple of Jerusalem in 70 CE, pointedly redirecting monies once due to the Temple to the rebuilding of the Temple of Capitoline Jupiter in Rome. After an atrocious episode in which the emperor Domitian stripped an elderly man to determine whether he was circumcised and thus required to pay the Jewish tax, liability for the tax was determined by self-identification from the age of Nerva (Josephus, *Jewish War*, 7.218; Suetonius, *Domitian*, 2.2; Goodman 1989).

More broadly, the Roman near monopoly on arbitration over the status of individuals and communities involves the Roman state and its representatives in the brokerage of genealogical and cultural value. This is well illustrated in an episode from 26 CE when cities of Roman Asia competed in the Roman senate to be granted the privilege of hosting a temple of the imperial cult. The claims of the finalists, Sardis and Smyrna, suggest the importance of two competing considerations in the Roman imperial world: prestige claims that rest particularly on antiquity and civilization (with all the arbitrariness and contingency associated with such values), on the one hand, and loyalty to Rome, on the other (Tacitus, *Annals* 4.55–6). Local distinctiveness is, then, a valuable currency in the Roman world.

At the same time, the new pre-eminence of Roman power challenges, reconfigures, and co-opts the binary distinction between Greeks and barbarians. Some Greek authors such as Polybius seem to wonder out loud where to place the Romans in this scheme (as barbarians, as taking the place that the Greeks should and did once hold, or somewhere between the two) (Millar 1987; Erskine 2000; Champion 2004). Others such as Dionysius of Halicarnassus, writing in the Augustan age, seem to protest a little too loudly that the Romans were ethnically Greek, even if their insistence in more recent history on taking in foreigners had somewhat muddied their memories of the Greek customs that once enacted this ethnicity (*Roman Antiquities*, 1.89–90; Dench 2005: ch. 1).

The Romans for their part offered the part-for-a-whole ethnic name that made the self-identifying Hellenes "Greek," a distinctively western counterpart to the Achaemenids' "Yauna" and its equivalents in ancient Egyptian, Sanskrit, and other languages. Even as the Romans assigned unifying dress and religious practice as well as language that created a new duality of "Greeks" and "Romans," they co-opted Greekness as both a social marker and an imperial possession. Roman bickering over the appropriate time, place, and variety of Greekness within upper-class Roman performance eloquently suggests appropriation of Hellenistic Greekness as cultural cachet, while the Emperor Claudius could by the mid-first century CE casually refer to Latin and Greek as "both of our languages" (Suetonius, *Claudius* 42.1; Woolf 1994; Scheid 1995; Wallace-Hadrill 1998). In a particularly ironic move, the emperor Hadrian would, in the second century CE, sponsor and be called to police membership of the Panhellenion, an exclusive organization of Greek cities, on the age-old criterion of descent from the common ancestor, Hellen (Spawforth and Walker 1985, 1986; Spawforth 1999; Jones 1996; Romeo 2002).

THE EXPERIENCE OF BEING AND BELONGING IN THE ROMAN EMPIRE

Both the direct imperial interventions of the Roman state and its officers and the indirect effects of Roman supremacy profoundly disrupted self-identification in the classical world. When it comes to tracing responses and experiences of citizens and subjects of the Roman empire, it is tempting to focus on a vocal and articulate minority that is to some extent the precursor of aspirational modern globalization. This is the cosmopolitan, international, well-connected, and highly cultured elite who celebrated their individual capacity to maintain multiple *personae* or who exposed the tensions between being a Roman citizen and being a citizen of a local community or a member of another group. Prime examples include Cicero in his attempt to formulate dual citizenship; Josephus reconciling Jewish priesthood with Flavian friendship (Dench 2005: ch. 5); the sophist Favorinus, an embodiment of three paradoxes ("although a Gaul he went Greek, although a eunuch he was tried for adultery, although he had quarreled with a king he was still alive;" Philostratus, *Lives of the Sophists* 489; cf. Favorinus, *Corinthian Oration* 22–36); and Philopappos, whose bilingual (Greek and Latin) monument looms over Athens portraying him simultaneously as Athenian *archon*, Roman consul, heir of the defunct Near Eastern kingdom of Commagene, and even heir of the defunct major imperial power of the Seleucids (Kleiner 1983; Gleason 1995).

While flamboyant multiculturalism and celebration of multiple *personae* is a feature of Roman imperial society directly connected to the peculiar tendency of the Roman imperial state to co-opt and reconfigure local elites, it is not the only or even the most important consequence of imperial disruption of modes of self-identification. Much more significant is the visibility of newly Roman citizen freedmen and freedwomen, especially in funerary monuments. Their numerousness is a symptom of a vast, global slave-trade facilitated by Roman conquest and the private enterprise that flourished on the back of Roman rule (including piracy and banditry, extreme forms of private enterprise officially at odds with the Roman state; cf. Lo Cascio, this volume), a long history of regarding citizenship as extendable, and a generalized culture of co-opting, reconfiguring, and displaying identities at the level of private households mirroring that of the state.

One well-known memorial from Rome commemorates a family, a freedman, freedwoman and their son: P(ublius) Servilius Q(uinti) f(ilius) / Globulus f(ilius) // Q(uintus) Servilius Q(uinti) l(ibertus) / Hilarus pater // Sempronia / C(ai) l(iberta) Eune uxor ("Publius Servilius, son of Quintus, 'Globulus' ['Blobby'], son, Quintus Servilius, freedman of Quintus, Hilarus ['Happy'], father, Sempronia, freedwoman of Gaius, Eune, wife") (*CIL* 6.26410). As is typical, the couple's personal names continue the former master's "clan" name (Servilius in the case of the husband, and Sempronius in the case of the wife), and combine these with the former slave name, now functioning as a *cognomen*, a hereditary nickname ("Hilarus" for the husband and "Eune" for the wife). Eune's name suggests Greek ethnic origin, which may have been false (Greek names were overwhelmingly used to suggest fancy origins for household slaves), while Hilarus, "Happy," suggests a register similar to that of modern animal pet names (or, to the great embarrassment of mainstream twentieth-century culture, that of the seven dwarves' names in Disney's *Snow White*). These new names elide the processes of forcible removal from original kin and homeland, and relocation as virtual kin of their former masters: the abbreviation *l.* for *libertus* or *liberta*, "freedman" or "freedwoman" of the former masters, stands in structurally for the *f.* for *filius* or *filia*, "son" or "daughter" of the father, used as kinship markers of Roman citizens (Y. Thomas 1986; Wallace-Hadrill 1989: 73–7; Purcell 1983; Joshel 1992: 35–6). At the same time, these monuments look to a new present and future. They claim and celebrate those most basic rights denied to slaves: ownership of one's body, to be joined in marriage, to be cared for by one's closest relatives after death, and, perhaps most importantly, to possess one's children, a stake in the future that mirrors the traditional elite's stake in the past (Andreau 1993; Mouritsen 2005; Petersen 2006; Dasen 2010; Baroin 2010).

The funerary monuments of freedpersons suggest the profound effects of forced removal from kinship and homeland bonds, a conspiracy of state and private processes. They also suggest some unexpected consequences, not least the complex interplay of kinship and kinship-inspired structures: even as Eune and Hilarus create and celebrate their nuclear family, they are both legally bound and facilitated by the kinship-inspired ties with their former masters. More broadly, recent scholarship has emphasized the role of imperial socialization structures in changing behavior and affinities. This includes Greg Woolf's model of subjects "becoming Roman" primarily by buying into an imperial preference for *humanitas*, "civilization," in all its eye of the beholder complexity (Woolf 1998), and Clifford Ando's rituals of communication that engender loyalty and affective bonds of individual to imperial center, through traffic in letters, honors and gifts, or through participating in the census or loyalty oaths (Ando 2000).

The most obvious case study of the processes and effects of Roman imperial socialization is the standing army from the Augustan period. Both citizen legionaries and non-citizen auxiliaries were subjected to the most comprehensive socialization processes, both deliberate and situational, of any group in the Roman empire, including the use of Latin (or, in the case of Roman army units in Egypt, code-switching from Greek to Latin in "super-high" contexts that required a sense of officialdom), the requirement to swear regular loyalty oaths, a ban on marriage recognized in Roman law, and, most scholars agree, unit-based participation in the rhythms of an adapted version of a city of Rome festival calendar, with its particular emphasis on the "imperial cult" (Shaw 1983; Phang 2001; Adams 2003: 393–6, 608–30; Rüpke 2011: 120). There is plenty of evidence for outsiders' association of soldiers with the power, efficacy, and culture of the Roman empire. The story of Jesus' exorcism from an unfortunate individual of a horde of demons who identify themselves by a term for a military unit borrowed from Latin ("my name is Legion"), and enter a herd of pigs (an unclean animal for Jews) to drown themselves (Mark 5:9; cf. Luke 8:30), is an extreme commentary on occupation by an alien force. In turn, occupational self-identification on the part of Roman soldiers is undoubtedly important (MacMullen 1984; Alston 1995; Goldsworthy and Haynes 1999; James 1999; Pollard 2000; Haynes 2013: 10–11).

If we dig a little deeper, however, we see that these block identifications sometimes co-exist with multiple overlapping or intersecting smaller group affinities, somewhere between virtual kin and virtual homelands. This shows up beautifully in the complex sub-groups united in religious worship, and in the focuses of worship themselves. Legions' standards and auxiliaries' signs functioned as portable *lieux de mémoire*, with all the fostered distinctiveness of a local city of the Roman empire: their birthdays were celebrated, they had origin stories, rich histories, and a competitive pride. Multiple *genii* (tutelary deities) were worshiped, on the analogy of the *genius* of a *paterfamilias* or city or host place, ritual embodiments of the grouphoods of legions or auxiliary divisions and any number of subdivisions and specialisms. Meanwhile, units or sub-units might continue links with a distant homeland by practicing the worship of that homeland's god or gods, enact an adopted homeland by worshiping its gods, often alongside the local population, and even take those gods with them when they moved on (Stoll 2001; 2007). Army units or sub-units regularly function as platforms for "imperial cult" dedications, prime enactments of grouphood in the Roman empire, but private dedications may incorporate verbal formulae associated with the "imperial cult" for purposes that have nothing to do with communicating with the imperial center (Haensch 2012; Haynes 2013: 216–17, 220–2).

Recent emphasis on the part played by imperial socialization processes in changing behavior and encouraging affinities usefully illuminates the deep level at which Roman imperial power functioned, but, as the case of the Roman army suggests, risks understating the situatedness or patchiness of participation, and overstating the exclusivity and directness of the relationship between individuals and the imperial center, and its effects on modes of self-identification. To describe these processes as being or becoming Roman (Woolf 1998; cf. Revell 2009) risks suggesting a coherence and singular direction of focus that must be complicated by the multiple allegiances and affinities suggested by soldiers' dedications and commemorations. The enactment of multiple small- to medium-sized grouphoods in the Roman army that mobilize the language and practices of shared kinship and homeland might be understood in part as compensation for dislocation from kinship and homeland bonds, although the regularity of commemoration of dead soldiers by their partners cautions us against taking that argument too far (Phang 2001). We might think instead of these grouphoods' reproductions of kinship and homeland in more positive terms, of the adaptive capability of such notions and the empowerment and opportunities that these grouphoods offer to their members.

Soldiers' re-creation of affinity groups, somewhere between legally recognized families and homeland as represented by village or city, alerts us to the broader phenomenon of elective groups, the "voluntary associations" that go viral throughout the Roman world, defining themselves by common worship, occupation, or provenance. Liable to suspicion on the part of the Roman state after they were mobilized intensively for political purposes in the late Republic, "voluntary associations" of the empire are most visibly concerned with shared feasts, honoring their patrons and illustrious members, and commemorating their dead. Usually spontaneous but on occasion actively encouraged by the imperial center, they claim space within the rituals and fabric of the city, with reserved theater seats, burial plots, and even latrines. Their language and institutions sometimes suggest the family, and sometimes the state, with its hierarchies, officials who performed benefactions, and platform for traffic in praise for city dignitaries or, well beyond the city, for the emperor himself. Some "voluntary associations" even organized tax collection.

While these associations were not necessarily exclusive, their bylaws could preclude membership of certain other groups. Associations might provide various funerary observances and celebrations as well as a burial or cremation plot, but they did not replace the care of the body and rituals normally conducted by family members. Nevertheless, the sparsest funerary commemorations give only the name of the individual and the association, so that within this context the association assumes all other possible reference points for being and belonging. Thus, an individual might be primarily or solely commemorated not in terms of family, tribe, or homeland, but as one of the linen-weavers, fullers, or builders. Recent scholarship has re-evaluated older assumptions that association members were primarily driven by poverty or by lack of kinship and homeland bonds because of servile or freedmen status.

Members were in fact drawn largely from the relatively prosperous "middling" classes of the Roman world, and we should emphasize rather the positive advantages of membership of these elective groups, with their reproduction and intensification through their small scale of the privilege and hierarchy benefits that are the sites of such competition in a world brokered by Roman authority. The vast majority of the associations' activities in the empire were innocuous and worked with rather than against city and imperial authorities. However, the cautiousness of the Roman state around associations, and infrequent tense incidents, highlight the potential for opportunism in the assumption of authority by groups of all kinds in the Roman world (including cities and military units), an opportunism that lends dynamism to imperial society at the cost of occasional risk (Kloppenborg and Wilson 1996; van Nijf 1997; Tran 2006; Bendlin 2011; Noreña forthcoming a).

Jewish synagogues and early Christian congregations have traditionally been characterized as reclusive and exclusive cultish outliers in the broader Roman world of "voluntary associations" clustered by shared cult, occupation, or provenance (Figure 8.4). But we should think rather in terms of a sliding scale running across "voluntary associations," synagogues, and congregations of interactions with the broader life of the city (including the "imperial cult") and

FIGURE 8.4: Menorah inscribed on stone column. Synagogue, Ostia, mid-first century CE. Accessed via Wikimedia Commons, CC BY-SA 3.0.

the exclusivity demanded of members (Harland 2003, 2009). In turn, when early Christian texts radically reject traditional bonds of kinship and homeland, actively making Christian grouphood in the process, they mobilize the strident rhetoric of exclusivity and essentialism that was one response to the social and geographical mobility and cultural eclecticism of the Roman world. If the Augustan vision of a toga-clad Roman race could include language of retaining blood purity, and membership of and place within the Panhellenion could be judged by close scrutiny of directness of a community's descent from the sons of Hellen, it is less of a surprise to see early Christians claim to be a "race." Early Christian "ethnic reasoning" claims the language of kinship and homeland even as it asserts Christians' deracination from ties of kinship, homeland, and the religious observance that were normally expected to align with these. The characterization of Christians as a *"new* race" in the anonymous *Epistle to Diognetus* (1.1) nicely points up the paradoxical juxtaposition of rootedness and deracination (Buell 2005; Eshleman 2012). In one of the starkest instances of early Christian profession of identity, Perpetua explains to her father that she could not recant her Christianity by saying that she cannot be "other than whom I am," just as a vase in the room could not be "other than what it is" (*Passion of Saints Perpetua and Felicitas* 3.1–2 van Beek). Perpetua's disavowal of her father's authority and kinship bond is meant to shock, even as it engages with broader contemporary notions of being and belonging: the essentialist discourse of race and purity, "elective" self-identification by occupation, religious affiliation, or expat origins, and even ancient philosophical questions about the relationship between names and things (Heffernan 2012: 156–7).

CONCLUSION

With nationalist and populist movements currently raging on both sides of the Atlantic, arguments are set to continue about who owns classical antiquity and how to characterize the ethnic composition of its societies. The issue of whether or not the history of classical antiquity is a history of white people, a central tenet of traditional notions of "western civilization," is currently raging again in the public arena. It is thus all the more important not to promote reductionist paradigms of ancient societies (however alarming or comforting), but to explore ancient modes and logics of being and belonging in all their cumbersome contradictoriness.

NOTES

Introduction

1. This is a composite definition, essentially Weberian in inspiration. For a comprehensive recent overview of definitions of the state, with a focus on the ancient period, see Scheidel 2013.
2. Important general treatments of (premodern) empire, on which this discussion draws, include Eisenstadt 1963; Doyle 1986; Finer 1997; Alcock *et al.* 2001; Motyl 2001; Howe 2002; Münkler 2007; Morris and Scheidel 2009; Burbank and Cooper 2010; Lavan *et al.* 2016.
3. For "hard" and "soft" power, see Nye 2005. For the role of culture generally in the state-formation process, see the essays in Steinmetz 1999.
4. In world-historical terms, the Roman empire does not stand out for its combination of size, longevity, and stability as such. The immense polities of premodern China, especially the Han empire, were equally impressive in those regards. Where the imperial system of ancient Rome differs most strikingly from that of early China—and from all other large, territorial empires in antiquity—is in its repubican, city-state roots. For systematic comparison between the Roman and Han empires, a rapidly developing field, see (e.g.,) Mutschler and Mittag 2009; Scheidel 2009, 2015a; Beck and Vankeerberghen forthcoming.

Chapter 1

1. For war in ancient Greece and Rome, and best current overview are provided by the contributions in Sabin *et al.* 2007. The accessible illustrations and sensible scholarship of Connolly 1981 (with many reprints) remains a useful gateway to the topic, as do the contributions in Hackett 1989. Lendon 2004 provides an invaluable survey of the intersection between culture and combat in the ancient Mediterranean.

2. On the evolution of the Roman army, see the contributions in Erdkamp 2007; Goldsworthy 1996 provides a monograph treatment of the army as a combat force, focusing on the imperial period.
3. For the population of Rome in 218, Brunt 1971 posits 325,000 adult male citizens, while de Ligt 2012 suggests the figure may have been somewhat higher, at 350,000.
4. The Sicilian expedition only numbered 5,100 heavy infantry, of which 2,100 were Athenians. (Thucydides 6.43). One need only compare this to a standard Roman expeditionary force in the Middle Republic: 16,000–25,000 legionary and Italian infantry (two legions and two allied wings), with around 2,000 cavalry.
5. Rosenstein 2004 argues that Roman peasant families organized their life cycle to accommodate long periods of military service by young men, tempering the notion advanced by Toynbee 1960, and modified by Brunt 1971 that heavy military deployments in the second century BCE sorely reduced the number of citizen landholders (*assidui*), liable for military service.
6. Not only was Roman manpower spread thin, but the Romans declined to build up a significant fiscal apparatus; see Taylor 2017 for a reconstruction of Roman finances, still modest in the second century BCE. Tan 2017 suggests that the Roman aristocracy declined to bolster finances in order to maintain a weak state that allowed room for aristocratic prerogatives.
7. Appian, *Iberian Wars* 60. Galba, the commander, was acquitted by the people after parading his children before them (Cicero, *Brutus* 89), leading to the creation of a new corruption court with a senatorial jury.
8. Luttwak 1976 remains the strongest vision of emperors producing coherent strategy, still compelling despite numerous subsequent critiques and caveats. For emperors and the courts hampered by limited geographic knowledge and ideological blinders, see Mattern 1999. For a study of the flow of information along frontiers in the late empire, Lee 1993.
9. Heads on stakes appear on Trajan's column; a disembodied skull found outside Vindolanda seems to have decorated the wall outside the post; now on display at the Vindolanda Museum.
10. Philostratus, *Life of Apollonius* 1.25. Even if these tapestries are fictional (as Philostratus' biography of Apollonius freely mixes fact and fiction), it nicely illustrates how easily truth might become a casualty in the process of imperial commemoration.

Chapter 2

1. The Roman contracts with Carthage before the Punic Wars of the third century BCE are the most famous examples; see Polybius 3.22.4–13.
2. Rickman 1980 and Erdkamp 2005: 206–60. From the late second century CE, free olive oil, pork, and (under Marcus Aurelius) price-reduced wine were added, while for the armies payments in kind rather than cash were much extended: Mitthof 2001.

3. We lack sufficient economically useful price information for analysing imperial price setting mechanisms; for a bold attempt, see Temin 2013; more cautiously, Rathbone and von Reden 2014.
4. Regional trade along the coast of Southern France is well attested, although it is difficult to ascertain which role individual cities played in this trade; Dietler 2007: 250–4, and Morel 2007.
5. Jerome, *Commentary on Daniel* 11.5 gives 1.5 million *artabas* of grain and 14,500 talents of cash per year as the income of Ptolemy II (279–243 BCE). For Alexandrian connections with Syracuse, see Hölbl 2001.
6. Mitthof 2001, which provides the most systematic analysis of the army supply in Egypt, gives ample evidence for the involvement of state agents; for the empire in general also Erdkamp 2002a. Elton 1996a and Roth 1999 argue that armies were paid in cash and supplied themselves via local markets.
7. The only possible example of a banker extending a maritime loan comes from Egypt (*SB* 14. 11850, mid-second century Theadelphia). This banker belonged to the wealthy Romanized elite in Egypt, and thus cuts across the categories of professional banker and élite financier.
8. *Emporion nomimon* seems to refer to a port of trade in which all commodities had to pass the control of the local king or his agents; see Casson 1989: 276.

Chapter 3

1. For the Capitol in its contemporary architectural context: Hopkins 2012a; 2016; Winter 2009.
2. For the Alban Hills and their mythistory, Grandazzi 2008, with Ziolkowski 2009. Drainage of the Alban Lake: Castellani and Dragoni 1992; Senay 1995
3. For the regional power and interactions of sixth-century Rome, see now Smith 2017.
4. An instance of the new caution about imperial spatialities, Gargola 2017.
5. On Nature in Augustan poetry, see Armstrong 2009. For the Augustan Golden Age, Wallace-Hadrill 1982. On Caesarian and Augustan time, Feeney 2007.
6. For Pliny, Wallace-Hadrill 1990b; Laehn 2013; Gibson and Morello 2011; Conte 1994. On similar naturalistic justifications for empire, Jones-Lewis 2012.
7. From a large bibliography on these topics, Leveau 1993 is particularly to be recommended.
8. On ancient responses to disaster, Ñaco del Hoyo et al. 2016.

Chapter 4

1. Temin 2013: 123. But one can observe that Weber in the *Agrarverhältnisse im Altertum* (1909) criticized Marx and the other theoreticians who thought free labor to be a *conditio sine qua non* of capitalism; Weber claimed that it would have been legitimate to use the term "capitalism" even where there was no free labor, or, better, where free labor was not the only available labor: Lo Cascio 2009: 308–12.

2. I am enormously grateful to Jane Johnson and Marco Maiuro for their invaluable help in the revision and translation of this chapter.

Chapter 5

1. The arguments in this chapter loosely employ legal scholar and critical race theorist Kimberlé Crenshaw's concept of "intersectionality" as a framework of analysis for how intersecting social identities in the Roman world fundamentally shaped the experience of mobility therein (Crenshaw 1989).
2. As Foubert 2016: 288–90 points out, archaeology and military studies in particular are at the forefront of change with regard to studying the mobility of women.
3. The lack of epigraphic documentation for the poor makes the problem of assessment particularly acute. Woolf 2013: 355.
4. Most Romans living outside of Italy, however, were required to pay the *tributum capitis* and *tributum soli*. All Romans were liable to the so-called "indirect" taxes, which included the manumission tax and inheritance tax. The privileges that Roman citizens enjoyed began to blur by the second century CE, when the social status of citizens came to reflect two ranks: *honestiores*, who were high status senators, equestrians, and so on, and low status *humiliores*. The former were granted legal immunity from cruelties like torture, forced labor and, most important, the death penalty. These exemptions were not granted to *humiliores*, even though they were Roman citizens. Hope 2000: 131–2.
5. Augustus, in turn, benefited from the loyalty of a few protégés, whose management of territories allowed him to control them while allowing them a superficial kind of autonomy. Eurycles eventually fell afoul of the emperor. Lindsay 1992: 290–1.
6. The division between the citizen legions and non-citizen auxiliaries became more flexible over the course of the Principate, and reflects the softening boundary between citizens and non-citizens that was occurring empire-wide. Southern 2007: 143.
7. The descendants of freedmen enjoyed all the privileges of the freeborn. Ibid.
8. These associations are known by a variety of Latin terms, such as *conventus* and *cives Romani consistentes*; and Greek terms, such as *hoi Rhomaioi katoikountes*. For a discussion of the phrase "association of Roman citizens," see Ramgopal 2017.
9. Caesarian evidence indicates that many associations played important roles in facilitating some Roman officials' rise to power in the Late Republic. In the Augustan era and later, others appear to have communicated directly with the emperor and maintained important roles in provincial cults dedicated to the worship of the emperor. Ramgopal forthcoming.
10. I am grateful to Carlos Noreña for the invitation to contribute to this volume, and for his and Nicole Julia Giannella's helpful comments on this chapter.

Chapter 6

1. See Foucault's 3-volume *History of Sexuality*, especially vol. 2 (1985): 253, and for criticisms of his failure to give due attention to ancient Greek and Roman women, Richlin 1998. Other criticisms include the *History*'s elite bias and its apparent neglect of colonial bodies (for which on vol. 1, see Stoler 1995). Recent attempts to

make the history of sexuality a history of empire include Whittaker 2004: 115–43; Richlin 2006; and Mattingly 2011: 94–124.
2. Tacitus *Annals* 14.31.3, 14.35.1 and *Histories* 4.14. For a discussion of the difficult category of "*stuprum*," and its implications of sex *crime*, Williams 2010: 103–36. Unless otherwise stated in the forthcoming notes, all citations of ancient texts are from the Loeb Classical Library.
3. As in the work of Stephen Maynard, discussed in Houlbrook 2001.
4. Nye 1999: 11 who argues that the "Who am I?" question is "arguably of more recent vintage." Perhaps this "replacement" enables us to ask the question raised by D'Ambra 2000: 111, "how did Roman women view these statues?" Already querying D'Ambra is Morales 2011: 92–3.
5. Morales 2011. Note here too Ovid, *Metamorphoses* 10.238–42, in which the mythical Propoetides, "the first prostitutes", are turned to stone for "denying" Venus. This is often read as meaning that Venus and prostitution are at odds with each other, but see Liveley 2011: 103 for prostitution as part of their punishment for celibacy.
6. Neal and Cosh 2002–10, vol. 3(2): 385, Tuck (2015) 353–4, and Cosh 2016, who also sees the inscription as parodying Martial.
7. Neal and Cosh 2002–10, vol. 2: 253–7 and Tuck 2015: 355–6. On the popularity of Venus on Romano-British pavements, Scott 2000: 120–1.
8. This epigraphic evidence from the Antonine Wall has been subject to a number of interpretations: Wright 1964: 178–9, Allason-Jones 1999: 44; Allison 2011: 165; Foubert 2013: 396–8.
9. See, for example, the *contubernalis*, mess-mate or concubine, mentioned in tablet 181 from Vindolanda on Hadrian's Wall: http://vindolanda.csad.ox.ac.uk/4DLink2/tablet-notes/181-notes.html (accessed April 18, 2017).
10. As discussed in Morales 2008: 47. Crucial here is Goldhill 1995 and on Roman "homosexuality;" more broadly, Williams 2010.
11. All Ausonius' epigrams are numbered according to Green 1991.
12. Zajko 2009 and Åshede 2015. Although important here, and not un-influential on my discussion, is Floridi 2015, who exculpates Ausonius by having him always "tone down" his literary inheritance and the "homosexuality" and "pederasty" it brings with it.
13. The text used here is *The Life of Saint Pelagia, Prostitute* (Migne, *Patrologia Latina* 73: cols. 663–72), and the most convenient translation, Ward 1987: 66–75. See Miller 2003 and Burrus 2004: 137–46.
14. I thank the editor, Carlos Noreña, and Ingo Gildenhard, Christopher Kelly, Rebecca Lees, Charles Manklow, and Robin Osborne.

Chapter 7

1. For detailed discussion of the varied reception of Spartacus in the twentieth century and beyond, see Wyke 1997: 34–72; Futrell 2001; Hardwick 2003: 37–43; Urbainczyk 2004: 106–30; Hunnings 2007; Langerwerf 2011: 353; Radford 2017.
2. Examples include Brunt 1959 (Vindex, 69 CE) and 1960 (Batavians, 69 CE); Webster 1978 (Boudicca, 60 CE); Goodman 1987 (First Jewish War, 66–70 CE), Schäfer 2003 (Bar Kochba, 132–5 CE); Popović 2011 (First Jewish War, 66–70 CE); Schiavone

2013 (Spartacus, 73–1 BCE), Horbury 2014 (Bar Kochba, 132–5 CE). Urban 1999, Mattingly 2006, Coltelloni-Trannoy and Le Bohec 2014 discuss rebellions in Roman Gaul, Britain, and Africa respectively.

3. For excellent recent overviews of outright rebellions, with a special focus on the role that religion played in them, see Goodman 1991 and 2014. Daniel Jolowicz is currently editing an exciting volume on resistance in cultural production in the Roman empire.
4. Bénabou 1978, Leveau 1978, and Thébert 1978 discuss this question in a special issue of the French journal *Annales*. Daube 1972, who writes about civil disobedience in Antiquity, could also be mentioned in this paragraph.
5. E.g., Josephus, *Jewish War* 2.261–3: in 54 CE an Egyptian prophet marched with 30,000 followers on Jerusalem. Woolf 1993: 187–8 mobilizes archaeological evidence for this purpose.
6. For later evidence for the same phenomenon in Rome see Ammianus Marcellinus 26.3.6. On urban crowds and protest in late Roman Africa, which ecclesiastical sources, especially Augustine, attest much better than any source from the early empire, see Magalhães de Oliveira 2012.
7. The precise origins and goals of the Bagaudae have been a subject of extensive debate. Thompson 1952, MacMullen 1966, van Dam 1985 made important contributions; most recently, see Couper 2015. Nobody has doubted their peasant origins.
8. Banditry has attracted more scholarship than urban unrest. Important contributions to the topic include Shaw 1984, Riess 2001, and Gruenewald 2004.
9. Thornton 2001 and 2008 and are the most recent attempts to reconstruct the sequence of events in Lycia. Şahin and Adak 2007: 49–62 and Bennett 2011 reconstruct the situation from the Roman perspective.
10. The literature on just what problem Roman authorities had with early Christians is vast. Sherwin-White 1952, de Ste Croix 1963 and Barnes 1968 are important contributions. For the idea that Christians could, and often did, appear like another suspicious association, see Corke-Webster 2017.
11. For more detailed treatment of unrest among the Roman plebs in relation to the emperor see Yavetz 1969: 18–32; Cameron 1976: 155–61; and Deininger 1979: 285–303.
12. I owe the interpretation of the evidence for the First Servile War adopted here to a talk that Peter Morton delivered at the 2017 Society for Classical Studies Annual Meeting in Toronto; his monograph on the Sicilian Slave Wars is in preparation.
13. I owe thanks to Daniel Jolowicz, for organizing a seminar series about resistance in the Roman empire at Corpus Christi College, Oxford in the fall of 2014, where I first became interested in the subject, and to Carlos Noreña for inviting me to write about the problem in this volume. Many of the ideas presented here were first articulated in conversations with Philipp Höhn; Sarah Bühler, Myles Lavan, Carlos Noreña, and Sebastian Schmidt-Hofner provided most helpful comments in the final stages of writing. I am grateful to all of them for their encouragement and support.

FURTHER READING

Abu-Lughod, Lilah (1990), "The Romance of Resistance: Tracing Transformations of Power Through Bedouin Women," *American Ethnologist*, 17: 41–55.
Adams, J. N. (2003), *Bilingualism and the Latin Language*, Cambridge: Cambridge University Press.
Adams, J. N. (2012), "Late Latin," in James Clackson (ed.), *A Companion to the Latin Language*, 257–83, Oxford: Blackwell.
Alcock, Susan (1993), *Graecia Capta: The Landscapes of Roman Greece*, Cambridge: University Press.
Alcock, Susan, Terence D'Altroy, Kathleen Morrison, and Carla Sinopoli, eds (2001), *Empires: Perspectives from Archaeology and History*, Cambridge: Cambridge University Press.
Alföldy, Géza (1972), "Die Freilassung von Sklaven und die Struktur der Sklaverei in der römischen Kaiserzeit," *Rivista Storica dell'Antichità* 2: 97–129.
Allason-Jones, Lindsay (1989), *Women in Roman Britain*, London: The British Museum.
Allason-Jones, Lindsay (1999), "Women and the Roman Army in Britain," in Goldsworthy and Haynes 1999: 41–52.
Allason-Jones, Lindsay (2012), "Women in Roman Britain," in Sharon James and Sheila Dillon (eds), *A Companion to Women in the Ancient World*, 467–77, Oxford and Malden, MA: Wiley-Blackwell.
Allison, Penelope (2011), "Soldiers Families in the Early Roman Empire," in Beryl Rawson (ed.) *A Companion to Families in the Greek and Roman Worlds*, 161–82, Chichester, West Sussex: Wiley-Blackwell.
Allison, Penelope (2013), *People and Spaces in Roman Military Bases*, Cambridge: Cambridge University Press.
Alston, Richard (1995), *Soldier and Society in Roman Egypt: a Social History*, London: Routledge.
Ameling, Walter (2013), "Carthage," in Bang and Scheidel 2013: 361–82.
Ampolo, Carmine, Maria Cecilia Parra, and Emilio Rosamilia (2014), "Kaulonia. La Tabula Cauloniensis: note preliminari," *Annali della Scuola Normale Superiore di Pisa*, s. 5, 6/2, supplemento, 72–80.

Ando, Clifford (2000), *Imperial Ideology and Provincial Loyalty in the Roman Empire*, Berkeley: University of California Press.
Ando, Clifford (2006), "The Administration of the Provinces," in David Potter (ed.), *A Companion to the Roman Empire*, 177–92, Oxford and Malden, MA: Blackwell.
Ando, Clifford (2012), *Imperial Rome AD 193 to 284: The Critical Century*, Edinburgh: Edinburgh University Press.
Ando, Clifford (2016), "Making Romans: Citizens, Subjects, and Subjectivity in Republican Empire," in Myles Lavan, Richard Payne, and John Weisweiler (eds), *Cosmopolitanism and Empire: Universal Rulers, Local Elites, and Cultural Integration in the Ancient Near East and Mediterranean*, 169–86, Oxford: Oxford University Press.
Andrade, Nathanael (2013), "Rebellions, Roman Empire," in Roger Bagnall (ed.), *The Encyclopedia of Ancient History*, 5742–7, Oxford and Malden, MA: Wiley-Blackwell.
Andreau, Jean (1993), "The Freedman," in A. Giardina (ed.), *The Romans*, 175–98, Chicago: University of Chicago Press.
Andreau, Jean (1999), *Banking and Business in the Roman World*, Cambridge: Cambridge University Press.
Arieti, James (1997), "Rape and Livy's View of History," in Susan Deacy and Karen Peirce (eds), *Rape in Antiquity*, 209–29, Swansea: Classical Press of Wales.
Armayor, O. Kimball (1978), "Herodotus' Catalogues of the Persian Empire in the Light of the Monuments and Greek Literary Tradition," *Transactions of the American Philological Association* 108: 1–9.
Armstrong, Rebecca (2009), "Against Nature? Some Augustan Responses to Man-Made Marvels," in Philip Hardie (ed.), *Paradox and the Marvellous in Augustan Literature and Culture*, 75–94, Oxford: Oxford University Press.
Arnaoutoglou, Ilias (2002), "Roman Law and collegia in Asia Minor," *Revue internationale des droits de l'antiquité* 49: 27–44.
Arrington, Nathan (2011), "Inscribing Defeat: The Commemorative Dynamics of the Athenian Casualty Lists," *Classical Antiquity* 30: 179–212.
Åshede, Linnea (2015), "Desiring Hermaphrodites: the Relations of Hermaphroditus in Roman Group Scenes," PhD diss., Institutionen för Historiska Studier, Gothenburg University, Gothenburg.
Assmann, Jan (2002), *The Mind of Egypt: History and Meaning in the Time of the Pharaohs*, Cambridge, MA: Harvard University Press.
Badian, Ernst (1968), *Roman Imperialism in the Late Republic*, Ithaca, NY: Cornell University Press.
Badian, Ernst (2013), *Collected Papers on Alexander the Great*, London and New York: Routledge.
Bagnall, Roger (2002), "Alexandria: Library of Dreams," *Proceedings of the American Philosophical Society* 146.4: 348–62.
Bagnall, Roger and Bruce Frier (1994), *The Demography of Roman Egypt*, Cambridge: Cambridge University Press.
Bagnall, Roger and Petre Derow, eds (2003), *The Hellenistic Period: Historical Sources in Translation*, 2nd edition, Oxford and Malden, MA: Wiley-Blackwell.
Bainaji, Jairus (2007), *Agrarian Change in Late Antiquity: Gold, Labour, and Aristocratic Dominance*, Oxford: Oxford University Press.
Bainaji, Jairus (2015), *Exploring the Economy of Late Antiquity: Selected Essays*, Cambridge: Cambridge University Press.
Bang, Peter (2007), "Trade and Empire: In Search of Organizing Concepts for the Roman Economy," *Past & Present* 195: 3–54.

Bang, Peter (2008), *The Roman Bazaar: A Comparative Study of Trade and Markets in a Tributary Empire*, Cambridge: Cambridge University Press.
Bang, Peter (2013), "The Roman Empire II: The Monarchy," in Bang and Scheidel 2013: 412–72.
Bang, Peter and Walter Scheidel, eds (2013), *The Oxford Handbook of the State in the Ancient Near East and Mediterranean*, Oxford: Oxford University Press.
Barjamovic, Gojko (2013), "Mesopotamian Empires," in Bang and Scheidel 2013: 120–60.
Barnes, Timothy (1968), "Legislation against the Christians," *Journal of Roman Studies* 58: 32–50.
Baroin, Catherine (2010), "Remembering One's Ancestors, Following in their Footsteps, Being Like Them: The Role and Forms of Family Memory in the Building of Identity," in Veronique Dasen and Thomas Späth (eds), *Children, Memory, and Family Identity in Roman Culture*, 19–48, Oxford: Oxford University Press.
Battistoni, Filippo (2010), *Parenti dei Romani. mito troiano e diplomazia*, Bari: Edipuglia.
Bauckham, Richard (1991), "The Economic Critique of Rome in Revelation 18," in Alexander Loveday (ed.), *Images of Empire*, 47–90, Sheffield: JSOT Press.
Beard, Mary (1999), "The Erotics of Rape: Livy, Ovid and the Sabine Women," in Päivi Setälä and Liisa Savunen (eds), *Female Networks and the Public Sphere in Roman Society*, 1–10, Rome: Institutum Romanum Finlandiae.
Beard, Mary (2009), *The Roman Triumph*, Cambridge MA: Harvard University Press.
Beck, Hans, and Griet Vankeerberghen, eds (forthcoming), *Citizens and Commoners in Ancient Greece, Rome, and China*, Oxford and Malden, MA: Wiley-Blackwell.
Beckmann, Martin (2011), *The Column of Marcus Aurelius: The Genesis and Meaning of a Roman Imperial Monument*, Chapel Hill: University of North Carolina Press.
Bekker-Nielsen, Tønnes (n.d.), "Mobility, Ethnicity and Identity: The Evidence of the Funerary Inscriptions from Pantikapaion," PDF online.
Bénabou, Marcel (1976), *La résistance africaine à la romanisation*, Paris: F. Maspero.
Bell, Sinclair and Teresa Ramsby, eds (2012), *Free at Last! The Impact of Freed Slaves on the Roman Empire*, London: Bristol Classical Press.
Bénabou, Marcel (1978), "Les Romains ont-ils conquis l'Afrique?" *Annales. Économies, Sociétés, Civilisations* 33: 83–8.
Bendlin, Andreas (2011), "Associations, Funerals, Sociality, and Roman law: The 'Collegium' of Diana and Antinous in Lanuvium (*CIL* 14.2112) Reconsidered," in M. Öhler (ed.), *Aposteldekret und antikes Vereinswesen: Gemeinschaft und ihre Ordnung*, 207–96, Tübingen: Mohr Siebeck.
Bennet, John (2013), "Bronze Age Greece," in Bang and Scheidel 2013: 235–58.
Bennett, Julian (2011), "Why did Claudius Annex Lycia?" *Adalya* 14: 119–36.
Benoit, Pierre and Jacques Schwartz (1948), "Caracalla et les troubles d'Alexandrie en 215 après J.-C," *Études de Papyrologie* 7: 17–33.
Benton, Lauren (2010), *A Search for Sovereignty: Law and Geography in European Empires, 1400–1900*, Cambridge, Cambridge University Press.
Ben-Yahuda, Nachman (1995), *Masada Myth: Collective Memory and Mythmaking in Israel*, Madison: University of Wisconsin Press.
Bergamini, Margherita, ed. (1992), *Gli Etruschi maestri di idraulica*, Perugia: Mondadori Electa.
Bernal, Martin (1987–91), *Black Athena: the Afroasiatic Roots of Classical Civilization*, 2 volumes, New Brunswick: Rutgers University Press.

Bertrand, Audrey (2010), "Y a-t-il un paysage religieux colonial? Entre prescription, mimétisme et adaptation: les mécanismes de l'*imitatio Romae*," *Revue de l'histoire des religions* 4: 591–608.

Bickerman, Elias (1939), "Notes et discussions: la cité grecque dans les monarchies hellénistiques," *Revue de philologie* 13: 335–49.

Bickerman, Elias (1952), "Origines gentium," *Classical Philology* 47: 65–81.

Birley, Anthony (1980), *The People of Roman Britain*, Berkeley: University of California Press.

Birley, Anthony (2012), "The Wars and Revolts," in Marcel Van Ackeren (ed.), *A Companion to Marcus Aurelius*, 217–34. Oxford and Malden, MA: Wiley-Blackwell.

Bishop, Michael and Jonathan Coulston (2006), *Roman Military Equipment From the Punic Wars to the Fall of Rome*, 2nd edition, Oxford: Oxbow.

Bland, Roger and Catherine Johns (1993), *The Hoxne Treasure: An Illustrated Introduction*, London: British Museum Press.

Blasius, Andreas and Bernd Schipper, eds (2002), *Apokalyptik und Ägypten: eine kritische Analyse der relevanten Texte aus dem griechisch-römischen Ägypten*, Leuven: Peeters.

Blok, Josine (1996), "Proof and Persuasion in *Black Athena*: The Case of K. O. Müller," *Journal of the History of Ideas* 57.4: 705–24.

Boatwright, Mary (2015), "Acceptance and Approval: Romans' non-Roman Population Transfers, 180 BCA–*ca*. 70 CE," *Phoenix* 69: 122–46.

Boedeker, Deborah and Kurt Raaflaub, eds (1998), *Democracy, Empire and the Arts in Fifth-century Athens*, Cambridge, MA: Harvard University Press.

Borg, Barbara (2012), "The Face of the Social Climber: Roman Freedmen and Elite Ideology," in Bell and Ramsby 2012: 25–49.

Bosworth, A. B. (1993), *Conquest and Empire: The Reign of Alexander the Great*, Cambridge: Cambridge University Press.

Bosworth, A. B. (2002), *The Legacy of Alexander: Politics, Warfare and Propaganda under the Successors*, Oxford: Oxford University Press.

Bowes, Kimberly (2008), *Private Worship, Public Values, and Religious Change in Late Antiquity*, Cambridge: Cambridge University Press.

Bowman, Alan (1994), *Life and Letters on the Roman Frontier*. London: British Museum Press.

Bowman, Alan, and Andrew Wilson, eds (2013), *The Roman Agricultural Economy: Organization, Investment, and Production*. Oxford: Oxford University Press.

Bowra, Cecil (1957), "Melinno's Hymn to Rome," *Journal of Roman Studies* 47: 21–8.

Boyle, Anthony J. (2003), *Ovid and The Monuments: A Poet's Rome*, Bendigo, Victoria: Aureal.

Bradley, Keith (1992), "'The Regular, Daily Traffic in Slaves': Roman History and Contemporary History," *The Classical Journal* 87: 125–38.

Bradley, Keith and Paul Cartledge, eds (2011), *The Cambridge World History of Slavery, Volume 1: The Ancient Mediterranean World*, Cambridge: Cambridge University Press.

Brélaz, Cédric (2005), *La sécurité publique en Asie Mineure sous le Principat (Ier – IIIème s. ap. J.-C.): institutions municipales et institutions impèriales dans l'Orient romain*, Basel: Schwabe.

Brennan, T. Corey (2000), *The Praetorship in the Roman Republic*, 2 volumes, Oxford: Oxford University Press.

Bresson, Alain (2016), *The Making of the Ancient Greek Economy*. Princeton: Princeton University Press.

Briant, Pierre (2002), *From Cyrus to Alexander: A History of the Persian Empire*, Winona Lake, IN: Eisenbrauns.
Broadhead, William (2000), "Migration and Transformation in North Italy: 2nd–1st centuries BC," *Bulletin of the Institute of Classical Studies* 44: 145–66.
Broodbank, Cyprian (2013), *The Making of the Middle Sea. A History of the Mediterranean from the Beginning to the Emergence of the Classical World*, Oxford: Oxford University Press.
Brooten, Bernadette J. (1996), *Love Between Women: Early Christian Responses To Female Homoeroticism*, Chicago: University of Chicago Press.
Brown, Peter (1971), *The World of Late Antiquity: AD 150–750*, London: Thames and Hudson.
Brown, Peter (1988), *The Body and Society: Men, Women and Sexual Renunciation in Early Christianity*, New York: Columbia University Press.
Brown, Peter (1990), "Bodies and Minds: Sexual Renunciation in Early Christianity," in David M. Halperin, John J. Winkler and Froma I. Zeitlin (eds), *Before Sexuality: The Construction of Erotic Experience in the Ancient Greek World*, 479–94, Princeton: Princeton University Press.
Brown, Peter (2012), *Through the Eye of a Needle: Wealth, The Fall of Rome, and the Making of Christianity in the West, 350–550 AD*, Princeton: Princeton University Press.
Brown, Peter (2013), *The Rise of Western Christendom: Triumph and Diversity, A.D. 200–1000*, revised edition, Oxford and Malden, MA: Wiley-Blackwell.
Brunt, Peter (1959), "The Revolt of Vindex and the Fall of Nero," *Latomus* 18: 531–59.
Brunt, Peter (1960), "Tacitus on the Batavian Revolt," *Latomus* 19: 494–517.
Brunt, Peter (1971), *Italian Manpower*, Oxford: Clarendon Press.
Brunt, Peter (1988), *The Fall of the Roman Republic and Related Essays*, Oxford: Oxford University Press.
Bruun, Christer (2007), "The Antonine Plague and the 'Third-Century Crisis'," in Olivier Hekster, Gerda de Kleijn, and Daniëlle Slootjes (eds), *Crises and the Roman Empire*, 201–18, Leiden: Brill.
Bruun, Christer (2016), "Tracing Familial Mobility: Female and Child Migrants in the Roman West," in de Ligt and Tacoma 2011: 176–204.
Bryce, Trevor (2013), "Anatolian States," in Bang and Scheidel 2013: 161–79.
Bryen, Ari (2013), *Violence in Roman Egypt*, Philadelphia: University of Pennsylvania Press.
Bryen, Ari (2016), "Reading the Citizenship Papyrus (*P.Giss.* 40)," in Clifford Ando (ed.), *Citizenship and Empire in Europe 200–1900: The Antonine Constitution after 1800 Years*, 29–44, Stuttgart: Franz Steiner Verlag.
Buckler, William (1923), "Labour Disputes in the Province of Asia," in William Buckler and William Calder (eds), *Anatolian Studies Presented to Sir William Mitchell Ramsay*, 27–50, Manchester: Manchester University Press.
Buell, Denise (2005), *Why This New Race: Ethnic Reasoning in Early Christianity*, New York: Columbia University Press.
Burbank, Jane and Frederick Cooper (2010), *Empires in World History: Geographies of Power, Politics of Difference*, Princeton: Princeton University Press.
Burrus, Virginia (2004), *The Sex Lives of Saints: An Erotics of Ancient Hagiography*, Philadelphia: University of Pennsylvania Press.
Calder, William (1912), "Colonia Caesareia Antiocheia," *Journal of Roman Studies* 2: 78–109.

Cameron, Alan (1976), *Circus Factions: Blues and Greens at Rome and Byzantium*, Oxford: Clarendon Press.

Carandini, Andrea (1988), *Schiavi in Italia: gli strumenti pensanti dei Romani fra tarda Repubblica e medio Impero*, Rome: La Nuova Italia Scientifica.

Caroll, Maureen (2012), "The Insignia of Women: Dress, Gender and Identity on the Roman Funerary Monument of Regina from Arbeia," *Archaeological Journal* 169: 281–311.

Cartledge, Paul (2002), *Sparta and Lakonia: A Regional History 1300–362 BC*, 2nd edition, London and New York: Routledge.

Casson, Lionel (1989), *The Periplous Maris Erythraei*, Princeton: Princeton University Press.

Castellani, V. and Water Dragoni (1992), "Opere arcaiche per il controllo del territorio: gli emissari sotterranei artificiali dei laghi albani," in Margherita Bergamini (ed.), *Gli Etruschi maestri di idraulica*, 43–60, Perugia: Mondadori Electa.

Champion, Craige (2004), *Cultural Politics in Polybius' Histories*, Berkeley: University of California Press.

Champlin, Edward (2003), *Nero*, Cambridge, MA: Harvard University Press.

Charles-Edwards, T. M. (2000), "Law in the Western Kingdoms Between the Fifth and Seventh Century," in *Cambridge Ancient History* 14, 260–87, Cambridge: Cambridge University Press.

Charles, Michael B. (2011), "Immortals and Apple Bearers: Towards a Better Understanding of Achaemenid Infantry Units," *Classical Quarterly* 61: 114–33.

Charles, Michael B. (2015), "Achaemenid Elite Cavalry: from Xerxes to Darius," *Classical Quarterly* 65: 14–35.

Cheng, Jack, and Marian Feldman, eds (2007), *Ancient Near Eastern Art in Context: Studies in Honor of Irene J. Winter by Her Students*, Leiden, Brill.

Cherry, David (2007), "The Frontier Zones" in Scheidel *et al.* 2007: 720–40.

Churchill, J. Bradford (1999), "Ex qua quod vellent facerent: Roman Magistrates' Authority over Praeda and Manubiae," *Transactions of the American Philological Association* 129: 85–116.

Claassen, Jo-Marie (1999), *Displaced Persons: The Literature of Exile from Cicero to Boethius*, Madison: University of Wisconsin Press.

Clark, Gillian (2004), *Christianity and Roman Society*, Cambridge: Cambridge University Press.

Clarke, John R. (1991), *The Houses of Roman Italy, 100 B.C.-A.D. 250: Ritual, Space and Decoration*, Berkeley: University of California Press.

Clarke, John R. (1996), "Hypersexual Black Men in Augustan Baths: Ideal Somatotypes and Apotropaic Magic," in Natalie Boymel Kampen (ed.), *Sexuality in Ancient Art*, 184–98, Cambridge: Cambridge University Press.

Clarke, John R. (1998), *Looking at Lovemaking: Constructions of Sexuality in Roman Art, 100 B.C.-A.D. 250*, Berkeley: University of California Press.

Clarke, John R. (2003), *Art in the Lives of Ordinary Romans: Visual Representation and Non-Elite Viewers in Italy, 100 B.C.-A.D 315*, Berkeley: University of California Press.

Clarysse, Willy (1985), "Greeks and Egyptians in the Ptolemaic army and administration," *Aegyptus* 65: 57–66.

Clarysse, Willy and Doroth J. Thompson (2006), *Counting the People in Hellenistic Egypt*, Cambridge: Cambridge University Press.

Cline, Eric and Marc Graham (2011), *Ancient Empires: From Mesopotamia to the Rise of Islam*, Cambridge: Cambridge University Press.

Cline, Eric, ed. (2010), *The Oxford Handbook of the Bronze Age Aegean*, Oxford: Oxford University Press.
Coarelli, Filippo (1996), "Fregellae, Arpinum, Aquinum. Lana e *fullonicae* nel Lazio meridionale," in Mireille Cébeillac-Gervasoni (ed.), *Les élites municipales de l'Italie péninsulaire des Gracques á Néron*, 199–205, Rome: École française de Rome.
Cohen, Edward E. (2005), "Commercial Law," in Michael Gagarin and David Cohen (eds), *The Cambridge Companion to Ancient Greek Law*, 290–304, Cambridge: Cambridge University Press.
Coleman, Kathleen (1990), "Fatal Charades: Roman Executions Staged as Mythological Enactments," *Journal of Roman Studies* 80: 44–73.
Collins, Rob, and Frances McIntosh, eds (2014), *Life in the Limes: Studies of the Peoples and Objects of the Roman Frontiers*, Oxford: Oxbow.
Coltelloni-Trannoy, Michèle and Yann Le Bohec (2014), *La guerre dans l'Afrique romaine sous le Haut-Empire*, Paris: Comité des travaux historiques et scientifiques.
Companion to Women in the Ancient World, 467–77, Oxford: Wiley-Blackwell.
Connolly, Peter (1981), *Greece and Rome at War*, London: MacDonald.
Connolly, Serena (2010), *Lives Behind the Laws: The World of the Codex Hermogenianus*, Bloomington, IN: Indiana University Press.
Conte, Gian Biaggio (1994), "The Inventory of the World: Form of Nature and Encyclopaedic Project in the Work of Pliny the Elder," in Gian Biaggio Conte (ed.), *Genres and Readers: Lucretius, Love-Elegy, Pliny's Encyclopaedia*, 67–104, Baltimore: Johns Hopkins University Press.
Corke-Webster, James (2017), "Trouble in Pontus: The Pliny-Trajan Correspondence on the Christians Reconsidered," *Transactions of the American Philological Association*, 147: 371–411.
Cornell, Tim (1995), *The Beginnings of Rome: Italy and Rome from the Bronze Age to the Punic Wars (c. 1000–264 BC)*, London and New York: Routledge.
Cornwell, Hannah (2017), *Pax and the Politics of Peace*, Oxford: Oxford University Press.
Cosh, Stephen R. (2016), "The Lullingstone Mosaic Inscription – A Parody of Martial?" *Britannia* 47: 262–6.
Cottier, M. *et al.*, eds (2008), *The Customs Law of Asia*. Oxford: Oxford University Press.
Coulston, James (2008), *All the Emperor's Men: Roman Soldiers and Barbarians on Trajan's Column*, Oxford: Oxbow.
Couper, Grant (2015), "Gallic Insurgencies? Annihilating the Bagaudae," in Timothy Howe and Lee Brice (eds), *Brill's Companion to Insurgency and Terrorism in the Ancient Mediterranean*, 312–34, Leiden: Brill.
Courrier, Cyril (2014), *La plèbe de Rome et sa culture (fin du IIe siècle av. J.-C. – fin du Ier siècle ap. J.C.)*, Rome: École française de Rome.
Crenshaw, Kimberle (1989), "Demarginalizing the Intersection of Race and Sex: A Black Feminist Critique of Antidiscrimination Doctrine, Feminist Theory and Antiracist Politics," *The University of Chicago Legal Forum* 140: 139–67.
Culham, Phyllis (1997), "Did Roman Women Have an Empire?" in Mark Golden and Peter Toohey (eds), *Inventing Ancient Culture: Historicism, Periodization, and the Ancient World*, 192–204, London and New York: Routledge.
Curchin, Leonard (1991), *Roman Spain: Conquest and Assimilation*, London and New York: Routledge.
Curtin, Philip (1984), *Cross-Cultural Trade in World History*, Cambridge: Cambridge University Press.

D'Ambra, Eve (1996), "The Calculus of Venus: Nude Portraits of Roman Matrons," in Natalie Boymel Kampen (ed.), *Sexuality in Ancient Art,* 210–32, Cambridge: Cambridge University Press.

D'Ambra, Eve (2000), "Nudity and Adornment in Female Portrait Sculpture of the Second Century AD," in Diana E. E. Kleiner and Susan B. Matheson (eds), *I Claudia II: Women in Roman Art and Society*, 101–14, Austin, TX: University of Texas Press.

Dasen, Veronique (2010), "Wax and Plaster Memories: Children in Elite and Non-Elite Strategies', in Veronique Dasen and Thomas Späth (eds), *Children, Memory, and Family Identity in Roman Culture*, 109–45, Oxford: Oxford University Press.

Daube, David (1972), *Civil Disobedience in Antiquity*, Edinburgh: Edinburgh University Press.

De la Bédoyère, Guy (2017), *Praetorian: The Rise and Fall of Rome's Imperial Bodyguard.* New Haven: Yale University Press.

De Ligt, Luuk (2000), "Governmental Attitudes towards Markets and Collegia," in Elio Lo Cascio (ed.), *Mercati permanenti e mercati periodici nel mondo romano*, 237–52, Bari: Edipuglia.

De Ligt, Luuk (2012), *Peasants, Citizens and Soldiers: Studies in the Demographic History of Roman Italy 225 BC-AD 100*, Cambridge: Cambridge University Press.

De Ligt, Luuk, and Laurens Tacoma, eds (2016), *Migration and Mobility in the Roman Empire*, Leiden: Brill.

De Nardis, Mauro (2016), "Terminologia e concetto di "lavoro" in età romana," in Marcone 2016: 79–91.

De Robertis, Francesco M. (1963), *Lavoro e lavoratori nel mondo romano*, Bari: Adriatica.

De Ste Croix, Geoffrey (1963), "Why were the Early Christians Persecuted?" *Past & Present*, 26: 6–38.

De Ste Croix, Geoffrey (1981), *The Cass Struggle in the Ancient Greek World: From the Archaic Age to the Arab Conquests*, London: Duckworth.

Dee, James (2003–4), "Black Odysseus, White Caesar: When Did 'White People' Become 'White'?" *The Classical Journal* 99.2: 157–67.

Deininger, Jürgen (1979), "Brot und Spiele. Tacitus und die Entpolitisierung der plebs urbana," *Gymnasium* 86: 278–303.

Delz, Josef (1988), "Harald F.," *Gnomon* 60: 80–2.

Dench, Emma (1995), *From Barbarians to New Men: Greek, Roman and Modern Perceptions of Peoples from the Central Apennines*, Oxford: Clarendon Press.

Dench, Emma (2005), *Romulus' Asylum: Roman Identities from the Age of Alexander to the Age of Hadrian*, Oxford: Oxford University Press.

Dench, Emma (2011), "Roman Imperial Pasts," in Stephane Benoist, Anne Daguet-Gagey, and Christine Hoët-van Cauwenberghe (eds), *Figures d'empire, fragments de mémoire: pouvoirs et identités dans le monde romain imperial (IIe s. av. n. è. – VI s. de n. è.)*, 487–502, Villeneuve-d'Ascq: Presses universitaires du Septentrion.

Derow, Peter (1989), "Rome, the Fall of Macedon and the Sack of Corinth," in *Cambridge Ancient History* 8, 290–323, Cambridge: Cambridge University Press.

Diamond, Jared (1999), *Guns, Germs, and Steel: The Fate of Human Societies*, New York: W. W. Norton & Company.

Dietler, Michael (2007), "The Iron Age in the Western Mediterranean," in Scheidel *et al.* 2007: 211–41.

Diller, Aubrey (1937), *Race Mixture among the Greeks before Alexander*, Urbana, IL: University of Illinois Press.

Dinkova-Bruun, Greti (2012), "Medieval Latin," in James Clackson (ed.), *A Companion to the Latin Language*, 284–302, Oxford and Malden, MA: Wiley-Blackwell.

Dmitriev, Sviatoslav (2011), *The Greek Slogan of Freedom and Early Roman Politics in Greece*, Oxford: Oxford University Press.

Dörner, Andreas (1995), *Politischer Mythos und symbolische Politik: Sinnstiftung durch symbolische Formen am Beispiel des Hermannsmythos*, Opladen: Westdeutscher Verlag.

Dossey, Leslie (2010), *Peasant and Empire in Christian North Africa*, Berkeley: University of California Press.

Dougherty, Carol (2001), *The Raft of Odysseus: The Ethnographic Imagination of Homer's Odyssey*, Oxford: Oxford University Press.

Doyle, Michael (1986), *Empires*, Ithaca, NY: Cornell University Press.

Drew-Bear, Thomas, and Askold Ivantchik (2011), "Honneurs a Apamée pour Proclus Manneius Ruso," in Lâtife Summerer, Askold Ivantchik, and Alexander von Kielin (eds), *Kelainai-Apameia Kibotos. Développement urbain dans le contexte anatolien*, 281–94, Bordeaux: Ausonius.

Drinkwater, John (1987), *The Gallic Empire: Separatism and Continuity in the North-western Provinces of the Roman Empire*, Stuttgart: Steiner Verlag.

Duncan-Jones, Richard (1996), "The impact of the Antonine Plague," *Journal of Roman Archaeology* 9: 108–36.

Dyson, Stephen (1971), "Native Revolts in the Roman Empire," *Historia* 20: 239–274.

Dyson, Stephen (1975), "Native Revolt Patterns in the Roman Empire," in *Aufstieg und Niedergang der römischen Welt* 2.3, 138–75, Berlin: Walter de Gruyter.

Eberle, Lisa (2016), "Law, Empire, and the Making of Roman Estates in the Provinces during the Late Republic," *Critical Analysis of Law*, 3.1: 50–69.

Eckstein, Arthur (2005), *Mediterranean Anarchy, Interstate War, and the Rise of Rome*, Berkeley: University of California Press.

Edwards, Catharine (1993), *The Politics of Immorality in Ancient Rome*, Cambridge: Cambridge University Press.

Edwards, Catharine (1997), "Unspeakable Professions: Public Performance and Prostitution in Ancient Rome," in Judith P. Hallett and Marilyn B. Skinner (eds) *Roman Sexualities*, 66–95, Princeton: Princeton University Press.

Edwards, Catharine (2001), Review of Hingley 2000, *Classical Review* 51.2: 366–7.

Ehrhardt, Norbert and Peter Weiss (2011), "Eine monumentale Dankesgabe: Trajans Neubau der Heiligen Straße von Milet nach Didyma," *Chiron* 41: 217–62.

Eisenstadt, Shmuel (1963), *The Political Systems of Empires*, New York: Free Press of Glencoe.

Eliav-Feldon, Miriam, Benjamin Isaac, and Joseph Ziegler, eds, (2009), *The Origins of Racism in the West*, Cambridge, Cambridge University Press.

Elsner, Jaś (1997), "The Origins of the Icon: Pilgrimage, Religion, and Visual Culture in the Roman East as 'Resistance' to the Centre," in Susan Alcock (ed.), *The Early Roman Empire in the East*, 178–99, Oxford: Oxbow.

Elsner, Jaś (2001), "Cultural Resistance and the Visual Image: The Case of Dura Europos," *Classical Philology* 96: 269–304.

Elton, Hugh (1996a), *Frontiers of the Roman Empire*. Bloomington, IN: Indiana University Press.

Elton, Hugh (1996b), *Warfare in Roman Europe: AD 350–425*, Oxford: Clarendon Press.

Erdkamp, Paul (2002a), "The Corn Supply of the Roman Armies during the Principate (27 BC–235 AD)," in Paul Erdkamp (ed.), *The Roman Army and the Economy*, 47–69, Amsterdam: J. C. Gieben.
Erdkamp, Paul (2002b), "'A Starving Mob has no Respect'–Urban Markets and Food Riots in the Roman World, 100 BC–400 AD," in Lukas de Blois and John Rich (eds), *The Transformation of Economic Life under the Roman Empire*, 93–115, Amsterdam: J. C. Gieben.
Erdkamp, Paul (2005), *The Grain Market in the Roman Empire: A Social, Political and Economic Study*, Cambridge: Cambridge University Press.
Erdkamp, Paul (ed.) (2007), *A Companion to the Roman Army*, Oxford and Malden, MA: Wiley-Blackwell.
Erskine, Andrew (2000), "Polybios and Barbarian Rome," *Mediterraneo Antico* 3.1: 165–82.
Eshleman, Kendra (2012), *The Social World of Intellectuals in the Roman Empire: Sophists, Philosophers and Christians*, Cambridge: Cambridge University Press.
Fagan, Garrett (2011), *The Lure of the Arena: Social Psychology and the Crowd at Roman Games*, Cambridge: Cambridge University Press.
Farney, Gary (2007), *Ethnic Identity and Aristocratic Competition in Republican Rome*, Cambridge: Cambridge University Press.
Feeney, Dennis (2007), *Caesar's Calendar: Ancient Time and the Beginnings of History*, Berkeley: University of California Press.
Feeney, Dennis (2016), *Beyond Greek: The Beginnings of Latin Literature*, Cambridge, MA: Harvard University Press.
Feldman, Marian (2005), "Mesopotamian Art," in Daniel Snell (ed.), *A Companion to the Ancient Near East*, 281–301, Oxford: Blackwell.
Feldman, Marian and Marlies Heinz, eds (2007), *Representations of Political Power: Case Histories from Times of Change and Dissolving Order in the Ancient Near East*, Winona Lake, IN: Eisenbrauns.
Fenoaltea, Stefano (1984), "Slavery and Supervision in Comparative Perspective: A Model," *Journal of Economic History* 44: 635–68.
Fentress, Elizabeth (2006), "Romanizing the Berbers," *Past & Present* 190: 3–33.
Ferguson, R. James (2016), "The Ancient Egyptian Concept of Maat: Reflections on Social Justice and Natural Order," *Center for East-West Cultural and Economic Studies Research Papers* 15. Bond University.
Ferrary, Jean-Louis (1988), *Philhellénisme et impérialisme. Aspects idéologiques de la conquête romaine du monde hellénistique*, Rome: École française de Rome.
Ferris, Iain (2009), *Hate and War: The Column of Marcus Aurelius*, Gloucestershire: Stroud.
Finer, Samuel (1997), *A History of Government from the Earliest Times, Volume 1: Ancient Monarchies and Empires*, Oxford: Oxford University Press.
Finley, Moses I. (1980), *Ancient Slavery and Modern Ideology*, New York: Viking.
Finley, Moses I. (1998), *Ancient Slavery and Modern Ideology*, expanded edition, Princeton: Princeton University Press.
Flaig, Egon (1992), *Den Kaiser herausfordern: die Usurpation im Römischen Reich*, Frankfurt am Main: Campus Verlag.
Floridi, Lucia (2015), "The Construction of a Homoerotic Discourse in the Epigrams of Ausonius," *Harvard Studies in Classical Philology* 108: 545–69.
Flower, Harriet (2010), *Roman Republics*, Princeton: Princeton University Press.
Formigé, Julius (1949), *Le Trophée des Alpes, La Turbie,* Paris: Centre national de la recherche scientifique.

Forni, Giovani (1953), *Il reclutamento delle legioni da Augusto a Diocleziano,* Rome: Bocca.
Foubert, Lien (2011), "The Impact of Women's Travels on Military Imagery in the Julio-Claudian Period," in Ted Kaizer and Olivier Hekster (eds), *Frontiers in the Roman World: Proceedings of the Ninth Workshop of the International Network Impact of Empire,* 349–61, Leiden: Brill.
Foubert, Lien (2013), "Female Travellers In Roman Britain: Vibia Pacata and Julia Lucilla," in Emily Hemelrijk and Greg Woolf (eds), *Women and the Roman City in the West,* 391–403, Leiden: Brill.
Foubert, Lien (2016), "Mobile Women in P.Oxy. and the Port Cities of Roman Egypt: Tracing Women's Travel Behaviour in Papyrological Sources," in de Ligt and Tacoma 2016: 285–304.
Foucault, Michel (1985), *The History of Sexuality,* volume 2: *The Use of Pleasure,* translated by Robert Hurley, New York: Random House.
Fowler, Robert, ed. (2004), *The Cambridge Companion to Homer,* Cambridge: Cambridge University Press.
Fraser, Peter (1972), *Ptolemaic Alexandria,* Oxford: Clarendon Press.
Frayne, Douglas (2008), *The Royal Inscriptions of Mesopotamia Volume 1: Presargonic Period (2700–2350 BC),* Toronto: University of Toronto Press.
Fuchs, Harald (1938), *Der geistige Widerstand gegen Rom in der antiken Welt,* Berlin: Walter de Gruyter.
Fuhrmann, Christopher (2012), *Policing the Roman Empire: Soldiers, Administration, and Public Order,* Oxford: Oxford University Press.
Futrell, Alison (2001), "Seeing Red: Spartacus as Domestic Economist," in Sandra Joshel, Margaret Malamud, and Donald McGuire (eds), *Imperial Projections: Ancient Rome in Modern Popular Culture,* 77–118, Baltimore: Johns Hopkins University Press.
Galinsky, K. (2012), *Augustus: Introduction to the Life of an Emperor,* Cambridge: Cambridge University Press.
Gallivan, Paul (1973), "Nero's Liberation of Greece," *Hermes* 101: 230–4.
Gambash, Gil (2015), *Rome and Provincial Resistance,* London and New York: Routledge.
Garfinkle, Steven (2013), "Ancient Near Eastern City-States," in Bang and Scheidel 2013: 94–119.
Gargola, Daniel (2017), *The Shape of the Roman Order: the Republic and its Spaces,* Chapel Hill: University of North Carolina Press.
Garnsey, Peter (1970), *Social Status and Legal Privilege in the Roman Empire,* Oxford: Clarendon Press.
Garnsey, Peter (1988), *Famine and Food Supply in the Graeco-Roman World: Responses to Risk and Crisis,* Cambridge: Cambridge University Press.
Garnsey, Peter (1996), *Ideas of Slavery from Aristotle to Augustine,* Cambridge: Cambridge University Press.
Garnsey, Peter (2004), "Roman Citizenship and Roman Law in the Later Empire," in Simon Swain and Mark Edwards (eds), *Approaching Late Antiquity: From Early to Later Empire,* 133–55, Oxford: Oxford University Press.
Gellner, Ernst (1983), *Nations and Nationalism,* Ithaca, NY: Cornell University Press.
Gibbon, Edward (1908), *The History of the decline and fall of the Roman empire,* 4th edition, London: Methuen.
Gibson, Roy and Ruth Morello (2011), *Pliny the Elder: Themes and Contexts,* Leiden: Brill.

Giddens, Anthony (1985), *The Nation-State and Violence*, Berkeley: University of California Press.
Giovannini, Adalberto (1985), "Le sel et la fortune de Rome," *Athenaeum* 73: 373–86.
Giovannini, Adalberto, ed. (1986), *Opposition et résistances à l'Empire d'Auguste à Trajan*, Geneva: Fondation Hardt.
Gleason, Maud (1995), *Making Men: Sophists and Self-Presentation in Ancient Rome*, Princeton: Princeton University Press.
Goldhill, Simon (1995), *Foucault's Virginity: Ancient Erotic Fiction and the History of Sexuality*, Cambridge: Cambridge University Press.
Goldstone, Jack and John Haldon (2009), "Ancient States, Empires, and Exploitation," in Morris and Scheidel 2009: 3–29.
Goldsworthy, Adrian (1996), *The Roman Army at War, 100 BC-AD 200*, Oxford: Clarendon Press.
Goldsworthy, Adrian (2016), *Pax Romana*. New Haven: Yale University Press.
Goldsworthy, Adrian and Ian Haynes, eds (1999), *The Roman Army as a Community*, Portsmouth, RI: Journal of Roman Archaeology Supplementary Series, no. 34.
Goodman, Martin (1987), *The Ruling Class of Judaea: The Origins of the Jewish Revolt Against Rome A.D. 66–70*, Cambridge: Cambridge University Press.
Goodman, Martin (1989), "Nerva, the fiscus Judaicus and Jewish identity," *Journal of Roman Studies* 79: 26–39.
Goodman, Martin (1991), "Opponents of Rome: Jews and Others," in Alexander Loveday (ed.), *Images of Empire*, 222–38, Sheffield: JSOT Press.
Goodman, Martin (2003), "Trajan and the Origins of the Bar Kochba War," in Peter Schäfer (ed.), *The Bar Kokhba War Reconsidered: New Perspectives on the Second Jewish Revolt against Rome*, 23–9, Tübingen: Mohr Siebeck.
Goodman, Martin (2014), "Enemies of Rome," in Peter Garnsey and Richard Saller (ed.), *The Roman Empire: Economy, Society and Culture*, 2nd edition, 53–67, London: Bloomsbury Academic.
Grandazzi, Alexandre (2008), *Alba Longa: histoire d'une légende: Recherches sur l'archéologie, la religion, les traditions de l'ancien Latium*, Rome: École françaises de Rome.
Grandazzi, Alexandre (2010), "Lavinium, Alba Longa, Rome: à quoi sert un paysage religieux?" *Revue de l'histoire des religions* 227: 573–90.
Green, Roger, ed. (1991), *The Works of Ausonius*, Oxford: Clarendon Press.
Grey, Campbell (2011), *Constructing Communities in the Late Roman Countryside*, Cambridge: Cambridge University Press.
Griffin, Miriam (1991), "Urbs Roma, Plebs, and Princeps," in Alexander Loveday (ed.), *Images of Empire*, 19–46, Sheffield: JSOT Press.
Grose-Hodge, H. (1944), *Roman Panorama: A Background for Today*, Cambridge: Cambridge University Press.
Grubbs, Judith Evans (2015), "Making the Private Public: Illegitimacy and Incest in Roman Law," in Clifford Ando and Jörg Rüpke (eds), *Public and Private in Ancient Mediterranean Law and Religion*, 115–42, Berlin: Walter de Gruyter.
Gruen, Erich (1969), *Roman Politics and the Criminal Courts, 149–78 B.C.*, Cambridge, MA: Harvard University Press.
Gruen, Erich (1984), *The Hellenistic World and the Coming of Rome*, 2 volumes, Berkeley: University of California Press.
Gruen, Erich (1990), *Studies in Greek Culture and Roman Policy*, Leiden: Brill.
Gruen, Erich (1992), *Culture and National Identity in Republican Rome*, Ithaca, NY: Cornell University Press.

Gruen, Erich (1996), "The Expansion of the Empire Under Augustus," in *Cambridge Ancient History* 10, 147–97, Cambridge: Cambridge Ancient History.
Gruenewald, Thomas (2004), *Bandits in the Roman Empire: Myth and Reality*, London: Routledge.
Hackett, John, ed. (1989), *Warfare in the Ancient World*, New York: Facts on File.
Haensch, Rudolph (2012), "The Roman army in Egypt," in Christina Riggs (ed.), *The Oxford Handbook of Roman Egypt*, 68–82, Oxford: Oxford University Press.
Haldon, John (2013), "The Byzantine Successor State," in Bang and Scheidel 2013: 475–97.
Hall, Edith (1989), *Inventing the Barbarian: Greek Self-Definition through Tragedy*, Oxford: Clarendon Press.
Hall, Edith (1992), "When is a myth not a myth? Bernal's 'Ancient Model'," *Arethusa* 25: 181–201.
Hall, Jonathan (1997), *Ethnic Identity in Greek Antiquity*, Cambridge: Cambridge University Press.
Hall, Jonathan (2002), *Hellenicity: Between Ethnicity and Culture*, Chicago: University of Chicago Press.
Hallett, Judith (1989), "Female Homoeroticism and the Denial of Roman Reality in Latin Literature," *Yale Journal of Criticism* 3: 209–27.
Halperin, David M., John J. Winkler and Froma I. Zeitlin eds (1990), *Before Sexuality: The Construction of Erotic Experience in the Ancient Greek World*, 479–94, Princeton: Princeton University Press.
Hammond, N. G. L. (1989), *The Macedonian State: Origins, Institutions, and History*, Oxford: Oxford University Press.
Hansen, Mogens (1988), *Three Studies in Athenian Demography*, Copenhagen: Danish Royal Academy of the Sciences.
Hansen, Mogens (1999), *The Athenian Democracy in the Age of Demosthenes*, 2nd edition, Bristol: Bristol Classical Press.
Hansen, Mogens (2006), *Polis: An Introduction to the Ancient Greek City-State*, Oxford: Oxford University Press.
Hansen, Mogens (2013), "Greek City-States," in Bang and Scheidel 2013: 259–78.
Hansen, Mogens, ed. (2000), *A Comparative Study of Thirty City-State Cultures: An Investigation Conducted by the Copenhagen Polis Center*, Copenhagen: Det Kongelige Danske Videnskabernes Selskab.
Hansen, Mogens and Thomas Nielsen, eds (2004), *An Inventory of Archaic and Classical Poleis*, Oxford: Oxford University Press.
Hardwick, Lorna (2003), *Reception Studies*, Oxford: Oxford University Press.
Harland, Philip (2003), *Associations, Synagogues, and Congregations: Claiming a Place in Ancient Mediterranean Society*, Minneapolis: Fortress Press.
Harland, Philip (2009), *Dynamics of Identity in the World of the Early Christians: Associations, Judeans, and Cultural Minorities*, London: T & T Clark.
Harland, Philip (2011), *Travel and Religion in Antiquity*, Waterloo: Wilfrid Laurier University Press.
Harper, Kyle (2010), "Slave Prices in Late Antiquity (and in the Very Long Term)," *Historia* 59: 206–38.
Harper, Kyle (2011), *Slavery in the Late Roman World, AD 275–425*, Cambridge: Cambridge University Press.
Harper, Kyle (2013), *From Shame to Sin: The Christian Transformation of Sexual Morality in Late Antiquity*, Cambridge, MA: Harvard University Press.

Harries, Jill (1999), *Law and Empire in Late Antiquity*, Cambridge: Cambridge University Press.
Harris, William (1979), *War and Imperialism in Republican Rome 327–70 BC*, Oxford: Oxford University Press.
Harris, William (1989), "Roman Expansion in the West," in *Cambridge Ancient History* 8, 107–62, Cambridge: Cambridge University Press.
Harris, William (1999), "Demography, geography and the sources of Roman slaves," *Journal of Roman Studies* 89: 62–75.
Harris, William (2006), "A Revisionist View of Roman Money," *Journal of Roman Studies* 96: 1–24.
Harris, William (2007), "The Late Republic," in Scheidel *et al.* 2007: 511–42.
Harris, William (2011), "Trade (70–192 AD)," in William Harris (ed.), *Rome's Imperial Economy*, 155–87, Oxford: Oxford University Press.
Harrison, Thomas (2013), "Exploring Virgin Fields: Henry and George Rawlinson on Ancient and Modern Orient," in Eran Almagor and Joseph Skinner (eds), *Ancient Ethnography: New Approaches*, 223–55, London: Bloomsbury Academic.
Hartmann, Udo (2001), *Das palmyrenische Teilreich*, Stuttgart: Steiner Verlag.
Hatzopoulos, Miltiades (1996), *Macedonian Institutions under the Kings*, 2 volumes, Athens: Research Centre for Greek and Roman Antiquity.
Havelock, Christine Mitchell (1995), *The Aphrodite of Knidos and Her Successors: A Historical Review of the Female Nude in Greek Art*, Ann Arbor: University of Michigan Press.
Haynes, Ian (2013), *Blood of the Provinces: The Roman Auxilia and the Making of Roman Provincial Society from Augustus to the Severans*, Oxford: Oxford University Press.
Heath, Malcolm (2008), "Aristotle on Natural Slavery," *Phronesis* 53: 243–70.
Heather, Peter (1991), *Goths and Romans: 332–489*, Oxford: Oxford University Press.
Heather, Peter (2010), *The Fall of the Roman Empire*, New York, MacMillan.
Heffernan, Thomas (2012), *The Passion of Perpetua and Felicity*, Oxford: Oxford University Press.
Hemelrijk, Emily (2015), *Hidden Lives, Public Personae: Women and Civic Life in the Roman West*, Oxford: Oxford University Press.
Hemelrijk, Emily, and Greg Woolf, eds (2013), *Women and the Roman City in the Latin West*, Leiden: Brill.
Henderson, Jeffrey (2007), "Drama and Democracy," in Loren J. Samons II (ed.), *The Cambridge Companion to the Age of Pericles*, 179–95, Cambridge: Cambridge University Press.
Hengel, Martin (1974), *Judaism and Hellenism: Studies in Their Encounter in Palestine During the Early Hellenistic Period*, translated by John Bowden, Philadelphia: Fortress Press.
Henig, Martin (1997), "The Lullingstone Mosaic: Art, Religion and Letters in a Fourth-Century Villa," *Mosaic* 24: 4–7.
Hicks, John (1969), *A Theory of Economic History*, Oxford: Oxford University Press.
Hingley, Richard (2000), *Roman Officers and English Gentlemen: The Imperial Origins of Roman Archaeology*, London and New York: Routledge.
Hirth, Friedrich (1975), *China and the Roman Orient: Researches into Their Ancient and Mediaeval Relations as Represented in Old Chinese Records*, Chicago: Ares.
Hölbl, Günther (2001), *A History of the Ptolemaic Empire*, London and New York: Routledge.

Hölkeskamp, Karl-Joachim (2010), *Reconstructing the Roman Republic: An Ancient Political Culture and Modern Research*, Princeton: Princeton University Press.
Holleran, Claire (2012), *Shopping in Ancient Rome: The Retail Trade in the Late Republic and Early Empire*, Oxford: Oxford University Press.
Holleran, Claire (2017), "Getting a Job: Finding Work in the City of Rome,' in Verboven and Laes 2017: 87–103.
Holliday, Peter (1997), "Roman Triumphal Painting: Its Function, Development, and Reception," *Art Bulletin* 79: 130–47.
Holloway, Ross (1991), *The Archaeology of Early Rome and Latium*, London and New York: Routledge.
Hölscher, Tonio (2006), "The Transformation of Victory into Power: From Event to Structure" in Sheila Dillon and Katherine Welch (eds), *Representations of War in Ancient Rome*, 27–48, Cambridge: Cambridge University Press.
Hope, Valerie (2000), "Status and Identity in the Roman World," in Janet Huskinson (ed.), *Experiencing Rome: Culture, Identity and Power in the Roman Empire*, 125–52, New York: Routledge.
Hope, Valerie (2003), "Trophies and Tombstones: Commemorating the Roman Soldier," *World Archaeology* 35: 79–97.
Hopkins, J.N. (2012a) 'The Capitoline Temple and the effects of monumentality on Roman temple design', in Thomas, M., and Meyers, G., (eds) *Monumentality in Etruscan and Early Roman architecture: ideology and innovation*, Austin, 111–27.
Hopkins, J.N. (2012b), 'The sacred sewer: tradition and religion in Rome's Cloaca Maxima', in Bradley, Mark (ed), *Pollution and propriety: dirt, disease and hygiene in Rome from antiquity to modernity*, Cambridge, 81–102.
Hopkins, John (2016), *The Genesis of Roman Architecture*, New Haven: Yale University Press.
Hopkins, Keith (1978), *Conquerors and Slaves*, Cambridge: Cambridge University Press.
Hopkins, Keith (1980), "Taxes and Trade in the Roman Empire (200 B.C.–A.D. 400)," *Journal of Roman Studies* 70: 101–25.
Horbury, William (2014), *Jewish War under Trajan and Hadrian*, Cambridge: Cambridge University Press.
Horden, Peregrine, and Nicholas Purcell (2000), *The Corrupting Sea: A Study of Mediterranean History*, Oxford and Malden, MA: Blackwell.
Horsley, Richard (1981), "Ancient Jewish Banditry and the Revolt against Rome, A.D. 66–70," *The Catholic Biblical Quarterly* 43: 409–32.
Houlbrook, Matt (2001), "Toward a Historical Geography of Sexuality," *Journal of Urban History* 27: 497–504.
Howe, Stephen (2002), *Empire: A Very Short Introduction*, Oxford: Oxford University Press.
Howe, Timothy and Lee Brice, eds (2016), *Brill's Companion to Insurgency and Terrorism in the Ancient Mediterranean*. Leiden: Brill.
Hoyos, Dexter, ed. (2011), *A Companion to the Punic Wars*, Oxford and Malden, MA: Wiley-Blackwell.
Humm, Michel (1996), "Appius Claudius Caecus et la construction de la via Appia," *Mélanges de l'école française de Rome* 108: 693–746.
Hunnings, Leanne (2007), "Spartacus: Pole, Proletariat or Christ?" in Christopher Stray (ed.), *Remaking the Classics: Literature, Genre and Media in Britain 1800–2000*, 1–19, London: Duckworth.
Hunt, Ailsa (2011), "Priapus as a Wooden God: Confronting Manufacture and Destruction," *Cambridge Classical Journal* 57: 29–54.

Hunt, Arthur Surridge, and C. C. Edgar (2014), *Select Papyri*, Cambridge, MA: Harvard University Press.
Isaac, Benjamin (1990), *The Limits of Empire: The Roman Army in the East*, Oxford: Oxford University Press.
Isaac, Benjamin (2004), *The Invention of Racism in Classical Antiquity*, Princeton, Princeton University Press.
James, George G. M. (1954), *Stolen Legacy: Greek Philosophy is Stolen Egyptian Philosophy*, New York: Philosophical Library.
James, Simon (1999), "The Community of the Soldiers: A Major Identity and Centre of Power in the Roman Empire," in Patricia Baker, Sophia Jundi, and Robert Witcher (eds), *TRAC 98: Proceedings of the Eighth Annual Theoretical Roman Archaeology Conference, Leicester 1998*, 14–25, Oxford, Oxbow.
Johnston, Andrew (2017), *The Sons of Remus: Identity in Roman Gaul and Spain*, Cambridge, MA: Harvard University Press.
Jones, A. H. M. (1964), *The Later Roman Empire, 284–602: A Social, Economic, and Administrative Survey*, 3 volumes, Oxford: Oxford University Press.
Jones, Christopher (1996), "The Panhellenion," *Chiron* 26: 29–56.
Jones, Christopher (1999), *Kinship Diplomacy in the Ancient World*, Cambridge MA: Harvard University Press.
Jones, David (2006), *The Bankers of Puteoli: Finance, Trade and Industry in the Roman World*, Gloustershire: Tempus.
Jones-Lewis, Molly Ayn (2012), "Poison: Nature's Argument for the Roman Empire," *Classical World* 106: 51–74.
Jördens, Andrea (2009), *Statthalterliche Verwaltung in der römischen Kaiserzeit: Studien zum praefectus Aegypti*, Stuttgart: Steiner Verlag.
Joshel, Sandra (1992), *Work, Identity and Legal Status at Rome: A Study of the Occupational Inscriptions*, Norman, OK: University of Oklahoma Press.
Kähler, Heinz (1965), *Der Fries vom Reiterdenkmal des Aemilius Paullus in Delphi*, Berlin: Mann.
Kallet-Marx, Robert (1995), *Hegemony to Empire: The Development of Roman Imperium in the East from 148 to 62 B.C.*, Berkeley: University of California Press.
Keaveney, Arthur (1987), *Rome and the Unification of Italy*, London: Croon Helm.
Keith, Alison and Stephen Rupp (2007), "After Ovid: Classical, Medieval, and Early Modern Receptions of Metamorphoses," in Alison Keith and Stephen Rupp (eds), *Metamorphosis: The Changing Face of Ovid in Medieval and Early Modern Europe*, 15–32, Toronto: Centre for Reformation and Renaissance Studies.
Kelly, Benjamin (2011), *Petitions, Litigation, and Social Control in Roman Egypt*, Oxford: Oxford University Press.
Kelly, Christopher (2004), *Ruling the Later Roman Empire*, Cambridge, MA: Harvard University Press.
Kelly, Christopher (2009), *End of Empire: Attila the Hun and the Fall of Rome*, New York: W. W. Norton.
Kemp, Barry (2006), *Ancient Egypt: Anatomy of a Civilization*, 2nd edition, London and New York: Routledge.
Keppie, Lawrence (1996), "The army and the navy," in *Cambridge Ancient History* 10, 371–96, Cambridge: Cambridge University Press.
Kim, Hyun Jin (2013), *The Huns, Rome and the Birth of Europe*, Cambridge: Cambridge University Press.
King, Anthony (1999), "Diet in the Roman World: A Regional Inter-site Comparison of the Mammal Bones," *Journal of Roman Archaeology* 12: 168–202.

Kleijwegt, Marc (2012), "Deciphering Freedwomen in the Roman Empire," in Ramsby and Bell 2012: 110–29.
Kleiner, Diana (1983), *The Monument of Philopappos in Athens*, Rome: G. Bretschneider.
Klockars, Leena (2013), "On the Essence of Sexuality," *The Scandinavian Psychoanalytic Review*, 36: 97–103.
Kloppenborg, John and Stephen Wilson, eds (1996), *Voluntary Associations in the Graeco-Roman World*, London and New York: Routledge.
Koortbojian, Michael (2013), *The Divinization of Caesar and Augustus: Precedents, Consequences, Implications*, Cambridge: Cambridge University Press.
Kosmin, Paul (2014), *The Land of the Elephant Kings: Space, Territory, and Ideology in the Seleucid Empire*, Cambridge, MA: Harvard University Press.
Kousser, Rachel (2007), "Mythological Group Portraits in Antonine Rome: The Performance of Myth," *American Journal of Archaeology* 111: 673–91.
Kovács, Péter (2009), *Marcus Aurelius' Rain Miracle and the Marcomannic Wars*, Leiden: Brill.
Krebs, Christopher (2011), "Borealism: Caesar, Seneca, Tacitus and the Roman Discourse about the Germanic North," in Erich Gruen (ed.), *Cultural Identity in the Ancient Mediterranean*, 212–31, Malibu, CA: Getty Research Institute Publications.
Kremer, David (2007), *Ius latinum: le concept de droit latin sous la République et l'Empire*, Paris: de Boccard.
Kuefler, Mathew (2001), *The Manly Eunuch: Masculinity, Gender Ambiguity, and Christian Ideology in Late Antiquity*, Chicago: University of Chicago Press.
Kuhrt, Amélie (1983), "The Cyrus Cylinder and Achaemenid Imperial Policy," *Journal for the Study of the Old Testament* 25: 83–97.
Kuhrt, Amélie (2002), *"Greeks" and "Greece" in Mesopotamian and Persian Perspectives*, Oxford: Leopard's Head Press.
Kuhrt, Amélie (2007a), *The Persian Empire: A Corpus of Sources from the Achaemenid Period*, 2 volumes, London: Routledge.
Kuhrt, Amélie (2007b), "Cyrus the Great of Persia: Images and Realities," in Marian Feldman and Marlies Heinz (eds), *Representations of Political Power: Case Histories from Times of Change and Dissolving Order in the Ancient Near East*, 169–91, Winona Lake, IN: Eisenbrauns.
Kulikowski, Michael (2000), "Barbarians in Gaul, Usurpers in Britain," *Britannia* 31: 325–45.
Kurke, Leslie (1992), "The Politics of *habrosyne* in Archaic Greece," *Classical Antiquity* 11: 91–120.
Laehn, Thomas (2013), *Pliny's Defense of Empire*, London and New York: Routledge.
Laird, A. G. (1921), "The Persian Army and Tribute Lists in Herodotus," *Classical Philology* 16: 305–26.
Lange, Carl and Frederik Vervaet, eds (2014), *The Roman Republican Triumph: Beyond the Spectacle*, Rome: Quasar.
Langerwerf, Lydia (2011), "Universal Slave Revolts: C.L.R. James's use of Classical literature in *Black Jacobins*," in Edith Hall, Richard Alston, and Justine McConnell (eds), *Ancient Slavery and Abolitions*, 353–84, Oxford: Oxford University Press.
Lapatin, Kenneth (2007), "Art and Architecture," in Loren J. Samons II (ed.), *The Cambridge Companion to the Age of Pericles*, 125–52, Cambridge: Cambridge University Press.
Lape, Susan (2010), *Race and Citizen Identity in the Classical Athenian Democracy*, Cambridge: Cambridge University Press.

Lavan, Myles (2017a), "Writing Revolt in the Early Roman Empire," in Justine Firnhaber-Baker and Dirk Schoenaers (eds), *The Routledge History Handbook of Medieval Revolt*, 19–38, London and New York: Routledge.

Lavan, Myles (2017b), "Peace and Empire: *Pacare, pacatus,* and the Language of Roman Imperialism," in Eoghan Moloney and Michael Williams (eds), *Peace and Reconciliation in the Classical World*, 102–14, London and New York: Routledge.

Lavan, Miles, Richard Payne, and John Weisweiler, eds (2016), *Cosmopolitanism and Empire: Universal Rulers, Local Elites, and Cultural Integration in the Ancient Near East and Mediterranean*, Oxford: Oxford University Press.

Leach, Stephany, Hella Eckardt, Carolyn Chenery, Gundula Müldner, and Mary E. Lewis (2010), "A Lady of York: Migration, Ethnicity and Identity in Roman Britain," *Antiquity* 84: 131–145.

Lee, A. (1993), *Information and Frontiers: Roman Foreign Relations in Late Antiquity*, Cambridge: Cambridge University Press.

Lefkowitz, Mary (1996), *Not Out of Africa: How Afrocentrism Became an Excuse to Teach Myth as History*, New York: Basic Books.

Lendon, J. E. (1997), *Empire of Honour: the Art of Government in the Roman World*, Oxford: Oxford University Press.

Lendon, J. E. (2004), *Soldiers and Ghosts,* New Haven: Yale University Press.

Lenski, Noel (1999), "Assimilation and Revolt in the Territory of Isauria, from the 1st Century BC to the 6th Century AD," *Journal of the Economic and Social History of the Orient* 42: 413–65.

Lenski, Noel (2003), *Failure of Empire: Valens and the Roman State in the Fourth Century AD*, Berkeley: University of California Press.

Lenski, Noel, ed. (2012), *The Cambridge Companion to the Age of Constantine*, Cambridge: Cambridge University Press.

Leppard, Frank and Sheppard Frere (2017), *Trajan's Column,* Oxford: Fonthill Media.

Leveau, Philippe (1978), "La situation coloniale de l'Afrique romaine," *Annales. Économies, Sociétés, Civilisations* 33: 89–92.

Leveau, Philippe (1993), "Mentalité économique et grand travaux: le drainage du lac Fucin. Aux originesd'un modèle," *Annales. Économies, Sociétés, Civilisations* 48: 3–16.

Levine, Philippa (2004), "Sexuality, Gender, and Empire," in Philippa Levine (ed.), *Gender and Empire*, 134–55, Oxford: Oxford University Press.

Lilja, Saara (1983), *Homosexuality in Republican and Augustan Rome*, Helsinki: Societas Scientiarum Fennica.

Lindsay, Hugh (1992), "Augustus and Eurycles," *Rheinisches Museum für Philologie* 135: 290–7.

Lintott, Andrew (1993), *Imperium Romanum: Politics and Administration*, London and New York: Routledge.

Lis, Catharina and Hugo Soly (2012), *Worthy Efforts: Attitudes to Work and Workers in Pre-industrial Europe*, Leiden: Brill.

Lis, Catharina and Hugo Soly (2017), "Work, Identity and Self-Representation in the Roman Empire and the West-European Middle Ages: Different Interplays between the Social and the Cultural," in Verboven and Laes 2017: 262–89.

Lively, Genevieve (2011), *Ovid's Metamorphoses: A Reader's Guide*, London: Continuum.

Liverani, Mario (2014), *The Ancient Near East: History, Society and Economy*, London and New York: Routledge.

Lo Cascio, Elio (2007), "La vita economica e sociale delle città romane nella testimonianza del *Satyricon*," in Luigi Castagna and Eckard Lefèvre (eds), *Studien zu Petron und seiner Rezeption–Studi su Petronio e sulla sua fortuna*, 3–14, Berlin: Walter de Gruyter.

Lo Cascio, Elio (2009), *Crescita e declino. Studi di storia dell'economia romana*, Roma: L'Erma di Bretschneider.

Lo Cascio, Elio, and Laurens Tacoma, eds (2017), *The Impact of Mobility and Migration in the Roman Empire, Proceedings of the Twelfth Workshop of the International Network Impact of Empire*, Leiden: Brill.

Luttwak, Edward (1976), *The Grand Strategy of the Roman Empire: From the First Century CE to the Third*, Baltimore: Johns Hopkins Press.

Ma, John (1999), *Antiochos III and the Cities of Western Asia Minor*, Oxford: Oxford University Press.

Ma, John (2013), "Hellenistic Empires," in Bang and Scheidel 2013: 324–57.

Ma, John, Nikolaos Papazarkadas, and Robert Parker, eds (2012), *Interpreting the Athenian Empire*, Bristol: Bristol Classical Press.

MacGeorge, Penny (2002), *Late Roman Warlords*, Oxford: Oxford University Press.

Mackil, Emily (2013), *Creating a Common Polity: Religion, Economy, and Politics in the Making of the Greek Koinon*, Berkeley: University of California Press.

MacMullen, Ramsay (1966), *Enemies of the Roman Order: Treason, Unrest, and Alienation in the Empire*, Cambridge, MA: Harvard University Press.

MacMullen, Ramsay (1970), "Market-Days in the Roman Empire," *Phoenix* 24: 333–41.

MacMullen, Ramsay (1984), "The Legion as Society," *Historia* 33: 440–56.

MacMullen, Ramsay (1988), *Corruption and the Decline of Rome*, New Haven: Yale University Press.

MacMullen, Ramsay (1990), "How to Revolt in the Roman Empire," in *Changes in the Roman Empire Essays in the Ordinary*, 198–204, Princeton: Princeton University Press.

MacMullen, Ramsay (2000), *Romanization in the Time of Augustus*, New Haven: Yale University Press.

Maehler, Herwig (2003), "Alessandria, il Museo, e la questione dell'identità culturale," *Atti della Accademia Nazionale dei Lincei, Rendiconti*, ser. 9ª.14.1: 99–120.

Magalhães de Oliveira, Julio Caesar (2012), *Potestas populi: participation populaire et action collective dans les villes de l'Afrique romaine tardive (vers 300–430 apr. J.-C.)*, Turnhout: Brepols.

Mahmood, Saba (2005), *Politics of Piety. The Islamic Revival and the Feminist Subject*, Princeton: Princeton University Press.

Malkin, Irad (2011), *A Small Greek World: Networks in the Ancient Mediterranean*, Oxford: Oxford University Press.

Manganaro, Giacomo (1990), "Un Philippeion di oro di Euno-Antioco in Sicilia," *Museum Helveticum* 47:181–3.

Mann, Michael (1986–2012), *The Sources of Social Power*, 3 volumes, Cambridge: Cambridge University Press.

Manning, Joseph (2007), "Hellenistic Egypt," in Scheidel *et al.* 2007: 434–59.

Manning, Joseph (2010), *The Last Pharaohs: Egypt under the Ptolemies, 305–30 BC*, Princeton: Princeton University Press.

Manning, Joseph (2013), "Egypt," in Bang and Scheidel 2013: 61–93.

Marchand, Suzanne and Anthony Grafton (1997), "Martin Bernal and His Critics," *Arion* 5:1–35.

Marcone, Arnaldo (2000), "Tra archeologia e storia economica: il mausoleo dei *Secundini* a Igel," *Athenaeum* 84: 485–98.
Marcone, Arnaldo, ed. (2016), *Storia del lavoro in Italia. I. L'Italia romana. Liberi, semiliberi e schiavi in una società premoderna*, Roma: Castelvecchi.
Marksteiner, Thomas and Michael Wörrle (2002), "Ein Altar für Kaiser Claudius auf dem Bonda tepesi zwischen Myra und Limyra," *Chiron* 32: 545–69.
Marzano, Annalisa (2011), "Agricultural Production in the Hinterland of Rome: Wine and Olive Oil," in Bowman and Wilson 2011: 85–106.
Master, Jonathan (2016), *Provincial Soldiers and Imperial Instability in the Histories of Tacitus*, Ann Arbor: University of Michigan Press.
Mattern, Susan (1999), *Rome and the Enemy: Imperial Strategy in the Principate*, Berkeley: University of California Press.
Mattingly, David (1994), *Tripolitana*. Ann Arbor: Michigan University Press.
Mattingly, David (2006), *An Imperial Possession. Britain in the Roman Empire*, London: Allen Lane.
Mattingly, David (2011), *Imperialism, Power and Identity: Experiencing the Roman Empire*, Princeton: Princeton University Press.
McCall, Jeremiah (2002), *The Cavalry of the Roman Republic: Cavalry Combat and Elite Reputation in the Middle and Late Republic*, New York: Routledge.
McCoskey, Denise (2012), *Race: Antiquity and its Legacy*, London: I. B. Tauris.
McEvoy, Meaghan (2014), *Child Emperor Rule in the Late Roman West, AD 367–455*, Oxford: Oxford University Press.
McGinn, Thomas (1998), *Prostitution, Sexuality and the Law in Ancient Rome*. Oxford: Oxford University Press.
McInerney, Jeremy and Ineke Sluiter, eds (2016), *Valuing Landscape in Classical Antiquity: Natural Environment and Cultural Imagination*, Leiden: Brill.
McLaren, James and Martin Goodman (2016), "The Importance of Perspective. The Jewish-Roman Conflict of 66–70 CE as a Revolution," in John Collins and Joseph Manning (eds), *Revolt and Resistance in the Ancient Classical World and the Near East*, 205–18, Leiden: Brill.
Mildenberg, Leo (1984), *The Coinage of the Bar Kokhba War*, Salzburg: Sauerländer.
Millar, Fergus (1977), *The Emperor in the Roman World*, Ithaca, NY: Cornell University Press.
Millar, Fergus (1981), "The World of The Golden Ass," *Journal of Roman Studies* 71: 63–75.
Millar, Fergus (1987), "Polybius between Greece and Rome," in John Koumoulides (ed.), *Greek Connections: Essays on Culture and Diplomacy*, 1–18, Notre Dame: University of Notre Dame Press.
Millar, Fergus (2002), *Rome, The Greek World, and The East, Volume 1: The Roman Republic and the Augustan Revolution*, Chapel Hill: University of North Carolina Press.
Miller, Margaret (1997), *Athens and Persia in the Fifth Century BC: A Study in Cultural Receptivity*, Cambridge: Cambridge University Press.
Miller, Patricia Cox (2003), "Is there a Harlot in this Text? Hagiography and the Grotesque," *Journal of Medieval and Early Modern Studies* 33: 419–35.
Millett, Martin (1990), *The Archaeology of Roman Britain*, Cambridge: Cambridge University Press.
Millett, Martin and Rebecca Gowland (2015), "Infant and Child Burial Rites in Roman Britain: A Study from East Yorkshire," *Britannia* 46: 171–89.

Mitchell, Stephen (2000), "Ethnicity, Acculturation and Empire in Roman and Late Roman Asia Minor," in Stephen Mitchell and Geoffrey Greatrex (eds), *Ethnicity and Culture in Late Antiquity*, 117–50, London: Duckworth.

Mitthof, Fritz (2001), *Annona Militaris. Die Heersversorgung im spätantiken Ägypten*, volume 1, Florence: Edizione Gonnelli.

Moatti, Claudia (2000), "Le contrôle de la mobilité des personnes dans l'Empire romain," *Mélanges de l'École française de Rome: Antiquité* 112: 925–58.

Moatti, Claudia (2010), "Mobility and Identity: The Cosmopolitanization of the Identities in the Roman Empire," in Claudia Rapp (ed.), *City-Empire-Christendom: Contexts of Power and Identity from Antiquity to the Middle Ages*, 130–52, Cambridge: Cambridge University Press.

Moatti, Claudia, ed. (2004), *La mobilité des personnes en Méditerranée de l'antiquité à l'époque moderne. Procédures de contrôle et documents d'identification*. Rome: École française de Rome.

Moatti, Claudia, and Wolfgang Kaiser, eds (2007), *Gens de passage en Méditerranée de l'Antiquité à l'époque moderne. Procédures de contrôle et identification*, Paris: Maisonneuve & Larose.

Moatti, Claudia, Wolfgang Kaiser, and Christophe Pébarthe, eds (2009), *Le monde de l'itinérance en Méditerranée de l'antiquité à l'époque moderne. Procédures de contrôle et identification*, Paris: Boccard.

Montiglio, Silvia (2005), *Wandering in Ancient Greek Culture*, Chicago: University of Chicago Press.

Morales, Helen (2007), *Classical Mythology: A Very Short Introduction*, Oxford: Oxford University Press.

Morales, Helen (2008), "The History of Sexuality," in Tim Whitmarsh (ed.), *The Cambridge Companion to the Greek and Roman Novel*, 39–55, Cambridge: Cambridge University Press.

Morales, Helen (2011), "Fantasising Phryne: The Psychology and Ethics of *Ekphrasis*," *Cambridge Classical Journal* 57: 71–104.

Morel, Jean-Paul (2007), "Early Rome and Italy," in Scheidel *et al.* 2007: 487–510.

Morley, Neville (1996), *Metropolis and Hinterland: The City of Rome and the Italian Economy, 200 BC-AD 200*, Cambridge: Cambridge University Press.

Morley, Neville (2007a), "The Early Empire: Distribution," in Scheidel *et al.* 2007: 570–91.

Morley, Neville (2007b), *Trade in Classical Antiquity*, Cambridge: Cambridge University Press.

Morley, Neville (2011), "Slavery under the Principate," in Bradley and Cartledge 2011: 265–86.

Morris, Ian (2009), "The Greater Athenian State (478–404 BC)," in Ian Morris and Walter Scheidel (eds), *The Dynamics of Ancient Empires*, 99–177, Oxford: Oxford University Press.

Morris, Ian and Walter Scheidel, eds (2009), *The Dynamics of Ancient Empires. State Power from Assyria to Byzantium*, Oxford: Oxford University Press.

Morton, Peter (2013), "Eunus: The Cowardly King," *Classical Quarterly* 63: 237–52.

Motyl, Alexander (2001), *Imperial Ends: The Decay, Collapse, and Revival of Empires*, New York: Columbia University Press.

Mouritsen, Henrik (1998), *Italian Unification: A Study in Ancient and Modern Historiography*, London: Institute of Classical Studies.

Mouritsen, Henrik (2005), "Freedmen and Decurions: Epitaphs and Social History in Imperial Italy," *Journal of Roman Studies* 95: 38–63.
Mouritsen, Henrik (2007), "The *civitas sine suffragio*: Ancient Concepts and Modern Ideology," *Historia* 56: 141–58.
Mouritsen, Henrik (2011), *The Freedman in the Roman World*, Cambridge: Cambridge University Press.
Mouritsen, Henrik (2017), *Politics in the Roman Republic*, Cambridge: Cambridge University Press.
Mullen, Alex (2012), "Introduction: Multiple Languages, Multiple Identities," in Alex Mullen and Patrick James (eds), *Multilingualism in the Graeco-Roman Worlds*, 1–35, Cambridge: Cambridge University Press.
Münkler, Herfried (2007), *Empires: The Logic of World Domination from Ancient Rome to the United States*, Cambridge: Polity Press.
Musurillo, Herbert (1961), *Acta Alexandrinorum*, Lipsiae: Teubner.
Mutschler, Fritz-Heiner, and Achim Mittag, eds (2009), *Conceiving the Empire: China and Rome Compared*, Oxford: Oxford University Press.
Ñaco del Hoyo, Toni, Roger Riera, and Daniel Gómez-Castro, eds (2016), *Ancient Disasters and Crisis Management in Classical Antiquity*, Gdansk: Akanthina.
Nagy, Gregory (1979), *The Best of the Achaeans: Concepts of the Hero in Archaic Greek Poetry*, Baltimore: Johns Hopkins University Press.
Neal, David and Stephen Cosh (2002–10), *Roman Mosaics of Britain*, London: Society of Antiquaries.
Nesselhauf, Herbert and Hans Lieb (1959), "Dritter Nachtrag zu CIL XIII, Inschriften aus den germanischen Provinzen une dem Trevererebiet," *Bericht der römisch-germanischen Kommission* 40: 120–229.
Nicolet, Claude (1976), *Tributum: Recherches sur la fiscalité directe sous la République romaine*, Bonn: Rudolf Habelt Verlag.
Nicolet, Claude (2000), *Censeurs et publicains. Économie et fiscalité dans la Rome antique*, Paris: Fayard.
Nippel, Wilfried (2002), "The Construction of the 'Other'," in Thomas Harrison (ed.), *Greeks And Barbarians*, 278–310, Edinburgh: Edinburgh University Press.
Noreña, Carlos (2003), "Medium and Message in Vespasian's Templum Pacis," *Memoirs of the American Academy in Rome*, 48: 25–43.
Noreña, Carlos (2007), "Hadrian's Chastity," *Phoenix* 61: 296–317.
Noreña, Carlos (2009), "The Ethics of Autocracy in the Roman World," in Ryan Balot (ed.), *A Companion to Greek and Roman Political Thought*, 266–79, Oxford and Malden, MA: Wiley-Blackwell.
Noreña, Carlos (2011), *Imperial Ideals in the Roman West: Representation, Circulation, Power*, Cambridge: Cambridge University Press.
Noreña, Carlos (forthcoming a), "Private Associations and Urban Experience in the Han and Roman Empires," in Beck and Vankeerberghen forthcoming.
Noreña, Carlos (forthcoming b), "Monarchy, Benefaction, and Honorific Practice in the Roman Imperial Greek *polis*," in Marc Domingo Gygax and Andries Zuiderhoek (eds), *Benefactors and the Polis: Origins and Development of the Public Gift in Greek Cities from the Homeric World to Late Antiquity*, Cambridge: Cambridge University Press.
North, Douglass, John J. Wallis, and Barry Weingast, eds (2009), *Violence and Social Orders: A Conceptual Framework for Interpreting Recorded Human History*, Cambridge: Cambridge University Press.

Northwood, Simon (2008), "Census and Tributum," in Luuk de Ligt and Simon Northwood (eds), *People, Land, and Politics: Demographic Developments and the Transformation of Roman Italy 300 BC–AD 14*, 257–70, Leiden: Brill.

Nye, Jr., Joseph (2005), *Soft Power: The Means to Success in World Politics*, New York: Public Affairs.

Nye, Robert A. (1999), *Sexuality*, Oxford: Oxford University Press.

O'Connor, David and Eric Cline (2012), "The Sea Peoples," in Eric Cline and David O'Connor (eds), *Ramesses III: The Life and Times of Egypt's Last Hero*, 180–208, Ann Arbor: University of Michigan Press.

Ober, Josiah (1989), *Mass and Elite in Classical Athens: Rhetoric, Ideology, and the Power of the People*, Princeton: Princeton University Press.

Ober, Josiah and Barry Weingast (forthcoming), "The Spartan Game: Violence, Proportionality, Austerity and Collapse," in Danielle Allen, Paul Christensen, and Paul Millet (eds), *How to Do Things with History*, Oxford: Oxford University Press.

Ohana, David (2012), *The Origins of Israeli Mythology: Neither Canaanites nor Crusaders*, Cambridge: Cambridge University Press.

Oliver, Jen (2015), "*Oscula iungit nec moderata satis nec sic a uirgine danda*: Ovid's Callisto Episode, Female Homoeroticism, and the Study of Ancient Sexuality," *American Journal of Philology* 136: 281–312.

Ormand, Kirk (2009), *Controlling Desires: Sexuality in Ancient Greece and Rome*, Westport, CT: Praeger Series on the Ancient World.

Osborne, Robin (1996), *Greece in the Making 1200–479 BC*, London and New York: Routledge.

Osgood, Josiah (2006), *Caesar's Legacy: Civil War and the Emergence of the Roman Empire*, Cambridge: Cambridge University Press.

Östenberg, Ida (2009), *Staging the World: Spoils, Captives, and Representations in the Roman Triumphal Procession*, Oxford: Oxford University Press.

Panella, Clementina and André Tchernia (2002), "Agricultural Wealth Transported in Amphorae," in Walter Scheidel and Sitta von Reden (eds), *The Ancient Economy*, 173–89, Edinburgh: Edinburgh University Press.

Parker, Anthony (1992), *Ancient Shipwrecks of the Mediterranean and the Roman Provinces*, BAR International Series, no. 580, Oxford: Oxbow.

Patterson, Orlando (1982), *Slavery and Social Death*, Cambridge, MA: Harvard University Press.

Payne, Richard (2015), *A State of Mixture: Christians, Zoroastrians, and Iranian Political Culture in Late Antiquity*, Berkeley: University of California Press.

Payne, Richard (2016), "The Making of Turan: The Fall and Transformation of the Iranian East," *Journal of Late Antiquity* 9: 4–41.

Payne, Richard and Mehrnoush Soroush, eds (2014), *The Archaeology of Sasanian Politics*, special issue of *Journal of Ancient History*, Berlin: Walter de Gruyter.

Peacock, David (1982), *Pottery in the Roman World: An Ethnoarchaeological Approach*, New York: Longman.

Pekáry, Thomas (1989), "*Seditio*. Unruhen und Revolten im römischen Reich von Augustus bis Commodus," *Ancient Society* 18: 133–50.

Penella, Robert J. (1980), "Caracalla and his Mother in the *Historia Augusta*," *Historia* 29: 382–5.

Pensabene, Patrizio and Clementina Panella, eds (1999), *Arco di Costantino: Tra archaeologia e archeometria*, Rome: Bretschneider.

Petersen, Lauren (2006), *The Freedman in Roman Art and Art History*, Cambridge: Cambridge University Press.

Pettegrew, David (2016), *The Isthmus of Corinth: Crossroads of the Mediterranean World*, Ann Arbor: University of Michigan Press.

Phang, Sarah (2001), *The Marriage of Roman Soldiers (13 B.C.-A.D.235): Law and Family in the Imperial Army*, Leiden: Brill.

Pilkington, Nathan (2013), "An Archaeological History of Carthaginian Imperialism," PhD Diss., Columbia University, New York.

Pittenger, Miriam (2008), *Contested Triumphs: Politics, Pageantry, and Performance in Livy's Republican Rome*, Berkeley: University of California Press.

Pitts, Martin (2013), *Alien Cities: Consumption and the Origins of Urbanism in Roman Britain*, London: Spoilheap Monograph 7.

Pitts, Martin (2015), "Globalisation, Circulation and Mass Consumption in the Roman World," in Martin Pitts and Miguel Versluys (eds), *Globalisation and the Roman World: World History, Connectivity and Material Culture*, 69–98, Cambridge: Cambridge University Press.

Poblome, Joroen (2015), "The Economy of the Roman World as a Complex Adaptive System: Testing the Case in Second to Fifth Century Sagalassos," in Paul Erdkamp and Koenraad Verboven (eds), *Structure and Performance in the Roman Economy*, Collection Latomus vol. 350, 97–140, Leuven: Peeters.

Pollard, Elizabeth (2009), "Pliny's Natural History and the Flavian Templum Pacis: Botanical Imperialism in First-Century C.E. Rome," *Journal of World History* 20: 309–38.

Pollard, Nigel (2000), *Soldiers, Cities and Civilians in Roman Syria*, Ann Arbor: University of Michigan Press.

Popović, Mladen, ed. (2011), *The Jewish Revolt against Rome: Interdisciplinary Perspectives*, Leiden: Brill.

Potter, David (2004), *The Roman Empire at Bay: AD 180–395*, London and New York: Routledge.

Prag, Jonathan (2007), "Auxilia and Gymnasia: A Sicilian Model of Roman Imperialism," *Journal of Roman Studies* 97: 68–100.

Prag, Jonathan (2014), "Bronze Rostra from the Egadi Islands off NW Sicily: The Latin Inscriptions," *Journal of Roman Archaeology* 27: 33–59.

Price, Simon (1984), *Rituals and Power: The Roman Imperial Cult in Asia Minor*, Cambridge: Cambridge University Press.

Pritchard, David (2015), *Public Spending and Democracy in Classical Athens*, Austin: University of Texas Press.

Purcell, Nicholas (1983), "The *Apparitores*: A Study in Social Mobility," *Papers of the British School in Rome* 51: 125–73.

Purcell, Nicholas (1996), "Rome and the Management of Water: Environment, Culture and Power," in John Salmon and Graham Shipley (eds), *Human Landscapes in Classical Antiquity: Environment and Culture*, 180–212, London and New York: Routledge.

Purcell, Nicholas (2005), "Romans in the Roman World," in Karl Galinsky (ed.), *The Cambridge Companion to the Age of Augustus*, 85–105, Cambridge: Cambridge University Press.

Quinn, Josephine (2017), "Translating Empire From Carthage To Rome," *Classical Philology* 112: 312–31.

Quint, David (1993), *Epic and Empire: Politics and Generic Form from Virgil to Milton*, Princeton: Princeton University Press.

Raaflaub, Kurt, ed. (2005), *Social Struggles in Archaic Rome: New Perspectives on the Struggle of the Orders*, 2nd edition, Oxford and Malden, MA: Wiley-Blackwell.

Raaflaub, Kurt (2009), "Learning from the Enemy: Athenian and Persian 'Instruments of Empire'," in Ma *et al.* 2009: 89–124.

Radford, Fiona (2017), "Hollywood Ascendant: *Ben Hur* and *Spartacus*," in Arthur Pomeroy (ed.), *A Companion to Ancient Greece and Rome on Screen*, 119–44, Oxford and Malden, MA: Wiley-Blackwell.

Raggi, Andrea (2006), *Seleuco di Rhosos. Cittadinanza e privilegi nell'Oriente greco in età tardo-repubblicana*, Pisa: Giardini editori e stampatori.

Rajak, Tessa (2016), "Josephus, Jewish Resistance and the Masada Myth," in John Collins and Joseph Manning (eds), *Revolt and Resistance in the Ancient Classical World and the Near East*, 219–33, Leiden: Brill.

Ramgopal, Sailakshmi (2017), "One and Many: Associations of Roman Citizens in Greece," in Athanasios Rizakis and Sophia Zoumbaki (eds), *Social Dynamics under Roman Rule: Mobility and Status Change in the Provinces of Achaia and Macedonia*, 407–25, Athens: Meletemata.

Ramgopal, Sailakshmi (forthcoming), *Romans Abroad: Associations of Roman Citizens from the Second Century BCE to the First Century CE*.

Ramsby, Teresa (2012), "'Reading' the Freed Slave in the Cena Trimalchionis," in Bell and Ramsby 2012: 66–87.

Rapp, Claudia (2005), *Holy Bishops in Late Antiquity: The Nature of Christian Leadership in an Age of Transition*, Berkeley: University of California Press.

Rathbone, Dominic (1990), "The Muziris Papyrus (SB XVIII 13167): Financing Roman Trade with India," *Bulletin de la Société royale d'archéologie d'Alexandrie* 46: 39–50.

Rathbone, Dominic (1993), "Egypt, Augustus and Roman taxation," *Cahiers du Centre Gustave Glotz* 4: 81–112.

Rathbone, Dominic and Peter Temin (2008), "Financial Intermediation in First-Century AD Rome and Eighteenth-Century England," in Koenraad Verboven, Kateijn Vandorpe, and Véronique Chankowski (eds), *Pistoi dia tèn technèn. Bankers, Loans, and Archives in the Ancient World*, 371–420, Leuven: Peeters.

Rathbone, Dominic and Sitta von Reden (2014), "Mediterranean Grain Prices in Classical Antiquity," in R. J. van der Spek, Bas van Leeuwen, and Jan Luiten van Zanden (eds), *A History of Market Performance: From Ancient Babylonia to the Modern World*, 148–238, London and New York: Routledge.

Revell, L. (2009), *Roman Imperialism and Local Identities*, Cambridge: Cambridge University Press.

Reynolds, Susan (2006), "Empires: A Problem of Comparative History," *Historical Research* 79: 151–65.

Rhee, Helen (2005), *Early Christian Literature: Christ and Culture in the Second and Third Centuries. The Apologies, Apocryphal Acts and Martyr Acts*, London and New York: Routledge.

Rhodes, Peter (2004), *Athenian Democracy*, Oxford: Oxford University Press.

Rhodes, Peter (2007), "The Impact of the Persian Wars in Classical Greece," in Emma Bridges, Edith Hall, and Peter Rhodes (eds), *Cultural Responses to the Persian Wars: Antiquity ot the Third Millennium*, 31–44, Oxford: Oxford University Press.

Rhodes, Peter (2009), "Ancient Athens: Democracy and Empire," *European Review of History: Revue européenne d'histoire* 16: 201–15.

Rice, Candice (2016a), "Shipwreck Cargoes in the Western Mediterranean and the Organization of Roman Maritime Trade," *Journal of Roman Archaeology* 29: 165–92.

Rice, Candice (2016b), "Mercantile Specialization and Trading Communities," in Andrew Wilson and Miko Flohr (eds), *Urban Craftsmen and Traders in the Roman World*, 97–114, Oxford: Oxford University Press.

Rich, John (1983), "The Supposed Manpower Shortage in the Second Century BC," *Historia* 32: 287–331.

Rich, John (2008), "Treaties, Allies and the Roman Conquest of Italy," in Philip de Souza (ed.), *War and Peace in Ancient and Medieval History*, 51–75, Cambridge: Cambridge University Press.

Richardson, John (1986), *Hispaniae: Spain and the Development of Roman Imperialism, 218–82 BC*, Cambridge: Cambridge University Press.

Richardson, John (2008), *The Language of Empire: Rome and the Idea of Empire from the Third Century BC to the Second Century AD*, Cambridge: Cambridge University Press.

Richlin, Amy (1983), *The Garden of Priapus: Sexuality and Aggression in Roman Humor*, New Haven: Yale University Press.

Richlin, Amy (1993), "Not Before Homosexuality: The Materiality of the *Cinaedus* and the Roman Law Against Love Between Men," *Journal of the History of Sexuality* 3: 523–73.

Richlin, Amy (1998), "Foucault's *History of Sexuality*: A Useful Theory for Women?" in David Larmour, Paul Allen Miller, and Charles Platter (eds), *Rethinking Sexuality: Foucault and Classical Antiquity*, 138–70, Princeton: Princeton University Press.

Richlin, Amy (2006), "Sexuality in the Roman Empire," in David Potter (ed.), *A Companion to the Roman Empire*, 327–53, Oxford and Malden, MA: Wiley-Blackwell.

Richlin, Amy (2014), "Talking to Slaves in the Plautine Audience," *Classical Antiquity* 33: 174–226.

Richmond, I. A. (1967), "Adamklissi," *Papers of the British School in Rome* 35: 29–39.

Rickman, Geoffrey (1980), *The Corn Supply of Ancient Rome*, Oxford: Oxford University Press.

Riess, Werner (2001), *Apuleius und die Räuber. Ein Beitrag zur historischen Kriminalitätsforschung*, Stuttgart: Steiner Verlag.

Riess, Werner (2015), "Bulla Felix: ein Sozialbandit zwischen Geschichte und Fiktion," in Sabine Panzram, Werner Riess, and Christoph Schäfer (eds), *Menschen und Orte*, 287–301, Rahden: Verlag Marie Leidorf.

Rihll, T. E. (2011), "Classical Athens," in Keith Bradley and Paul Cartledge (eds), *The Cambridge World History of Slavery Volume 1: The Ancient Mediterranean World*, 48–73, Cambridge: Cambridge University Press.

Ripat, Pauline (2011), "Expelling Misconceptions: Astrologers at Rome," *Classical Philology* 106: 115–54.

Rives, James (2010), "Venus," in Hubert Cancik and Helmuth Schneider (eds), *Brill's Encyclopaedia of the Ancient World: New Pauly*, 283–7, Leiden: Brill.

Robinson, Ronald, John Gallagher, and Alice Denny (1961), *Africa and the Victorians: The Official Mind of Imperialism*, London: Macmillan.

Robson, Eleanor (2007), "Literacy, Numeracy, and the State in Early Mesopotamia," in Kathryn Lomas, Ruth Whitehouse, and John Wilkins (eds), *Literacy and the State in the Ancient Mediterranean*, 29–52, London: Accordia Research Institute.

Rodríguez-Almeida, Emilio (2002), *Formae urbis antiquae. Le mappe marmoree di Roma tra la repubblica e Settimo Severo*, Rome: École françaises de Rome.

Roisman, Joseph, ed. (2003), *Brill's Companion to Alexander the Great*, Leiden: Brill.

Romeo, Ilaria (2002), "The Panhellenion and Ethnic Identity in Hadrianic Greece," *Classical Philology* 97: 21–39.
Root, Margaret (1979), *The King and Kingship in Achaemenid Art*, Leiden: Brill.
Root, Margaret (1985), "The Parthenon Frieze and the Apadana Reliefs at Persepolis: Reassessing a Programmatic Relationship," *American Journal of Archaeology* 89: 103–122.
Rosenstein, Nathan (1990), *Imperatores Victi: Military Defeat and Aristocratic Competition in the Middle Republic*, Berkeley: University of California Press.
Rosenstein, Nathan (2004), *Rome at War: Farms, Families and Death in the Middle Republic*, Chapel Hill: University of North Carolina Press.
Rossi, Lino (1997), "A Synoptic Outlook of Adamklissi Metopes and Trajan's Column Frieze: Factual and Fanciful Topics Revisited," *Athenaeum* 85: 471–86.
Roth, Jonathan (1999), *The Logistics of the Army at War (264 BC–AD 235)*, Leiden: Brill.
Roth, Martha (1997), *Law Collections from Mesopotamia and Asia Minor*, 2nd edition, Atlanta: Society for Biblical Literature.
Roth, Ulrike (2007), *Thinking Tools: Agricultural Slavery Between Evidence and Models*, London: Institute of Classical Studies.
Rüpke, Jörg (2011), *The Roman Calendar from Numa to Constantine: Time, History and the Fasti*, Oxford and Malden, MA: Wiley-Blackwell.
Russell, Ben (2013), *The Economics of the Roman Stone Trade*, Oxford: Oxford University Press.
Sabin, Philip, Hans Van Wees, and Michael Whitby, eds (2007), *The Cambridge History of Greek and Roman Warfare*, 2 volumes, Cambridge: Cambridge University Press.
Şahin, Sencer and Mustafa Adak (2007), *Stadiasmus Patarensis: Itinera Romana Provinciae Lyciae*. Istanbul: Yayınları.
Sallaberger, Walther and Aage Westenholz, eds (1999), *Mesopotamien: Akkade-Zeit und Ur III-Zeit*, Freiburg, Universitätsverlag.
Sarris, Peter (2015), *Byzantium: A Very Short Introduction*, Oxford: Oxford University Press.
Schäfer, Peter (1981), *Der Bar-Kokhba-Aufstand: Studien zum zweiten jüdischen Krieg gegen Rom*, Tübingen: Mohr Siebeck.
Schäfer, Peter, ed. (2003), *The Bar Kokhba War Reconsidered: New Perspectives on the Second Jewish Revolt against Rome*, Tübingen: Mohr Siebeck.
Scheid, John (1995), "*Graeco Ritu*: A Typically Roman Way of Honoring the Gods," *Harvard Studies in Classical Philology* 97: 15–31.
Scheidel, Walter (1997), "Quantifying the Sources of Slaves in the Early Roman Empire," *Journal of Roman Studies* 87: 156–69.
Scheidel, Walter (2004), "Human Mobility in Roman Italy, I: The Free Population," *Journal of Roman Studies* 94: 1–26.
Scheidel, Walter (2005a), "Human Mobility in Roman Italy, II. The Slave Population," *Journal of Roman Studies* 95: 64–80.
Scheidel, Walter (2005b), "Real Slave Prices and the Relative Cost of Slave Labor in the Greco- Roman World," *Ancient Society* 35: 1–17.
Scheidel, Walter (2007a), "Demography," in Scheidel *et al.* 2007: 38–86.
Scheidel, Walter (2007b), "Marriage, Families, and Survival: Demographic Aspects," in Paul Erdkamp (ed.), *A Companion to the Roman Army*, 417–34, Oxford and Malden, MA: Wiley-Blackwell.
Scheidel, Walter (2008), "The Comparative Economics of Slavery in the Greco-Roman World," in Enrico Dal Lago and Constantina Katsari (eds), *Slave Systems: Ancient and Modern*, 105–26, Cambridge: Cambridge University Press.

Scheidel, Walter (2011), "Monogamy and Polygyny," in Beryl Rawson (ed.), *A Companion to Families in the Greek and Roman Worlds*, 108–15, Oxford and Malden, MA: Wiley-Blackwell.

Scheidel, Walter (2012), "Slavery" in Walter Scheidel (ed.), *The Cambridge Companion to the Roman Economy*, 89–113, Cambridge: Cambridge University Press.

Scheidel, Walter (2013), "Studying the State," in Bang and Scheidel 2013: 5–57.

Scheidel, Walter (2014), "The Shape of the Roman World: Modelling Imperial Connectivity," *Journal of Roman Archaeology* 27: 7–32.

Scheidel, Walter, ed. (2009), *Rome and China: Comparative Perspectives on Ancient World Empires*, Oxford: Oxford University Press.

Scheidel, Walter, ed. (2015a), *State Power in Ancient China and Rome*, Oxford: Oxford University Press.

Scheidel, Walter (2015b), "State Revenue and Expenditure in the Han and Roman Empires," in Scheidel 2015a: 150–80.

Scheidel, Walter, Ian Morris, and Richard Saller, eds (2007), *The Cambridge Economic History of the Greco-Roman World*, Cambridge: Cambridge University Press.

Schiavone, Aldo (2013), *Spartacus*, Cambridge, MA: Harvard University Press.

Scott, James (2017), *Against the Grain: A Deep History of the Earliest States*, New Haven: Yale University Press.

Scott, Sarah (2000), *Art and Society in Fourth-Century Britain: Villa Mosaics in Context*, Oxford: Oxford University School of Archaeology.

Senay, Pierre (1995), "Le romain fantassin irréductible, réalité ou mythe. Le prodige du lac d'Albe de 398 av. J.-C. ou l'amorce d'une stratégie hégémonique," *Cahiers des études anciennes* 29: 165–70.

Severy, Beth (2003), *Augustus and the Family at the Birth of the Roman Empire*, London and New York: Routledge.

Shapiro, H. A., ed. (2007), *The Cambridge Companion to Archaic Greece*, Cambridge: Cambridge University Press.

Shaw, Brent (1983), "Soldiers and Society: The Army in Numidia," *Opus* 2.1: 133–59.

Shaw, Brent (1984), "Bandits in the Roman empire," *Past & Present* 105: 3–52.

Shaw, Brent (1990), "Bandit Highlands and Lowland Peace: The Mountains of Isauria-Cilicia," *Journal of the Economic and Social History of the Orient* 33: 199–233.

Shaw, Brent (2000), "Rebels and Outsiders," in *Cambridge Ancient History* 11, 361–404, Cambridge: Cambridge University Press.

Shaw, Brent (2003), "Judicial Nightmares and Christian Memory," *Journal of Early Christian Studies* 11: 533–63.

Shaw, Brent (2013), *Bringing in the Sheaves: Economy and Metaphor in the Roman World*, Toronto: University of Toronto Press.

Sherratt, Melanie and Alison Moore (2016), "Gender in Roman Britain," in Martin Millett, Louise Revell, and Alison Moore, eds (2016), *The Oxford Handbook of Roman Britain*, 363–80, Oxford: Oxford University Press.

Sherwin-White, Adrian (1952), "The Early Persecutions and Roman Law Again," *Journal of Theological Studies* 3: 199–213.

Sherwin-White, Adrian (1973), *The Roman Citizenship*, 2nd edition, Oxford: Clarendon Press.

Sidebotham, Steven, E. (2011), *Berenike and the Ancient Mediterranean Spice Route*, Berkeley: University of California Press.

Simmel, Georg (2009), *Sociology: Inquiries into the Construction of Social Forms*, Leiden: Brill.

Simonton, Matthew (2017), *Classical Greek Oligarchy: A Political History*, Princeton: Princeton University Press.
Skinner, Joseph (2013), "Imperial Visions, Imagined Pasts: Ethnography and Identity on India's North-Western Frontier," in Eran Almagor and Joseph Skinner (eds), *Ancient Ethnography: New Approaches*, 203–22, London: Bloomsbury Academic.
Skinner, Marilyn (1993), "*Ego mulier*: The Construction of Male Sexuality in Catullus," *Helios* 20: 107–30.
Skinner, Marilyn (2005), *Sexuality in Greek and Roman Culture*, Oxford and Malden, MA: Wiley-Blackwell.
Smith, Christopher (2017), "Ager Romanus antiquus," *Archeologia Classica* 68: 1–26.
Smith, R. R. R. (1987), "The Imperial Reliefs from the Sebasteion at Aphrodisias," *Journal of Roman Studies* 77: 88–138.
Smith, R.R.R. (1998), "Cultural Choice and Political Identity in Honorific Portrait Statues in the Greek East in the 2nd Century A.D.," *Journal of Roman Studies* 88: 56–93.
Snodgrass, Anthony (2000), *The Dark Age of Greece: An Archaeological Survey of the Eleventh to the Eighth Centuries BC*, London and New York: Routledge.
Southern, Pan (2007), *The Roman Army: A Social and Institutional History*, Oxford: Oxford University Press.
Spawforth, Antony (1999), "The Panhellenion again," *Chiron* 29: 339–52.
Spawforth, Antony and Susan Walker (1985), "The World of the Panhellenion 1: Athens and Eleusis," *Journal of Roman Studies* 75: 78–104.
Spawforth, Antony and Susan Walker (1986), "The World of the Panhellenion 2: Three Dorian Cities," *Journal of Roman Studies* 76: 88–105.
Speidel, Michael (2006), *Emperor Hadrian's Speeches to the African Army: A New Text*, Mainz: Koch Neff & Volckmar.
Speidel, Michael and Hans Lieb, eds (2007), *Militärdiplome: die Forschungsbeiträge der Berner Gespräche von 2004*, Stuttgart: Steiner.
Squire, Michael (2011), *The Art of the Body: Antiquity and its Legacy*, London: I. B. Tauris.
Steel, Catherine (2013), *The End of the Roman Republic 146 to 44 BC: Conquest and Crisis*, Edinburgh: Edinburgh University Press.
Steinmetz, George, ed. (1999), *State/Culture: State-Formation After the Cultural Turn*, Ithaca, NY: Cornell University Press.
Stewart, Peter (1997), "Fine Art and Course Art: The Image of Roman Priapus," *Art History* 20: 575–88.
Stoler, Ann Laura (1995), *Race and the Education of Desire: Foucault's History of Sexuality and the Colonial Order of Things*, Durham, NC: Duke University Press.
Stoll, Oliver (2001), *Zwischen Integration und Abgrenzung: Die Religion des Römischen Heeres im Nahen Osten*, St. Katharinen: Scripta Mercaturae Verlag.
Stoll, Oliver (2007), "The Religions of the Armies," in Paul Erdkamp (ed.), *A Companion to the Roman Army*, 451–76, Oxford and Malden, MA: Wiley-Blackwell.
Syme, Ronald (1939), *The Roman Revolution*, Oxford: Oxford University Press.
Talbert, Richard (2004), "Rome's Provinces as Framework for World-view', in Luuk De Ligt, Emily Hemelrijk, and H. W. Singor (eds), *Roman Rule and Civic Life: Local and Regional Perspectives*, 21–37, Amsterdam: J.C. Gieben.
Tan, James (2017), *Power and Public Finance at Rome, 264–49 BCE*, Oxford: Oxford University Press.

Taylor, Michael (2016), "The Battle Scene on Aemilius Paullus's Pydna Monument: A Reevaluation," *Hesperia* 85: 559–76.
Taylor, Michael (2017), "Roman State Finances in the Middle Republic: A Reevaluation," *American Journal of Philology* 138: 143–80.
Taylor, Rabun (1997), "Two Pathic Subcultures in Ancient Rome," *Journal of the History of Sexuality* 7: 319–71.
Temin, Peter (2004), "The Labor Market of the Early Roman Empire," *Journal of Interdisciplinary History* 34: 513–38.
Temin, Peter (2013), *The Roman Market Economy*, Princeton: Princeton University Press.
Terpestra, Taco (2013), *Trading Communities in the Roman World: A Micro-Economic and Institutional Perspective*, Leiden: Brill.
Thébert, Yvon (1978), "Romanisation et déromanisation en Afrique: histoire décolonisée ou histoire inversée?" *Annales. Économies, Sociétés, Civilisations* 33: 64–82.
Thomas, Charles (1998), *Christian Celts: Messages and Images*, Tempus: Stroud.
Thomas, Rosalind (2000), *Herodotus in Context: Ethnography, Science and the Art of Persuasion*, Cambridge: Cambridge University Press.
Thomas, Y. (1986), "A Rome, pères citoyens et cité des pères II siècle avant J.C.–IIè siècle apres J.C.," in André Burguière, Christiane Klapisch-Zuber, Martine Segalene, and Françoise Zonabend (eds), *Histoire de la famille*, vol. 1, 195–229, Paris: Armand Colin.
Thompson, Dorothy (2001), "Hellenistic Hellenes: The case of Ptolemaic Egypt," in Irad Malkin (ed.), *Ancient Perceptions of Greek Ethnicity*, 301–22, Cambridge, MA: Harvard University Press.
Thompson, Edward (1952), "Peasant Revolts in Late Roman Gaul and Spain," *Past & Present*, 2: 11–23.
Thompson, Lloyd (1989), *Romans and Blacks*, Norman: University of Oklahoma Press.
Thonemann, Peter (2004), "The Date of Lucullus' Quaestorship," *Zeitschrift für Papyrologie und Epigraphik* 149: 80–2.
Thonemann, Peter (2010), "The Women of Akmoneia," *Journal of Roman Studies* 100: 163–78.
Thornton, John (2001), "Gli *aristoi*, l'*akriton plethos* e la provincializzazione della Llicia nel monumento di Patara," *Mediterraneo antico* 4: 427–46.
Thornton, John (2008), "*Lesteiai* nella dedica a Claudio del monumento di Patara: una sommessa proposta d'interpretazione," *Mediterraneo antico* 11: 175–98.
Tilly, Charles (1985), "War Making and State Making as Organized Crime," in Peter Evans, Dietrich Rueschemeyer, and Theda Skocpol (eds), *Bringing the State Back In*, 169–91, Cambridge: Cambridge University Press.
Tilly, Charles (1992), *Coercion, Capital, and European States AD 990–1992*, Cambridge, MA: Harvard University Press.
Todd, Malcolm (1996), *The Early Germans*, Oxford and Malden, MA: Wiley-Blackwell.
Todman, Don (2007), "Childbirth in Ancient Rome: From Traditional Folklore to Obstetrics," *Australian and New Zealand Journal of Obstetrics and Gynaecology* 47: 82–5.
Toynbee, Arnold (1965), *Hannibal's Legacy: The Hannibalic War's Effects on Roman Life*, 2 volumes, Oxford: Oxford University Press.
Tran, Nicolas (2006), *Les membres des associations romaines: le rang social des collegiati en Italie et en Gaules sous le haut-empire*, Rome: École française de Rome.

Tran, Nicolas (2017), "*Ars* and *doctrina*: The Socio-economic Identity of Roman Skilled Workers (first century BC-third century AD)," in Verboven and Laes 2017: 246–61.
Treggiari, Susan (1991), *Roman Marriage: Iusti Coniuges From the Time of Cicero to the Time of Ulpian*, Oxford: Clarendon Press.
Trigger, Bruce (2003), *Understanding Early Civilizations: A Comparative Study*, Cambridge: Cambridge University Press.
Tuck, Steven L. (2015), *A History of Roman Art*, Chichester, West Sussex: John Wiley & Sons.
Turner, Brian (2013), "War Losses and Worldview: Reviewing the Roman Funerary Altar at Adamclisi," *American Journal of Philology* 134: 277–304.
Tuval, Michael (2012), "Doing without the Temple: Paradigms in the Judaic Literature of the Diaspora," in Daniel Schwartz and Zeev Weiss (eds), *Was 70 CE a Watershed in Jewish History?*, 181–239, Leiden: Brill.
Tyrrell, William Blake (1984), *Amazons: A Study in Athenian Myth-Making*, Baltimore: Johns Hopkins University Press.
Urbainczyk, Theresa (2004), *Spartacus*, Bristol: Bristol Classical Press.
Urban, Ralf (1999), *Gallia rebellis: Erhebungen in Gallien im Spiegel antiker Zeugnisse*, Stuttgart: Steiner Verlag.
Vaahtera, J. (1990), "The Origin of Latin *suffragium*," *Glotta* 71: 66–80.
Van Dam, Raymond (1985), *Leadership and Community in Late Antique Gaul*, Berkeley: University of California Press.
Van Nijf, Onno (1997), *The Civic World of Professional Associations in the Roman East*, Amsterdam: J. G. Gieben.
Van Wees, Hans (2013), *Ships and Silver, Taxes and Tribute: A Fiscal History of Archaic Athens*, London: I.B. Tauris.
Vasunia, Phiroze (2013), *The Classics and Colonial India*, Oxford: Oxford University Press.
Verboven, Koenraad (2002), *The Economy of Friends. Economic Aspects of* Amicitia *and Patronage in the Late Republic*, Collection Latomus vol. 269, Leuven: Peeters.
Verboven, Koenraad (2007), "The Associative Order: Status and Ethos among Roman Businessmen in the Late Republic and Early Empire," *Athenaeum* 95: 861–93.
Verboven, Koenraad and Laes, Christian, eds (2017), *Work, Labour, and Professions in the Roman World*, Leiden: Brill.
Versluys, Miguel John (2014), "Understanding Objects in Motion: An Archaeological Dialogue on Romanization," with responses by Richard Hingley, Tamar Hodos, Tesse Stek, Peter van Dommelen, and Greg Woolf, *Archaeological Dialogues* 21: 1–64.
Vervaet, Fredrick (2014), *The High Command in the Roman Republic: The Principle of the summum imperium auspiciumque from 509–19 BCE*, Stuttgart: Franz-Steiner.
Viglietti, Cristiano (2011), *Il limite del bisogno. Antropologia economica di Roma arcaica*, Bologna: Il Mulino.
Vlassopoulos, Kostas (2009), "Slavery, Freedom and Citizenship in Classical Athens: Beyond a Legalistic Approach," *European Review of History: Revue européenne d'histoire* 16: 347–63.
Von Reden, Sitta (2010), *Money in Classical Antiquity*, Cambridge: Cambridge University Press.
Vout, Caroline (1996), "The Myth of the Toga: Understanding the History of Roman Dress," *Greece and Rome* 43: 204–20.

Vout, Caroline (2007), *Power and Eroticism in Imperial Rome*, Cambridge: Cambridge University Press.
Vout, Caroline (2013), *Sex on Show: Seeing the Erotic in Greece and Rome*, London: The British Museum Press.
Waebens, Sofie (2012), "Reflecting the 'Change in A.D. 140': The Veteran Categories of the Epikrisis Documents Revisited," *Zeitschrift für Papyrologie und Epigraphik* 180: 267–77.
Walker, Susan and Peter Higgs (2001), *Cleopatra of Egypt: From History to Myth*, London: The British Museum Press.
Wallace-Hadrill, Andrew (1981), "Family and Inheritance in the Augustan Marriage Laws," *Proceedings of the Cambridge Philological Society* 27: 58–80.
Wallace-Hadrill, Andrew (1982), 'The golden age and sin in Augustan ideology', *Past & Present* 95, 19–36.
Wallace-Hadrill, Andrew (1989), "Patronage in Roman Society: From Republic to Empire," in Andrew Wallace-Hadrill (ed.), *Patronage in Ancient Society*, 63–87, London and New York: Routledge.
Wallace-Hadrill, Andrew (1990a), "Pliny the Elder and Man's Unnatural History," *Greece & Rome* 37: 80–96.
Wallace-Hadrill, Andrew (1990b), "Roman Arches and Greek Honours: The Language of Power at Rome," *Proceedings of the Cambridge Philological Society* 36: 143–81.
Wallace-Hadrill, Andrew (1998), "To Be Roman, Go Greek: Thoughts on Hellenization at Rome," in M. M. Austin, Jill Harries, and Christopher Smith (eds), *Modus Operandi: Essays in Honour of Geoffrey Rickman*, 79–91, London: Institute of Classical Studies.
Wallace-Hadrill, Andrew (2008), *Rome's Cultural Revolution*, Cambridge: Cambridge University Press.
Wallerstein, Immanuel (1974–89), *The Modern World System*, 3 volumes. New York: Academic Press.
Ward, Benedicta (1987), *Harlots of the Desert: A Study of Repentance in Early Monastic Sources*, Kalamazoo, MI: Cistercian Publications.
Ward-Perkins, Bryan (2005), *The Fall of Rome and the End of Civilization*, Oxford: Oxford University Press.
Webster, Graham (1978), *Boudica: The British Revolt Against Rome AD 60*, New York: Routledge.
Webster, Jane (1999), "At the End of the World: Druidic and Other Revitalization Movements in Post-Conquest Gaul and Britain," *Britannia* 30: 1–20.
Weeks, Jeffrey (1986), *Sexuality*, London and New York: Routledge.
Welch, Katherine (2006), "*Domi Militaeque*: Roman Domestic Aesthetics and War Booty in the Republic," in Sheila Dillon and Katherine Welch (eds), *Representations of War in Ancient Rome*, 223–68, Cambridge: Cambridge University Press.
Whitmarsh, Tim (2013), "Resistance is Futile: Greek Literary Tactics in the Face of Fevolt," in Paul Schubert and Luc van der Stockt (eds), *Les Grecs héritiers des Romains*, 57–85, Geneva: Fondation Hardt.
Whitmarsh, Tim, ed. (2010), *Local Knowledge and Microidentities in the Imperial Greek World*, Cambridge: Cambridge University Press.
Whittaker, C. Richard (2004), *Rome and its Frontiers: the Dynamics of Empire*, London and New York: Routledge.
Wickham, Chris (1984), "The Other Transition: From the Ancient World to Feudalism," *Past & Present* 103: 3–36.

Wierschowski, Lothar (1995), *Die regionale Mobilität in Gallien nach den Inschriften des 1. bis 3. Jahrhunderts n. Chr.: quantitative Studien zur Sozial- und Wirtschaftsgeschichte der westlichen Provinzen des römischen Reiches*, Stuttgart: Franz Steiner.
Wiesehöfer, Josef (2013), "Iranian Empires," in Bang and Scheidel 2013: 199–231.
Williams, Craig. A. (2010), *Roman Homosexuality*, 2nd edition, Oxford: Oxford University Press.
Wilson, Andrew (2008a), "Economy and Trade," in Edward Bispham (ed.), *Roman Europe*, 170–202, Oxford: Oxford University Press.
Wilson, Andrew (2008b), "Large Scale Manufacturing, Standardization, and Trade", in John Peter Oleson (ed.), *The Oxford Handbook of Engineering and Technology in the Classical World*, 393–417, Oxford: Oxford University Press.
Wilson, Andrew (2009), "Approaches to Quantifying Roman Trade," in Alan Bowman and Andrew Wilson (eds), *Quantifying the Roman Economy: Methods and Problems*, 213–49, Oxford: Oxford University Press.
Wilson, Andrew, Morris Silver, Peter Bang, Paul Erdkamp, and Neville Morley (2012), "A Forum on Trade," in Walter Scheidel (ed.), *The Cambridge Companion to the Roman Economy*, 287–317, Cambridge: Cambridge University Press.
Winter, Irene (1995), "Homer's Phoenicians: History, Ethnography, or Literary Trope?" in Joseph Carter and Sarah Morris (eds), *The Ages of Homer: A Tribute to Emily Townsend Vermeule*, 247–71, Austin: University of Texas Press.
Winter, Nancy (2009), *Symbols of Wealth and Power: Architectural Terracotta Decoration in Etruria and Central Italy, 640–510 B.C.*, Ann Arbor: University of Michigan Press.
Witschel, Christian (2013), "The Public Presence of Women in the Cities of Roman North Africa. Two Case Studies: Thamugadi and Cuicul," in Hemelrijk and Woolf 2013: 85–106.
Wohl, Victoria (2002), *Love Among the Ruins: The Erotics of Democracy in Classical Athens*, Princeton: Princeton University Press.
Wolters, Reinhard (2017), *Die Schlacht im Teutoburger Wald: Arminius, Varus und das römische Germanien*, München: Verlag C. H. Beck.
Wood, Ian (2013), "The Germanic Successor States," in Bang and Scheidel 2013: 498–517.
Woolf, Greg (1990), "World System Analysis and the Roman Empire," *Journal of Roman Archaeology* 3: 44–58.
Woolf, Greg (1993), "Roman peace," in John Rich and Graham Shipley (eds), *War and Society in the Roman World*, 171–94, London and New York: Routledge.
Woolf, Greg (1994), "Becoming Roman, Staying Greek: Culture, Identity, and the Civilizing Process in the Roman East," *Proceedings of the Cambridge Philological Society* 40: 116–43.
Woolf, Greg (1998), *Becoming Roman: The Origins of Provincial Civilization in Gaul*, Cambridge: Cambridge University Press.
Woolf, Greg (2011), "Provincial Revolts in the Early Roman Empire," in Mladen Popović (ed.), *The Jewish Revolt against Rome: Interdisciplinary Perspectives*, 27–44, Leiden: Brill.
Woolf, Greg (2013), "Female Mobility in the Roman West," in Hemelrijk and Woolf 2013: 351–68.
Wrede, Henning (1981), *Consecratio in Formam Deorum: vergöttlichte Privatpersonen in der römischen Kaiserzeit*, Mainz am Rhein: von Zabern.

Wright, R. P. (1964), "Roman Britain in 1963: I. Sites Explored, II. Inscriptions," *Journal of Roman Studies* 54: 152–85.
Wyke, Maria (1997), *Projecting the Past: Ancient Rome, Cinema, and History*, London and New York: Routledge.
Yavetz, Zvi (1969), *Plebs and Princeps*, Oxford: Clarendon Press.
Yavetz, Zvi (1986), "The Urban Plebs in the Age of the Flavians, Trajan and Nerva," in Adalberto Giovannini (ed.), *Opposition et résistances à l'Empire d'Auguste à Trajan*, 135–86, Geneva: Fondation Hardt.
Yoffee, Norman (2005), *Myths of the Archaic State: Evolution of the Earliest Cities, States, and Civilizations*, Cambridge: Cambridge University Press.
Zajko, Vanda (2009), "Listening with Ovid: Intersexuality, Queer Theory, and the Myth of Hermaphroditus and Salmacis," *Helios* 36: 175–202.
Zanker, Paul, ed. (1976), *Hellenismus in Mittelitalien*, Göttingen: Vandenhoeck und Ruprecht.
Zeitlin, Froma (1986), "Thebes: Theater of Self and Society in Athenian drama', in J. Peter Euben (ed.), *Greek Tragedy and Political Theory*, 101–41, Berkeley: University of California Press.
Ziolkowski, Adam (2009), "The Legend of Alba or a Discourse on the Method," *Archeologia* 60: 1–10.

NOTES ON CONTRIBUTORS

Emma Dench is the McLean Professor of Ancient and Modern History and of the Classics at Harvard University. She is the author of *From Barbarians to New Men: Greek, Roman, and Modern Perceptions of Peoples from the Central Apennines* (1995); *Romulus' Asylum: Roman Identities from the Age of Alexander to the Age of Hadrian* (2005); and *Empire and Political Cultures in the Roman World* (2018).

Lisa Eberle is Assistant Professor of Ancient History at the University of Tübingen, Germany. She is the author of "Making Roman Subjects: Citizenship in the Time of Augustus," *Transactions of the American Philological Association* 147.2 (2017), 321–70 and, together with Énora LeQuéré, of "Landed Traders, Trading Agriculturalists? Land in the Economy of the Italian Diaspora in the Greek East," *Journal of Roman Studies* 107 (2017), 27–59.

Elio Lo Cascio is Professor of Roman History at Sapienza Università di Roma. He has written extensively on the institutions of the Roman Republic, on the administrative history of the High and Late Empire, on Roman social and economic history and on the history of Roman population. He is the author of *Il princeps e il suo impero. Studi di storia amministrativa e finanziaria romana* (2000); "The Emperor and his Administration," *Cambridge Ancient History* 13 (2005), 131–83; "The Early Roman Empire: The State and the Economy," in W. Scheidel *et al.* (eds.), *The Cambridge Economic History of the Greco-Roman World* (2007), 619–47; *Crescita e declino. Studi di storia dell'economia romana* (2009); and *Die neue Wirtschaftsgeschichte des Römischen Reiches. Paradigmen und Ansätze* (2017).

Carlos Noreña is Associate Professor of History, and Chair of Ancient History and Mediterranean Archaeology, at the University of California, Berkeley. He is the author of *Imperial Ideals in the Roman West* (2011); co-editor, with Björn Ewald, of *The Emperor and Rome: Space, Representation, and Ritual* (2010); and co-editor, with Nikolaos Papazarkadas, of *From Document to History: Epigraphic Insights into the Greco-Roman Word* (2018).

Nicholas Purcell is Camden Professor of Ancient History at the University of Oxford. He works on Roman social, cultural, and economic history. He is joint author, with Peregrine Horden, of *The Corrupting Sea: A Study of Mediterranean History* (2000).

Sitta von Reden is Professor of Ancient History at the University of Freiburg, Germany. She is a specialist in Greco-Roman economic history, having published *Money in Ptolemaic Egypt* (2007); *Money in Classical Antiquity* (2010); *Die Antike Wirtschaft* (2015); and, as editor, *Économie et inégalité: ressources, échanges et pouvoir dans l'antiquité classique* (2017). She is currently conducting an interdisciplinary research project on the economies along the ancient "Silk Road."

Sailakshmi Ramgopal is College Fellow in Ancient History at Harvard University. She is the author of "One and Many: Associations of Roman Citizens in Greece," *Meletemata* 74 (2017), 407–25. Her research examines cultural change in the Roman Empire as a consequence of interactions between Romans and non-Romans in the absence of state actors.

Michael J. Taylor is Assistant Professor of History at the State University of New York at Albany. He is the author of several articles on Roman military history, and is working on a monograph exploring taxation and conscription in the Hellenistic Mediterranean.

Caroline Vout is Reader in Classics at the University of Cambridge and a Fellow of Christ's College. Her publications include *Power and Eroticism in Imperial Rome* (2007); *The Hills of Rome: Signature of an Eternal City* (2012); *Sex on Show: Seeing the Erotic in Greece and Rome* (2013); and *Classical Art: A Life History from Antiquity to the Present* (2018).

INDEX

Abu-Lughod, Lila 190
accountability, generals in Republican Rome 46–8
Achaemenid empire 7–9
  conquest of 19–20
  logistical sophistication of 41
  military forces of 9, 42
  multiculturalism in 208
  religion and power in 11–12
  and trade in the Mediterranean 70–1
  wealth of 39
Adrianople (378 CE) 58, 59
adultery 159
Aegean islands 13
Aemilianus, Scipio 53
Aemilius Paullus 55
Aeneas 164–5
Aeneid 131, 163
agency, of women 152
aggression, sexual 154
Agricola 194
agriculture 5, 6, 74, 122–4, 128–9
Agrippa, Marcus Vipsanius 100
Akkade 5–6
Alban Lake 90–1
Alexander III of Macedon (the Great) (334–323 BCE) 19–20, 42, 70–1
Alexandria 70, 72
Alföldy, Geza 120
Anatolia 7
Ando, Clifford 217

Annals 25
antichrematistic ideology 118–19
Antigonid kingdom 20
Antigonus I (r. 306–301) 20
Antinous 171, 173
Antiochus IV Epiphanes 96, 195, 210
Antonine plague 107, 128
Antoninus Pius (138–61 CE) 50, 184, 192
Appian 215
Appius Claudius 91, 93
Apuleius 158, 182, 184
Aqua Claudia *103*
Aquae Sextiae (101 BCE) 55
aqueducts 91
Arcadius 51
archē, Athenian 16–17
Archelaus of Macedon 96
architecture
  Capitoline Hill 88–90, 93, 94
  controlling nature 100
  development of cities 99–100
  Roman 90, 94, 97
Aristotle 207
Arminius 178
army(ies)
  of the Achaemenid state 9, 42
  atrocities committed by 168
  Augustus's reform of the Roman 40, 44, 54
  command and role of military forces 45–52

deployment and recruitment of military forces 41–5
deployment of auxiliary troops 198
ethnic units 211
imperial armies 29, 40
military culture 54–5
Roman and citizenship 144
Roman and trade 76–8
sexual abuses by 154
socialization processes 218 (*see also* Romanization)
soldiers marrying/sexual relations of 165
supply of 77–8, 225n.6
ars 92, 94, 99
Artemidorus 189
artes 113
assimilation, Roman Empire 32–3 (*see also* Romanization)
associations of Roman citizens 149–51, 188, 219–21, 226n.9
Assur 7
astrologers 186
Athens
 democracy 15–18
 resources of and warfare 41, 42
 as a slave society 17
 wealth of the Athenian empire 39
Athronges 182, 184
Attalus III of the Seleucid kingdom 23
Attila 59
Augustales 146
Augustine, the bishop of Hippo 60, 174–5
Augustus (27 BCE –14 CE)
 Augustan peace 102
 building projects of 100
 and grain supply 73
 and manumission 119–21, 145–6
 military career of 49
 reform of the army 40, 44, 54
 and Roman citizenship 212
 Roman power under 131
 rule of 28
 and sexuality 154
 statue of 213
Ausonius 170, 173

Babylon 7, 12
Bacchae 208
banditry 135, 137, 185, 186, 187

banks 82
Bar Kochba revolt 193–4, 196
"barbarian" peoples 206–7
Batavian rebellion (69 CE) 198
battles. *See* names of individual battles
Bénabou, Marcel 179
benefactions 32, 37, 147–9, 151
Bernal, Martin 204
Black Athena 204
Bleda 59
Boniface 60
brigandage 135, 137, 185
Brill's Companion to Insurgency and Terrorism in the Ancient Mediterranean 179
Britannia, sexuality in 159–68
building projects, of emperors 100, 103–5
Byzantine empire 34, 35–6

Calgacus 194
canalization 90, 104
Capitoline Hill 88–90
Capitoline Temple 93, 94
Caracalla 172, 188, 214
Carthage 23, 24, 42, 46, 69, 70
Cassius Dio 77, 184
Cato the Elder 81
Catullus 171–2
Celer 103
Chaeronea (338 BCE) 19
chattel slavery 110, 111–12 (*see also* slavery)
childbearing 158, 166
Christianity
 Christian clergy and war 60
 Christians as a race 221
 early Christians 220–1
 and gender 174–5
 and identity 173, 221
 as a religion of empire 36–7, 107
 and sexuality 154, 172, 173–6
Christology 172
Cicero 112, 113, 211, 216
cities, development of 99–100 (*see also* city-states)
citizenship
 in the Greek *polis* 14–15
 Roman 21, 22, 27, 30–1, 73, 120, 143–4, 166, 211–14, 216–17
 of the Sabines 211

city-states 2–3 (*see also* cities)
  Carthage 23 (*see also* Carthage)
  Greek 14–15, 18, 19
  Mesopotamia 5–6, 71
  Rome 21, 22 (*see also* Rome)
  West Asia 7
civil war 44, 48, 51, 168, 172, 180
Civilis 198
Claudius (41–54 CE) 28, 73, 103, 144,
   160–1, 187–8, 216
Cloaca Maxima 90
"Coasting-voyage of Pseudo-Scylax" 92
Cocles, Horatius 52
coercion
  and empires 8–9
  and the Roman empire 29, 91
coinage
  Denarius of Julius Caesar 27
  first use of 69
  Roman 79
colonization, Greek 14
Colosseum 104
Columella 74
comitatenses 45
comitia centuriata 52
Commodus 192
communication(s)
  molding a landscape of 92–5,
    102, 104
  rituals of 217
Connolly, Serena 190
consensus
  and empires 9, 11
  Roman Empire 29–30
Constantine (306–37 CE) 35, 36, 51, 172
consumption
  city of Rome 74–6
  of elites 74–5, 79–80
  trade and acculturation 78–81
  trade and empire 71–6
Corbulo 49
Corinth 24
Cornwell, Hannah 180
corvée labor 6
cosmopolitanism, Romanization as
   29–30, 32
Crastinus 48
Crete 13
cult, Roman 89
culture(s)

adoption of Greek cultural forms in
   Rome 25
and consensus 9
cultural construction of labor 112–18
cultural history xiv–xvi
cultural production 18
and elites 4
gods in Roman culture 89, 95, 218
Greek 12–20, 25, 208, 209–10, 215–16
imperial 30, 32, 36, 218, 220
military 54–5
and overcoming nature 87–8
political in ancient Greece 12–20
Romanization 29–30, 31–2, 78–9, 179
and states/empires 3–4
visual expressions of 18
and war in ancient empire 52–5
Cynoscephalae (197 BCE) 55
Cyrus Cylinder 12
Cyrus the Great (r. 559–530 BCE) 8, 48

Darius 71
Dark Age (c. 1100–800 BCE) 13
daughter-settlement establishment 91
debt-bondsmen 111
Decline and Fall of the Roman Empire
   33, 37
Delian League 16
Delos 16, 71
Demeter 195
democracy, Athenian 15–18
demographic mobility 91–2 (*see also*
   mobility)
Denarius of Julius Caesar 27
Dentatus, Manius Curius 91, 93
*Der geistiger Widerstand gegen Rom in der
   antiken Welt* 178
dictator perpetuo, Julius Caesar 27
Dido 164–5
Diocletian 35, 51, 190
Dionysius, Aurelius 188–9
diplomas 144, *145*, 165
diseases 106 (*see also* plague)
display, and architecture/environmental
   engineering 97
diviners 186
divorce 159
Domitian (r. 81–96) 50, 58, 215
Druids in Gaul 193
Drusus 49

economic development 72, 80
economic systems, Mediterranean Hellenistic–Carthaginian 71
economy, Roman and labor 121–3
education, and self-promotion 118
Egypt
   Indian Ocean trade 63–5, 83–4
   Pharaohs 6–7, 11
   pharaonic tombs/pyramids 9–10, *11*
   Ptolemaic kingdom in 20, 71, 208, 209
   state-formation of 6–7
elites
   and adultery 159
   buildings of 100
   consumption of 74–5, 79–80
   and culture 4
   multiple *personae* of 216
   Roman 25, 26–8, 30, 31–3, 53–4
   snobbery of 147
   and trade 63, 68, 81
   villas of 72, 98, 162–4, 169, *183*
empires
   Athenian 16–17
   and coercion and consensus 8–9, 12, 29, 91
   defined 4
   empire-building as masculine 160, 168
   legitimating mechanisms of 9–10, 12
   periphery and core model of 3, 29, 41, 45, 50, 55
   pre-modern 41
   proto empires 7, 8
   and slavery 17, 132–3
   and states 2–4
   war and culture in ancient empires 52–5
Enemies of the Roman Order 178
enfranchisement, Roman 211
Ennius 25
environmental engineering, Roman 90–3, 95, 97 (*see also* road building)
essentialism 221
Euripides 208
Europa 162, *163*, 174
exceptionalism, Roman 88–9, 92, 95
exclusivity 219, 221
expropriation, and conquest 193

Favorinus 216
Fenoaltea, Stefano 123
Fertile Crescent 5, 7, 20

finance, maritime loans 81–2
Finley, Moses 124
First Servile War in Sicily 135–132 BCE 195, 196
Flavius 95
Foucault, Michel 153, 168–9
freedpeople
   and associations of Roman citizens 151
   manumission 112, 119–21, 122, 127–8, 144, 145
   memorials to 120, 216–17
   mobility of 133, 137–41, 143, 144
   and "open" slave societies 121–2
   social marginalization of 138, 146–7
   status of freedwomen 146
   successful freedmen 118
Fuchs, Harald 178–9

Gaius Julius Caesar Augustus Germanicus (Caligula) 103
Galba 49, 50, 224n.7
Ganymede 169
gatherings, banning of 188 (*see also* associations of Roman citizens)
gender (*see also* women)
   and Christianity 174–5
   empire-building as masculine 160, 168
genealogical thinking 206
Gibbon, Edward 33–4, 37, 110, 181
gods (*see also* names of individual gods)
   in Roman culture 89, 95, 218
   and sexuality 154–5
Gordian III 192
Goths 59
grain doles 67, 73
grain supplies 73, 77–8
Gratian 59
Great Transformation, The 122
Greece (*see also* Athens)
   Aegean islands 13
   city-states 14–15, 18, 19
   culture 12–20, 25, 208, 209–10, 215–16
   emergence of tyranny 15
   Greek Bronze Age (c. 3000–1050 BCE) 13
   Greek identity 14, 19, 215–16
   Greekness 215–16
   Hellenistic age 20
   influence on Rome 25, 95–6

INDEX

law 71
literature 25
male–male desire 168–9
poleis 14–15
political culture in ancient Greece 12–20

Hadrian (117–138) 50, 104–5, 156, 171, 216
Hadrian's Wall 104
Hannibal 23, 40, 46
Harper, Kyle 127
Hellenistic age 20
Herodotus 15, 39, 95–6, 205, 207
Hicks, John 124–5
hierarchy, visual expressions of 9
Histories 205
historiography 18
Hittites 7
homeland 205, 218–19, 221
Homer 204
Homeric epics 14
Homeric Hymn to Aphrodite 158
homosexuality 170–1 (*see also* sexuality)
honestiores and *humiliores* 213–14, 226n.4
Honorius 51
Hopkins, Keith 120
Horace 25
House of Israel 196
human trafficking 133

identity(ies)
 and Christianity 173, 221
 disruption of 210–11
 Greek 14, 19, 215–16
 and labor 118–19
 and mobility 137
 and profession 116
 Roman 165
 sexual 156, 158
 and social hierarchy 113
Iliad 14
images, erotic 159–60
imperialism
 and cultural history xiv–xvi
 imperial armies 29, 40
 imperial culture 30, 32, 36, 218, 220
 imperial statuary 32
 Macedonia 19

natural history of Roman 95–100
socialization structures 217–19
imperium 24, 46
imports, to Rome 67
Indian Ocean, trade with Egypt 63–5, 83–4
inequalities, Roman Empire 35
infamia 159
infrastructural control 93
Italian Sacred Spring 91

Jewish synagogues 220
Jewish uprisings (66–73, 115–17, 131–6 CE) 29, 196
Josephus 40, 216
Julius Caesar 27, 47, 48, 100, 103, 139, 150, 155, 171
Junian Latins 144
Juno 163
Jupiter 95, 155, 162, 163, 169
justice, Roman 189

kingship 5, 12, 19
kinship 205–6, 218–19, 221
kleos 14
Knossos 13

La résistance africaine à la romanisation 179
labor
 corvée labor 6
 cultural construction of 112–18
 dependent laborers 111
 free labor 111, 122
 and identity 118–19
 and the Roman economy 121–3
 and self-promotion 113–16, 118
 and slavery 109–12, 128–9 (*see also* slavery)
 and the structuring of Roman society 119–21
 unified view of the labor market 123–7
 of women 141, 146
landscape, and communications 92–5, 102, 104
language, and Roman citizenship 212
late antiquity 36
Latin War (341–338 BCE) 22
Latins 90, 211

law(s)
   against diviners and astrologers 186
   Greek 71
   Roman 30, 138
   and sexual issues 160–1
liberales 112
Liebknecht, Karl 177
Life of Pelagia 175
limitanei 45
Linear A/Linear B scripts 13
Lis, Catharina 119
literacy 9
literary genres, fifth-century Athens 18
literature, Latin 25
Livy 89, 135, 214
locatio 94
logistics, and warfare 41, 77–8
Lucius 53
Lucretius 159
Luxemburg, Rosa 177

Macedonia 19–20, 23, 24, 208, 214
Macedonian War, Third (171–168 BCE) 43–4
MacMullen, Ramsay 178
manumission 112, 119–21, 122, 127–8, 144, 145–6
Marcus Aurelius 50, 156
Mariccus 183, 184
maritime trade 81–5, 225n.7
Marius 47
marketing, and urbanization 75–6
markets, ancient 66–7
marriage 158, 166
Marx, Karl 177
Massalia 69–70
Maximinus the Thracian 50–1
Maximus of Tyre 118
Mediterranean
   early trade in 67–8, 70
   and mobility 134
Melinno 95
memorials to freedpeople 120, 216–17
Mesopotamia 5–6, 71
Metamorphoses 158, 182, 184
Metrodoros of Skepsis 194
migration, and trade 71–2
migration crisis, Roman Empire 59–60
militarism 52 (*see also* army(ies))

military expansion, and economic development 72
Miltiades 46
Minoans 13
Mithridates VI of Pontus 150, 194–5
mobility
   dangers of 135
   demographic 91–2
   and exclusivity and essentialism 221
   and identity 137
   legal and social 210
   physical 133–7
   and Roman conquest 131
   Roman Empire 79
   and slaves/freedmen 132–3, 137–41, 143, 144
   social mobility 113–16, 119, 132, 133, 143–52
   upward and labor 113–16
   of women 133–4, 141–3
monarchy (*see also* kingship)
   Egypt 6
   Roman Empire 21, 28
monasticism 173
money
   coinage 69
   Denarius of Julius Caesar 27
   Greek monetary practice 71
   Roman 79
Mons Albanus 90
monumental statements 9–10, 18, 30
multiculturalism 204, 208, 216
Musonius Rufus 118
Muziris papyrus 63–5, 68, 75, 80
Mycenaean civilization (c. 1600–1200 BCE) 13–14
Myos Hormos 63, *64*

Naram-Sin Victory Stele 9, *10*
Narmer, King 6
nation-states, and state power 2, 3
Natural History 102
nature, the overcoming of 87–8, 91, 95, 98, 100–1, 103–7
navicularii 73–4
Near East. *See* West Asia
Neo-Assyrian state (934–610 BCE) 7, 8
Neo-Babylonian state (626–539 BCE) 7
neolithic revolution. *See* agricultural revolution

Nero 49–50, 103–4, 160, *162*, 198–9
networks
    associations of Roman citizens 149–51, 188, 219–21, 226n.9
    trade 69–71
Nicene Creed 174
Nicomedes of Bithynia 171

obaerarii 111
Octavian. *See* Augustus
Odoacer 35, 51–2
Odyssey 14, 204
oligarchies 15
On Clemency 110
On Duties 112
On the Interpretation of Dreams 189
On the Nature of Things 159
organization, Roman 94
Ostia 72, 73, 75
Otherness 154
Otho 50
Ovid 57, 162

Parthenon *18*
patriarchy 159
Patrick, Saint 60
pax (peace) 40, 102, 180–9
peculium 120, 122
pederasty 171
Pekáry, Thomas 181
Pelagius 60
performance, and Athenian democracy 17–18
Pergamum 23
Pericles 39, 46
periphery and core model of empire 3, 29, 41, 45, 50, 55
Perseus of Macedonia 23
Persian empire. *See* Achaemenid empire
petitioning as refuge 189–93
Petronius 116, 118, 146–7
Pharaohs 6–7, 11
Philip II (r. 360–336 BCE) 19
Philip V of Macedon 23, 96, 210
Philopappos 216
Phoenician traders 69, 70
Phryne 159
Pietrabbondante 209
plague 106, 107, 128
Plato 18

Plautus 25
Pliny the elder 102, 104
Pliny the Younger 135, 185
Polanyi, Karl 122
poleis, Greek 14
Politics 207
politics
    absolutist 12
    political culture in ancient Greece 12–20 (*see also* culture(s))
    political economy of the Roman Empire 34
    Roman political system 21
    and sexuality 159
Polybius 40, 72, 215
pomerium 53
Pompeius Magnus 100
Pompey 48, 55, 150
population transfers 98
pornography 164
Postumus 197
power
    and architecture/environmental engineering 97, 101–2
    autocratic of Egypt 7
    delegated 49
    hard 9
    religious and political 11–12
    Roman under Augustus 131
    ruralization of Roman 34
    and sexuality 153
    state power in West Asia 7–8
    within states 2–3
    visual representation of 9
Praeneste, sanctuary of Fortune the First-born 97
Praetorian Guard 44
Prefect of the Grain 73
Priapus 154–5
priesthoods, containing former slaves 146
property tax (*tributum*) 22
prostitutes 159
provincia 24
Prudentius 173
Ptolemaic kingdom 20, 71, 208, 209
Ptolemy I 20
Ptolemy II 71
Punic Wars 42, 71
punishments, Roman 189

race
- being and belonging in the Roman Empire 216–21
- being, belonging and categorization 204–10
- blood purity 212
- Christians as a race 221
- race science 212
- and Rome 210–16
- skin color and physiognomy 202

rape, and Rome 161–2
Red Sea coast, map of 65
religion (*see also* Christianity)
- and building new landscape 107
- and imperial authority 11–12
- and overcoming nature 94

resettlement policy, Roman 98
resistance
- petitioning as refuge 189–93
- and revolt 193–9
- in the Roman empire 178–9, 181–5
- ruling through 185–93

resource deficiency, and the decline of the Roman Empire 59–60
revolt(s)
- Bar Kochba revolt 193–4, 196
- Batavian rebellion (69 CE) 198
- and resistance 193–9

Rhodes 70, 71
Ripat, Pauline 186
ripenses 45
Risorgimento 178
road building 92–3, 101–2, 104, 187
Roman Empire (*see also* Rome)
- accountability of Generals 46–8
- ambition to transform the world 100–5
- army of. *See* army(ies)
- being and belonging in 216–21
- citizenship 21, 22, 27, 30–1, 73, 120, 143–4, 166, 211–14, 216–17
- civil wars 44, 48, 51, 168, 172, 180
- consensus in 29–30
- decline and fall of 33–7, 58–61
- elites 25, 26–8, 30, 31–3, 53–4
- extent of trade in 63–5 (*see also* trade)
- Greek influence on 25, 95–6
- and interdependence 91
- late empire (from 284 CE) 45, 58–61, 127–8
- logistics of 42
- male–female relations in 156–68
- maximum territorial extension 28
- migration crisis 59–60
- periphery and core model of 3, 29, 41, 45, 50, 55
- and race 210–16
- resistance in. *See* resistance
- rise of 96–7
- the Roman emperor 31–2
- Roman frontiers 77
- and sexuality as a power base 155
- slavery. *See* slavery
- state, culture and cosmopolitanism in 20–33
- and the status of individuals/communities 215
- structural transformation of 100
- taxation 64, 65, 72, 73, 74, 76, 214–15, 226n.4
- third-century crisis 34, 45
- urbanization 30, 72
- "year of the four emperors" 50

Romanization 29–30, 31–2, 78–9, 179
Rome (*see also* Roman Empire)
- centrality of 102
- as a city-state 21, 22
- consumption in the city 74–6
- early Republic (509–264 BCE) 21–4
- environmental engineering 90–1
- imperial expansion of 21–8
- imports to 67
- late Republic (133–44 BCE) 26–8, 48
- as a mega-city 72–3
- middle Republic (264–133 BCE) 44–5, 99
- war and culture in the Roman Republic 52–3

Romulus and Remus 135, 137
Romulus Augustulus 35, 51
Roth, Ulrike 126
Rustica, Iunia 148

Sabines 211
sacrificial Altar with Image of Cow's Head *31*
Samnites 209
Sassanian empire (Persian) (224–651 CE) 35–6
Satyricon 118
Scheidel, Walter 125–6

scopophilia 155
Sebasteion 168
Second Athenian Sea League (378–338 BCE) 16
Seleucid kingdom 5, 7, 20, 23, 208
Seleucus I (r. 305–281) 20
self-identification
  elective 221
  of Roman soldiers 218, 219
  and Roman supremacy 216
self-location 92
self-perception, Roman 95
self-promotion, and labor 113–16, 118
self-representation, of Greece and the Roman Empire 99
Seneca the Younger 91, 110, 113, 132, 135, 146
Septimius Severus 45, 50, 172
Servile War in Sicily (First) (135–132 BCE) 195, 196
Severinus of Noricum 60–1
Severius Emeritus, Gaius 188–9
Severus 103
Severus Alexander 50
seviri 146
sex workers 142
sexuality
  and Christianity 154, 172, 173–6
  female same-sex love 172
  male–female relations in Rome 156–68
  male–male desire 168–73
  permissiveness 154–5
  and politics 159
  and power 153
  in the provinces 165
  in Roman Britain 155, 159–68
  sexual identity 156, 158
  sexually explicit images 154–5
  as a threat to empire 160
slavery
  Athens as a slave society 17
  atrocities perpetrated against slaves 132–3, 140–1, 154
  and empires 17, 132–3
  evolution of 128–9
  extent of 133
  versus free labor 123–5
  in late antiquity 127–8
  memorials to freedpeople 120, 216–17
  and mobility 132–3, 137–41, 143, 144
  open and closed 121–2
  Roman Empire 80, 109–12, 119
  slaves petitioning of emperors 192
  social status of former slaves 145
  transaction costs model of 123
"Slavery and supervision in comparative perspective: a model" 123
social control, in ancient cities 2
social hierarchy, and identity 113
social marginalization, of freedpeople 138, 146–7
social mobility 113–16, 119, 132, 133, 143–52
social status, of former slaves 145
social stratification 5, 9
Social War (91–89 BCE) 27, 73, 211
socialization structures, imperial 217–19
  (*see also* Romanization)
Socrates 18
soldiers, atrocities committed by 168
Solon 17
Soly, Hugo 119
Sophists 207
sordidi 112–13
sovereignty
  in non-monarchic empires 46
  and territoriality 3
Sparta 15, 16, 41, 58
Spartacus 177–8
Standard of Ur 9
standardization, and empires 10
states
  and empires 2–4
  state-formation 4–7, 19, 21
  state power in West Asia 7–8
statues, as places of refuge 191–2
Stoicism 25
Strabo 64–5, 98, 186
Struggle of the Orders 21
subordination, and the Roman Empire 91
Suetonius 212
Sulla 27, 47–8, 215
Sumer 4–5
superiority, Roman 95

Tacfarinas 137
Tacitus 28, 40, 45, 103, 137, 145, 168, 184, 194, 198

taxation
    and conquest 193
    Jewish tax 215
    property tax (*tributum*) 22
    Ptolemaic "salt-tax" system 209
    Roman Empire 64, 65, 72, 73, 74, 76, 214–15, 226n.4
technological innovations 5
Temin, Peter 121–2, 127
Temple of Venus and Rome 156
Temple of Venus Genetrix 156
terra sigillata 80–1
territoriality, and sovereignty 3
Theodosian Code 190
Theodosius I (379–95 CE) 51, 174
Theory of Economic History, A 124
Third-Century Crisis (235–84 CE) 34, 45
Third Macedonian War (171–168 BCE) 43–4
Thucydides 16, 18, 39, 46
Tiber river 90, 92
Tiberius 42, 49, 78
Titus 49
toga 212
Tomb of the Manilii 157, 158
trade
    consumption and acculturation 78–81
    consumption and empire 71–6
    early trade in the Mediterranean 67–8, 70
    and elites 63, 68, 81
    extent of in the Roman Empire 63–5
    maritime loans 81–2
    maritime trade 81–5, 225n.7
    the organization of 81–5
    and the Roman army 76–8
    in the Roman economy 66–7
    trade networks and the coming of Rome 69–71
Trajan (r. 98–117 CE) 28, *33*, 50, 55, 77, 104, 185–6
Trajan's Column, Rome *57*, 58, 139
tribus 93, 96
tributum 22
triumphal parades 56–7
Tucciana, Cornelia Valentina 148
tyranny, emergence of 15

Ulpian 186

Ur III 6
Ur, Standard of 9
urban form, and the overcoming of nature 99
urbanization
    and marketing 75–6
    Roman Empire 30, 72

Vaballathus 197
Valens (364–78 CE) 51, 58–9
Valentinian (364–75 CE) 51
Vandals 60
Varro 99, 111, 112
Velleius Paterculus 78
Venus 155, 156–8, 164
Vergil 99, 131, 163
Vespasian 49, 50, 180–1
Via Appia 93, 104, 157
Via Latina 92
villas
    of elites 72, 98, 162–4, 169, *183*
    fortified villa-estates 72
    Hadrian's Villa 104–5
    villa agriculture 74
    villa system and slavery 126–7, 128
Vitellius 50
Volkswanderung 60
voluntary associations 149–51, 188, 219–21, 226n.9
voyeurism 155

warfare (*see also* names of battles and wars)
    Christian clergy and war 60
    city-states 5–6
    command and role of military forces 45–52
    commemoration of 55–8
    and culture in ancient empire 52–5
    deployment and recruitment of military forces 41–5
    early Roman Republic 22
    imperial warfare 39–40
    and logistics 41, 77–8
    resourcing of 41
    and Roman trade 77
Warka vase 9
water, management of 90–1
West Asia, state-formation, empire and culture in 4–12
western civilization 221

whiteness 202
women
   adultery and divorce 159
   agency of 152
   and Christianity 174–5
   collective action of 151–2
   female same-sex love 172
   labor of **141**, 146
   and marriage and childbearing 158, 166
   mobility of 133–4, 141–3
   prostitutes 159
   social mobility of 147–9
   status of freedwomen 146

Woolf, Greg 217
work. *See* labor
work ethic, Roman Empire 118–19 (*see also* labor)
Worthy Efforts. Attitudes to Work and Workers in Pre-Industrial Europe 119
writing
   emergence of 5
   Linear A/Linear B scripts 13

Zama (202) 23
Zeno 52
Zenobia 197, 198